W9-BFE-521

Economics

for Christian Schools®

Economics

for Christian Schools®

Alan J. Carper

Bob Jones University Press, Greenville, SC 29614

NOTE:
The fact that materials produced by other publishers are referred to in this volume does not constitute an endorsement by Bob Jones University Press of the content or theological position of materials produced by such publishers. The position of Bob Jones University Press, and the University itself, is well known. Any references and ancillary materials are listed as an aid to the student or the teacher and in an attempt to maintain the accepted academic standards of the publishing industry.

ECONOMICS for Christian Schools®
Alan J. Carper, M.B.A.

Contributing Writer
Pamela B. Creason, M. Ed.

Produced in cooperation with the Bob Jones University School of Business Administration, the Department of Social Studies of the College of Arts and Science, and Bob Jones Academy.

©1991 Bob Jones University Press
Greenville, South Carolina 29614

Printed in the United States of America
All rights reserved

ISBN 0-89084-521-2

20   19   18   17   16   15   14   13   12   11   10   9   8   7   6

CONTENTS

Unit IV: Economics of the Financial Market

Unit V: Economics of the Government

Unit VI: Economics of the Household

Featured Personalities in Economics

Featured Countries of the World

Unit I: Economics: The Science of Choice

CHAPTER 1

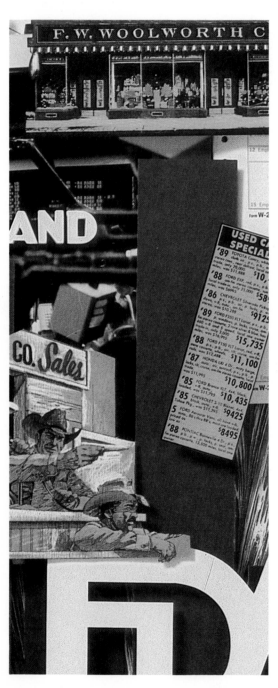

What Is Economics?

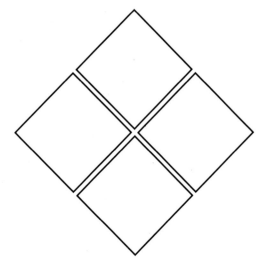

Therefore take no thought, saying, What shall we eat? or, What shall we drink? or, Wherewithal shall we be clothed? (For after all these things do the Gentiles seek:) for your heavenly Father knoweth that ye have need of all these things. But seek ye first the kingdom of God, and his righteousness; and all these things shall be added unto you.

Matthew 6:31-33

I. Economics:
The Science of Choice

What image does your mind conjure up when you hear the word *economics?* Some students think of old gray-headed professors writing technical equations on blackboards in dimly lit university classrooms. Others think of Congress and its confusing economic policies; while still others think of the complex interaction between American businesses.

Even though all of these things certainly fall within the sphere of economics, it is not nearly as difficult a subject as you might imagine. In fact, you probably know a lot more about economics than you think because economics plays a part in everyone's life.

The Science of Economics

What, then, is economics? **Economics** is the common-sense science of how and why people, businesses, and governments make the choices they do. Economics is as much a science as biology, chemistry, or physics for the following reasons:

1. Science always begins with observation. The economist observes how and why choices are made.
2. Scientists use their observations as a basis to predict the future. Economists make observations of the past actions of the economy to predict the future choices of households, business firms, and governments.
3. In many cases scientists go one step further by attempting to control future events through altering important variables. Some economists attempt to control the economy (lowering unemployment, lowering prices, etc.) by manipulating key variables involved in economic choices.

Why Do We Make Choices?

Most students do not realize that they already are economists because of the multitude of choices they must make every day: *Should I get out of bed or sleep just a few more minutes? Do I want oatmeal or pizza for breakfast? Shall I drink milk or orange juice? How will I get to school—walk, drive, or take the bus?*

Our lives are composed of millions of small economic choices with each choice, no matter how insignificant it appears, acting like an individual gold bead, one following another until a chain is formed. The quality of a person's life, like the beauty of a completed chain, is directly related to the quality of each choice he has made in life. Therefore, to understand choice is to understand life itself, and to understand economics is to understand choice. The first step in understanding economics is to learn why choices are necessary.

Like everyone else, you are constantly in the middle of an unavoidable predicament caused by two contradictory ideas: insatiability and scarcity. **Insatiability** means that everyone has unlimited wants.

If you were to write down everything you could possibly desire, the list would help to illustrate this idea of insatiability. How long would it take for you to complete your list? An hour? A day? A year? Fifty years?

Consider the things that might go on your list. First, you would list basic needs such as food, shelter, and clothing; but then it quickly would become a list of wants: what kinds of foods would you want? This part of the list alone could take years to complete. What about shelter? Would you really be content with basic shelter when you could have a mansion? Would you be happy with just one mansion when you could have one at the lake and one in the mountains? How about one (or several) in each major city of the world? Next is clothing. No sooner would you finish your immense clothing list than it would require rewriting, because tastes,

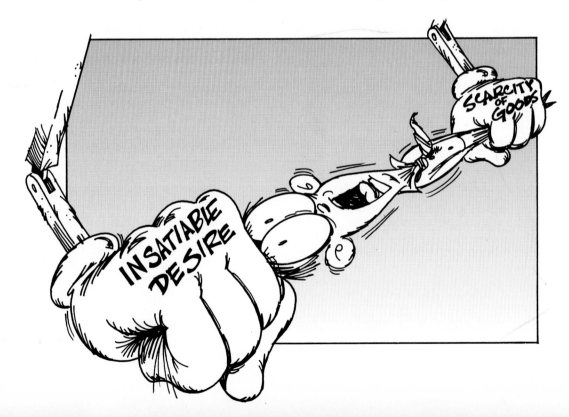

preferences, and styles change.

Continue your list to include cars, boats, jewelry, books, music, tools, and ten thousand other things, and you will come to the conclusion that your desires are infinite. Solomon in his wisdom made this observation when he penned the book of Ecclesiastes nearly three thousand years ago:

> The sun also ariseth, and the sun goeth down, and hasteth to his place where he arose. The wind goeth toward the south, and turneth about unto the north; it whirleth about continually, and the wind returneth again according to his circuits. All the rivers run into the sea; yet the sea is not full; unto the place from whence the rivers come, thither they return again. All things are full of labor; man cannot utter it: the eye is not satisfied with seeing, nor the ear filled with hearing.
>
> (Ecclesiastes 1:5-8)

Unsaved man views material wealth as the product of his own labor, something to be desired and acquired. Scripture, on the other hand, points out that the Christian should realize that God knows His children and will provide for their needs when they are seeking to please Him. (See Matt. 6:31-33.)

To seek those things that God does not want for us will shift our focus away from Christ and bring us to grief. This is a trap of Satan into which many Christians have fallen.

> But godliness with contentment is great gain. For we brought nothing into this world, and it is certain we can carry nothing out. And having food and raiment let us be therewith content. But they that will be rich fall into temptation and a snare, and into many foolish and hurtful lusts, which drown men in destruction and perdition. For the love of money is the root of all evil: which while some coveted after, they have erred from the faith, and pierced themselves through with many sorrows. But thou, O man of God, flee these things; and follow after righteousness, godliness, faith, love, patience, meekness.
>
> (I Timothy 6:6-11)

Insatiability leads people always to want more—perhaps a house like Biltmore, the 255-room mountain chateau of the Vanderbilts.

The second concept in the predicament is **scarcity.** To the economist scarcity does not mean that everything is in short supply. Rather it means that everything is finite, or limited in quantity.

There are only so many hours in a day, so many dollars in circulation, so many tasks that one may perform at any given time, and so many barrels of oil in the earth. We say, therefore, that time, money, labor, and natural resources are scarce or limited in quantity.

When insatiability and scarcity combine, choices become necessary. Since time is limited, one must choose which of the many desirable time-consuming activities one wishes to perform. Since money is scarce, one must choose what one wishes to buy. Although making choices is not a pleasant predicament, it is especially perplexing to the unsaved. Life's choices constantly remind the unregenerate man that he can never be truly happy in a world that defines happiness as satisfaction of all wants. To maximize happiness, therefore, he devotes his energies and activities to an endless cycle of desiring, seeking, acquiring, and consuming those things he believes will bring him satisfaction. The Bible points out the grim predicament of the unsaved man in his search for happiness:

> But the wicked are like the troubled sea, when it cannot rest, whose waters cast up mire and dirt. There is no peace, saith my God, to the wicked.   (Isaiah 57:20-21)

The natural man, no matter how long he searches or how hard he tries, can never achieve total satisfaction or peace apart from having Jesus Christ as Saviour:

> Peace I leave with you, my peace I give unto you: not as the world giveth, give I unto you. Let not your heart be troubled, neither let it be afraid.   (John 14:27)

The dilemma of scarcity and choice is such a fundamental idea in economics that it has become the underlying theme of every economic concept. Indeed, even the word *economics* implies scarcity and choice. The word economics is the product of two Greek words: *oikos* (OY kahs), which means *house,* and *nomos* (NAH mahs), which means *administration of.* To the Christian the word *economics* means much more than the day-to-day administration of a household; it means wise care in making all choices. We could say, then, that a Biblical economist is a believer who exercises wise care in making all his choices, with the goal of pleasing Jesus Christ:

> And the Lord said, Who then is that faithful and wise steward [*oikonomos* or *economist*], whom his lord shall make ruler over his household, to give them their portion of meat in due season? Blessed is that servant, whom his lord when he cometh shall find so doing.   (Luke 12:42-43)

Section Review

1. List three reasons economics is considered a science.
2. What two contradictory ideas result in the necessity of choice?
3. Why should Christians not be continually striving to acquire material wealth?

II. Economic Cost: The Evidence of Choice

Everything is scarce, but not all things are equally desirable and therefore equally scarce. The more desirable and scarce a good or service becomes, the higher its **economic cost.** Economic cost is the value people place on a good or service and is reflected in its price. What exactly is a good or a service?

A **good** is any tangible (physical) thing that has a measurable life span. This textbook is a good in that it is a physical thing and its life may be measured. Your shoes, clothing, car keys, eyeglasses, and goldfish are all goods.

Services, on the other hand, are intangible items. Services include the labor of the accountant, the performance of the singer, and the work of the teacher. Those goods and services that bear a positive economic cost (a price tag higher than zero) are known as **economic goods** and **economic services.**

Goods and services that you are paid to take are said to bear a negative economic cost and are

Garbage is a nuisance good that bears a negative economic cost.

called **nuisance goods and services.** Nuisance goods include toxic waste, garbage, and sewage. Some firms make significant profits by taking nuisance goods and turning them into economic goods, a process called **recycling.**

Goods and services with a price tag of zero are called **free goods** and **free services.** Free goods are those free gifts of God such as air and water. As free goods become more scarce, they become economic goods. For example, the free air that the farmer in the country enjoys may be an economic good to the citizen of the large polluted city. If the city dweller wants to breathe pure air, either he must pay for it through higher taxes to have the polluted air cleaned up, or he must pay to move to the country. Free services include the service provided by the wind on a windmill, a rushing stream on a water wheel, and geothermal steam on an electrical power generator.

Intrinsic Versus Subjective Value

What has more economic value: a handful of diamonds or a single glass of water? Keep in mind that the phrase *economic value* means the value of a good or service in dollars.

Before 1871 this economic riddle, known as the **Diamond-Water Paradox,** had not been solved. The obvious reply was that diamonds, of course, were more valuable, but this answer was incorrect when one considered that a person dying of thirst would give every diamond he possessed for one glass of water.

The riddle was thought to have no correct answer before 1871 because the "obvious" solution depended upon the principle of **intrinsic value.** This principle holds that a thing is valuable because of the nature of the product such as its scarcity or the amount of labor and natural resources that went into its production. Diamonds, therefore, were considered valuable because they were scarce and required much human labor to get out of the ground. Water, on the other hand, was believed to have no value since it was free.

An Austrian economist named Karl Menger put the riddle to rest when his book *Principles of Economics* was published in 1871. In it he argued that there is not just one economic value for every good. The value of an object is not determined by anything having to do with the good, but rather by the subject, the person buying the good or service. Therefore every good's value differs from person to person. The answer to the question "What is more valuable, a handful of diamonds or a glass of water?" is "it depends upon the state of mind of the one answering the riddle"–there is no wrong answer! Menger called his new idea the principle of **subjective value.** Subjective value means that the worth of everything is determined by its usefulness to the buyer. Economists have another word for usefulness: **utility.** Utility, of course, varies from person to person. For a person living beside a stream, diamonds would provide far more utility and therefore be far more valuable than water; while for the man dying of thirst in the desert, diamonds would hold little or no utility relative to the value of water.

This idea of subjective value is very important to keep in mind, for many people too easily fall into the intrinsic value trap. For example, a pilot of a jumbo jet may believe that his labor is worth $500,000 per year because of the stress involved, the years of study he had to endure, and the responsibility of having several hundred lives in his care. Economically speaking, however, the pilots' service is worth whatever his passengers are willing to pay. If he were the only pilot of jumbo jets in the world, they might be willing to pay him $500,000. However, if there were 200 million jumbo jet pilots, his relative value would decrease.

Opportunity Cost Is the Basis of Choice

Critical to understanding Menger's Principle of Subjective Value is an understanding of the twin concepts of opportunity benefit and opportunity cost. The **opportunity benefit** of a choice is the satisfaction a person receives from it. **Opportunity cost,** on the other hand, is the satisfaction one gives up by not choosing what was second best.

Suppose you are walking down the sidewalk with a spring in your step, a song in your heart, and a smile on your face because you have a $10 bill in your pocket, and you are on your way to your local steakhouse for a long awaited dinner. As you pass by an old storefront, this sign in the window catches your eye:

You are now forced to make a choice because you are being pulled between the two concepts of scarcity and insatiability. Your money is scarce, but you want both the dinner and the shoes.

Subconsciously your mind begins calculating opportunity benefits and opportunity costs. If you choose to ignore the shoes and keep on walking, you will enjoy the utility (satisfaction) that the steak dinner will afford, but you will also experience a degree of opportunity cost (regret) for not purchasing the shoes.

A rational person will always make the choice in which the satisfaction received is greater than the regret experienced. Suppose that before you left home to go to the steakhouse an economist attached a meter to your brain that has the ability to measure satisfaction. Imagining the delicious dinner that awaits you, the meter jumps to 10 utils. The **util** (YOO till) is a word economists use to describe an imaginary unit of satisfaction.

The Broken Window

Most people naively assume that the cost of something is limited to what is written on a price tag. In his book *Economics in One Lesson*, Henry Hazlitt points out that there are hidden opportunity costs lurking behind every decision.

A young hoodlum, say, heaves a brick through the window of a baker's shop. The shopkeeper runs out furious, but the boy is gone. A crowd gathers, and begins to stare with quiet satisfaction at the gaping hole in the window and the shattered glass over the bread and pies. After a while the crowd feels the need for philosophic reflection. And several of its members are almost certain to remind each other or the baker that, after all, the misfortune has its bright side. It will make business for some glazier. As they begin to think of this, they elaborate upon it. How much does a new plate glass window cost? Two hundred and fifty dollars? That will be quite a sum. After all, if windows were never broken, what would happen to the glass business? Then, of course, the thing is endless. The glazier will have $250 more to spend with still other merchants, and so ad infinitum. The smashed window will go on providing money and employment in ever-widening circles. The logical conclusion from all this would be, if the crowd drew it, that the little hoodlum who threw the brick, far from being a public menace, was a public benefactor.

Now let us take another look. The crowd is at least right in its first conclusion. This

While admiring the shoes and imagining their comfort and style, you notice that the meter registers 9 utils. If you choose to buy the shoes, you will receive 9 utils of opportunity benefit, or satisfaction, but you will also experience 10 utils of opportunity cost, or regret, for not buying the steak dinner for a net utility of negative 1 util. If you purchase the steak dinner, however, you will experience a positive 1 util of overall satisfaction.

little act of vandalism will in the first instance mean more business for some glazier. The glazier will be no more unhappy to learn of the incident than an undertaker to learn of a death. But the shopkeeper will be out $250 that he was planning to spend for a new suit. Because he has had to replace a window, he will have to go without the suit (or some equivalent need or luxury). Instead of having a window and $250 he now has merely a window. Or, because he was planning to buy the suit that very afternoon, instead of having both a window and a suit he must be content with the window and no suit. If we think of him as part of the community, the community has lost a new suit that might otherwise have come into being and is just that much poorer.

The glazier's gain of business, in short, is merely the tailor's loss of business. No new 'employment' has been added. The people in the crowd were thinking only of two parties to the transaction, the baker and the glazier. They had forgotten the potential third party involved, the tailor. They forgot him precisely because he will not now enter the scene. They will see the new window in the next day or two. They will never see the extra suit, precisely because it will never be made. They see only what is immediately visible to the eye.

Hazlitt therefore concludes,

The whole of economics can be reduced to a single lesson, and that lesson can be reduced to a single sentence. The art of economics consists in looking not merely at the immediate but at the longer effects of any act or policy; it consists in tracing the consequences of that policy not merely for one group but for all groups.

Figure 1-1

	purchase the dinner forgo the shoes	purchase the shoes forgo the dinner
opportunity benefit	10 utils	9 utils
minus opportunity cost	-9 utils	-10 utils
net utility	1 util	-1 util

Under these circumstances a rational person would choose to purchase the steak dinner, but it is not a happy choice. Had you never passed the shoe store, you would have enjoyed the dinner in the amount of 10 utils, but now that satisfaction has evaporated to 1 util. Your satisfaction is diminished because, while you eat your dinner, you will be thinking of what you gave up. You would have been better off had you never passed the shoe store!

Every decision has opportunity benefits and opportunity costs. When people spend money on one good, they must necessarily give up the satisfaction that a different good would have provided. When a business chooses to produce shoes, it must forego the profit it could have made on purses. And when the government hires an unemployed person, someone else in the economy will lose a job since the money he would have received has been taxed away from his customers to pay for the government program. The wise consumer should always ask himself, "What is the hidden cost of making this decision?"

This concept of opportunity cost is the reason that the unregenerate world views economics as the *dismal science*. Every decision brings with it some degree of regret, and that regret varies according to the subjective value placed on the opportunity costs. To the believer, however, one's own subjective value of life's choices are to be examined in light of the principles of God's Word. Making godly choices helps the Christian to be satisfied with the knowledge that he has made right decisions, and thereby he minimizes his regret. When the believer allows the Holy Spirit to renew his mind, he can become truly capable of making godly value judgments:

> I beseech you therefore, brethren, by the mercies of God, that ye present your bodies a living sacrifice, holy, acceptable unto God, which is your reasonable service. And be not conformed to this world: but be ye transformed by the renewing of your mind, that ye may prove what is that good, and acceptable, and perfect, will of God.
>
> (Romans 12:1-2)

Section Review

1. What is economic cost?
2. What is the difference between intrinsic value and subjective value?
3. What is an opportunity cost?

III. Economic Scope and Purpose

Microeconomics Versus Macroeconomics: The Scope of Choice

Economists study their subject on two levels. The first is **microeconomics,** which concerns itself with choices made by individual units: individual people, individual households, or individual business firms. What causes a person to save money? How does one business firm set its prices? How will the closing of a factory affect the individual community?

The second level of economic study is **macroeconomics,** which is concerned with large-scale economic choices and issues. What causes bank interest rates to rise and fall? What causes large scale national unemployment? Why do the Japanese sell more goods to the United States than the United States sells to Japan?

Positive Economics Versus Normative Economics

The approach of observing economic choices and predicting economic events is referred to as **positive economics** while **normative economics** makes value judgments about existing or proposed economic policies. Because normative economics leads economists to judge polices and conditions as good or bad, it often leads to an active attempt to manipulate the economy by altering key economic variables. This intervention may cause trouble because economists, calling upon their personal values, declare what should be.

Everyone makes normative economic statements from time to time such as "Everyone should save 10% of his income," "It is unpatriotic to buy a car made in a foreign country," or "Our nation is becoming a country of hamburger flippers and accountants. The government must get our nation back into being a major producer of the world's goods." The government makes choices based on normative economics such as when it passed the Social Security Act, which requires people to save

Karl Menger (1840-1921)
Founder of the Austrian School of Economics

Karl Menger was born on February 23, 1840 in New Sandec, Galicia. At that time Galicia was a part of Austria, but today it lies within Poland. Karl was one of three brothers who distinguished themselves in some way. Karl became famous in the field of economics while his brothers gained their fame in law and politics. Karl was educated in law at the universities of Prague and Vienna and later studied economics at the University of Kracow, where in 1867 he received a Ph.D.

In that same year the liberals (at that time "liberals" were those who desired individual freedom) persuaded the Austrian emperor to draw up a new constitution promoting the ideas of free trade, equality of individuals under the law, and representative government. Menger, however, studied in the universities that were full of the nonliberal professors of the day. He was taught that the economic affairs of individuals were best controlled by government. Menger thought that this teaching was wrong, that governmental decision making was inefficient, and that it led to the enslavement of the individual to the state.

Menger then tried to determine just how efficient economic choices are made. In the work that resulted from his research, *Grundsatze der Volkswirthschaftslehre* (Principles of Economics), he noted that people make their decisions more efficiently than government because their decisions are based upon personal utility as opposed to some vague notion of the "public good." Menger explained that utility is what gives value to anything. This idea exploded the myth that an object's value is determined by the quality of raw materials or quantity of labor that went into its creation.

Answering the Diamond-Water Paradox, Menger questioned that if a diamond was worth a vast amount simply because it took so much labor to get it out of the ground, how could a diamond found on the surface of the ground possibly sell for the same price as one that "took a thousand days' labor" to produce? As a result of his liberal ideas, which advocated personal freedom, the German government prohibited any of his followers from teaching in any German university.

Because his work emphasized individual economic freedom, Karl Menger has come to be regarded as the father of Austrian Economics, the school of thought that emphasizes the free market, private ownership of property, and limited government.

for retirement in spite of their personal desires, or when it passes laws forbidding certain imports in spite of the desire of citizens to purchase these foreign goods.

Section Review
1. What kind of economics limits its scope to the study of individual people, businesses, or other small economic units?
2. What is positive economics?

GNP: $667.0 billion*
Per Capita GNP: $11,730*
Population: 57,028,000 (1989)
Monetary Unit: pound

The United Kingdom

BANK OF ENGLAND £20
47E 952623 I PROMISE TO PAY THE BEARER ON DEMAND THE SUM OF
TWENTY POUNDS
LONDON FOR THE GOVR AND COMPY OF THE BANK OF ENGLAND
20 POUNDS
47E 952623

Like other Western European countries, the United Kingdom began to rebuild its economy after World War II by using government controls and management in an attempt to give all of its citizens a decent standard of living. As a result, Britain gradually developed a welfare state, and the government took over many key industries. Taxes grew as the government sought funding for its programs, and top rates on the income tax scale soared to over 80%. In order to please workers, the government passed regulations that guaranteed high wages and protected labor from unemployment. High taxes and government regulations stifled efficiency and discouraged business investment. By 1979 the United Kingdom was racked with strikes, inflation, and a generally despondent business climate that gave Britons little opportunity to raise their standard of living.

Into that depressed setting came a new government led by Prime Minister Margaret Thatcher. She led Britain into a program of gradually lowering taxes, privatizing state industries (selling government-owned businesses to private owners), decreasing the power of labor unions, and eliminating many subsidies that had

propped up unprofitable industries. The initial effects of this policy, which was intended to encourage a more competitive and productive nation, were not exactly pleasant. Inflation continued and even grew, and unemployment skyrocketed as industries shed themselves of unproductive workers and as inefficient businesses folded.

However, Britain remained true to its new economic course, and the economy turned upward in the 1980s. Businesses have become more competitive and efficient, and more people are reaping the benefits of improved productivity. Home ownership has risen significantly, and an increasing number of people are investing in Britain's industries. Despite the obvious economic improvements, the British are still reluctant to give up further governmental assistance programs such as national health care and government-controlled industries such as railways and coal mines. If Britons insist that the government return to policies of supplying popular wants out of the public treasury, the nation will undoubtedly fall back into its economic malaise.
*figures for 1987 from the 1990 *Statistical Abstract*

Chapter Review

Terms

economics
insatiability
scarcity
economic cost
goods
services
economic goods
economic services
nuisance goods and services
recycling
free goods
free services
Diamond-Water Paradox
intrinsic value
subjective value
utility
opportunity benefit
opportunity cost
util
microeconomics
macroeconomics
positive economics
normative economics

Content Questions

1. What is economics?
2. Why must we make choices?
3. What language did the word *economics* come from, and what was its original meaning?
4. What are the differences among economic goods, nuisance goods, and free goods? (Give an example of each.)
5. How is it possible for a handful of diamonds to be worth less than a single glass of water?
6. When an economist uses the word *utility*, what does he mean?
7. Why is economics considered a dismal science to an unsaved man? How should the economic choices of Christians differ from those of the unsaved?
8. Define microeconomics and macroeconomics.
9. Define normative economics.

Application Questions

1. Is it possible for an unsaved person to be truly happy in an economic sense? Use Scripture to support your response.
2. List three economic choices you made today. Discuss how you subconsciously or consciously made your choice being sure to include the concepts of opportunity benefit and opportunity cost.
3. Using what you have learned so far in this chapter, explain why the price of Christmas wrapping paper rises before Christmas and then generally falls after December 25th.

CHAPTER 2 _____

Value and Demand

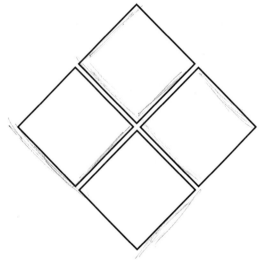

The full soul loatheth an honeycomb; but to the hungry soul every bitter thing is sweet.
Proverbs 27:7

I. Value

Danny loved auctions and this one was no exception. As he elbowed his way to the front of the crowd, he heard the auctioneer call out, "All right, ladies and gentlemen, let's begin the bidding on this fine lamp at five dollars," as he pointed to what, by some stretch of the imagination, might be called a lamp. Actually the object for sale was one of the ugliest things Danny had ever seen. His amusement was turned to shock and disbelief as twelve people began clamoring to purchase it. Several minutes later, after the hectic bidding had died down, the gavel fell. "Sold to the gentleman in the pin-striped suit for three hundred forty-seven dollars!" Danny's mind was reeling, "Who on earth would be willing to pay any price for that thing? What a waste of money!" As the victor happily paid the clerk and strode out the door clutching his prize, several people overheard Danny muttering to himself, "It just doesn't make sense!"

Actually the buyer's actions make perfect sense. Danny is just forgetting Karl Menger's rule of value, which states that value is in the mind of the buyer, not in the thing being purchased. Danny is also forgetting that in a free market in which people are protected from fraud and force they will almost always make choices designed to suit their own needs. Perhaps the buyer of the lamp was interested in it for personal reasons. Perhaps it was like a lamp his grandparents had, and it would be a very special link with his past. Perhaps the lamp contained some hidden treasure, or it may be that the man collected curious lamps and this was a needed addition to his collection.

Being unfamiliar with another's circumstances and frame of mind, we, like Danny, may believe others are acting economically foolishly when, in fact, they are acting quite rationally. People dislike Menger's Principle of Subjective Value because it is unsettling to think that their way of valuing goods and services is not *the* way. In fact, the theory of subjective value lends itself to the possibility that a good actually may possess millions of different values, as many values as there are people on earth.

Diminishing Marginal Utility

While Menger's principle states that values are not constant from one person to another, a second principle holds that values are not constant even for a single person. Those things that a person holds dear right now may be held in lower esteem five minutes from now. For example, let us assume that you enjoy eating Yum-Yum brand candy bars and that you are so hungry that you place a value of $1.20 on the first Yum-Yum bar you can get. This is not to say that the price of a bar is $1.20, merely that you value one so much that you would be *willing to pay* $1.20 for one. Will you always be willing to pay that price? Would you be willing to pay $1.20 for a second bar, a fifth bar, a fiftieth? Probably not. How, then, is it possible for a person's value system to change dramatically in just a matter of moments? How could a person at one moment be willing to pay $1.20 for a candy bar and a few minutes (and several bars) later be unwilling to buy one at any price?

William Stanley Jevons, an English economist, tackled and solved this riddle in 1871. In his book *Theory of Political Economy,* Jevons developed the **Principle of Diminishing Marginal Utility,** which states that people tend to receive less and less (di-

William Stanley Jevons

minishing) additional (marginal) satisfaction (utility) from any good or service as they obtain more and more of it during a specific period of time.

Figure 2-1 Marginal Utility Schedule ᵗ

candy bar number	total satisfaction after this candy bar	minus	total satisfaction before this candy bar	equals	satisfaction this candy bar provided— "marginal utility"
1	6 utils	–	0 utils	=	6 utils
2	10	–	6	=	4
3	13	–	10	=	3
4	15	–	13	=	2
5	16	–	15	=	1
6	16	–	16	=	0
7	15 $\frac{1}{2}$	–	16	=	$-\frac{1}{2}$
8	14	–	15 $\frac{1}{2}$	=	$-1\frac{1}{2}$
9	12	–	14	=	–2
10	2	–	12	=	–10

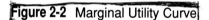

To illustrate, let us return to the candy shop. If we attach to your brain the utility meter referred to in Chapter 1, we find that after eating your first bar your satisfaction level jumps to 6 utils. After eating a second bar, which you enjoyed but not quite as intensely as the first, the meter jumps by 4 additional utils to a total of 10. Your third bar results in a rise of 3 additional utils to a total of 13. Notice how your total satisfaction is rising, but each increase tends to be less than the previous increase. This is diminishing marginal utility. Eventually a point will be reached where additional candy bars will provide no added satisfaction. In fact, past this point, eating more bars will cause dissatisfaction.

Figure 2-1 is an example of a **marginal utility schedule,** a tabular model based upon the observation of our eating the hypothetical candy bars. Figure 2-2 is a **marginal utility curve,** a graphic representation of the marginal utility schedule.

Figure 2-2 Marginal Utility Curve

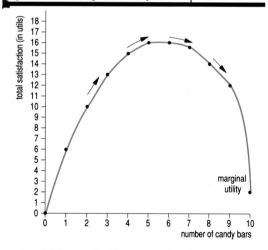

The Function of Prices

In every transaction each person compares his value of an item being purchased with the price tag on the good or service. If a person holds a value for an item that is greater than or equal to its price, a sale will be made. If, on the other hand, a person finds the price higher than what he thinks the item is worth, a sale will not take place. We understand the concept of value, but what about the other part of the transaction? What is this thing called price? Prices are much more than numbers on little stickers affixed to merchandise. Prices serve to transmit information, provide incentives, and redistribute income.

Scripture and the Principle of Diminishing Marginal Utility

The principle of diminishing marginal utility worsens the predicament of unregenerate man because it reveals that man cannot find satisfaction in material things. As William Jevons pointed out, those few things that a man can bring into his possession tend to satisfy less and less as more and more are acquired.

Many do not recognize this and, as a result, spend their lives searching for more material possessions, hoping that ultimate satisfaction might be achieved. The search for happiness in material wealth is futile because the accumulation of possessions only enflames one's desire for more.

But they that will be rich fall into temptation and a snare, and into many foolish and hurtful lusts, which drown men in destruction and perdition. (I Timothy 6:9)

The Bible points out that a person can be totally satisfied only within the context of a close personal relationship with God through trust in the saving work of God's Son, Jesus Christ:

Ho, every one that thirsteth, come ye to the waters, and he that hath no money; come ye, buy, and eat; yea, come, buy wine and milk without money and without price. Wherefore do ye spend money for that which is not bread? and your labor for that which satisfieth not? hearken diligently unto me, and eat ye that which is good, and let your soul delight itself in fatness. (Isaiah 55:1-2)

The principle of diminishing marginal utility not only explains one's disaffection with possessions, but also goes a long way toward explaining other problems. For example, as people grow more familiar with others, they sometimes begin to esteem them less. Those who live in seemingly glamorous or luxurious places often do not enjoy their advantages. And after growing up in Christian homes and being surrounded by Scripture, godly examples, and spiritual blessings, some children grow weary of their blessings and come to despise the Bible, their parents, and their churches. God warned His children that they need to be on guard against the insensitivity that grows out of familiarity.

And it shall be, when the Lord thy God shall have brought thee into the land which he sware unto thy fathers, to Abraham, to Isaac, and to Jacob, to give thee great and goodly cities, which thou buildedst not, And houses full of all good things, which thou filledst not, and wells digged, which thou diggedst not, vineyards and olive trees, which thou plantedst not; when thou shalt have eaten and be full; Then beware lest thou forget the Lord, which brought thee forth out of the land of Egypt, from the house of bondage.
(Deuteronomy 6:10-12)

Suppose that for some unknown reason millions of people begin placing a greater value on Yum-Yum candy bars. Thousands of stores will experience greater demand and, therefore, place larger orders with their wholesalers. Wholesalers, realizing that they have nowhere near the number of candy bars needed to satisfy the stores' demand, place larger orders with the candy manufacturers. The makers of the candy bars, now overwhelmed with orders from stores all over the country, need to purchase greater amounts of ingredients from suppliers. In order to persuade producers to sell them more cocoa, milk, cream, and eggs, the candy makers must offer them higher prices. Seeing a potential for huge profits, cocoa producers will increase their production; dairy farmers will purchase more milk cows and will hire more farm hands. Egg ranchers will purchase more laying hens. On and on this process continues until information is transmitted virtually all over the world telling business firms what ought to be produced.

The price mechanism also provides incentives. As buyers demand more Yum-Yum bars, the higher prices that producers offer farmers act as incentives for them to divert their production to those goods

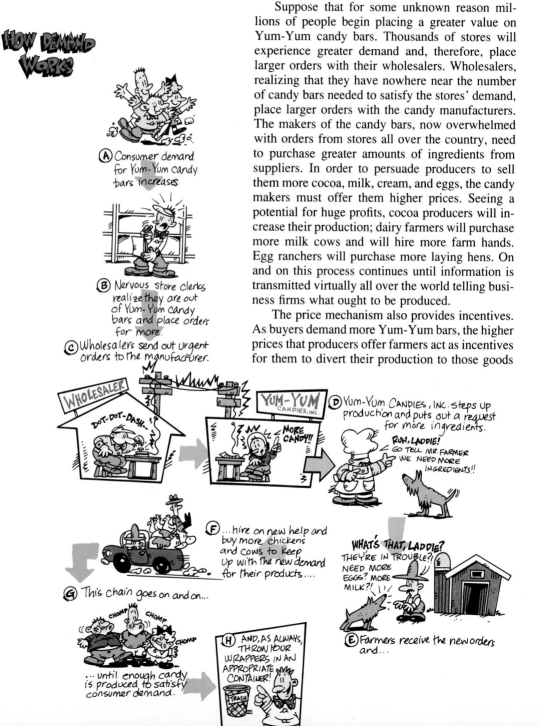

How Demand Works

(A) Consumer demand for Yum-Yum candy bars increases.

(B) Nervous store clerks realize they are out of Yum-Yum candy bars and place orders for more.

(C) Wholesalers send out urgent orders to the manufacturer.

(D) Yum-Yum Candies, Inc. steps up production and puts out a request for more ingredients.

RUN, LADDIE! GO TELL MR. FARMER WE NEED MORE INGREDIENTS!!

(F) ...hire on new help and buy more chickens and cows to keep up with the new demand for their products....

(G) This chain goes on and on...

WHAT'S THAT, LADDIE? THEY'RE IN TROUBLE?! NEED MORE EGGS? MORE MILK?!

(E) Farmers receive the new orders and...

...until enough candy is produced to satisfy consumer demand.

(H) AND, AS ALWAYS, THROW YOUR WRAPPERS IN AN APPROPRIATE CONTAINER!

Friedrich von Hayek (1899-)
Champion of the Market Price System

Born in Vienna, Friedrich von Hayek rose to prominence by his contributions to the "Austrian School" of economic thought. This approach to economics asserts the ability of markets to adjust to changing circumstances and opposes government interference in these natural market adjustments.

Hayek's first major work, the widely read *The Road to Serfdom,* was an assault on government intervention in the market process. In 1945, one year after the appearance of that celebrated work, he wrote an important article entitled "The Use of Knowledge in Society." In that article Hayek described how prices automatically transmit information to producers and consumers in such a way that each responds and adjusts to market disturbances regardless of their knowledge about the original causes of those disturbances.

Hayek's writings and teaching in Europe and the United States gave him opportunity to add to the development of macroeconomics and monetary theory. In 1974 he won the Nobel Prize for economics.

that the economy wants. Financial institutions, eager to make loans to candy makers and candy shops, offer savers higher rates of interest on savings to create a larger pool of money to lend.

Prices also serve a third function of redistributing income. As a result of redirecting their factors of production into those activities that satisfy buyers, farmers, chemists, and inventors will find that their incomes have increased. On the other hand, those producers who have ignored the information transmitted by the price mechanism and who are not persuaded by its incentive function to produce what the economy desires will find their incomes being redistributed to others—that is, they will go broke.

Section Review
1. Who identified the Principle of Diminishing Marginal Utility?
2. What does that principle state?
3. What are the three functions of prices?

II. True Prices Determined by Supply and Demand

It is easy to observe that prices transmit information, provide incentives, and redistribute income, but *where do prices come from* might very be your next question. Do producers charge whatever price they want? Do price tags somehow mysteriously appear in the night on items in stores? Does the government declare what prices shall be? In a free-market economy, prices are determined by both the sellers *and* the buyers. If a price is too high, sellers will have to lower their price or risk going out of business for a lack of buyers. If buyers are willing to pay only a ridiculously low price, they will go unsatisfied, because firms will refuse to produce.

Undoubtedly you have heard that many things occur because of *supply and demand.* Exactly what are supply and demand and how do they work together to create prices? The rest of this chapter will be devoted to discussing demand–its definition and its operation. Supply and prices will be examined in Chapter 3.

The Law of Demand

Most people believe that demand is the same thing as "want." The economist sees **demand** not as just a willingness to buy but as the act of buying.

Figure 2-3

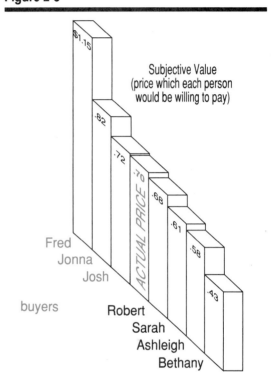

Subjective Value
(price which each person would be willing to pay)

$1.15

.82

.72

.70 ACTUAL PRICE

.68

.61

.58

.43

Fred
Jonna
Josh

buyers

Robert
Sarah
Ashleigh
Bethany

The **law of demand** states that, everything else being held constant, the lower the price charged for a good or service, the greater the quantity people will demand and vice versa.

The law of demand is nothing but common sense. If the price of a Yum-Yum bar at Candy City, our new hypothetical candy store, is 70¢, then only those people who value a bar greater than or equal to 70¢ will demand one. Figure 2-3 shows the subjective values seven people have for a Yum-Yum bar. At a price of 70¢ per bar, Candy City will sell only three bars to these seven people.

Now suppose that a discount from the manufacturer enables Candy City to lower its price to 60¢. Figure 2-4 illustrates that the price has dropped to a level where it is now attractive to two more buyers.

Figure 2-4

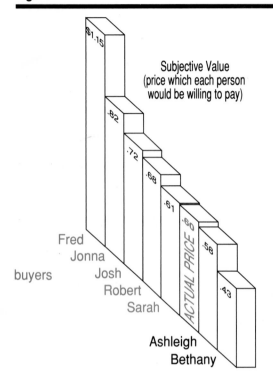

Subjective Value
(price which each person
would be willing to pay)

$1.15
.82
.72
.68
.61
.60
.58
.43

ACTUAL PRICE

buyers

Fred
Jonna
Josh
Robert
Sarah
Ashleigh
Bethany

Figure 2-5 Demand Schedule

PRICE CHARGED PER CANDY BAR	QUALITY DEMANDED
$1.60	2,000 BARS
1.25	2,250
.70	3,500
.50	6,000
.45	6,750

GIFFEN - they don't make it till you buy it

Economists, wishing to observe the effects of price changes on a product's demand, construct a **demand schedule,** a table listing various quantities demanded at various prices. Figure 2-5 is a demand schedule for Candy City's Yum-Yum bars.

To visualize the law of demand better, economists take the information from the demand schedule and put it into line-graph form. The result is called a **demand curve.** Notice how the demand schedule contains only a limited number of observations. However, when put into line graph form such as in Figure 2-6, the information is expanded into an infinite number of points. Thus the observer has a better idea of the demand for the product at any given price.

Whenever a change in price causes a change in the number of items demanded, a **change in quantity demanded** has occurred. Suppose that Candy

Figure 2-6 Demand Curve

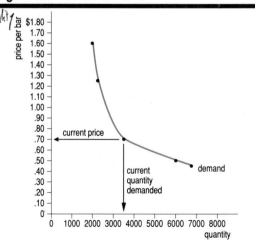

Figure 2-7 Change in Quantity Demanded

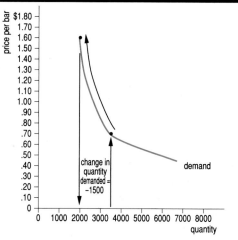

Figure 2-8 Increase in Demand

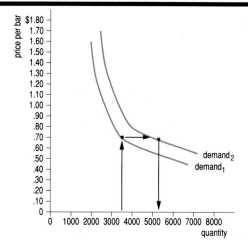

City has been selling Yum-Yum bars for 70¢, but because of increases in the prices of ingredients, it must charge $1.60. Looking at Figure 2-7, we find that at a price of $1.60 per bar, the quantity demanded will be only 2,000 bars, a change of 1,500 bars.

Change in Demand

When a demand curve shifts, it is said that the product is experiencing a **change in demand.** A rightward shift, an **increase in demand,** represents a willingness on the part of buyers to demand more of a good or service at every price. The opposite is the case if a leftward shift, or **decrease in demand,** occurs.

Figure 2-8 illustrates an increase in demand. At a price of 70¢ per bar on the first demand curve (D₁), the quantity demanded is 3,500 bars. A rightward shift of the demand curve to D₂ leads to a quantity demanded of 5,250 bars at that same 70¢ price. A decrease in demand is seen in Figure 2-9. The leftward shift of the demand curve means that at any given price less will be demanded than before. Whereas 3,500 bars were originally demanded at 70¢, only 2,750 bars will be sold after a leftward shift of the demand curve to D₂.

Common sense tells us that if the price of a good falls, people tend to buy more of it and vice

Figure 2-9 Decrease in Demand

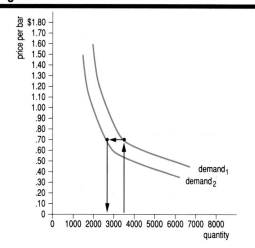

versa, but what could cause people to buy more or less of a good or service when the price stays the same? Economists have discovered four things that may cause a change in demand.

1. A change in people's incomes
2. A change in the price of related goods
3. A change in people's tastes and preferences
4. A change in people's expectations

Saudi
Arabia

GNP: $98.1 billion*
Per Capita GNP: $7,571*
Population: 16,109,000 (1989)
Monetary Unit: riyal

Oil was first discovered in Saudi Arabia in 1938, but little development of that resource took place until after World War II. Then, as petroleum provided a growing source of wealth for the impoverished desert kingdom, the Saudis moved from an economy characterized by oasis date farmers, camel caravans, and markets of open stalls along village streets to one noted for developing industries and growing modern cities with superhighways and shopping malls.

Saudi Arabia has about 25% of the world's known oil reserves, and it produces five million barrels of oil a day. The tremendous income the nation has received from the sale of this resource since the late 1940s has provided money for the Saudis to improve their standard of living, develop a growing industrial economy, and contribute aid to other needy lands. The government has controlled and developed much of Saudi Arabia's economic ventures. Such government activity was necessitated by the original lack of educated and skilled Saudis and capable Saudi businesses to handle large modernization and development projects. Foreign firms, including many American businesses, were called to provide needed manpower and technical assistance. Nevertheless, the Saudi government has made provisions to train the Saudi people to assume responsibility for future development as well as to encourage private Saudi businesses to acquire control of many of the growing industries.

Although Saudi Arabia's present economy is noticeably dependent on oil exports, diversification is under way. Some of these projects involve the manufacture of petrochemicals and metal products, food processing, and even desert agriculture. The arid land of Saudi Arabia has actually produced some wheat for export. The rapid transformation of this weak and backward desert country of a few million people into a world economic power has been made possible by the oil that lies under its sands.

*figures for 1986 from the 1990 *World Almanac*

Change in Income—*One of the most important causes of a shift of the demand curve is a change in people's incomes. When people receive paychecks, they must divide their limited incomes among those goods and services they want most. For example, some families budget a given amount for eating in a nice restaurant once per month. When their incomes rise they will probably allot more for this activity even though the price of dinners at the restaurant has not changed. Likewise with our candy bars, as buyers receive greater incomes, they will want to buy more. Parents will buy more for their children, boyfriends will buy more for their girlfriends, and some will buy more for themselves. Whereas 3,500 bars were purchased at 70¢ each, now, with their higher incomes, purchasers are able to buy 5,250 bars at the same price.

If demand increases for a good because the buyer's income goes up, then that good is called a **normal good.** While most goods are normal goods, some goods actually experience a decline in popularity as buyers' incomes increase. These **inferior goods** include such things as recapped tires, travel on city buses, used cars, secondhand clothing, and powdered milk. Not only do inferior goods experience a decrease in demand as people's incomes increase, but they also see an increase in demand as consumer incomes fall. As incomes decline, more used cars, powdered milk, and recapped tires are sold. No single good or service can be definitely called a normal good or an inferior good since an inferior good to one person may be a normal good to another. A wealthy person may consider a used car to be an inferior good while a less wealthy person may consider it to be a normal good.

Change in the Price of Related Goods—A second reason that demand may increase or decrease for a product without its price changing is that it may be replaced by a similar good. Goods that may be used in place of others are called **substitute goods.** They include chicken and beef, hot dogs and hamburgers, ice cream and ice milk. As the price of one of the goods rises, consumers tend to buy more of the substitute. For example, as the price of beef rises, consumers will decrease their purchases of beef. Needing to make up for the decrease, consumers will purchase more chicken, even though its price has not changed. This increase in demand for chicken corresponds to a rightward shift of its demand curve.

Figure 2-10a good #1-beef

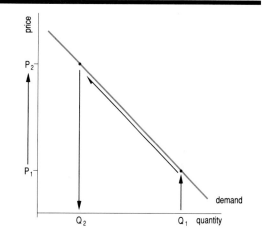

Figure 2-10b good #2-chicken

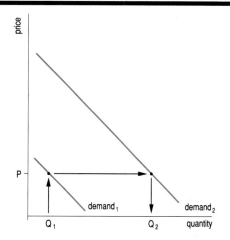

An increase in the price of beef causes a decrease in the quantity demanded for beef, which eventually leads to an increase in demand for chicken, a substitute for beef.

Not only are there goods that act as substitutes, but there also exist **complementary goods,** goods that are usually purchased or used together. Examples of complementary goods include film and cameras, gasoline and automobiles, hamburgers and french fries, and peanut butter and jelly. When the price of one of the complementary goods rises, demand for the other good decreases even though its price has not changed. For example looking at Figure 2-11a, let us assume that the price of peanut butter rises from $1.80 to $4.50 per jar. Naturally, since the price has gone up, the quantity demanded will decrease, in this case, from three jars to one. Since many customers purchase peanut butter for peanut butter and jelly sandwiches, they will cut their demand for jelly from three jars to one even though the price of jelly has not changed. (See Figure 2-11b.)

Change in Tastes and Preferences–A third reason that people change their demand for goods and services is a change in their tastes and preferences. As a product gains popularity, its demand curve experiences a rightward shift as people demand more at any given price. As the product loses popularity, its demand curve begins to shift to the left. The products that most people associate with shifts

Film and cameras are examples of complementary goods.

Figure 2-11a Good #1-peanut butter

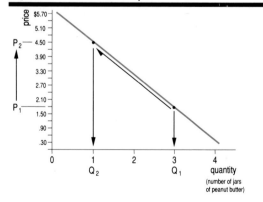

Figure 2-11b Good #2-jelly

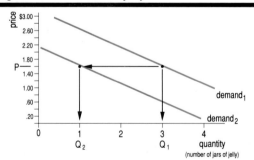

An increase in the price of peanut butter causes a decrease in the quantity demanded for peanut butter, which eventually leads to a decrease in demand for jelly, a complementary good.

in demand due to changes in taste and preferences are fad items. Fad items are those goods and services that appear quickly on the scene, are advertised heavily, and are sold in great quantities over a short period of time. As quickly as it caught the market's fancy, the product loses favor and sales plummet. Examples of fad items in the past have included certain styles of haircuts, pet rocks, and gourmet ice cubes.

Virtually all items, however, suffer the same fate as fad items only over a longer period of time. Consider the horse and buggy, the top hat, and hooped skirts. As time progressed, each of these items gradually became less popular, causing left-ward shifts of their demand curves until there was virtually no demand left.

Change in Expectations–The final reason for a shift in the demand curve is a change in people's expectations of future prices. Suppose you have just received word from a reliable source that the price of frozen concentrated orange juice, which is currently selling for $1.25 per can, will be going up to $3.00 per can because of a drought in both California and Florida. Chances are, if you have the money, you will make a trip to the supermarket to purchase more cans than usual to beat the expected price increase.

Fad items sell in great quantities for short periods of time, but demand for them quickly fades.

Since the price has not yet changed but you demanded more, your orange juice demand curve has just made a rightward shift. The opposite also holds true: as people believe prices are going to decline, they postpone purchases so that they may buy at a lower price later. Assume you hear from your reliable source that both California and Florida will be harvesting record-breaking crops of oranges, causing a decline in the price of frozen concentrated orange juice from $1.25 per can to 50¢ per can. Chances are great that you will shift your demand curve to the left. That is, you will postpone purchases of orange juice today in the hope of purchasing more tomorrow at the lower price.

Section Review

1. What is the economic definition of the word demand?
2. What is the law of demand?
3. What is the name for the graph that illustrates the demand for certain products?
4. What four conditions may change the demand for a product?

Chapter Review

Terms
principle of diminishing marginal utility
marginal utility schedule
demand
law of demand
demand schedule
demand curve
change in quantity demanded
change in demand
increase in demand
decrease in demand
normal good
inferior goods
substitute goods
complementary goods

Content Questions
1. Explain in your own words the principle of diminishing marginal utility. Give an example.
2. Explain how prices act to transmit information.
3. Explain how the law of demand works in light of Figures 2-3 and 2-4.
4. Looking at Figure 2-6 calculate what will be the approximate quantity demanded at a price of 90¢? 60¢? $1.10?

5. List five goods that you consider normal goods and five that you consider inferior goods.
6. Why is it that when the price of the original good rises we tend to purchase more substitute goods and fewer complementary goods?

Application Questions
1. Discuss the moral implications of the following statement: *I like General Motors; therefore, it should be illegal for anyone to demand a different brand of car.* How is this type of reasoning evidencing itself in some of our laws?
2. What should be the Christian's attitude toward the principle of diminishing marginal utility? Does the Christian's attitude disagree with the attitude of the unsaved person? Use the Bible to support your answer.
3. If the market price for a candy bar should be 50¢ but the government, in its desire to decrease candy consumption, requires stores to charge $5.00 per bar, what disruptions may occur in the economy? (Hint: Review the list of the three functions of prices.)
4. How do business firms use advertising to shift an individual household's demand curves? Is it morally right for them to do so?

CHAPTER 3 _____

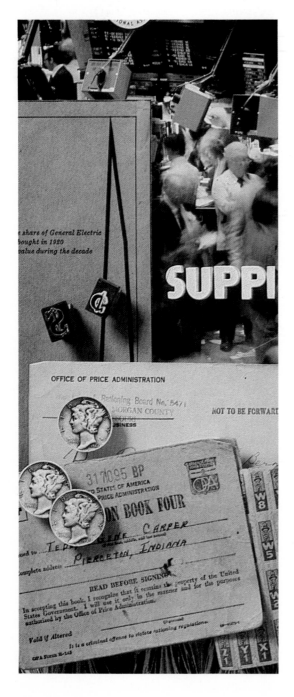

Supply and Prices

I. Supply
    A. The Law of Supply
    B. Changes in Supply
II. Determining Prices
    A. Equilibrium
    B. Surplus
    C. Shortage

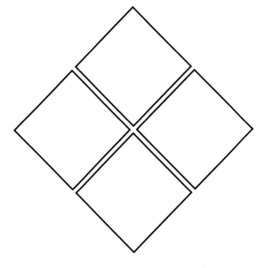

In the American economy, products generally sell at the market price.

Labour not to be rich: cease from thine own wisdom.   Proverbs 23:4

"How could we have been so wrong?" muttered the government official to himself late one winter afternoon as he sat in his comfortable office gazing out at the long line of blank-faced peasants stoically waiting for bread. Running through his mind was a vision of the painful personal consequences he and his family would experience as a result of his department's horrendous decision. The date: the early 1960s. The place: the Soviet Union. The problem: the Kremlin's decision to standardize all Soviet owned trucks and tractors to diesel rather than gasoline-powered engines. "It all seemed so perfect–diesel fuel is safer and more efficient than gasoline. At 30 rubles per ton it's cheaper than gasoline, which costs 80 rubles per ton. Even most American companies have switched to diesel equipment; what went wrong?"

Indeed, what did go wrong? Actually the Soviet planners made several mistakes. First, rather than calculating the cost of the equipment using the market interest rate on borrowed money, Soviet planners used a rate dictated by the state. That rate, which was too low, caused them to seriously underestimate the total cost of new diesel equipment.

Second, forgetting that the quality of Soviet diesel fuel was inferior to the rest of the world's and unsuitable for use, Soviet planners were deceived into thinking that diesel fuel was significantly cheaper at their "official" price. The market price of higher-quality, non-Soviet diesel fuel was not much less than gasoline. Later, attempting to avoid paying the higher market price, they began using their inferior diesel fuel. The high sulfur content of the fuel quickly damaged or destroyed almost all the engines in state-owned equipment.

While several problems contributed to the Soviet "dieselization" fiasco, the fundamental error was that the Soviet planners did not realize that there can never be an "official price" contrary to the market price. The price of a good is not like an elevator, which can be raised and lowered at the whim of some controller. The market price of anything–money, equipment, and diesel fuel–comes not from an edict, but from a compromise, an agreement between a buyer and a seller. Chapter 2 examined the demand side, or the buyer's point of view. We now examine the seller's perspective, or the supply side, and later we will see how buyers and sellers agree, reaching a market price.

I. Supply

Supply is defined as the amount of goods and services business firms are willing and able to provide at different prices. As far as economists are concerned, business firms include *all* sellers of goods and services, not just major corporations.

The Law of Supply

The law of demand stated that as the price of a good or service falls, other things being held constant, people will demand more of it and vice versa. The **law of supply,** on the other hand, holds that the higher the price *buyers* are willing to pay, other things being held constant, the greater the quantity of the product a supplier will produce, and vice versa.

Let us now turn the table and assume that you are no longer a customer but the owner of Candy City and that it costs you 40¢ to produce each Yum-Yum candy bar. Common sense tells us that if customers are willing to pay only 39¢, you would be unwilling to produce any, since you would find yourself losing 1¢ on every bar sold. As the price buyers are willing to pay rises above this 39¢ level, you would be willing to produce more candy. A hypothetical observation was made and the results are found in Figure 3-1. This table of data is known as a **supply schedule.**

Whether their product be shoes or sheets of steel, generally speaking, suppliers will produce a greater quantity as the price rises.

Figure 3-1 Supply Schedule

PRICE OFFERED PER CANDY BAR	QUANTITY SUPPLIED
$1.60	5,000 BARS
1.25	4,750
.70	3,500
.50	1,000
.45	250

Information contained in a supply schedule may be made more useful if it is plotted on a graph called a **supply curve.** Supply curves are positively sloped, demonstrating that as the price consumers are willing to pay rises, suppliers become willing to provide greater quantities; and as the price falls, producers are led to produce fewer quantities. Whenever a change in the price consumers are willing to pay causes a change in the number of goods produced and sold, a **change in quantity supplied** has occurred as seen in Figure 3-2.

Changes in Supply

Just as a demand curve may shift to the left or right, a supply curve may shift in a similar way, causing a **change in supply.** A leftward shift indicates a **decrease in supply,** a situation in which suppliers will produce less of their product at any given price. An **increase in supply,** a rightward shift of the supply curve, demonstrates the willingness of business firms to produce more at any given price. Figure 3-3 and 3-4 illustrate these two situations. Figure 3-3 illustrates a decrease in supply. Where Candy City was willing to supply, for example, 3,500 candy bars at 70¢ (Supply₁), it is now willing to supply 1,750 candy bars at the same price. Figure 3-4, on the other hand, demonstrates a rightward shift of the supply curve. Where Candy City previously was willing to provide 3,500 bars at 70¢, it is now willing to supply 4,250.

It is understandable why business firms would be willing to provide more or less of a good as customers become willing to pay more or less, but what could cause a business to supply more or less of a good *at the same price?* Economists have

Figure 3-2 Change in Quantity Supplied

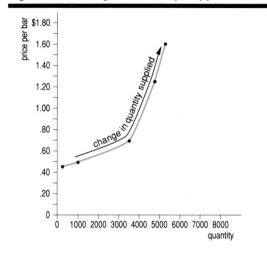

Figure 3-3 Decrease in Supply

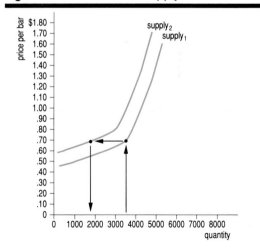

pinpointed three factors that lead to this phenomenon.
1. Changes in technology
2. Changes in production costs
3. Changes in the price of related goods

Figure 3-4 Increase in Supply

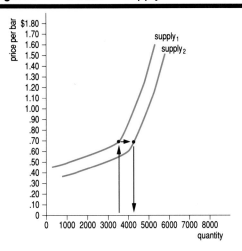

Changes in Technology–Technological advances are improvements in the tools used to produce goods and services. Recent technological advances include the use of computers and automated production machinery. As the tools of production are improved, businesses are able to offer more of the product at the same price (or the same amount at a lower price).

Consider the case of the electronic calculator. In the early 1970s a "pocket" electronic calculator (which was in fact very large) had the ability to perform only limited mathematical functions, and it cost the average consumer around $75. As time passed the tools of production improved, the components were miniaturized, and quality increased dramatically. As the tools used in producing calculators improved, businesses were able to manufacture them less expensively. The same amount of money that the producers once spent to manufacture a few early calculators now allowed them to make many more of the modernized versions. Supplies increased rapidly, and prices began to drop. For the $75 a person had to pay for a single calculator in 1973, he could buy fifteen or more now.

Changes in technology caused the functional calculators of the early 1970s to be replaced by smaller, more powerful, and more economical models.

Figure 3-5

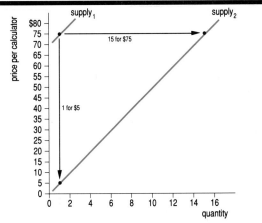

A Change in Technology Kills the Caboose

The following article from the *Washington Post* illustrates how technology has improved the efficiency of the railroads.

Mighty Microchip Derails the Caboose
Roads Switch to Mini-Monitor

SALT LAKE CITY–The caboose is headed for the last roundhouse.

The venerable piece of Americana that has brought up the rear of countless trains for more than a century is headed for extinction, replaced by a shoebox-size microelectronic monitor–most of them built in Rockville, Maryland–designed to do the work traditionally entrusted to a crew member perched in the caboose's cupola.

"We're replacing a manned caboose that weighs 25 tons and costs $70,000 with an automatic 35-pound black box that costs about $4,000," said Dick Tincher, an executive with the Union Pacific, which is buying hundreds of the electronic monitors, which indicate whether the train and its air brakes are working properly.

But as in other confrontations between man and microchip, this leap into the future has not been entirely smooth. The caboose question has become a major economic and political battle.

Prodded by rail unions, three federal agencies, including a special inquiry board set up by President Reagan, have contemplated the caboose controversy. All three eventually agreed that the caboose is an anachronism.

"Five years, maybe eight years from now, and you won't ever see a caboose," said Tincher. Even A. W. Westphal of the United Transportation Union conceded that "the caboose is probably doomed unless we get some regulatory or legislative changes pretty fast."

The beneficiaries of this change would be the railroads, which would save $400 million annually in maintenance and fuel costs, according to the Association of American Railroads. Also benefiting would be a handful of inventive new companies that have brought the glamour of high-tech electronics to the workaday world of the freight yard.

The largest U.S. supplier of the microelectronic train-end monitor is Pulse Electronics on Frederick Avenue in Rockville.

Pulse was started in 1977 by a pair of Cuban refugees, Emilio Fernandes and Angel Beban, who knew both microelectronics and railroading. Today their privately held company has 100 employees and offers a full line of train-monitoring gear.

Pulse is selling its caboose replacement–called Trainlink–to Union Pacific, Burlington Northern, and other roads.

Mark Kane, marketing director at the Rockville firm, has ambitious dreams for Trainlink. "It's got to be a multimillion-dollar product," he said. "There are 12,000 cabooses out there now, and every one is going to be replaced with technology."

Caboose history is somewhat shrouded in mystery, but, according to rail historians, the friendly little car with the cupola probably was invented about 1850 when trains were getting so long that the crew could not watch every car from the engine.

At first, the railroads erected a wooden shanty on a flatcar and hooked it to the rear of the train. This makeshift car eventually was named the caboose, evidently from the Dutch word "kabuis," meaning "cabin house."

Railroad men have battled for years over the proper plural of this term. "Cabeese" was the accepted form for some time; "cabooses" seems to be standard now.

The caboose matured into a separate car, serving as the train's office, where the conductor kept records of his freight, and as a rolling dormitory for the crew.

Around 100 years ago, railroads added the cupola–a raised, windowed box sticking out of the caboose's roof. A crew member, either the conductor or the rear brakeman, was assigned to sit there and keep an eye out for derailments, dragging equipment, and overheated axles, called "hot boxes."

In later years, some railroads opted for bay windows on the side of the caboose rather than a cupola.

Over time, however, many of the caboose's functions were rendered unnecessary. With computerized record-handling, train personnel no longer needed a rolling office. Changing work rules meant crews no longer spent the night on the caboose.

Most railroads placed electronic monitors every 50 miles or so along the track to detect dragging gear and "hot boxes," making the brakeman in the cupola less important.

Gradually, the railroads concluded that the expense of buying and maintaining the caboose, and the fuel used in hauling the 25-ton car across the continent, could no longer be justified.

–T. R. Reid
February 17, 1985

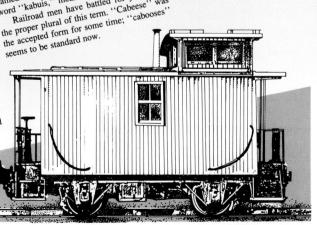

Changes in Production Costs–Business firms must pay for the natural resources, labor, and financial capital that go into their products. If a firm's costs rise, it must decrease the quantity it provides at the same price. For example, Beth, a business-minded ten-year-old, decided to open a lemonade stand in her front yard. Since a 100-ounce bottle of lemonade cost $1, Beth charged 10¢ per 10 ounce glass (we are ignoring profit for the moment). Her venture was so successful that she had to buy another 100-ounce bottle the next day. To her surprise the price had risen to $2. Making some quick mental calculations, she determined that for the same 10-ounce glass she would have to raise her price to 20¢. After Beth changed her sign to reflect the higher price, her business dropped off dramatically. Figuring that the price was out of the reach of her young customers, she decided to offer a second alternative corresponding to a leftward shift of the supply curve: a 5-ounce glass for the old 10¢ price (Figure 3-6).

Had the price of lemonade at the store *declined* to 50¢ per bottle, Beth would have been able to shift the supply curve to the right, offering a 20-ounce glass for the 10¢ price.

Changes in the Price of Other Goods–As the price people are willing to pay for a substitute rises, business firms naturally become willing to sell more of that good or service. To devote more resources to the higher-priced substitute, firms will decrease their supply of the original good even though its price has not changed.

Suppose Beth's best friend Brenda opened a much more popular iced-tea stand next door selling a 10-ounce glass for 10¢ yielding her a 3¢ profit. Receiving no profit on her lemonade and seeing her customers attracted to Brenda's stand, Beth decided to quit selling lemonade and to sell iced tea instead. The result: Even though the price of Beth's lemonade did not change, her supply curve shifted to the left. Where once she was willing to produce ten glasses at 10¢ each, she now became willing to produce zero glasses of lemonade at the same price.

Section Review

1. What is the law of supply?
2. Which way does a supply curve slope and why?
3. What three factors could lead to a change in supply?

Figure 3-6

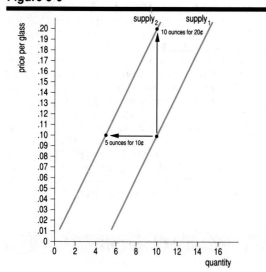

Figure 3-7

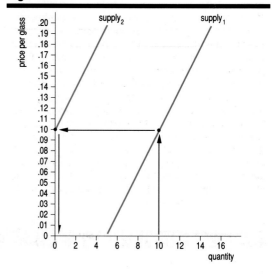

Thomas Robert Malthus (1766-1834)
Economic Prophet of Doom

Economics earned its reputation as "the dismal science" largely because of the work of Thomas Robert Malthus, a British minister who turned to a career in political economics. Malthus often discussed issues of the day with his learned father. In one of these conversations it appeared that the son disagreed with his father's view that economic conditions were improving and society would soon become free from want. As a part of their ongoing discussion on the matter, the younger Malthus wrote down his arguments in a well-reasoned paper. The father was so impressed by the work that he encouraged Malthus to publish it. In 1798 the treatise appeared anonymously as *An Essay on the Principle of Population as It Affects the Future Improvement of Society.*

In this work Malthus explained that populations expand at geometric rates. For example, when families have four children that live to adulthood and each child with his spouse has four more children, the population doubles every generation. Although the rate of this multiplication may vary, the potential for tremendous population growth is evident. Malthus pointed out that at the same time that the population is expanding geometrically, the growth of the food supply is limited to a slower rate of increase. A few more plows may cultivate a few more fields, but arable land is limited. Food production cannot multiply at the same fast rate as population. Therefore, Malthus predicted the inevitability that the demand for food by a multiplying population would soon outstrip the supply of food available. The result would be food shortages, giving rise to famine, pestilence, and war. These in turn would reduce the population to levels at which the food supply could again meet the demand. However, the population would begin to multiply again and eventually bring about another wave of famine and death. The only

remedy for this awful cycle, according to Malthus, was an effort to check population growth by moral restraint and by avoiding assistance to the poor so that their misery would discourage their propagation.

Malthus's prognosis certainly dampened the optimistic prospects of his contemporaries, but as the years progressed, his dire prediction was not fulfilled. Malthus could not foresee two important developments of the nineteenth and twentieth centuries–the agricultural improvements that greatly increased food supplies, and the tendency of people in industrial societies to have smaller families. Nonetheless, the work of Malthus has not been proved false. The potential for extreme population growth and resulting famine is seen all too clearly in Third World countries today.

Lactaid

II. Determining Prices

The beginning of this chapter stated that the market price of every good or service represents an agreement, a meeting of the minds, between the buyer and the seller. How, though, can there be a meeting of the minds when the motives of both participants are exactly opposite? When prices are high and suppliers are willing to supply great quantities, buyers are unwilling to buy. On the other hand, when prices are low, suppliers are willing to produce less than buyers are willing to buy.

Indeed the two laws are in continual conflict except at one and only one critical point. At this point both parties to the transaction will agree that the price is fair, permitting goods to freely clear the market. Once again using the Candy City candy shop for illustration, Figure 3-8 gives us a graphic representation of the plans both of the buyers and sellers.

Equilibrium

Figure 3-8 is a consolidated view of the plans of both the consumers and the suppliers. The critical intersection point at which both parties agree is called the **market equilibrium point** and represents that price at which consumers are willing

If a product is priced above the market equilibrium price, a surplus will result.

Figure 3-8 Market Equilibrium

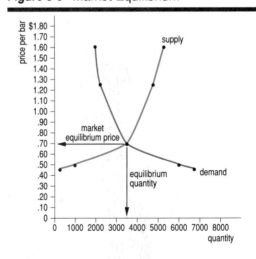

to pull out of the market the exact quantity of product that suppliers are willing to push into the market. The price at which this meeting of the minds occurs is called the **market equilibrium price.** For Candy City and its customers, this market equilibrium price is 70¢.

Surplus

Causes of Surplus–At this point you may be asking yourself why Candy City would limit its price to 70¢ per bar. After all, we have been brought up to believe that businesses can charge any price they desire. Reality is quite different. No one is totally exempt from the laws of demand and supply.

If a supplier raises the price of his product above the market equilibrium price, he will be led by the law of supply to push a greater quantity into the market than before. At the same time, however, the law of demand compels buyers to pull less out of the market. The combined effect of the two opposite laws will result in a **surplus,** an excess of unsold products.

Looking at Figure 3-9, let us assume that Candy City's management has become greedy and has decided to raise the price of its Yum-Yum bars to $1.25 each. Because of the higher price, Candy City stands to make a profit of 85¢ per bar sold ($1.25 minus its 40¢ cost to produce) as opposed to the 30¢ per bar profit it was making before. This rosy profit picture prompts Candy City's management to produce 4,750 candy bars, 1,250 more than it produced at the equilibrium price. Deciding that the price is too high, customers reduce total demand by 1,250 bars. With the firm producing 1,250 candy bars more and buyers demanding 1,250 less, the combined result will be a surplus of 2,500 bars.

Because of the high costs associated with carrying large inventories, business firms do not like surpluses. If a surplus continues for too long, carrying costs will drive many suppliers out of business.

Solutions to Surplus–Obviously something must be done: the surplus must be eliminated, and the carrying costs must decrease, but the question is how? Three possible solutions exist: increase demand, decrease supply, or allow the price to fall to the market equilibrium point.

The first and best solution, from the standpoint of the supplier, is the one in which he may both produce the greater quantity and charge the higher price at the same time. The only way this could occur would be for the demand curve to shift to

Figure 3-9 Surplus

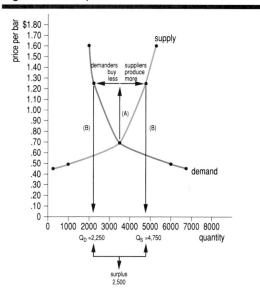

GNP: $7.6 billion*
Per Capita GNP: $340*
Population: 24,346,000 (1989)
Monetary Unit: shilling

Following its independence from Britain in 1963, Kenya quickly established itself as one of the most promising countries of sub-Saharan Africa. Although it had a large, poor population and lacked abundant supplies of natural resources, Kenya sought to build private industry and encourage foreign aid and investment. Kenya's efforts were rewarded with the introduction of new processing plants and refineries and several manufacturing industries to meet domestic needs. Also, the fertile land of the Kenya Highlands added significant crops of coffee and tea for export, and Kenya's spectacular wildlife attracted many tourists.

Even though Kenya made economic progress during the 1960s and 1970s, it did face several problems that have been common to much of sub-Saharan Africa. Contentions among tribal divisions tended to undermine the stability of the democratic government and thus encouraged leaders to take almost dictatorial pow-

ers to resist opposition. As a result, these leaders were able to give political and economic favors to those in their own ethnic group to preserve their power base. The contentions and the graft worsened in the 1980s as Kenya's leaders bought property, industries, and banks and then used their political power to control the economy and create personal fortunes from these ventures. Meanwhile, the majority of Kenyans continued in poverty. Unemployment, a lack of land for the country's poor farmers and herders, and diminishing opportunities for economic growth are some of the problems that have grown worse in recent years. Because of political corruption, ethnic division, and economic control, the prospects for Kenya's political and economic stability are poor; and without that stability Kenya will have difficulty acquiring the aid and investments it needs for future economic improvements.

*figures for 1987 from the 1990 *Statistical Abstract*

Figure 3-10 Demand Solution to a Surplus

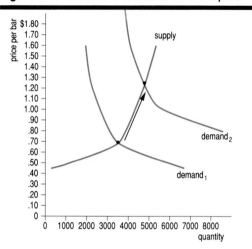

Figure 3-11 Supply Solution to a Surplus

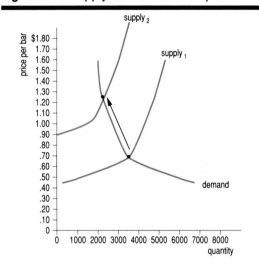

the right. In the case of Candy City the managers want their customers' demand curve to shift rightward so that the new market equilibrium point would allow them to continue charging $1.25 per bar. The problem is, how can this be accomplished?

Some firms try to shift the demand curve for their products by increasing consumers' tastes and preferences through advertising (Figure 3-10). Firms may also attempt to eliminate substitute goods by driving competitors out of business, buying rival firms, or persuading the government to forbid foreign competitors' products from entering the country. Some groups of firms band together to persuade the government to purchase the surplus. When the government purchases surpluses of commodities in order to raise their prices, it is said to be establishing a **price floor,** a barrier preventing the price from falling lower.

If suppliers are unsuccessful in their attempts to increase demand for their products and they still insist on keeping the price artificially high, they have a second course of action: decrease supply. The object of decreasing supply is to shift the supply curve to the left where the new intersection point is at the desired price. Figure 3-11 illustrates this alternative.

Figure 3-12 Market Solution to a Surplus

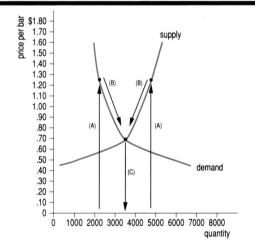

Businesses often place items on sale to reduce surplus merchandise; but if sale prices are below the market equilibrium level, shortages may result.

To decrease the supply of a good, a firm must cut production. As the product becomes scarcer, consumers become willing to pay a higher price. This solution is very easy for the firm that has no competition but poses serious problems for those that share the market with other firms. Typically, as one firm decreases its production, its competitors immediately increase their production, keeping the product's price at the lower level. By cutting production in a competitive market, a firm will drive itself out of business.

The simplest solution to the problem of a surplus is to allow the market to work. As you can see in Figure 3-12 (page 39), a supplier, realizing that a surplus exists, responds by slowly lowering his price. As he lowers his price, he discovers that his surplus is shrinking, so he continues to lower his price until the quantity supplied exactly matches the quantity demanded. At this point all surplus inventory disappears, and the supplier would have no reason to continue lowering his price.

Shortage

Think back to some shortage you have heard about or experienced. Chances are the experience went something like this: you heard that there was a terrific sale at a department store. The store is discounting goods by 95%. By the time you got to the store, however, it was too late; everything worth buying was sold out. Why?

Figure 3-13 Shortage

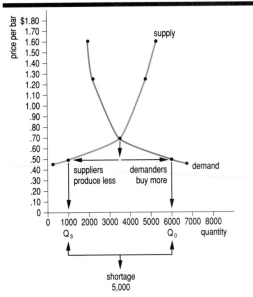

Causes of Shortage–A **shortage** is caused by the price of a good being held lower than its market equilibrium price. Figure 3-13 graphically illustrates a shortage. Suppose that for some reason the price of Yum-Yum candy bars was set at 50¢ each, 20¢ below the market equilibrium price of 70¢. At the lower price the quantity demanded would rise to 6,000 bars while, due to a lack of producer incentives, the quantity supplied would fall to 1,000 bars. The shortage, therefore, would be 5,000 bars.

Virtually no supplier would deliberately sell his products at a price lower than the market price if profit is his goal. Many supermarkets advertise certain products for sale at prices below the market equilibrium price, but these items are deliberately underpriced to lure customers into the store to pur-

chase items that do provide a profit. What, therefore, could compel producers to act in a manner contrary to common sense and their own best interest? The government, often with the best of motives, such as the desire to make certain products available to the poor at an affordable price, attempts to set aside the laws of supply and demand by passing regulations informing firms in selected industries that certain prices may not rise under penalty of law. Such mandates are called **price ceilings** because they prevent prices from rising to the equilibrium market price. Imposing a price ceiling will always cause shortages when the market price is higher. If the price is held below the market price too long, affected businesses will eventually suffocate from a lack of profits and will die, making

Because simple price ceilings on rent result in housing shortages for the poor, government must subsidize most low-income housing to in- *sure that while the rent is kept low, the landlords receive a fair market price.*

The American Revolution, Price Controls, and Misery

Those who think that price ceilings are a modern phenomenon, and long for the "good old days" of our forefathers when the market was allowed to operate freely should consider the following.

General George Washington was surrounded during the winter of 1777-1778 by many foes: the British, the mercenaries hired by the British, traitors among his own ranks, and the bitter winter weather. The biggest enemy of all, however, was the one that nearly wiped out his entire force without firing a shot—the well-intentioned legislature of the Commonwealth of Pennsylvania. The legislature, realizing the high cost of outfitting and maintaining an army, sought some legislative way of helping out the Continental forces.

the good or service unavailable to anyone at any price, including the targeted needy group.

The noblest of motives, when not tempered with common sense, can have disastrous consequences. For example, the desire to provide affordable housing has led many cities to pass rent-control laws compelling landlords to charge rents lower than the market price. As inflation drives up the costs of maintaining and running apartment com-

plexes, the low rents become insufficient for the landlord to pay the bills, make necessary repairs, and realize a profit. The landlord is now faced with a choice of either continuing to operate the apartment complex, paying for losses each month out of his own pocket, or evicting the residents, boarding up the windows and doors, and walking away, leaving the apartment building to crumble. Most rational landlords choose the latter, and the poor

The legislature passed laws setting maximum prices Pennsylvanians could charge for commodities purchased by the army. The legislated prices were far below the market price. The result of the price ceilings was as disastrous then as it is today. The prices of the same commodities when imported from states not having similar controls rose to record heights. Pennsylvania farmers refused to sell their produce at controlled prices, which were lower than their cost to produce the goods. Many farmers believed they were left no alternative but to sell their goods to the British troops, who willingly paid the market price in gold.

A final note, however, is that our forefathers learned from their mistake. On June 4, 1778, the Continental Congress adopted the following resolution:

Whereas . . . it hath been found by experience that limitations upon the prices of commodities are not only ineffectual for the purpose proposed, but likewise productive of very evil consequences to the great detriment of the public service . . . resolved, that it be recommended to the several states to repeal or suspend all laws or resolutions within the said states respectively limiting, regulating or restraining the Price of any Article, Manufacture or Commodity.

become even more impoverished than before the government sought to "help" them.

Solutions to Shortage–Just as there are three possible solutions to a surplus, there are three possible solutions to a shortage: decrease demand, increase supply, or allow the price to rise to the market equilibrium point.

Figure 3-14 Demand Solution to a Shortage

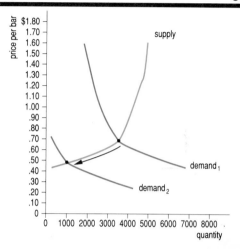

First, suppliers could respond to a shortage by discouraging demand for their product, shifting the demand curve to the left. Business firms could accomplish this by sponsoring advertising geared to discourage consumption. For example, during periods when demand exceeds their ability to produce, many electric power companies instruct customers in methods of conserving electricity (Figure 3-14).

A second solution to the problem of shortage lies in the management of supply. Consumers tend to view a shortage as a problem of undersupply, with the solution being to boost production, an action corresponding to a rightward shift of the supply curve (Figure 3-15). Two ways of increasing supply are improving technology and boosting productivity.

Increases in the technology used in production would certainly increase supply, but new tools and new production methods cannot be developed overnight. Technological advances occur gradually, certainly not fast enough to eliminate an immediate shortage. A more practical technique to boost supply would be for the firm to increase productivity,

Figure 3-15 Supply Solution to a Shortage

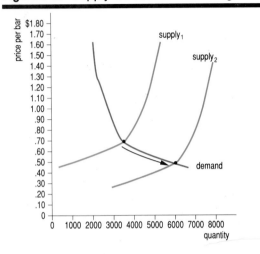

Figure 3-16 Market Solution to a Shortage

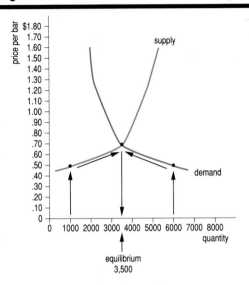

getting more production out of each machine and employee each hour. To boost employee productivity many businesses furnish training, award production incentives, and provide counseling and rehabilitative services for problems that decrease productivity such as drug addiction and alcoholism.

The third and in many cases the most sensible solution to a shortage is to allow the price of the good to rise to the market equilibrium level. Many might argue that for the government to allow some prices to rise would be cruel to the poor and the elderly. The problem with this line of reasoning is a belief that at the lower price supplies would exist in quantities large enough to satisfy everyone. In a sense the government forgets the existence of the law of supply. Allowing the price to rise to its market equilibrium point may be a better way of solving the plight of the poor for two important reasons: first, a realistic market price encourages conservation and discourages wastefulness. By establishing a price ceiling lower than the equilibrium price, the government sends out a signal that the supply of the commodity is so abundant that it may be squandered. Second, a realistic market price acts as an incentive for entrepreneurs to enter the market

either to produce more of the good at a lower cost or to invent less expensive substitutes that will fill the need.

Figure 3-16 graphically illustrates the market solution for Candy City. The manager of Candy City first notices that there is a greater demand for the product than is being produced; in this case the shortage is 5,000 bars. Responding to the excess demand, the manager gradually raises the price. As he does so, he is pricing some consumers out of the market while creating an incentive for higher production. The manager keeps on raising the price until the quantity demanded is exactly equal to the quantity supplied.

Section Review

1. At what point do supply and demand intersect?
2. What occurs when the price of a product is higher than the price at which supply equals demand?
3. What is the simplest solution to a surplus?
4. What causes a shortage, and what are its possible solutions?

Chapter Review

Terms
supply
law of supply
supply schedule
supply curve
change in quantity supplied
change in supply
decrease in supply
increase in supply
market equilibrium point
market equilibrium price
surplus
price floor
shortage
price ceiling

Content Questions
1. Define supply. Who are suppliers?
2. In the example on page 34, Beth had to decrease her supply because the cost of her main input, lemonade, had gone up. Besides materials, what other costs constitute ''input costs'' that may affect the supply curve?
3. Define and describe the ''market equilibrium point.''

4. Why does a price above the equilibrium price result in surplus?
5. List the three possible methods of solving a surplus.
6. What causes a shortage?

Application Questions
1. What would the supply curve look like for a product for which there is a finite supply: for example, seats at a stadium for a ball game?
2. What are the benefits and problems associated with technological improvements from the standpoint of the business owner and the employee? Would the limitation of technology save jobs?
3. ''Scalpers'' are people who purchase tickets for concerts and sporting events at a low price and attempt to sell them for significantly higher prices. Discuss the advantages and disadvantages of ''scalping,'' using demand and supply curves to illustrate your points.
4. What would be the immediate effects if the government set a price ceiling, which was *above* the market equilibrium price, on a product?

Assignment Due Tue. 10th
Career field
Starting salary
Obstacles
locations
MOS

CALL
LBNS

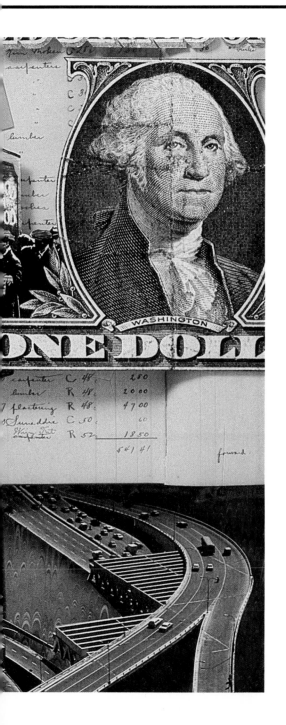

Unit II: Economics of the Nation

CHAPTER 4

The Workings of a National Economy

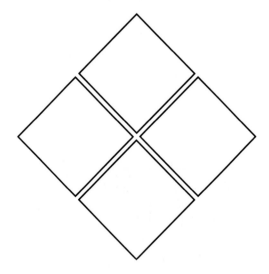

For by him were all things created, that are in heaven, and that are in earth, visible and invisible, whether they be thrones, or dominions, or principalities, or powers: all things were created by him, and for him: And he is before all things, and by him all things consist.   Colossians 1:16-17

I. Models: The Tools of the Economist

There are models of almost everything imaginable. A glance at the shelves of hobby stores will reveal models of cars, submarines, airplanes, trains, horses, solar systems, and spaceships. While models differ in the things that they represent, they also greatly differ in complexity. Have you noticed that a child's train set is usually very simple? The toy train is easily assembled and taken apart, inexpensive, travels in a circle, and has a life expectancy of three weeks. An adult's model train, on the other hand, is usually a technological marvel. It has a whole room devoted to its permanent containment; usually costs several months' salary; resembles a small country complete with rivers, mountains, roads, citizens, and army bases; and is expected to last well beyond the life of the owner.

Economic Models

A model is a simplified representation of something. It need not be made of wood or plastic but may be even a simplification of an idea. Scripture records many instances where Jesus Christ used parables–models of theological truths–to help people understand. An example of a parable as a model occurs in Matthew 18:23-35 where the Saviour likened the kingdom of God to a king requiring his servants to give account of themselves.

Economists also use models. An **economic model,** like a parable, is not a tangible thing but rather a simplification of how factors in our environment affect our choices.

Economic models, like models in a science class, are used for two purposes. The first is instruction. Models are used to explain to students the appearance and operation of more complex objects. The biology teacher finds it much easier to use a plastic model of a heart to explain its workings since it is more durable, less costly, and simpler to use than a real human heart.

Second, models are used to assist economists in predicting future events. Just as architects use models of bridges to predict their ability to hold their designed weight capacities, economists use

The Day Welfare Hit The Classroom

Economic models may take many forms. Steven Spetz, a high school economics teacher in Canada, found an interesting method to model the way in which governments finance and administer social programs.

I have often heard it expressed that the classroom should be a small window upon life and prepare students for the world they will soon enter as adults. I accept this idea, and introduced a magnificent scheme of marking that would alert students to economic factors they should appreciate. When I gave back a major assignment, the students noted some peculiar entries on their papers.

Sir, what does it mean, minus six marks for the Student Pension Plan?

Well, Bob, the Student Pension Plan is one that I invented similar to a government pension plan. You put aside some of your marks each week into a fund, which will be *available should you decide to retire toward the end of the school year.*

Do I get them back?

Yes, but in the meantime inflation will have eroded the marks terribly, so you will probably get back only a small part of what you set aside.

Yes, Mary?

Sir, what does it mean, minus four marks for Unemployed Student Insurance?

Ah, good question. Suppose you are absent or for some reason fail to hand in your assignment? Then, you are authorized to draw marks from the Unemployed Student Insurance Fund to make sure you don't suffer a drop in marks.

But what happens to my marks if I do all my assignments–do I get my marks back?

Certainly not. The marks are needed by the less fortunate.

Sir . . . Fred got a 55% on his assignment and he didn't even do it!

Yes, I know. You see how the Unemployed Student Insurance works? Fred didn't do anything, but we can't let him fail, so I authorized him to draw 55 marks from the Insurance Fund.

But the reason he didn't do it was he went to the hockey game and . . .

It doesn't matter. Each of us owes a duty to our neighbors to see that they encounter no hardships. It's their birthright.

Even if they don't do anything?

Perhaps he was unable to do it.

Sir, what would happen if we all didn't do the assignment? I mean, suppose we all just asked for 55 marks, what would happen?

Tsk, tsk, Tom. I assume that each of you wants to work. That you seek work and savor it. I know none of you would deliberately turn down the opportunity to work.

Sir, what does it mean, minus five marks for Student Health Plan?

That is in case you are ill for a prolonged period of time. The plan will pay you 60 marks per week while you are convalescing.

Why didn't you deduct any marks from Hilda for the Student Health Plan?

She comes from a low-income family. Can't expect her to pay anything, can you?

Sir, you took fifteen marks from me for Student Income Tax, but you only took four from Ralph.

Well, you are in a higher bracket than Ralph. You had a mark of 86% while Ralph only had a 57%. You should pay more than he.

Why?

Just because it always works that way.

Sir, I had a mark of 58%. After you deducted Student Income Tax, Student Health Plan, Student Pension Plan, and Unemployed Student Insurance I ended up with only 39%. I passed the assignment, but all of your deductions made me fail. I would have been better off if I hadn't done it at all like Fred.

He didn't do anything but got a higher mark than I did.

Yes, unfortunately there are a few cases where it does work out like that. Some people are financially better off not working than working.

You mean it's better to refuse work rather than work and get a low passing mark?

Yes, but again I want to emphasize that I know each of you would not want to take advantage of such an idea. The thrill of the job alone should drive you onward even though you end up with fewer marks. Besides, you wouldn't feel morally right knowing you were drawing marks from your fellow students when you were perfectly capable of getting them yourself.

Sir, do people really live like this?

Certainly, it's part of the great social scheme of life.

As the bell rang, I knew I had succeeded beyond my utmost dreams. The students were actively talking about incorporating so they could defer taxes, bringing in large numbers of immigrant students to do their assignments at a low pay scale while they collected from the Unemployed Student Fund year around, applying for government assistance to pay their Student Health Plan premiums because they came from low-income families, and had started a Strike Fund to keep their marks up while they were busy picketing the school for higher marks, a four-day week. . . .

As I watched them happily thinking of ways to obtain extra marks from the Unemployed Student Insurance Fund by enrolling in the plan under more than one name, I recalled the words from the musical, My Fair Lady: "By George, she's got it!"

Source: Spetz, Stephen. "The Day Welfare Hit the Classroom," *The Freeman*. May 1982, pp. 302-4.

models to answer questions such as ''What would happen to interest rates on loans if the number of dollars in circulation increased by 25%?'' or ''What would happen to consumer spending if the government increases purchases of military hardware by $100 billion without increasing taxes to pay for it?''

What Do Economic Models Look Like?

You may wonder at this point how it is possible to make an economic model. Unlike plastic airplane models, economic models take the form of theories or explanations of how people make choices, and usually are expressed as tables or graphs.

The **tabular model,** also known as a **schedule,** is a popular method of explaining simple relationships between pairs of variables. For example, Fig-

Figure 4-2

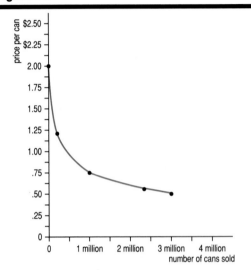

ure 4-1 shows how a limited number of changes in the price of Fizzo Cola affects the number of cans sold.

Tabular models are helpful in showing relationships between variables, but the information they provide is limited to only a few observations. The **line graph,** on the other hand provides significantly more data. For example, Figure 4-1 tells us only the number of cans that have been sold at 50¢, 55¢, 75¢, $1.20, and $2.00, a rather limited number of observations. The line graph, however, can tell the economist approximately how many cans will be sold at any given price that falls between 50¢ and $2.00. To construct a line graph, economists place ''price'' on the vertical axis and ''quantity'' on the horizontal axis. The limited number of observations is then plotted on the graph, and lines are drawn connecting the observed points. Figure 4-2 is an illustration of a line graph for Fizzo Cola.

Section Review

1. What are the two purposes for economic models?
2. What are the two popular forms of economic models?

Figure 4-1 Tabular Model for Fizzo Cola

Price Per Can	Quantity Sold Per Month (cans)
$.50	3,000,000
.55	2,300,000
.75	1,000,000
1.20	200,000
2.00	0

II. The Circular Flow Model

The Basic Circular Flow

So far you have been reading about microeconomic models: how the price of a single product affects the quantity sold. Not only do economists create models of individual behavior, but they also model the behavior of entire nations. The **circular flow model** attempts to explain how an entire national economic system works. Figure 4-3 shows the starting point of the circular flow model.

Virtually every economic system is made up of two basic groups: households and business firms.

Business firms create billions of dollars of goods and services, which are sold to the nation's households. If you were to add up all goods and services businesses produced and sold to final consumers, you would have a figure economists call the gross national product. The total of all households' expenditures is referred to as **consumption expenditures.**

Factors of Production–Figure 4-4 is only part of the picture, however. The resources that business firms use to create goods and services do not somehow mysteriously appear. Figure 4-5 illustrates that

Figure 4-3

Figure 4-4

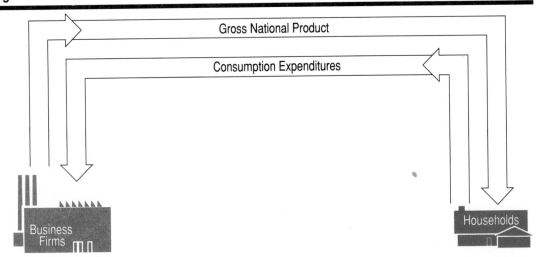

Gross National Product

Consumption Expenditures

Business Firms

Households

the resources used in producing the gross national product are supplied by the households and are called the **factors of production.** Economists have identified four factors that go into the production of every good and service.

- **Land** refers to all of the natural resources that go into the production of goods. Every economic good contains some form of animal, vegetable, or mineral resource. An automobile, for example, is made of glass, steel, and other materials composed of minerals, and its plastics and textiles may be formed from petroleum and many other natural resources.
- **Labor** is all human effort that goes into the creation of goods or services. Labor includes mental work of the manager as well as the physical effort of the employee.
- **Financial capital** is the third factor of production and is defined as all money loaned directly to the business firms from the household sector. Business firms use the borrowed financial capital to purchase **real capital,** the tools the business firm uses to produce goods and services.

Natural resources, such as the petroleum from this offshore well, are part of the factor of production called land.

A C D B

Figure 4-5

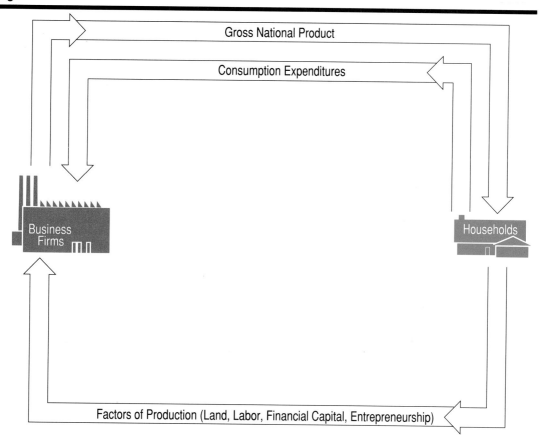

Gross National Product

Consumption Expenditures

Business Firms

Households

Factors of Production (Land, Labor, Financial Capital, Entrepreneurship)

- **Entrepreneurship** (on tra pra NEWER ship) is the activity of creatively combining natural resources, human labor, and financial capital in unique ways to develop new and useful products and services.

    Although natural resources, human labor, and financial capital are necessary to produce goods and services, entrepreneurship is the most important factor of production since it directs, organizes, and plans the production process. Without the direction entrepreneurship provides, extensive pockets of resources within a nation would remain unused. Without its organizing function, human labor would remain idle. Without the planning it provides, financial resources would remain untapped.

    People become entrepreneurs for a host of reasons, including personal recognition, the ability to use their talents, and a desire for financial rewards. If the benefits associated with entrepreneurship are discouraged in a nation, the flow of new and useful products and services will be significantly reduced. Therefore, it is of great importance to the economic growth of a nation that entrepreneurs be free both to use their talents and to receive the profits they have earned.

Factor Costs–Although the factors of production are provided by households, they are not provided without cost. The arrow going from the business sector to the households in Figure 4-6 represents the payments business firms make in exchange for the four factors of production:

- **Rent** includes all payments for the use of an owner's property. Rent includes not only payments for use of buildings and land, but also payments such as royalties to authors.
- **Wages** include all payments for labor used to produce goods or services. Wages include all salaries, hourly wages, and bonuses, in addition to other payments not directly received by the worker such as medical and dental benefits, unemployment compensation payments, worker's compensation payments, and the employer's portion of social security payments. Wages make up the largest portion of all the factor costs.
- **Interest** is the payment business firms make on borrowed money. Households lend money to business firms by purchasing bonds. The buyer of a bond is entitled to receive not only his original principal but also periodic interest payments.

Figure 4-6

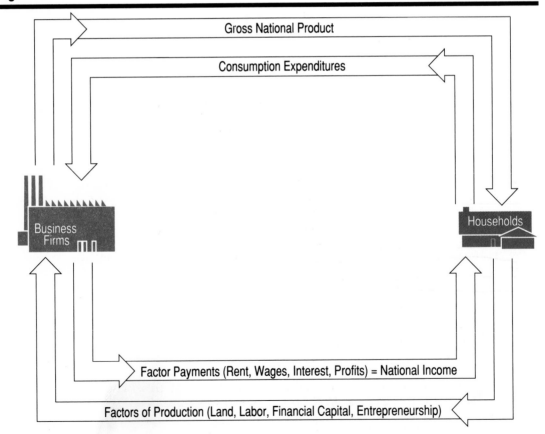

• **Profits** are the rewards entrepreneurs receive for successful risk-taking. Entrepreneurial risks are great. The entrepreneur must detect an unmet need, create a product to meet the need, produce it at a cost lower than the price buyers are willing to pay, and get it to the customer. If the entrepreneur is successful, he will realize a profit. It is very important to recognize that profits are not just another expense. Profit is the difference between revenues received from the sale of a product and the cost of the land, labor, and financial capital that went into its production. Therefore, if an entrepreneur wishes to increase profits, he usually cannot simply raise his price. He must instead lower his costs.

We now have a simple idea of how an economic system operates: households provide business firms the land, labor, financial capital, and entrepreneurship necessary to produce goods and services. In exchange, the households receive rents, wages, interest, and profits. Households then use their incomes to purchase the goods and services the business firms produce.

The Government as an Economic Entity

In its present form this model is too simple and unrealistic. To add a greater degree of reality, we need to include another participant with whom we have contact every day of our lives: government.

Figure 4-7 illustrates the circular flow model after the government has been added. The term *government* refers to all levels of civil government, including federal, state, and local authorities.

In order to continue operating, the government, like households and business firms, incurs necessary expenses. The government purchases goods and services ranging from mops and buckets to nuclear weapons and satellites. In addition to purchasing goods and services, government provides transfer payments to households. **Transfer payments** are payments of money or goods to persons for which no specific economic repayment is expected. Examples of transfer payments include the payment of social security benefits to the retired, welfare benefits to the poor, and payment of un-

Transfer payments are sometimes made in the form of food distributions by the U.S. Department of Agriculture.

employment compensation to those out of work.

Occasionally, the government will distribute goods instead of money to households. An example of this is the U.S. Department of Agriculture's distribution of milk, cheese, and other food products to the poor.

To pay for its spending, the government imposes taxes on households, which may be levied as sales taxes, income taxes, or property taxes. Governments may also obtain funds by taxing business firms through corporate income taxes, social security taxes, unemployment taxes, and a host of other business taxes. Usually government spending exceeds the amount it receives in taxes. When this happens, it is said that the government is operating under a **budget deficit.** If the government receives more in taxes than it is paying out, it is said to be operating under a **budget surplus.**

Figure 4-7

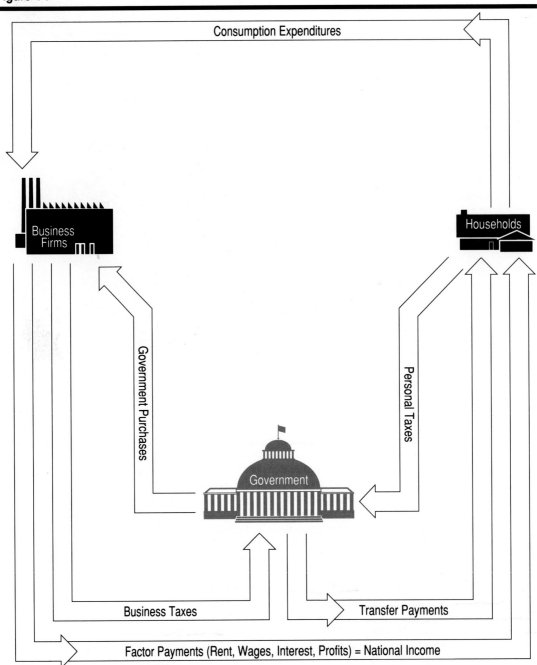

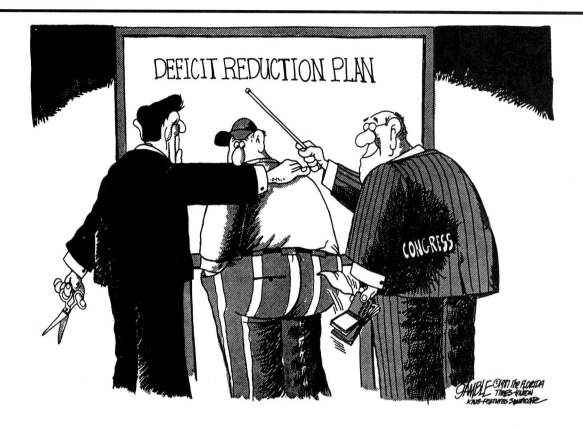

Financial Markets

The **financial market** is that vast collection of financial institutions that receive deposits of excess funds from households and lend to business firms. It is the heart of the economy. As a heart circulates blood throughout the body, the financial market efficiently circulates money from the nation's households to its business firms. The financial market is made up of commercial banks, savings and loan associations, credit unions, insurance companies, finance companies, and stock brokerage firms. Looking at Figure 4-8, note that households both save and dissave.

Economists consider households to be saving whenever money is put into a financial institution; when, for example, a person deposits money in a savings account or makes a payment on a loan. On the other hand, households are said to be **dissaving** when money is withdrawn from an account or borrowed.

A well-developed financial market is essential to the economic growth of a nation. A successful economy is characterized by a growing number of profitable business firms that have access to financial capital. As population grows and tastes change, business firms must have access to available funds to modernize their equipment. A well-developed financial market is able to meet this need efficiently by taking the savings of households and channeling them to businesses.

Ideally, all savings in the financial market should be lent to business firms, but the government often diverts some of the funds to itself to finance its budget deficit. It was mentioned earlier

Figure 4-8

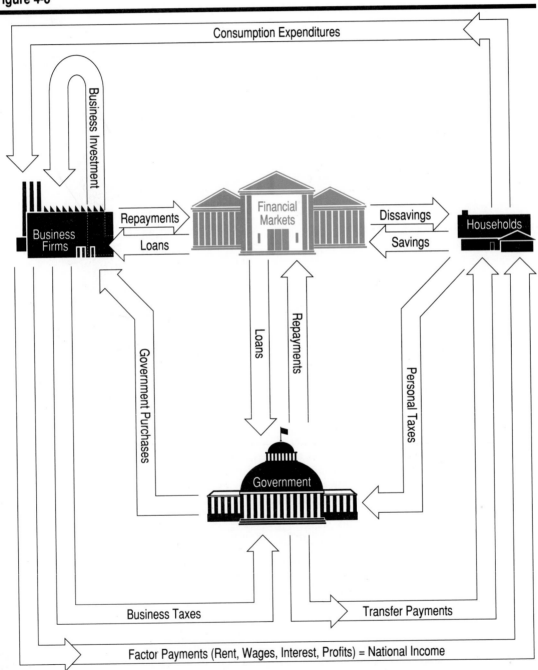

James Buchanan (1919-)
Leader in the Study of Public Choice

Raised on a farm near Murfreesboro, Tennessee, James Buchanan planned to become a lawyer. But when financial limitations kept him out of law school, he found the means to pursue studies in economics. In 1945 he earned a doctorate in this field from the University of Chicago. His later contributions to economics and public choice theory brought him the honor of receiving the Nobel Prize for economics in 1986.

Buchanan is considered the founder of the field of public choice theory. This area of economics attempts to analyze the economic choices made by government. In the marketplace individual producers and consumers make choices according to their own personal interests, weighing the amount of profit or utility they will receive for their choice. The government is theoretically supposed to make its choices in a similar manner according to the best interests of society. However, as Buchanan has pointed out, the realities of governmental procedures result in laws and expenditures that do not necessarily promote the public good.

The public choice theory observes that elected representatives, although they may display some altruistic actions, ultimately make most governmental decisions according to their own personal interests rather than for the true benefit of the public. What course of action will help them get reelected? What special-interest groups contribute the most to their political campaigns? What legislation can they support for fellow lawmakers so that those lawmakers will support, or "logroll," legislation for them? These and other similar questions continuously prompt representatives to make governmental choices according to their own best interests. Similarly, bureaucrats in government agencies such as the Department of Housing and Urban Development or the Social Security Administration often use the public funds available to them in ways that maximize their own utility rather than the utility of the public they

serve. The public often ignores the subtle neglect of its welfare, but even when it does recognize that its interests are not being served by these "public servants," its ability to remove excessively selfish representatives from office or punish wasteful bureaucrats is hampered by the quagmire of the political election process or the impediments of existing governmental procedures.

Despite the impossibilities of making government totally committed to making the best possible choices for the public good, Buchanan's ideas promote methods of making governmental decisions more responsive to public interests. Among these methods are the fostering of greater public awareness of government economic activity, the support of legislation that would help free representatives from some of the pressures that encourage them to be self-seeking, and the increase of accountability for government bureaucrats.

GNP: $868.3 billion*
Per Capita GNP: $15,620*
Population: 55,994,000 (1989)
Monetary Unit: franc

France

France, along with much of Western Europe, emerged from World War II with its industries in rubble and its agriculture in a backward and inefficient condition. However, the continual building of new industries and the introduction of improved agricultural techniques have lifted France to the position of the world's fifth most powerful economic and industrial country. Even so, with the arrival of the 1990s, economic progress has been overshadowed by France's participation in the developing economic union of the European Economic Community (EEC or Common Market).

In 1958 France was one of six Western European nations that gave original approval to the union of their economies in a common market. This union of diverse peoples and economies made few immediate changes. Ten years passed before the EEC removed internal tariffs and began coordination of external tariffs. A little over ten years more elapsed before it established the European Monetary System to regulate exchange rates among the currencies of the member countries. (The European Currency Unit [ECU] was established to facilitate this process.) While these slow changes took place, the EEC countries continued to operate as independent national economies.

However, dramatic changes came into view when in 1985 the EEC released a timetable for eliminating all remaining internal Community trade barriers and controls by December 31, 1992. Suddenly, France and the other five original EEC members, along with six more members added during the 1970s and 1980s, began to feverishly prepare guidelines for the completion of the economic union. Three hundred specific agreements deemed necessary for the union would have to be approved by the twelve EEC members. These agreements deal with economic issues involving everything from manufacturing guidelines and labor contracts to banking procedures and investment regulations. The EEC members must agree to relinquish their own national standards in these areas and to comply with the terms of the final EEC agreements. France and the other EEC members are willing to give up their economic independence in an attempt to establish a single Western European economy that will rival that of the United States. This unified economy will combine all the industrial and agricultural assets of the member nations and allow businesses to shift resources freely from country to country for greatest efficiency and profit. Nations and corporations that participate in this new venture are expected to reap benefits in the resulting free trade. France, as a member of the EEC, will be a part of a new winning team if the union can fulfill its objectives.

*figures for 1987 from the 1990 *Statistical Abstract*

TEST

Figure 4-9

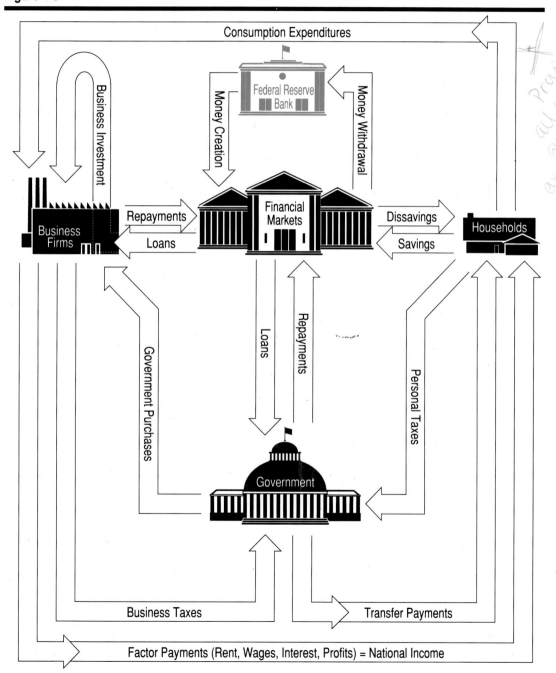

Consumption Expenditures

Federal Reserve Bank

Money Creation

Money Withdrawal

Business Investment

Business Firms

Repayments

Loans

Financial Markets

Dissavings

Savings

Households

Government Purchases

Loans

Repayments

Personal Taxes

Government

Business Taxes

Transfer Payments

Factor Payments (Rent, Wages, Interest, Profits) = National Income

that a budget deficit results when the government pays out more money than it receives in taxes. Suppose you go to the grocery store and write a check for $120; but after you leave the store, you find that you have only $50 in your account. You must find $70 to deposit to your account before your check returns to the bank. Likewise, when the government operates under a budget deficit, it must either increase taxes, an option that is considered politically unwise, or borrow the difference between its tax receipts and its expenses.

To borrow money from the financial market the government does not go to a bank, hat in hand, and fill out loan applications. Instead it sells bonds with very attractive interest rates to financial institutions. The federal government, for example, sells U.S. Savings Bonds, Treasury Bills, and Treasury Notes.

On the surface there appears to be little difference in the effect on the overall economy if the borrowing is done by business firms or by the government; however, there is one subtle difference. Government borrowing leads to a problem called **crowding out.** Money is finite like all other resources; therefore every dollar borrowed by the government is one less dollar available for business

firms to use in purchasing the real capital they need to produce goods consumers want and need. It is in this way that business firms are "crowded out" of the financial market by government budget deficits. Because the financial market is the heart of the economy, the money it provides to business firms is vital. If too much money is diverted for too long, business firms will die, their plants will lie idle, and widespread unemployment will result.

The Federal Reserve

The fifth and final player in our circular flow model is the Federal Reserve. Elected representatives are not ignorant of the effects of their deficit spending. They realize that in the long run their deficits could lead to business stagnation and unemployment, but given the desires of their constituents for greater spending and lower taxes and their desires for re-election, they feel powerless to stop themselves. They do not like to borrow, but the taxation alternative is unthinkable. In 1913 Congress created a solution to this dilemma by developing the Federal Reserve System, a government agency that has the ability to create new money (Figure 4-9).

Financing the deficit with newly created money may cause other serious problems in the economy. We will examine them and more thoroughly discuss the Federal Reserve System in Chapter 10.

Section Review

1. What model attempts to explain how an entire national economic system works?
2. What do we call the total of all goods and services businesses produce and sell to households?
3. What are the four factors of production?
4. What four payments do business firms make in exchange for the factors of production?
5. Who are the five participants in circular flow activities?

The federal government sells savings bonds and other bonds as its means of borrowing money.

Chapter Review

Terms
economic model
tabular model
schedule
line graph
circular flow model
consumption expenditures
factors of production
land
labor
financial capital
real capital
entrepreneurship
rent
wages
interest
profits
transfer payments
budget deficit
budget surplus
financial market
dissaving
crowding out

Content Questions
1. What is a model? Give an example of an economic model.
2. What advantage does the line graph have over the tabular model?
3. Draw the basic circular flow (where the only participants are households and business firms), labeling each of the flows.
4. What is the difference between financial capital and real capital?
5. What is the most important factor of production? Why?

6. What economic functions does the government perform as illustrated by the circular flow model?
7. Why is the financial market necessary for the effective functioning of a developed society?
8. Describe crowding out.

Application Questions
1. A recent hypothetical survey of high school students revealed the following table of information equating hours of study per weeknight with grade point averages. Draw a line graph using the above information. Is the slope of the curve positive or negative? Approximately how many hours of study would be necessary for a student to receive a G.P.A. of 2.5?

Hours of study	G.P.A.
2.25	4.0 (A)
1.25	3.0 (B)
0.75	2.0 (C)
0.25	1.0 (D)

2. Select one product currently on the market and try to list all of the natural resources, types of labor, entrepreneurship, and financial capital that went into its production.
3. What does the Bible say about entrepreneurship (business ownership and risk taking)?
4. You have just awakened to find that all financial institutions have vanished. (Deposits have been put back into the pockets of depositors.) What will be the repercussions on the economy?

CHAPTER 5

What Is the Economic Problem?

I. National Economic Goals
   A. A Low Level of Unemployment
   B. A Stable Price Level
   C. A Healthy Rate of Economic Growth
   D. A Fair Distribution of Income
II. The Economic Questions
   A. The Output Question: What Will Be Produced?
   B. The Input Question: How Will the Nation's Goods Be Produced?
   C. The Distribution Question: Who Will Receive What Is Produced?

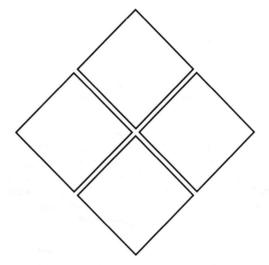

For which of you, intending to build a tower, sitteth not down first, and counteth the cost, whether he have sufficient to finish it?

Luke 14:28

It is early morning and the sun is casting its first amber streams of light across the land. Midwestern farmers are starting up their heavy equipment while hundreds of miles to the east, Wall Street financiers begin flooding into the stock exchanges. Detroit assembly line workers in clean coveralls break the silence of factories with the sound of a thousand echoing footsteps while the first of a caravan of bread trucks rolls out of bakery parking lots.

A new day is beginning like thousands of days before it, and again a miracle is passing unnoticed. The massive machinery of an entire economic system once again has been roused and set in motion. People will be commuting, producing, negotiating, buying, and selling. Millions of people, though oblivious of each other, will work separately yet collectively to solve the economic problem.

I. National Economic Goals

Simply stated, the economic problem of a society is how it may best achieve its economic goals. Most societies have identified four primary economic goals.

Goal #1: A Low Level of Unemployment

Unemployment exists when someone who wishes to work cannot find a job. Governments have found it in the interests of both society in general and the individual in particular that everyone who is able and wants to work be gainfully employed. High unemployment is usually accompanied by poverty, crime, despair, and a tremendous waste of human labor. Work is noble and commanded in Scripture:

Because of the problems caused by unemployment, the government has identified its most important economic goal as a low unemployment rate.

For even when we were with you, this we commanded you, that if any would not work, neither should he eat. (II Thessalonians 3:10)

Let him that stole steal no more: but rather let him labour, working with his hands the thing which is good, that he may have to give to him that needeth. (Ephesians 4:28)

Goal #2: A Stable Price Level

History has demonstrated that inflation and deflation, periods of generally rising and falling pric-es, cause economic disruptions as people become unsure of their economic future. For example, if prices are rapidly rising, people will decrease savings and spend greater portions of their incomes in an effort to beat the next price increase. As household spending rises, shortages of many goods and services may occur.

Goal #3: A Healthy Rate of Economic Growth

The term *economic growth* refers to an increase in the quantity of goods and services a nation can produce. Economic growth may be achieved in two ways. The first is through **extensive growth,** the increase of goods and services produced by business firms that are using more land, labor, or financial capital than previously. It was through extensive growth that the Soviet Union experienced phenomenal increase in production in the 1950s. As the tremendous supplies of labor and natural resources were tapped, the nation was able to produce more goods and services. After the U.S.S.R. more fully exploited its untapped resources, the economic growth slowed significantly. The second source of national economic growth is through **intensive growth,** the increase of goods and services produced when business firms use existing factors of production with greater efficiency.

Goal #4: A Fair Distribution of Income

The final goal of most nations is a fair distribution of income, but many problems and controversies arise as policymakers attempt to use different definitions of fairness. For example, should everyone be guaranteed equality of income, should a ''safety net'' of economic benefits be provided, or should the government let the market determine each person's income?

Section Review

1. What is the economic problem?
2. How is unemployment a problem for society?
3. What term denotes a period of generally rising prices?
4. What is the difference between extensive growth and intensive growth of an economy?

We're men we're men in tights tigh—t tights
We roam around the forest looking for
fights! ♪

II. The Economic Questions

In meeting the four economic goals, every society must answer three critical questions. Each of these questions must be answered either by imposing commands from some central authority or by allowing the free market to work.

1. The Output Question: What will be produced?
2. The Input Question: How will the nation's goods be produced?
3. The Distribution Question: Who will receive what is produced?

The Output Question: What Will Be Produced?

To some extent every society must determine what will be produced. Since resources are scarce and wants are limitless, every nation is faced with the predicament that it cannot produce everything that it wants; therefore, choices concerning what will and will not be produced are unavoidable.

Rather than asking a question concerning which particular goods (such as toasters, hammers, and breakfast cereals) to produce, economists ask which *types* of goods the nation should create. Generally speaking, nations produce only two types of goods–**consumer goods** and **capital goods.** Consumer goods are those that are purchased for personal use such as books, film, coffee, and ballpoint pens. Capital goods is another name for real capital, those goods that are used to produce consumer goods. Examples of capital goods include printing presses, farm equipment, welding machines, and factories.

Since a nation cannot produce everything its people desire, it is faced with the **consumer good/capital good tradeoff.** If a nation were to produce only consumer goods, no new factories, tools, or replacement parts would be created. Within a matter of months, factories and equipment would begin to deteriorate. In a few years they would fall into disrepair and would quit operating, leaving households without a source of consumer goods. If, on the other hand, a society were to produce only capital goods, the economy would collapse much sooner since the production of food, shelter, clothing, medical supplies, and other consumer goods would be abandoned in favor of producing tools of production. Of course, no society would hold to either of these extremes; the best combination lies somewhere between the two, but what combination is ideal, and how may it be achieved?

Both command economists and market economists recognize that the consumer good/capital good tradeoff is essentially a question of spending versus saving. When people spend money, they buy consumer goods. When people save, they in a sense ''buy'' capital goods as a result of their savings' being lent to businesses that purchase real capital.

A nation needs both capital goods, such as this heavy machinery in a steel mill, and consumer goods, such as these pound cakes from a bakery.

The Command Economists' Solution–The "command" answer to the output question lets some authority or committee decide the proportion of consumer goods to capital goods to produce. The justification is usually given that the decision is too important to be left to the whims of the market. Those who favor a command economy point out that if people save too much of their incomes, the reduction in spending will cause fellow citizens to become unemployed.

Critics of the command solution ask three compelling questions which are usually met with embarrassing silence. First, if one person can make a wrong choice judging how much to spend in relation to how much to save, would a wrong decision by a central committee not cause even worse negative consequences? Second, is it morally justifiable to punish someone for saving or spending more of his own income than the government allows? Finally, if too much consumer spending is encouraged, will not our factories and equipment fall into disrepair as spending on real capital declines?

The Market Economists' Solution–The "market" solution resolves this dilemma with an ease that causes the observer to marvel at the miracle of the economic laws that God has set in place.

Unlike a command economy's committee, the free market is able to sense the need for more or

The stagnation of the Soviet economy in the 1980s illustrates how a command economy approach to the consumer goods/capital goods tradeoff can have unsatisfactory results.

less capital goods spending and, without force, adjust proportionately the consumer's spending, quickly and efficiently. The key to the market's ability to match consumers' buying with businesses' producing and consumers' saving with businesses' borrowing is the regulating mechanism of the interest rate.

Like a thermostatic valve that regulates the flow of cooling water to an automobile's engine, the market's interest rate on money regulates the flow of money from households to business firms via the financial market. When interest rates are too low, consumers have little incentive to save; therefore, they choose to spend a large portion of their money on consumer goods. Business firms, unable to satisfy the tremendous demand with their old equipment, proceed to borrow from banks and other financial institutions in order to purchase more capital goods. To lure additional funds, banks offer consumers a higher interest rate on savings. As consumers save more, they spend less on consumer goods, further reducing the pressure on old equip-

ment. The market interest rate will continue to rise until increasing productive capacity matches the consumer's decreasing desire to purchase.

If, on the other hand, business firms have too much invested in capital goods, falling interest rates will bring the market back into equilibrium. Since businesses have too much equipment, they will stop borrowing from banks. Banks in turn will lower the interest rate they pay on savings accounts since they no longer need as much loanable money. As consumers save less, they will spend more, allowing businesses to use their previously idle equipment.

When the market is allowed to work, consumers wishing to buy goods will be satisfied, people desiring to save will be able to do so, and business firms will be able to borrow enough to meet their demands. The optimum proportion of consumer goods and capital goods will be reached, and the output question will have been answered in a way that satisfies both consumers and business firms.

The Input Question: How Will the Nation's Goods Be Produced?

Every economic good or service is created by a unique combination of the factors of production, but in many cases two of the factors of production, labor and capital, may be substituted one for the other. The input question, therefore, asks, ''Should the firm use either a greater amount of human labor or a greater amount of capital goods (equipment) in the production process?'' A business firm that uses a great deal of human labor relative to real capital is referred to as being **labor intensive,** while one that uses relatively more automated equipment is said to be **capital intensive.**

Businesses that choose to be labor intensive enjoy certain advantages over their capital intensive counterparts. By using a great deal of human labor, a business firm is contributing to a low unemployment rate, which has the effect of reducing crime and poverty. Human labor also is trainable and thus versatile; that is, workers may be taught to perform many tasks. Capital equipment, on the other hand, is generally limited in its applications. Business firms also can remain more flexible to meet changes in demand by using human labor. As demand increases, the exact number of workers needed may be hired; and some workers may be laid off if demand decreases. A slight increase in demand for the capital intensive firm may require the purchase of expensive equipment, an investment that will continue even if demand decreases and the equipment goes unused.

Capital intensive business firms, however, possess several advantages of their own. First, in addition to not having to meet large payrolls, capital intensive business firms do not pay great amounts in those hidden costs associated with employing workers—costs such as unemployment compensation, sick pay, vacation and holiday pay, medical and dental insurance, social security contributions, and profit sharing. Capital intensive firms also do not have to maintain as large an employee infirmary, cafeteria, or lounge. Second, the capital intensive business firm does not have hovering over it the constant threat of union agitation or labor unrest. Third, by using capital equipment, the firm assures itself of a nearly constant rate of productivity, whereas a human worker's productivity rises and falls with changes in the weather, the day of the week, family problems, or the number of hours worked in a day.

Of course, no firm could be totally capital intensive; and, as most operations require some tools, only those businesses in the simplest of industries could be totally labor intensive. Therefore, some combination of labor and capital is ideal for each business firm, but what combination is best?

The Command Economists' Solution–The ''command'' answer to the input question depends upon who is doing the commanding and what he hopes to achieve. Some command economies, such as the Soviet Union and the People's Republic of China, have desired business firms to be labor intensive in order to ensure a fully employed work force.

While labor intensive firms might bring about a lower unemployment rate, it is not logical to infer that a nation with a low unemployment rate is necessarily economically prosperous. The Soviet Union, the *workers' state,* boasted a population of 286 million and a 0% unemployment rate, but the average annual income per person in 1985 was $7,635 compared to America's $16,240. The People's Republic of China, with its population of over 1 billion also boasted an unemployment rate of 0%, but during the year 1985 the average worker there earned only $342.

The Market Economists' Solution–The free market recognizes that the question of labor versus capital is not a problem that can be efficiently answered by a single central authority for all firms. Rather the issue must be addressed by each firm's taking into consideration its unique needs. Whereas command authorities look to the immediate effects on unemployment, the market looks instead at production costs. Under the free market, business firms generally choose the mixture of labor and capital that will lower their costs and thereby allow them to sell their products at lower prices, satisfy more customers, capture a larger share of the market, and reap a greater profit.

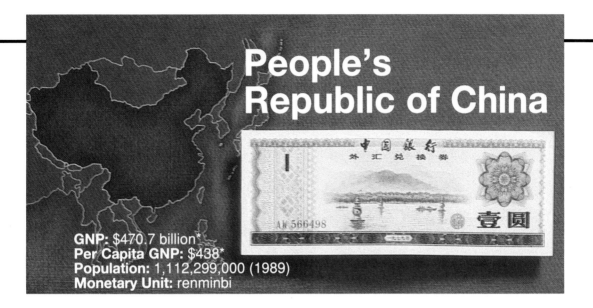

People's Republic of China

GNP: $470.7 billion*
Per Capita GNP: $438*
Population: 1,112,299,000 (1989)
Monetary Unit: renminbi

When Mao Zedong (Mao Tse-tung) led communism to victory over Mainland China in 1949, he started that nation on a winding economic path. The Communists gradually took control of private industries and farmland during the early 1950s, and because China's economy had suffered long from internal problems, the ravages of World War II, and a civil war, Mao's early reforms seemed to bring great improvement. At that time China benefited from Soviet economic aid and the rapid build-up and organization of large industries and collective farms. The initial economic successes, however, were achieved with great losses of personal freedom. Workers were no longer able to find jobs that met their skills and interests but instead were arbitrarily and permanently assigned to positions, and those assigned to the less prosperous agricultural regions were particularly dismayed to learn that they were forbidden to migrate to the more inviting cities. Along with this loss of freedom came shortages of food and manufactured goods because the communistic bureaucracy could not easily adapt to changing demands.

Once conversion to the Communist rule of the economy was complete, these dismal results clearly brought hardships and discontent. To deal with the problems of the economy, however, the Communist leaders had to compromise between allowing some economic freedoms and keeping total economic and political control. In the late 1950s Mao introduced the "Great Leap Forward," an economic plan that spread regimented production to small rural centers. That strict program was a disastrous failure that served only to make conditions worse. In the early 1960s China eased up on some of its economic controls and began to allow some freedom in the marketplace. The results were economic improvement and a weakening of the Communist party's political power. Mao countered this decline in power by instituting the "Cultural Revolution," a program that ruthlessly eradicated all manifestations of free thought and action and brought the nation into total conformity with Communist dogma. Then, after Mao's death in 1976, the nation again began to ease economic restraints. Trade with the West was encouraged, and individual Chinese more freely became entrepreneurs in Chinese markets. The new economic freedoms once again inspired more economic prosperity and more expressions of discontent with the continuing strict political control by the Communists. These calls for greater freedoms were met with violence in 1989 when the Communist government cracked down on its people. The years ahead will see a continued conflict between the determination of the Communist leaders to keep firm political control over the country and the necessity of allowing economic freedoms to help meet the material needs of this populous land.

*figures for 1987 from the 1990 *Statistical Abstract*

A labor intensive economy may increase the number of people working, but the nation may not necessarily be more prosperous as a result.

The Distribution Question: Who Will Receive What Is Produced?

Of the three economic questions none is so hotly debated as the distribution question. Who *should* receive the goods and services that the nation produces? Should the rich receive more than the poor? Are the intelligent entitled to a greater portion than the ignorant? Should a person's age determine his share? What is the fairest method of distributing a nation's limited goods and services? Since most of a nation's goods and services are purchased with money, economists recognize that the distribution question is really an issue of "who will receive the nation's money?"

The Command Economists' Solution–That there exists a gap separating the rich from the poor is an undeniable fact. Usually those who favor the command solution seek to close this gap out of an egalitarian concern for fairness. **Egalitarian fairness** maintains that each person in the nation has a right to a part of the nation's wealth simply because he is part of the human race. Some egalitarians argue in favor of **economic leveling,** equally distributing the nation's income regardless of each

person's ability to contribute to its pool of wealth. Less extreme egalitarians argue that society is obligated to maintain an economic "safety net" protecting the poor from the most devastating of economic hardships. This idea of safety-net egalitarianism is the basis of many of today's social programs including social security, unemployment compensation, Medicare, Medicaid, Aid to Families with Dependent Children, food stamps, Women with Infant Children Nutrition Assistance, and housing assistance.

Those who favor the command solution generally favor taxing income from those with above-average incomes and transferring that money to those whose incomes are below average.

The Market Economists' Solution–Those who favor the market solution maintain that wealth should be distributed solely to those who successfully satisfy the needs of others. They argue that people who cannot or will not create products or services for which others will pay are not deserving of a portion of the nation's wealth.

The market solution holds to a libertarian concept of fairness. Where egalitarianism maintains

Karl Marx (1818-1883)
Father of Communism

Karl Heinrich Marx was born in Trier in the German Rhineland, and his father intended that he become a lawyer. When Marx began his university training, however, he soon turned from studying law to exploring the philosophical and political developments of his day. He became associated with a group of radical students and teachers who openly criticized the government. They deplored the poor living conditions of the masses in nineteenth century Europe and detested the wealthy landowners and businessmen who enjoyed their wealth while the lower classes struggled to eke out a living. Marx, writing articles expounding these ideas, soon became an outcast in Germany. He went to Paris to continue his work, but again his radical ideas brought censure. He spent the last half of his life in exile in Britain. Because his work brought no steady income, he and his family lived in poverty, surviving by the charity of Marx's friend, Friedrich Engels.

Marx tirelessly studied the philosophical and economic ideas of his day and then meticulously wove the details of his own beliefs. His bitter atheistic outlook on life centered on the ongoing conflicts of society. Marx agreed with the then popular Hegelian thought that society continuously developed two antagonistic groups of people who would conflict. The conflict would become a revolution that would bring these groups together into a new society. That society would eventually split into two new groups destined to conflict. Seeing around him the upper classes (or bourgeoisie) and the lower classes (or proletariat), he believed that these groups would come into conflict because of their differences in wealth and living conditions. But he set forth his own opinion that man could change this pattern of history by using the conflict of the bourgeoisie and the proletariat to usher in an enlightened society. Marx's new harmonious society would strive for the betterment of all people by taking ''from each according to his ability'' and giving ''to each according to his need.'' All greed would then be overcome in this setting in which society owns all things in common. Marx called this utopia *communism*.

Marx tried to encourage the fulfillment of his dreams by inciting the proletariat to rebel against the bourgeoisie capitalists or owners of capital–the means of production. He despised capitalists, believing they gained their profits not by their own physical labor but by that of the oppressed proletarian workers. In 1848 Marx collaborated with Engels to write *The Communist Manifesto,* an appeal to the working classes to revolt against the capitalists. Europe was in political upheaval at that time, but even so, it rejected and suppressed Marx's radical ideas. Marx continued his study and his writings, especially the voluminous exposition of his ideas in a work called *Das Capital*. Marx was a revolutionary with some obviously un-Scriptural beliefs and erroneous predictions, but his ideas of perfecting society by human effort still appeal to men seeking human solutions for spiritual problems. His ideology also lends support to those who would increase their personal power by taking control of a nation's economic activities.

that every person deserves a share of the nation's wealth by virtue of his humanity, **libertarian fairness** argues that the only economic right to which citizens are entitled is the right to own and use property free of government interference. The accumulation of wealth is solely the responsibility of each individual. If a person is unable to earn a living because of a lack of education, libertarians maintain that it is his responsibility to secure the instruction he needs to gain a marketable skill. If one is unable to work because of physical limitations, it is his responsibility either to discover a skill that is compatible with his handicap or to secure private charity.

The libertarian concept of fairness has been dubbed **"economic Darwinism"** referring to Charles Darwin's principle of survival of the fittest. Libertarians argue that to transfer income from the productive members of society to less productive members would penalize those who are more productive while rewarding indolence.

The Bible As It Relates to the Distribution Question–Christians have a distressing tendency to hold to one or the other of the extreme views of economic fairness. Christian libertarians scoff at their "bleeding heart" egalitarian counterparts, carefully pointing out that Christ himself stated that eco-

Governments around the world decide whether they will take an egalitarian or a libertarian view toward the distribution of wealth to their peoples.

nomic leveling is an impossibility "for ye have the poor always with you" (Matt. 26:11). Christian egalitarians counter their "heartless" libertarian brethren with Christ's admonition: "If thou wilt be perfect, go and sell that thou hast, and give to the poor" (Matt. 19:21). Soon both groups march out their intellectual champions rattling their sabres in both the religious and secular press.

Christians occasionally need to be reminded that economic issues take a distant second place to the true mission of the Word of God: providing doctrine, reproof, correction, and righteous instruction (II Tim. 3:16). Students, teachers, pastors, and scholars who search the Scriptures for nothing more than justification of their libertarian or egalitarian economic philosophies run the risk of being side-tracked and missing the true lessons that God has in store.

Nevertheless, Scripture does present some clear economic principles regarding the distribution of wealth. First, the primary means whereby one is to have income transferred to himself is through his own labor. This principle began with Adam and Eve and continues today.

> Cursed is the ground for thy sake; in sorrow shalt thou eat of it all the days of thy life; Thorns also and thistles shall it bring forth to thee; and thou shalt eat the herb of the field; In the sweat of thy face shalt thou eat bread, till thou return unto the ground.
> (Genesis 3:17-19)

Obviously, therefore, Scripture maintains that economic leveling, providing equal economic benefits regardless of productivity, is clearly wrong. In fact, Paul the apostle stated in no uncertain terms:

> For even when we were with you, this we commanded you, that if any would not work, neither should he eat.
> (II Thessalonians 3:10)

Of course, Paul was referring to those who "*would not* work," as opposed to those who were unable to care for themselves. Time and again, Scripture points out that it is the responsibility of God's people to care for those who are poor in

spite of their own efforts; it is very careful to describe how this is to be accomplished. First, one is to care for the economic needs of his own family.

> But if any provide not for his own, and specially for those of his own house, he hath denied the faith, and is worse than an infidel.
> (I Timothy 5:8)

What if Christians and their churches fail to meet their Biblical obligation of providing charity? Should the state assume a role in caring for the poor? Citing passages such as Leviticus 23:22,

Christians have a responsibility to help care for those who are poor in spite of their own efforts.

many believe that, contrary to Christian libertarian thought, there is Scriptural precedent for government to use its power of taxation in providing a ''safety net'' for the truly poor. They point out that in a practice similar to modern day income taxation, the Israelites were forbidden by law from harvesting all of their produce, being required instead to leave a portion of it for the poor children of God and heathen alike:

And when ye reap the harvest of your land, thou shalt not make clean riddance of the corners of thy field when thou reapest, neither shalt thou gather any gleanings of thy harvest: thou shalt leave them unto the poor, and to the stranger: I am the Lord your God.

(Leviticus 23:22)

It should be noted especially that the government did not harvest, store, and later distribute the food to the poor. Rather, as in the case of Ruth's gleaning in Boaz's field, the poor were required to work to receive charity. Likewise, many states in the United States have redesigned their welfare programs to require labor on the part of the recipient. These redesigned programs have been dubbed ''workfare.''

Section Review

1. What are the three critical questions that every society must answer as it seeks to meet its economic goals?
2. How is the consumer good/capital good trade-off a matter of spending versus saving?
3. What term describes a business that uses a large amount of automated equipment?
4. Describe the egalitarian concept of fairness.
5. What Bible verse indicates that government may play some role in caring for the poor?

Chapter Review

Terms

extensive growth
intensive growth
consumer goods
capital goods
consumer goods/capital goods tradeoff
labor intensive
capital intensive
egalitarian fairness
economic leveling
libertarian fairness
economic Darwinism

Content Questions

1. What are the four economic goals of most societies? Describe.
2. How does the market solve the consumer goods-capital goods production dilemma? How does the command system attempt to solve it?

3. What are the advantages and disadvantages of labor intensive and capital intensive business firms?
4. How does the market decide who should receive what the nation produces? How does the command system address the problem? Are these solutions totally Biblical?

Application Questions

1. Read a news magazine or watch a television news report. List the circumstances in which the three economic questions were involved. Did the writer or broadcaster take the egalitarian or the libertarian point of view? Discuss your findings with others in your class.
2. Describe the activities of some business firms in your community. Do they produce consumer goods or capital goods? Are they labor intensive or capital intensive?

4 Goals

A. Output -
A. Command Economist
A. Market Economists

A2 Input -

A3 Distribution -

economic Karl Marx

CHAPTER 6 BUNGHOLIO

Economic Systems

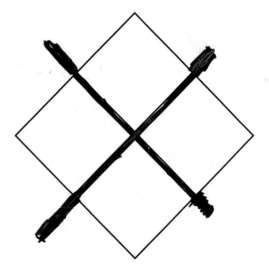

The Castillo de San Marcos at St. Augustine, Florida, a point of defense for the Spanish mercantilist system.

Thou shalt not covet thy neighbor's house, thou shalt not covet thy neighbor's wife, nor his manservant, nor his maidservant, nor his ox nor his ass, nor any thing that is thy neighbor's.

Exodus 20:17

I. Early Economic Systems

Throughout history man has sought to control others not only politically, but economically as well. He has attempted to control the economic choices of others in order to answer the three economic questions (see p. 69) according to his own dictates. In the latter part of the eighteenth century, something happened to upset this historical constant.

Mercantilism

From around the year 1500 until 1776, the nations of Western Europe operated under an economic philosophy known as **mercantilism.** Under mercantilism ruling monarchs had but one economic goal–to increase their holdings of gold and silver. These monarchs of the relatively new European nations did so out of the naive belief that the stockpiling of money was the same as accumulating wealth. In their efforts to amass fortunes, they subscribed to a five-point program:

1. Discover new sources of gold and silver both by sending explorers abroad to plunder less developed civilizations and by supporting pirates to steal from neighboring nations.
2. Increase the exportation of goods and services (selling to other nations), while decreasing the importation of foreign goods (buying from other nations). If a nation sold more goods abroad than it purchased, it was said to enjoy a **favorable balance of trade** since more gold was coming into the nation than flowing out.
3. Increase domestic manufacturing (manufacturing within the country) so that more goods might be sold abroad. Under mercantilism the manufacture of goods for the nation's own people was considered secondary since the sale of goods to them did not increase the nation's stockpile of gold and silver.
4. Encourage colonization of new territories and conquest of European neighbors so that new factors of production would become available. The motherland would use the new raw materials to produce goods that competing nations could not produce. To ensure maximum profit, the mother country usually forbade the colonies from selling their raw ma-

terials to competing nations, even when they were offered higher prices. This policy usually led to heightened tensions between the colonists and their monarchs.

5. Arrange all foreign relationships in a way that minimizes competition.

Laissez-Faire Liberalism

Naturally mercantilism fostered political discontent and economic distress both at home and in the colonies. By the mid-1700s political philosophers, arguing in favor of abolishing monarchies and replacing them with representative governments, were abundant, but those favoring economic freedom had no prominent champion around which they could rally. Then in 1776 an obscure economist with the unassuming name of Adam Smith became the focus of attention. Smith published a treatise against mercantilism which was so logical in its presentation, so explicit in its condemnations, and so specific in its remedies that the world took notice and was changed forever.

In his lengthy book with a title to match, *An Inquiry into the Nature and Causes of the Wealth of Nations,* Adam Smith argued that a nation is not made wealthy by the childish accumulation of shiny metals, but is enriched by the economic prosperity of its people. Mercantilism, he maintained, was illogical. When taken to its ultimate conclusion, the "wealthiest" nation would be the one that had laid its land waste in the production of food that foreigners had consumed. Its people would be cold, hungry, and angry as a result of its leaders' selling its goods to others. The nation would be despised by the other countries of the world as a result of its hostile behavior as it pursued its singular goal of accumulating gold and silver. Far from being the wealthiest, the nation that pursues a policy of accumulating money will actually become the most miserable.

The root problem, according to Smith, is the misconception that money is wealth. From a purely economic standpoint, money only provides the ability to purchase wealth: food, clothing, cars, homes, and other goods and services that provide utility. Money provides no utility of itself. It may not be eaten, worn, driven, or lived in. Money is only a tool to be used in acquiring economic wealth. To assume that the hoarding of money is the accumulation of wealth is like saying that the most successful carpenter is the one who accumulates the most hammers and screwdrivers.

After destroying the "money is wealth" myth, Adam Smith then presented what he saw as the true path to national enrichment: **laissez faire** (leh say FAIR). Loosely translated from the French, laissez faire means to "let alone." Smith argued that the monarch of a nation who wished his country to prosper should leave his subjects alone and allow them to seek their own profit. People must be free first to specialize in those jobs for which they feel best suited and second to exchange their products with others. Because of Smith's philosophy of limited government and personal responsibility, he became known as the father of laissez-faire or "let alone" economics.

Critics of Adam Smith's new approach argued that his laissez-faire liberalism (in the eighteenth century "liberalism" meant liberty) would create a nation of selfish, greedy, and antisocial people. Smith argued in *The Wealth of Nations* that, on the contrary, being left to their own devices and constrained by laws preventing theft and fraud, people will actively seek out the needs of others in order to profitably satisfy them: a system far more satisfactory, he believed, than mercantilism.

> But man has almost constant occasion for the help of his brethren, and it is in vain for him to expect it from their benevolence only. He will be more likely to prevail if he can interest their self-love in his favor, and show them that it is for their own advantage to do for him what he requires of them. It is not from the benevolence of the butcher, the brewer, or the baker that we can expect our dinner, but from their regard to their own interest.

As a result of seeking their own profit, Smith argued, people will eventually make the nation wealthier since a nation is merely a collection of individuals.

As every individual, therefore, endeavors as much as he can both to employ his capital in the support of domestic industry, and so to direct that industry that its produce may be of the greatest value, every individual necessarily labours to render the annual revenue of the society as great as he can. He generally, indeed, neither intends to promote the public interest, nor knows how much he is promoting it. By preferring the support of domestic to that of foreign industry, he intends only his own security; and by directing that industry in such a manner as its produce may be of the greatest value, he intends only his own gain, and he is in this, as in many other cases, led by an invisible hand to promote an end which was no part of his intention. Nor is it always worse for the society that it was no part of it. By pursuing his own interest he frequently promotes that of the society more effectually than when he really intends to promote it.

Section Review

1. What economic system prevailed in Europe from the 1500s to the 1700s?
2. What was the major economic goal of European countries from the 1500s to the 1700s?
3. Who was the father of laissez-faire liberalism?

II. Modern Economic Systems

In Adam Smith's day the great debate in economics focused on his laissez-faire liberalism and government-regulated mercantilism. The debate still continues between those who favor economic freedom and those who believe that the state should control economic events, but today the two sides of the argument are **capitalism** and **socialism**. It is very easy to determine whether a nation is capitalistic or socialistic by determining the answers to two fundamental questions:

1. Who owns the nation's factors of production?
2. Who answers the three economic questions?

If a central authority, committee, or the people in common own the factors of production and make all economic decisions, then the economic system is relatively socialistic. If, on the other hand, individuals both own the factors of production and make the economic decisions, the economic system is said to be relatively capitalistic.

Rather than being two distinct economic systems, however, capitalism and socialism are actually general categories that contain many systems that are variations on the themes of ownership and decision making. One could actually place the two categories on a line and arrange the various systems on the line relative to one another.

Adam Smith (1723-1790)
Father of Laissez-Faire Economics

Adam Smith was born on June 5, 1723, in the small town of Kirkcaldy, Scotland, a few weeks after his father died. Reared by a loving mother in a nation famous for the preaching of the gospel, Adam Smith undoubtedly came into contact with the gospel of Christ at an early age, but no evidence has been found attesting to his salvation. A rather humorous (although at the time distressful) incident occurred when Adam was three years old. While his mother was visiting her brother, Hercules Smith, in his Strathenry home, Adam was left to play in the front yard. While playing he was kidnapped by a band of wandering gypsies. During the chase that ensued, Adam was dropped in a forest to hasten the gypsies' escape. "He would have made," said one biographer, "I fear, a poor gypsy."

Adam proved to be a bright student and entered the University of Glasgow at the age of fourteen. While studying there he came under the influence of Francis Hutcheson, a professor of moral philosophy who, while a good, moral, and upright man, instilled in Adam the philosophy that human reason is to be held in high esteem, even above the Word of God.

After three years at the University of Glasgow, young Adam received a scholarship to attend England's prestigious Oxford University in Oxford. The scholarship was set up for the purpose of helping to train Scotsmen for the ministry of Jesus Christ. He accepted the scholarship but pursued a course of study leading to a degree not in religion, as was expected, but in political philosophy.

Because he knew that he would never become a minister of the gospel, Smith left Oxford in 1746, one year before graduation. He returned to Kirkcaldy intending to become a tutor, but parents were reluctant to hire him since he tended to be of "absent manner and bad address" (he was forgetful and sloppy). He

did find employment as a traveling lecturer in 1748, and later, in 1751 he was given the position of chairman of the department of Logic and Moral Philosophy at his old school, the University of Glasgow. He remained in this position until 1764 when he resigned to become the personal tutor of the young Duke of Buccleugh. While touring Europe with his young pupil, Smith met many of the influential European philosophers of the day, but eventually he became bored and began work on *The Wealth of Nations,* a classic work that earned him the title of "the economist's Shakespeare."

On July 17, 1790, at the age of sixty-seven Adam Smith, the brilliant but probably unregenerate economic philosopher, gathered his small band of followers around his deathbed. As the group quietly looked on their leader, he whispered the following words before passing into eternity, "I believe we must adjourn this meeting, gentlemen, to some other place."

Figure 6-1

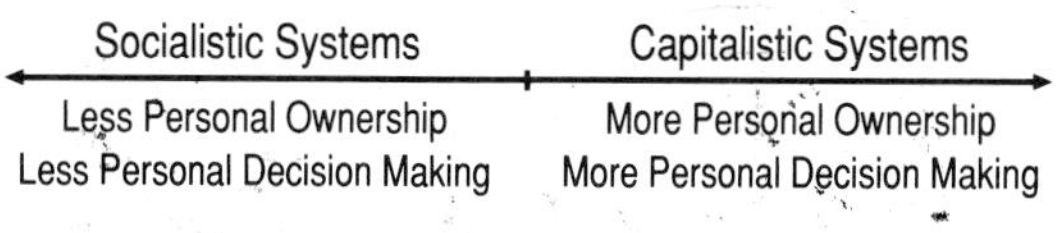

Socialistic Systems   Capitalistic Systems

Less Personal Ownership   More Personal Ownership
Less Personal Decision Making More Personal Decision Making

Figure 6-2 Radical Capitalism

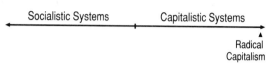

Socialistic Systems   Capitalistic Systems

Radical
Capitalism

Capitalism

***Radical Capitalism*–Radical capitalism** is capitalism in its most extreme form. Under it, private citizens own *all* factors of production and make *all* decisions regarding what will be produced, how it will be produced, and who will receive the production.

According to radical capitalism no government exists and the market is free to work unencumbered. Although it may be attractive at first glance, radical capitalism is both un-Scriptural and impractical. Radical capitalism is un-Scriptural because it denies the legitimacy of government. Indeed, if all decisions were to be made by individuals, no room would be left for any higher power. Under radical capitalism each individual is his own government. Scripture, on the other hand, stresses that government is a divine institution created by God and placed over us for our good:

> Let every soul be subject unto the higher powers. For there is no power but of God: the powers that be are ordained of God. For he is the minister of God to thee for good. But if thou do that which is evil, be afraid; for he beareth not the sword in vain: for he is the minister of God, a revenger to execute wrath upon him that doeth evil. (Romans 13:1, 4)

In addition to being un-Scriptural, radical capitalism is impractical. First, as puzzling as it may sound, the free market cannot exist without government. By maintaining property laws and affording a means to enforce these laws, the government provides an environment that fosters free enterprise. Without these laws there would be nothing hindering men from defrauding their neighbors. Second, in most economic systems the government plays the role of coordinator of many essential activities including national defense and police protection. To place these responsibilities in the hands of individuals would invite anarchy and leave a nation open to foreign invasion.

***Classic Liberal Capitalism*–Classic liberal capitalism** is the form of capitalism envisioned by Adam Smith. It accepts the idea that government must exist but allows it only minimal ownership of resources and decision-making power to perform its responsibilities.

What are the responsibilities of government under classic liberal capitalism? In *The Wealth of Nations* Smith declared that for citizens to enjoy economic and political liberty, government must be strictly limited to the performance of three major duties. The first of these responsibilities is that government is to protect its citizens from foreign aggression. This is accomplished by maintaining a national defense system:

> The first duty of the sovereign, that of protecting the society from the violence and invasion of other independent societies, can only be performed by means of a military force.

The second responsibility of government in a classic liberal capitalistic economy is to protect the rights of its citizens from infringements by others. Smith recognized that man's nature is depraved,

Figure 6-3 Classic Liberal Capitalism

Socialistic Systems   Capitalistic Systems

Classic
Liberal
Capitalism

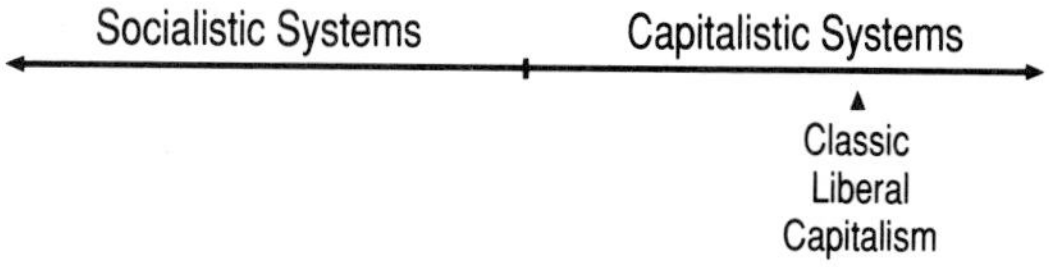

and left unrestrained, a free market would destroy itself. For example, a citizen might bargain with another to work for a certain wage, but without the threat of punishment the employer could at the end of the day refuse to pay the employee. To protect citizens from one another, Adam Smith argued that government should provide a legislature to enact just laws, a police force to restrain lawbreakers, and courts of law to judge and punish them:

> The second duty of the sovereign [is] that of protecting, as far as possible, every member of the society from the injustice or oppression of every other member of it. Men may live together in society with some tolerable degree of security, though there is no civil magistrate to protect them from the injustice of those passions. But avarice and ambition in the rich, in the poor the hatred of labour and the love of present ease and enjoyment, are the passions which prompt to invade property, passions much more steady in their operation, and much more universal in their influence.

The third responsibility of a classic liberal government is to provide **public goods.** Public goods are goods and services that are impossible for private firms to create at a profit. Highways, navigational aids, national parks, and a monetary system are all examples of public goods. In short, public goods are necessary goods and services which, if not provided by the government, would usually not be available.

> The third, and last duty of the sovereign or commonwealth is that of erecting and maintaining those public institutions and those public works, which, though they may be in the highest degree advantageous to a great society, are however of such a nature, that the profit could never repay the expense to any individual. . . . Works and institutions of this kind are chiefly those for facilitating the commerce of the society, and those for promoting the instruction of the people.

Public goods and services, such as highway construction and maintenance, are provided by the government in a classic liberal economy.

GNP: $155 billion*
Per Capita GNP: $18,490*

SVERIGES RIKSBANK

10

TIO KRONOR 10

SVERIGES RIKSBANK

Fem KRONOR

1974 BY
R 523715

Sweden

Population: 8,401,000 (1989)
Monetary Unit: krona

Sweden has developed a mixed economy with private industries that operate in an open market and a government that makes most of the decisions regarding the distribution of many vital services to the people. The Swedes are well off by most world standards. Their salaries are high, and they live in a modern industrial society that offers a wealth of comforts. Government programs provide money and care in sickness and in old age, and children receive state-sponsored child care and free education–even college tuitions. Yet these apparent benefits of Sweden's welfare state have a darker side as well.

Although private corporations account for about 90% of Swedish industry, government has pulled about one-third of the working population out of private enterprise and into the government bureaucracy. This bureaucracy and the many government programs and services it administers are not cheap. The Swedes pay income taxes amounting to 50% to 75% of their income, and what is left is further reduced by sales taxes

of over 20% on all purchases. The heavy tax burden has prompted the people to decline almost all opportunities to perform more work for more pay. They realize that the government will just tax the extra money away. Not only do the Swedes shy away from extra work, but they also find ways to decrease their normal work hours. All are entitled to a five-week vacation, and absenteeism from work is very high. This situation reduces industrial labor by an estimated 20% and diminishes industrial output. By encouraging people to work and earn less, Sweden's high taxes have also hurt government income. Tax receipts from lower salaries are insufficient to pay for government programs, and so the leaders must consider raising taxes even higher in order to pay for the social welfare. Where this web of taxes and social spending will lead Sweden is uncertain. Unfortunately, the future may not be as comfortable as the past.

*figures for 1987 from the 1990 *Statistical Abstract*

Figure 6-4 State Capitalism

Figure 6-5 European Social Democracy

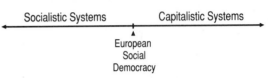

State Capitalism–Under **state capitalism** the vast majority of natural resources, financial capital, and labor is owned by private citizens, but the government intervenes widely in the decision-making process to ensure that its egalitarian goals are carried out.

To see this variation of capitalism at work one need only observe the day-to-day interventions of the U.S. government in the American economy. For example, Americans are free to own houses and factories, but the decisions of how buildings are to be built, who may build them, where they may be placed, and hundreds of other factors are decided by the government. People may own businesses but the government decides such things as ratios of various ethnic groups that must be represented among the employees, the minimum wage that must be paid to the workers, and the jobs that may or may not be performed by certain workers.

A nation under extreme state capitalism is known as a **welfare state.** In a welfare state, taxes are very high (generally averaging over 50%), and funds are redistributed in such a way that citizens are cared for from the "cradle to the grave." Several European nations could be classified as welfare states with Sweden being perhaps the best example.

Socialism

At this point you may be asking, "Just where does capitalism end and socialism begin?" While capitalism and socialism are relative terms, there does appear to be a clear dividing line between the two. As nations move further to the left on the economic spectrum, the government tends to take upon itself more ownership of resources and the making of more decisions. At the point, however, where the government actually steps in and takes

possession of business firms on a grand scale, that nation has crossed the line into socialism.

European Social Democracy–**European Social Democracy** is a transitional economic system bridging the gap between capitalism and socialism and is characterized by the state's taking possession of those industries that are the cornerstones of the economy.

These vital industries include transportation (auto manufacturers, airlines, wharfs, and trucking and shipping companies), communication (telephone and telegraph companies), energy (petroleum drilling, refining, and distribution companies as well as nuclear power), finance (banks, finance companies, and insurance companies), and health care (hospitals, clinics, and pharmaceutical businesses). Individual ownership of smaller, nonessential businesses is tolerated but highly regulated. When a nation's government assumes ownership of companies on such a large scale, it is said to be engaging in **nationalization.** Having experimented with nationalization and found it too expensive to maintain unprofitable companies for the sake of providing employment and low cost goods and services, many Western European governments are selling their nationalized businesses back to private stockholders, an action referred to as **privatization.**

Worker Management Socialism–As we move farther to the left on our spectrum, we encounter **worker management socialism.** Under worker management socialism, the government owns all business firms to prevent workers from being "enslaved" by private owners, but it realistically recognizes that it cannot operate all of the business firms from afar. To better manage the firms, the workers of each company are given that task. The workers collectively decide what will be produced,

*Centralized Socialism–*Centralized socialism maintains that the government should be both the central owner and the decision maker in all economic affairs of the state. It is this brand of socialism that Karl Marx envisioned for the world.

Marx in his *Communist Manifesto* argued that any arrangement of the tools of production short of total state ownership would be counterproductive. Beginning his **manifesto** with the statement "The history of all hitherto existing society is the history of class struggle," Marx announced that historically it has been the nature of mankind to oppress one another, most notably the rich against the poor. Karl Marx believed that being an employee in a capitalistic system was nothing more than being a slave. The wealthy business owner would pay his employees poverty wages which would have to be accepted meekly. After all, the business owner owns the tools necessary to create goods. Without the tools, the employees would have no work. Marx held that *all* of the money recovered from the sale of goods rightfully belonged to the employees who created those goods. Instead, the capitalists were diverting the employees' money to themselves in the form of profits. Marx maintained that eventually employees of firms in capitalist economies would realize that they are nothing more than slaves, would rise up in rebellion against their masters, and would take possession of the tools of production so that the fruit of their labor would be theirs indeed, not profits for indolent capitalist factory owners. The tools of production would then be turned over to the state, which would ensure that everyone would be employed at a fair wage and that no one would ever again be used as a tool to make profits for another.

France, having nationalized many of its vital industries, is an example of a European Social Democracy.

in what quantities, styles, and so forth. They also decide how the goods will be produced. As an incentive for greater productivity, workers are paid a base wage that increases as their individual productivity increases. As a further incentive, workers are paid a percentage of the firm's profits, much like stockholders in the United States. The most notable example of a nation that has used worker management socialism is Yugoslavia.

Figure 6-6 Worker Management Socialism

Socialistic Systems	Capitalistic Systems
▲ Worker Management Socialism	

Figure 6-7 Centralized Socialism

Socialistic Systems	Capitalistic Systems
▲ Centralized Socialism	

Since the state owns all factories and equipment, centralized socialism treats the nation's economy like one big company with the nation's leaders acting like a board of directors. Centralized socialism has been criticized by some as being inefficient in the extreme. First, by taking over the tools of production and outlawing profits, it has destroyed the incentive for entrepreneurs to take the risks necessary to develop new products and services. Thus, a centralized socialistic society is doomed to live either with outdated products, or the fruits of stolen technology. Second, leveling wages eliminates the incentive of individual workers to produce more and better goods and services. Thus, the society must tolerate shoddy merchandise. Finally, by controlling prices in such a way that they are unrealistically low, the centralized socialistic society is forced to live either with shortages or an ever growing black market.

Communism–Economically speaking, **communism** is socialism in its most extreme form. Ac-

The Soviet Union established a centralized socialist economy but has never achieved true economic communism.

Figure 6-8 Communism

Socialistic Systems	Capitalistic Systems

Communism

cording to Marx, centralized socialism is merely a stepping stone to a better society. When schoolchildren in the Soviet Union are asked in catechism fashion, "What is socialism?" they reply, "Socialism is the long, hard struggle between capitalism and communism." Marx wrote that centralized socialism is a transition time: a "time out" in which the government wrests ownership and control of the factors of production from the capitalists, purges the state of the greedy, and teaches the new generation the glories of sharing. After capitalism has been eradicated and the people have been properly prepared, Marx promised that the government would happily disband, leaving the factors of production to be managed by everyone in common, much as training wheels are discarded after a child has outgrown them. After socialism has been eliminated, the communist nation would automatically govern itself. Everyone in the society would selflessly concern himself with the welfare of all other members. Each person would voluntarily contribute as much as he possibly could and would demand of society only that which he absolutely needed. Obviously no nation has ever achieved this degree of socialism, nor will it ever be possible as long as mankind is depraved.

Section Review

1. The answers to what two questions can determine whether a nation is capitalistic or socialistic?
2. Name the three forms of capitalism.
3. What did Adam Smith declare to be the three functions of government?
4. What kind of economy does the United States have?
5. Name four forms of socialism.

Capitalism Versus Socialism

After examining libertarianism and egalitarianism, Adam Smith and Karl Marx, and capitalism and socialism, one comes to the inevitable question: which economic system is best? Capitalists point to their higher standard of living, their abundance of cars, television sets, coffee makers, and computers. Socialists, however, point to their low unemployment rate and their classless society in which there are no greedy businessmen exploiting the working class.

Before answering this question, Christians should recognize that any system created by man, whether it be political, social, or economic, is flawed because man himself is tainted by sin. Therefore there is nothing inherently godly in capitalism, nor inherently godless in socialism. Rather than supporting capitalism because it is "conservative" or "efficient" or socialism because it is "liberal" or "compassionate," Christians need to analyze the two systems in the light of the Word of God.

Although the Bible was not intended to be used as an economics text, it appears to support a number of principles that are more closely associated with capitalism while advocating many of the nobler motives of socialism. First, the Scriptures support the principle of accountability to God, the idea that everyone is answerable to the Lord for his decisions. In Matthew 25:14-30, the parable of the talents illustrates this principle. The master of the estate gave certain amounts of money to his three servants prior to his departure. One received five talents, another received two, and the third received one. The first two servants invested their talents wisely, doubling their master's money, but the third, fearful of making a poor investment, did nothing with his portion. Upon the master's return the first two servants were rewarded while the third was punished. While capitalistic systems foster accountability as a result of each person and each firm making most economic decisions, socialistic systems tend to rob their people of some of their accountability as a result of the government's vast decision-making power.

Second, Scripture supports the principle of rewarding the diligent and penalizing the indolent. Notice how, in Matthew 25, those who responsibly carried out their duties were honored while the careless servant was punished. Socialistic systems, on the other hand, tend to reward laziness as a consequence of their egalitarian goal of leveling incomes.

Third, and closely related to accountability, Scripture supports the principle of personal ownership of property. Acts 5 illustrates this position in the story of Ananias and Sapphira, who sold a possession, donated a portion of the proceeds, and lied by saying they contributed all of the money. Peter rebuked them, saying, "Whiles it remained, was it not thine own? and after it was sold, was it not in thine own power?" (verse 4) The two were punished, not for refusing to give away their property, but for lying to God as to what they did with it. Also, one of the first laws given by God to the Israelites in the Old Testament dealt with the sanctity of property: "Thou shalt not remove thy neighbor's landmark, which they of old time have set in thine inheritance, which thou shalt inherit in the land that the Lord thy God giveth thee to possess it" (Deut. 19:14). Socialists, on the other hand, argue that the primary evil in the world is the capitalist principle of property ownership. They believe that people who own homes will rob the poor by charging exorbitant rents or that capitalistic businessmen who own the tools of production will exploit their employees by threatening to fire them if they do not provide maximum labor for slave wages. With these fears in mind socialism denies the right of people to own property.

While Scripture gives strong support for many capitalistic principles, it also exhorts Christians to temper the baser characteristics that the absolutely free market permits, such as greed for material possessions, lust for power, and inordinate ambition. For example, to counteract the greed that property ownership may fuel, Scripture admonishes Christians to exercise good stewardship by giving to the Lord's work and supporting the poor. To hinder the materialism that capitalism may foster, the Bible commands the children of God to

> Lay not up for yourselves treasures upon earth, where moth and rust doth corrupt, and where thieves break through and steal: But lay up for yourselves treasures in heaven, where neither moth nor rust doth corrupt, and where thieves do not break through nor steal: For where your treasure is, there will your heart be also. (Matthew 6:19-21)

To prevent employers from exploiting their workers, Scripture instructs Christian business owners to treat their employees with respect, pay them a decent wage, and pay them on time.

> Masters, give unto your servants that which is just and equal; knowing that ye also have a Master in heaven. (Colossians 4:1)

> Woe unto him that buildeth his house by unrighteousness, and his chambers by wrong; that useth his neighbor's service without wages, and giveth him not for his work.
> (Jeremiah 22:13)

> Thou shalt not defraud thy neighbor, neither rob him: the wages of him that is hired shall not abide with thee all night until the morning.
> (Leviticus 19:13)

For all of its vaunted goals of sharing, intolerance of oppression, and the dignity of labor, socialism departs from Scripture on two critical points. First, socialism, in its struggle to establish a new economic order for the ''working classes,'' ignores the needs of individuals and indeed, is ready to sacrifice the individual for the needs of the state. Scripture, however, constantly maintains the importance of the individual:

> For the Son of man is come to seek and to save that which was lost. How think ye? if a man have an hundred sheep, and one of them be gone astray, doth he not leave the ninety and nine, and goeth into the mountains, and seeketh that which is gone astray? And if so be that he find it, verily I say unto you, he rejoiceth more of that sheep, than of the ninety and nine which went not astray. Even so it is not the will of your Father which is in heaven, that one of these little ones should perish. (Matthew 18:11-14)

Second, socialism departs from Scripture when it argues that the hearts of people can be changed by altering the environment within which they live in order to pave the way for a perfect society. Contrary to Karl Marx, Scripture maintains that man's primary struggle is not against external economic oppression; rather, man's greatest struggle is with the sin that resides in every person.

> From whence come wars and fightings among you? come they not hence, even of your lusts that war in your members?
> (James 4:1)

Neither socialism nor capitalism can meet the ultimate craving of the human heart, a need that can be met only through salvation in Christ.

Section Review

1. Name three capitalistic principles supported by Scripture.
2. What are some of the potential problems of capitalism?
3. What two particular beliefs of socialism are un-Scriptural?

2 ?'s - who owns nations factors?
    Who answers economic ?'s?

Chapter Review

Terms
mercantilism
favorable balance of trade
laissez faire
capitalism
socialism
radical capitalism
classic liberal capitalism
public goods
state capitalism
welfare state
European social democracy
nationalization
privatization
worker management socialism
centralized socialism
manifesto
communism

Sets,
Mercantilism

Content Questions
1. What two characteristics did Adam Smith point out as being the keys to economic prosperity in a nation?
2. Describe laissez faire capitalism.
3. What is liberalism according to its classical meaning?
4. Describe the differences between capitalism and socialism.
5. Why is radical capitalism un-Scriptural?
6. Socialism occurs when the government nationalizes which key industries?

Application Questions
1. Is the United States becoming a welfare state? Why or why not?
2. Which economic system does the nation of Mexico currently have? Discuss.
3. Report on the privatizing efforts of a Western European nation.

100% Socialist

100% Capitalism

```
|——X————X——X——X——X————X————————X——|
   1    2   3   4   5        6          7
```

Communism

Centralized Socialism

worker management system

European Social Democracy

state capitalism

classical liberal capitalism

Radical Capitalism

Unit III: Economics of the Business Firm

◇ 7 Forms of Business Ownership

◇ 8 Market Structure and Competition

CHAPTER 7

Forms of Business Ownership

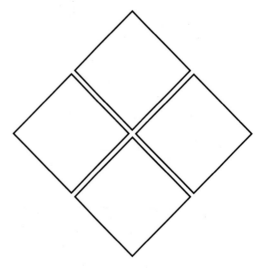

Seest thou a man diligent in his business? he shall stand before kings; he shall not stand before mean men. Proverbs 22:29

Take a moment to observe the various objects that surround you; virtually all of the goods you see are the result of successful entrepreneurship. Entrepreneurship, as you recall, is the ability to take risks and coordinate the factors of production in order to produce a good or service for a profit.

An entrepreneur has been likened to an orchestra conductor who first determines what the audience wishes to hear, organizes a team of talented musicians, motivates them, and leads them in a performance that will be attended and applauded. Likewise, the entrepreneur determines what the market wishes to purchase, hires managers and workers, encourages their efforts, and leads them. Hopefully, profits will materialize, but in many cases the entrepreneur comes out the loser. Over 30% of all new businesses fail within their first year, and 50% are out of business within two years.

Once an entrepreneur has decided to start a new business, one of the most important decisions he must make is to determine which form of business ownership he will use. Virtually all businesses in the United States today fall within three categories: sole proprietorships, partnerships, and corporations. Each form of ownership has distinct advantages and disadvantages, depending on factors such as the size of the firm, the abilities of the owner, and the firm's tax situation.

I. Sole Proprietorship

A **sole proprietorship** is a business firm that is owned by one person. Examples of sole proprietorships include chimney cleaning services, part-time sales businesses run out of the home, and lawn care services. While sole proprietorships are always owned by one person, many are operated by a number of managers or employees.

Sole proprietorships are the most popular form of business in America today, accounting for about 74% of the nation's 16 million business firms.

Advantages of Sole Proprietorship

The sole proprietorship is the most popular form of business ownership because of the tremendous freedom it affords.

Freedom to Enter and Exit the Market Easily–In most cases a sole proprietorship may be started simply by the owner's registering the new company's name with the clerk of court of the county in which the proprietor resides. In some cases (notably those involving medical doctors, dentists, daycare owners, and food handling enterprises) various licenses must be obtained, but usually starting a sole proprietorship is as easy as locating and renting a building, putting out an ''open for business'' sign, and selling the product or service.

Getting out of business is just as easy; the proprietor sells any remaining goods, collects the debts due him, pays off his bills, and quits.

Freedom from Outside Control–While being accountable to obey laws that apply to all businesses, sole proprietors have no special ''sole proprietorship laws'' imposed upon them. As far as the government is concerned, the business and the proprietor are one and the same.

In addition to having no special accountability to government, the sole proprietor reports to no one as far as his business decisions are concerned. He has no partners with which to negotiate or stockholders to please. The proprietor may apply for bank loans, offer new products or services, discontinue old product lines, expand or contract the business, change prices, or take all of the money out of the cash register for a vacation to the Bahamas without having to answer to anyone.

Freedom to Retain Information–One of the greatest fears of a business person is having his strategies, financial information, and production methods discovered by his competitors. Except for a possible audit by the Internal Revenue Service, the proprietor may keep his business information as secret as he wishes. He has no board of directors with which to consult and no stockholders to inform.

The owners of many restaurants and other small businesses enjoy the freedoms allowed by the sole proprietorship form of business ownership.

Freedom from Paying Excessive Taxes–All income of a sole proprietorship is subject to taxation at the personal income tax rate. While this does not sound like an advantage, it is of great benefit since taxes on corporations tend to be significantly higher.

Freedom from Being an Employee–Sole proprietors possess the unique advantage of being self-employed. The age-old ideal of rugged individualism, independence, and personal responsibility is most attainable under this form of business ownership. The sole proprietor is free to come and go without having to punch a time clock. The fruits of his labor (as well as the fruits of his failures) belong to him alone.

Disadvantages of Sole Proprietorship

Because of the attractive advantages of becoming one's own boss, many people jump into business for themselves without thinking about the limitations and problems it carries with it.

Unlimited Personal Financial Liability–If a proprietor is unable to pay the obligations of his business firm out of the income it generates, he will be required to make up the difference with his own funds. For example, if a sole proprietor is sued for several million dollars and loses the lawsuit, he personally will have to do all that is necessary to pay the debt, including selling all the business assets, using his personal savings, and selling his personal possessions. The Christian needs to pay careful attention to the Biblical principle of "counting the cost" before becoming a sole proprietor. Unlike the unsaved man, the child of God has more at stake in a business failure than the loss of dollars and cents: his Christian testimony is on the line.

> For which of you, intending to build a tower, sitteth not down first, and counteth the cost, whether he have sufficient to finish it? Lest haply, after he hath laid the foundation, and is not able to finish it, all that behold it begin to mock him. (Luke 14:28-29)

Limited Management and Employee Skills–In most sole proprietorships the proprietor performs all of the duties needed to keep the business going. He often acts as the owner, manager, salesman, bookkeeper, secretary, manufacturer, service technician, and janitor. The chances are great that he is not performing many of these tasks exceptionally well. Lack of expertise poses a problem for the proprietor, since he may find himself competing with firms that have entire departments filled with skilled personnel.

Most proprietors would like to hire the same skilled talent available to their competition, but usually they cannot match the high salaries, bene-

fits, and prestige that the larger firms can offer. Employees of sole proprietors, therefore, tend to be friends or relatives of the owner or people with limited education, experience, or abilities.

Limited Life–By their very nature sole proprietorships tend to be unstable. The continuation of the business depends on many things that could change in an instant. Notable among these factors are the life and health of the proprietor. If he should become seriously ill, the business would cease functioning. If he were to die, the business would die with him, possibly leaving many legal entanglements for his survivors to resolve.

Limited Availability of Money–As long as the business remains a sole proprietorship, the owner cannot sell a portion of his ownership interest to others in order to raise money to expand or continue operations. The only alternative, therefore, besides the owner's use of limited personal savings, is debt. When applying for a bank loan, many proprietors find that this source, too, is limited. When deciding whether to grant the loan, the **creditor,** or lender, must determine the probability of the proprietorship's staying in business long enough to repay the loan. Given the fact that proprietors have unlimited financial liability and limited management skills and that the life of the business is not perpetual, most creditors are reluctant to lend money without the deed to the proprietor's home or other valuable property to stand behind the loan. In addition, if a loan is granted, creditors may charge a high rate of interest to compensate for the high risk involved. In still other cases when the risk is too high, a lender may refuse to make the loan under any conditions.

Section Review
1. What are the three forms of business organization, and which is the most common in the United States?
2. What are the advantages of sole proprietorship?
3. What are the disadvantages of sole proprietorship?

Mexico

GNP: $139.2 billion*
Per Capita GNP: $1,701*
Population: 86,366,000 (1989)
Monetary Unit: peso

The country just "south of the border" has been a land of great economic potential and great economic problems. Mexico both imports more from and exports more to the United States than it does to any other country. Its cities have become a source of economical labor for American industries, and its agricultural products and petroleum deposits are important assets. Yet Mexico is a land of poverty and debt. Its unemployment rate was 18% in 1989. Hundreds of thousands of its people live without running water, sanitation, schools, or other vital services in crude slum areas of its major cities. Millions more live in a slightly higher class of poverty on small farms or in crowded cities where they struggle to make a living. Their government has had difficulty providing public services for these millions in recent years largely because it owes foreign creditors about $100 billion, and the interest payments alone are draining the country of any means it might have to improve domestic conditions.

Current leaders are attempting to overcome Mexico's economic difficulties by a number of means. They are selling many government-owned industries to the private sector in order to gain income and foster private enterprise. These leaders are tearing down some trade and investment barriers in order to attract foreign capital. They are seeking to adjust their debt payments to levels that they can afford, and thereby avoid defaulting on loans and ruining Mexico's credit. If these attempts are successful, Mexico may turn itself around and begin to reach its economic potential. If not, Mexico may become even poorer.

*figures for 1987 from the 1990 *Statistical Abstract*

II. Partnership

A **partnership,** also known as a **general partnership,** is a business enterprise owned by two or more people. The partnership is the least popular form of business ownership, accounting only for around 8% of all American businesses. While a majority (around 80%) of all partnerships are formed by only two individuals, some have over one hundred partners.

A written contract between the partners generally is not required by the laws of most states, but attorneys recommend that partners compose a partnership agreement that specifically answers the following questions:

1. Who are the partners?
2. What is each partner responsible to do?
3. How are profits to be divided?
4. How may a partner withdraw from the partnership?
5. How can the partnership be dissolved?

Advantages of Partnership

Partnerships have several advantages that overcome many of the problems posed by the sole proprietorship.

Greater Management Skills–The logic behind engaging in a partnership is simple: partnerships combine the complementary talents of two or more people. One partner may be proficient at financial management while the other may have skills in marketing or manufacturing. Two surgeons may form a partnership in order to replace each other during vacations, to share the cost of an office building and staff, or to share medical knowledge. By combining the strengths of two or more people, a business firm has a much greater chance of succeeding.

Greater Chance of Keeping Competent Employees–One great disadvantage of the sole proprietorship is its inability to attract or keep qualified and experienced personnel. Partnerships, on the other hand, have the ability to promote exceptionally well-qualified employees to the status of partner. Promotion acts as a great incentive for employees both to work harder and to remain with the firm.

Many law and accounting firms use this incentive to their advantage.

Greater Sources of Financing–Partnerships have a definite advantage over sole proprietorships where financing is concerned. Financing a sole proprietorship is virtually limited to the personal savings of a single owner, but because the partnership has a greater number of owners than the proprietorship, a greater quantity of money is available to it. Also, because the partnership has a more specialized management team and more competent employees, creditors are often more willing to lend money to the firm.

Ease of Formation and Freedom to Manage–Like the proprietorship, the partnership is relatively easy to form and operate. Though the firm is subject to several laws unique to partnerships, it is relatively free to carry out its business activities with a minimum of government interference.

Disadvantages of Partnership

When a form of business ownership represents only 8% of all American business firms, one wonders why it is relatively unpopular. Several advantages do exist, but many overwhelming disadvantages make this form of ownership unacceptable to most businesspeople.

Unlimited Personal Financial Liability–Perhaps the greatest drawback to the partnership form of business ownership is the unlimited personal financial liability with which each partner must live. Just as a sole proprietor is obligated to pay all company debts from his own personal wealth if need be, each general partner is responsible to pay all obligations of the firm. History is littered with sad stories of partners who have abandoned unprofitable businesses, leaving the other partners saddled with company debts to pay out of their own pockets. Not only is each partner liable for all of the firm's debts, but each general partner has the power to obligate the firm without the other partner's knowledge. Thus one partner could purchase thousands of dollars' worth of personal items under the firm's name and leave town, making the other partner liable to pay the debt.

Uncertain Life–Of all the forms of business ownership, partnerships historically have the shortest lives. Many reasons may contribute to the dissolution of partnerships, including death, withdrawal, insanity, bankruptcy, or the failure of any of the partners to carry out their responsibilities as listed in the partnership agreement.

Conflicts Between Partners–Many partnerships begin their existence with smiles, handshakes, and bright hopes but later end with conflicts, bitterness, anger, and occasionally violence. There are many reasons why partners have a change in attitude, but they all stem from one basic problem: for any endeavor it is impossible to have two masters.

In a general partnership each partner has an equal voice in matters of policy. When significant differences of opinion present themselves, as in decisions involving company policies, finances, salaries, and business practices, each partner feels that his opinion is the correct one.

Scripture and Partnerships

What does the Bible have to say about partnerships? Specific rules for business partnerships are not mentioned directly in Scripture, but it does give us some general principles we may use when considering entering into a partnership.

First, a born-again believer should never consider entering into a business partnership with an unsaved person. Such an association would constitute an unequal "yoking." "Be ye not unequally yoked together with unbelievers: for what fellowship hath righteousness with unrighteousness? and what communion hath light with darkness?" (II Cor. 6:14). Many Christians ask, what is "yoking"? Yoking is a situation in which two or more people are tied together in a common endeavor, striving toward a common goal, each one having the ability to influence, affect, or control the other. A Christian should not be yoked together with an unbeliever because their goals are not the same. The unregenerate man has a single-minded goal of increasing profits, whereas the believer's primary goal is to magnify Jesus Christ.

Second, Scripture implies that a general partnership between two saved persons would be very unwise because each would become a **surety**, or **cosigner**, for debts that the other may incur.

Every Scriptural reference to surety admonishes the child of God to avoid becoming obligated for another's debts:

> He that is a surety for a stranger shall smart for it: and he that hateth suretiship is sure.
> (Proverbs 11:15)

> A man void of understanding striketh hands, and becometh surety in the presence of his friend. (Proverbs 17:18)

> Be not thou one of them that strike hands, or of them that are sureties for debts. If thou hast nothing to pay, why should he take away thy bed from under thee? (Proverbs 22:26-27)

While some argue that becoming a surety for another's debts is totally forbidden by Scriptures, others maintain that certain exceptions are allowed such as when a parent cosigns on a loan for a son or daughter who is attempting to establish a good credit record. In such cases one should cosign for another only *after* determining that he has the ability to pay the debt in full.

NOTICE TO COSIGNER

You are being asked to guarantee this debt. Think carefully before you do. If the borrower doesn't pay the debt, you will have to. Be sure that you can afford to pay if you have to, and that you want to accept this responsibility.

You may have to pay up to the full amount of the debt if the borrower does not pay. You may also have to pay late fees or collection costs, which increase this amount.

The bank can collect this debt from you without first trying to collect from the borrower. The bank can use the same collection methods against you that are used against the borrower, such as suing you, etc. If this debt is ever in default, that fact may become part of your credit record.

This notice is not the contract that makes you liable for the debt.

FURTHER NOTICE

You agree to pay the debt identified below although you may not personally receive any property, services, or money. You may be sued for payment although the person who receives the property, services, or money is able to pay. This notice is not the contract that obligates you to pay the debt. Read the contract for the exact terms of your obligation.

IDENTIFICATION OF DEBT YOU MAY HAVE TO PAY

Dustin Polentz
(Name of Debtor)

Dustin Bob Polentz
(Name of Creditor)

4/20f
(Date)

Herbal Medicines
(Kind of Debt)

I have received a copy of this notice.

4/20   Robt Polentz
(Date)   (Signed)

Consumer 2 (12-86)

This cosigner's agreement for a loan gives a stern warning to someone willing to become a surety for another's debts.

To counter some of the biggest objections of the general partnership, the limited partnership was developed. A **limited partnership** is one in which there is at least one general partner who has unlimited personal financial liability and at least one **limited partner.** A limited partner invests money in a partnership, has the right to inspect the books of the business, and has the right to share in the profits of the firm, but he has no responsibilities in the management of the firm and makes no business decisions for the partnership. He is called a limited partner because his personal financial liability is limited to his total investment. The most money he could lose is the amount he has invested in the partnership.

Section Review
1. What are the two forms of partnership?
2. What are the disadvantages of a partnership?
3. What does it mean to be surety for another?

III. Incorporation

A corporation is created when a person or group incorporates, that is, when owners legally declare the business to be separate from themselves. A **corporation,** therefore, is a separate entity created by the law. The government recognizes the right of the corporation to buy, sell, enter into contracts, own property, sue, and be sued, just like any legal person. The most famous definition of the term *corporation* appeared in 1803 when Supreme Court Chief Justice John Marshall stated in his opinion of the case of *Dartmouth College* vs. *Woodward:*

> A corporation is an artificial being, invisible, intangible, and existing only in contemplation of law. Being the mere creature of law, it possesses only those properties that the charter of its creation confers upon it, either expressly or as incidental to its very existence. Among the most important are immortality, and, if the expression may be allowed, individuality; properties, by which a perpetual succession of many persons are considered as the same, and may act as a single individual.

Types of Corporations

When one thinks of the corporate form of ownership, what usually comes to mind is the private corporation. A **private corporation** is one that is owned by private citizens. Examples of private corporations include IBM, Exxon, Disney, Coca Cola, and General Electric. While most private corporations have many (sometimes hundreds of thousands) owners, some, such as Reader's Digest and Hallmark Cards, are held by relatively few people.

A second type of corporation is the **public corporation,** which is owned by the general public and managed by the government. Among public corporations are the Tennessee Valley Authority (TVA), some state-run liquor stores, and some nuclear power plants.

Ownership of a Corporation

A person becomes an owner of part of a corporation by purchasing its **stock.** A stockholder's ownership is evidenced by share certificates that declare the number of shares owned.

Each stockholder's degree of ownership is determined by the number of shares he owns divided

Ownership of a corporation is evidenced by share certificates.

James Cash Penney
(1875-1971)
American Merchant

Born on a farm near Hamilton, Missouri, J. C. Penney was the son of a poor farmer who preached on Sundays at a Primitive Baptist church. Although the family remained in debt and barely kept food on the table, Penney's parents made certain that their children obtained a proper education and that they learned Scriptural principles as well. The golden rule was drilled into him at an early age. When the lad was only eight, his father informed him that from then on, he would have to buy his own clothes. Penney decided that to earn money for this new responsibility he would use a small sum he had saved to buy a pig, which he could fatten and sell for profit. He gathered table scraps from the neighbors to feed his animal and then sold it and bought more pigs. However, one day his father ordered him to sell the pigs immediately. Penney protested that they were not fat enough yet and would not bring a good price. Even so, the father was firm because, as he explained, the smell of the pigs was beginning to bother the neighbors. The right thing to do was to follow the golden rule: "All things whatsoever ye would that men should do to you, do ye even so to them" (Matt. 7:12). Young Penney sold the pigs.

Penney's principled upbringing became a major asset as he grew up. He decided that farming was not the life for him; he wanted to be a merchant. His hard work at the new trade earned him a good job as a store clerk in his hometown. Poor health prompted him to move west, where he lost his savings while trying to run a butcher shop. Dejected but not defeated, he returned to the merchant trade and found work as a clerk. Again, his hard work and determination to succeed won him the admiration of his employers. The partners eventually offered Penney one-third interest in a new store that he would manage. Penney opened that store in Kemmerer, Wyoming, in 1902, and his fairness and eagerness to serve his customers brought him a loyal clientele. In 1907 Penney was able to buy out his partners' interest in the Kemmerer store and two other stores. He quickly expanded this chain that he called the "Golden Rule Stores." By 1913 he had forty-eight stores, and in 1924 he opened the five-hundredth J.C. Penney store at his old hometown of Hamilton. As his wealth grew, Penney became a generous philanthropist, supporting many religious organizations and charitable causes. Although he lost his fortune in the stock market crash of 1929 and the following depression, he won it back again in later years by continuing to follow what were called the "Penney Principles":

1. To serve the public, as nearly as we can, to its complete satisfaction.
2. To offer the best possible dollar's worth of quality and value.
3. To strive constantly for a high level of intelligent and helpful service.
4. To charge a fair profit for what we offer–and not all the traffic will bear.
5. To apply this test to everything we do: "Does it square with what is right and just?"

by the total number of shares outstanding. For example, if one million shares are outstanding in a firm and you own 500,000 shares, then you own one-half of the firm.

Advantages of Incorporation

Limited Personal Financial Liability of Stockholders–After studying proprietorships and partnerships with their disadvantages of unlimited personal financial liability, one can understand why limited financial liability is the primary advantage of the corporate form of ownership. Stockholders have the advantage of risking only their investment in the firm. The firm's creditors cannot touch the personal property of the shareholders. For example, if you purchased $1,000 worth of stock in a corporation, and it went out of business owing $1 million, you might lose your entire investment of $1,000, but your personal wealth would otherwise be left untouched. Your bank accounts would not be seized, your home would not be auctioned, and your personal possessions would be left undisturbed.

Experienced Management and Specialized Employees–A corporation is run by a board of directors, who are elected by votes of their stockholders. A board of directors represents the interests of the stockholders and usually is composed of people with experience in running other corporations. The board of directors appoints a Chief Executive Officer, or CEO, who usually serves as president of the corporation. The CEO in turn appoints qualified people to fill necessary top, middle, and lower management positions, who themselves hire and train the other employees.

Because of the specialization and experience of both the management and the firm's employees, the corporate form of ownership tends to be more profitable than either the proprietorship or partnership.

Continuous Life–If a proprietor or partner dies, the proprietorship or partnership also dies. In a corporation, however, if a board member dies, he is replaced. If a manager or employee dies, another is hired to take his place. If a stockholder dies, his stock is inherited by his heirs or sold on the open market to other investors. In any case, the corporation keeps living.

Ease in Raising Financial Capital–Since a corporation may have an unlimited number of owners, it may sell more ownership shares if it needs additional funds. Corporations usually borrow money at lower interest rates than proprietorships or partnerships because their higher caliber of management, limited financial liability, and unlimited life enable their firms to repay their debts with less risk of default.

Disadvantages of Incorporation

Obviously the corporate form of business ownership is not perfect, else the other forms would not exist. Five specific disadvantages of incorporation are higher taxes, greater regulation, lack of secrecy, impersonality, and rigidity.

Higher Taxes–One of the greatest disadvantages of incorporation is the high taxes levied on the firm's earnings. First, corporations pay taxes on a higher graduated scale than the personal income

Figure 7-1 Corporate Organizational Structure

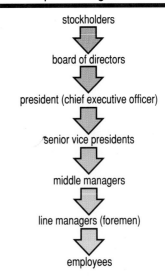

stockholders

board of directors

president (chief executive officer)

senior vice presidents

middle managers

line managers (foremen)

employees

An advantage of a corporation is that it may attract an experienced management team with the specialized abilities needed to help the business succeed.

tax rate. Second, after profits are paid out to the stockholders, they must pay personal income taxes on the dividends. This ''double taxation of earnings'' would be similar to having payroll taxes removed from your earnings before you get your paycheck, then paying taxes again on your after-tax income.

Greater Government Regulation–Because the government ''created'' the corporation, the government has the right of control. Thousands of regulations apply to all forms of businesses, including rules on hiring, paying, retiring, and firing employees. Standards on safety and health for the workers and the general population must be observed. In addition to following these business regulations, however, corporations must obey laws on such matters as merging with other companies, selling new stocks and bonds, and setting prices of certain products. Corporations spend a great deal of time and money interpreting and obeying laws in addition to keeping records and reporting to various government agencies.

Lack of Secrecy–As a result of required reporting, corporations find that keeping secrets is more difficult than for proprietorships or partnerships. By law, corporations must keep the government and their stockholders aware of the firm's sales, profits, advertising expenditures, costs of research and development, and other information of vital interest not only to the shareholders but to the firm's competitors as well. Some corporations have solved the secrecy problem by ''going private,'' a situation where the managers of the firm purchase all outstanding stock, allowing the corporation to keep sensitive information from reaching the public.

Impersonality–Many large corporations suffer because employees become demotivated by the sheer size of the firm. Workers who feel that they are only a small part of the giant corporate machinery tend to minimize the overall importance of their work. To counteract this problem, many large corporations have sponsored activities ranging from company picnics and softball teams to actually giving the workers a voice in running the business.

Rigidity–The owners of proprietorships and partnerships can react quickly to market changes. Corporations tend to move at a much slower pace. For example, a proprietor may develop a new product one day and begin selling it the next. The proprietor's complete control of the business operations allows him to make speedy adjustments. In contrast, a corporation's new product ideas may take months or years to gain approval of the various decision makers.

Section Review

1. According to the law, what is a corporation, and what important properties does it possess?
2. How does one become an owner of part of a corporation?
3. What are the advantages of incorporation?

Chapter Review

Terms

sole proprietorship
creditor
partnership
· general partnership
, surety
cosigner
limited partnership
, limited partner
corporation
private corporation
public corporation
stock

Content Questions

1. List three advantages and disadvantages of a sole proprietorship.
2. What are the key differences between a general partnership and a limited partnership?
3. What does the Bible say about the partnership form of ownership?
4. Describe a share certificate.
5. What is the primary advantage of being incorporated?

Application Questions

1. If you were given $100,000 to start your own business, what kind of business would you like to undertake (a bicycle shop, craft supply store, bookstore, etc.)? Assuming that this business is a sole proprietorship, what will be some of the necessary tasks that you will have to complete in order to form your business and begin operation?
2. Some believe that investing in stock is the same as gambling. Others believe that it is not. What does the Bible say about it?

CHAPTER 8

Market Structure and Competition

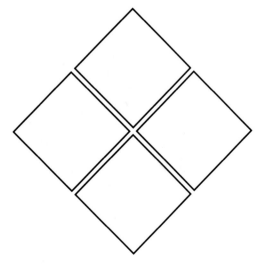

And every man that striveth for the mastery is temperate in all things. Now they do it to obtain a corruptible crown; but we an incorruptible.   I Corinthians 9:25

The owner of a business firm created a product for which there was a great need and produced the product in such a way that it was of very high quality. Seeing the potential for expansion, he examined the advantages and disadvantages of the proprietorship, partnership, and corporate forms of business organization. Although the owner chose the best form for his firm, he was bankrupt after six months–a scenario having become all too common in American business.

Why is the American business firm such an endangered species? Indeed, within the first year of operation, one out of every three new businesses closes its doors. The answer to this question may be found in one word: competition.

Having examined the various forms of business organization along with their respective advantages and disadvantages, Chapter 7 made clear that choosing the right form of organization is not enough to ensure a business's success. Every business firm must also be able to meet its customers' needs better than other business firms. That is, it must compete successfully in the market.

When most people first hear the word market, they tend to think either of a *place* such as a supermarket or department store, or of a particular *group of buyers* such as the "fast food market," the "new car market," or the "student market." From an economist's point of view, however, the word **market** refers to the arrangements that people have developed for trading with one another.

This chapter will examine three basic market questions. First, what are the fundamental differences that distinguish markets from one another? Second, based upon these differences, what types of competition exist in the market? And third, how does the U.S. government attempt to preserve market competition through federal laws?

I. Differences Between Markets

Every business has unique characteristics and differing ways of bringing products and services to customers. But firms tend to be grouped into specific markets, such as automobile production, banking, book publishing, plumbing, or construction. Each of these markets is referred to as an **industry.** Industries are families of common concerns—groups of businesses that sell a similar product, sell to a certain group of customers, or produce their products in a similar way. Each industry is distinguished from every other industry by a great many things, but economists have identified five key differences.

1. Number of Firms in the Industry

The first and most obvious way in which industries differ is in the number of firms that make up that industry. Some, such as the fast food industry, are made up of a large number of separate companies while others, such as the jet airplane manufacturing industry, may have only a handful of competitors.

2. Differences in the Products Sold

The differences in the goods that they sell also distinguish many industries from one another. Many industries are composed of firms that sell **differentiated products,** products that are visibly different from one firm to another. Other industries produce **undifferentiated products,** products that are exactly alike from firm to firm. For example, dairy farmers produce an undifferentiated product—milk. The milk coming from one farm is virtually indistinguishable from that coming from a neighboring farm. Producers of undifferentiated products often go to great lengths to set their product apart from that of their competitors.

3. Availability of Market Information

A third characteristic that distinguishes one industry from another is the extent to which vital information is known by both competing business firms and their customers.

In some industries all firms are fully aware of the prices they and their competitors are

paying for factor inputs (natural resources, labor, and financial capital). In some industries, however, some firms may even find it difficult to determine the price competing firms are charging.

Firms in the automotive industry sell differentiated products. These two brands of luxury cars may both provide transportation, but they are not just alike.

4. Control of Price

Some industries are composed of companies that have the ability to control the price of the products they sell while firms in other industries do not. For example, some industries may have so little competition that customers must either accept the seller's price or go without the product. Other industries may have so many competitors that when one firm raises its price, all of its customers flee to the other firms with lower prices.

5. Ease in Entering and Exiting the Industry

The final difference among industries is the degree of difficulty that firms experience in entering and leaving the market. Imagine how easy it would be to start a term-paper typing service–simply purchase a typewriter and a few supplies and let students know that you are in business. Conversely, think how difficult it would be to start a nuclear power plant. In addition to meeting thousands of regulations, you would need to locate and purchase a great deal of land, skilled labor, and technical machinery. These requirements, among others, would make it virtually impossible for you to enter the market.

Economists use the term **barrier to entry** to refer to any unusual obstacle that would prevent a new firm from entering the industry and competing on an equal basis with established firms. Normal difficulties, however, such as financing, attracting customers, hiring managers, and producing a product are not included in this definition.

Barriers to entry may be either natural or artificial. **Natural barriers to entry** occur when firms in the industry already own all of a vital natural resource necessary for new firms to enter the business. **Artificial barriers to entry** are caused by government regulations. In some cases the government makes it impossible for new businesses to take root in some selected industries.

Basing their analysis upon these five characteristics, economists have identified four major types of competition and have placed them on a continuum. As one moves further to the left on the line, the number of firms in the industry declines, differences in products increase, availability of market information decreases, firms are more able to control the market price, and it becomes more difficult to enter and exit the industry.

Section Review

1. From an economist's point of view, what is a market?
2. What is an industry?
3. What is the difference between a natural barrier to entry and an artificial barrier to entry?

Figure 8-1

Fewer number of firms in the industry	← →	Greater number of firms in the industry
More differences in products	← →	Fewer differences in products
Less market information available	← →	More market information available
Greater ability to control price	← →	Less ability to control price
Harder to enter and leave the industry	← →	Easier to enter and leave the industry

II. Types of Competition

Perfect Competition

Perfect competition exists when there is a very large number of sellers who are selling an identical product, when each seller and buyer is perfectly aware of all the information available in the market, when no seller can affect the price, and when sellers find it relatively easy to enter and exit the market. One of the best examples of perfect competition is the farming of crops, such as soybeans, corn, or wheat.

Number of Firms in the Industry–With perfect competition there exists a very large number of sellers, each of which has a very small share of the total market. For example, the number of soybean farmers in the United States is so large that even if one farmer owned a 100,000-acre farm and produced over 3 million bushels of soybeans annually, he would produce less than one-fifth of 1% of the total U.S. soybean production.

Differences in the Products Sold–Another characteristic of perfect competition is that each firm in the industry sells an undifferentiated product. For example, the soybeans produced on one farm are indistinguishable from the soybeans grown on any other farm. Since there are no differences between the products, customers are indifferent to whose product they buy. Therefore, they base their buying decisions solely on the lowest price.

Availability of Market Information–In a perfectly competitive market all buyers and sellers are completely aware of all vital information. Through newspapers, periodicals, and farmers' groups, the soybean farmer can determine the prices his competitors are paying for factor inputs. He also is aware of the prices offered for his product in various parts of the country so that he may move his

Figure 8-2 Perfect Competition

Perfect
Competition

product to an area where he may receive more money for his goods.

Control of Price–Because there are so many sellers producing identical products, no individual firm can control the price. Imagine what would happen if Old MacDonald, a soybean farmer, decided to raise his price from $5.00 to $6.00 per bushel. All of Mr. MacDonald's customers would immediately abandon his product and purchase soybeans from other producers. Likewise when many firms are producing for price-conscious buyers, each company tries to sell its product for a price lower than the other companies. Eventually, the price is driven down to an unprofitable level. Thus, profit-minded business people generally shy away from involving themselves in perfectly competitive industries.

Ease in Entering and Exiting the Industry–Under perfect competition, firms may enter and exit the market with ease. All that one would need to enter the soybean farming industry is a little ground, some inexpensive seed, fertilizer, pesticide, sunshine, and rain. Exiting the industry would be just as easy: one simply grows a different crop or sells the farm.

Andrew Carnegie (1835-1919)

Businessman and Philanthropist

In 1848 Andrew Carnegie immigrated to America from Scotland with his family. After locating in the Pittsburgh area, the thirteen-year-old set out to help provide for his poor family. Working first in a cotton factory and then in a bobbin factory, the lad eagerly accepted a new job in 1850 as a messenger boy for the telegraph office. Although it paid only $2.50 per week, the position became an important steppingstone for an amazing career. While quickly learning about Pittsburgh and its prominent people, Carnegie proved that he was a dependable, hard worker worthy of greater responsibilities. He learned telegraphy on his own initiative and became a telegraph operator at age seventeen. His skill was noticed by Thomas Scott, a superintendent for the Pennsylvania Railroad, who hired the young man as his personal clerk and telegraph operator. As Scott's able assistant, Carnegie climbed through the ranks of the railroad company. In 1859 Carnegie became superintendent of the Pittsburgh division and earned a yearly salary of $1,500–an impressive sum in those days, especially for a man not yet twenty-five.

Carnegie's earnings from his work with the railroad allowed him to begin investing in promising industries. He made it a practice to avoid stock speculation (which he regarded as gambling), but rather to invest his money in businesses he knew and believed in. Although he acquired considerable stock in several companies, it was his investments in iron and steel that multiplied his wealth. First he formed the Keystone Bridge Company, a successful partnership that replaced hazardous wooden bridges with iron ones and spanned great rivers like the Mississippi and the Ohio. The need for high quality iron for these bridges led Carnegie to build iron mills and expand his interests to all phases of iron production. His business acumen, his determination to manufacture quality products, and his practice of bringing talented men into these businesses as partners mul-

tiplied his wealth. In 1865 Carnegie resigned from the railroad to oversee these other interests. Three years later he was making $50,000 per year and was considering retiring at the age of thirty-three. However, he continued in his business activities and soon jumped into the emerging steel industry, realizing that steel would be a major construction material in the future. He and his partners built their own steel mills in Pittsburgh, and later they bought the Homestead Mills. These operations and their subsidiaries were consolidated into the Carnegie Steel Company in 1899 and were sold two years later to J. P. Morgan. Carnegie received more than $250 million for his interests in this industry alone.

In later years Carnegie became determined to dispose of his wealth by philanthropic endeavors. He wrote, "The man who dies . . . rich dies disgraced. Surplus wealth is a sacred trust which its possessor is bound to administer in his lifetime for the good of the community." Accordingly, he donated vast sums (eventually amounting to about $350 million) in America and abroad to build libraries, further education, aid the needy, and support other charitable concerns. Despite his generosities and his admirable diligence and integrity, Carnegie was an unbeliever who scorned divine authority and judgment and discounted some of Scripture as "positively pernicious and even poisonous refuse." (*Autobiography of Andrew Carnegie,* Houghton Mifflin, 1920, p. 306)

Imperfect Competition

Imperfect competition is probably the most prevalent form of competition in America today. Imperfect competition exists when there are many sellers of slightly differentiated goods, when sellers and buyers are reasonably aware of conditions that may affect the market, when each seller has some control over his good's price, and when sellers find it relatively easy to enter and exit the market.

Number of Firms in the Industry and Differences in the Products Sold–Under imperfect competition a large number of firms exist, and their products are differentiated in some way. Product differentiation may take many forms. First, the product itself may be differentiated, as with perfumes, which differ in scent from brand to brand. Second, products may be superficially differentiated by distinctive packaging or persuasive advertising.

Figure 8-3 Imperfect Competition

▲
Imperfect
Competition

Distinctive packaging helps some manufacturers to differentiate their products from those of their competitors.

What's in a Name?

Inventors may apply for patents to protect their designs from being copied, and authors can gain copyrights to preserve their works from unauthorized duplication. Manufacturers also have an interest in protecting the name of their product, and they gain a measure of protection by registering their product's name as a trademark. Trademarks, names and symbols for a particular brand of product, have legal protection. Some familiar trademarks are Mountain Dew (soft drink), Oreo (cookies), and Ford (automobiles). No one but the owners of these trademarks is allowed to put these names on products. The trademark may cover even pictorial designs such as McDonald's golden arches. The owner of a trademark can legally prosecute anyone who uses that name or symbol without authorization.

Businesses have a vital interest in keeping their product names and symbols from being used by impostors. The owner of a trademark has undoubtedly spent an enormous sum of money on advertisements in order to build the reputation of a product. If a company markets a product using the same name, it will be taking unfair advantage of the advertising done by the original company without bearing any of the expense. Also, products of poor quality that are counterfeited as a name brand can severely damage the

reputation of the brand. Clothing is particularly susceptible to product name infringements. Violators may easily sew on a designer label or an identifying ornament to exploit a trademarked name such as Levi Strauss or Izod. However, manufacturers other than those in the fasion industry must also beware, because everything from counterfeit auto parts to bogus food products has appeared on the market with phony logos.

Businesses must not only beware of willful name infringements but also protect their name from becoming a ''generic'' term. If a trademark becomes too commonly used as a term for a class of products, it can lose its protection under the law. Linoleum, aspirin, and shredded wheat are just a few of the familiar names that once held trademark protection but lost it. Companies today must be ready to legally prosecute every infraction in order to preserve trademarks for such names as Coca-Cola, Kleenex, Xerox, and Scotch tape, because they are often used in a general manner.

Availability of Market Information–Unlike firms under perfect competition, those operating under imperfect competition are not "all-knowing," but they do possess reasonably complete information about the factors that will affect their business. For example, soft drink companies have a relatively good idea of what their competitors are paying for natural resources, labor, and financial capital; how the overall economy will affect their own sales; and what customers desire to buy. In order to gain more information, some firms conduct extensive market research studies by surveying customers and analyzing competing products.

Control of Price–Imperfectly competitive firms have the ability to affect the price of their products slightly. The degree of a firm's ability to control price is directly related to the degree of product differentiation it is able to achieve. Some firms are highly successful in setting their products apart from their competitors' products and gaining customers' "brand loyalty." Such loyalty allows the business to raise its prices and gain a greater profit. This phenomenon may be seen in the market for clothing with designer labels. While not significantly different from competing brands, these products have the ability to command a higher price than nondesigner clothing.

Ease in Entering and Exiting the Industry–"Relative ease" is the phrase economists use to describe the level of difficulty that firms under imperfect competition experience when trying to enter or leave their industry. The costs of entering and exiting the industry may be higher than under perfect competition, but there are certainly no insurmountable barriers.

Oligopoly

As we move further to the left on our continuum of market organization, we encounter the **oligopoly.** The word *oligopoly* literally means "selling by a few." The following circumstances exist in an oligopoly: only a few firms are selling either highly differentiated or undifferentiated products, sellers and buyers are not fully aware of all the information that may affect the market, each seller has a great deal of control over the price, and sellers find it relatively difficult to enter and exit the industry.

Number of Firms in the Industry–When can an industry be considered an oligopoly? When two firms dominate the market? six? nine? The term *oligopoly,* in fact, may be used quite broadly. The U.S. automobile industry is dominated by three firms while approximately eight dominate the petroleum refining industry; yet both are considered oligopolies. To narrow the distinction, economists call those industries in which the top four firms account for 75% of the market sales **tight oligopolies.** A **loose oligopoly** is one in which the top four firms account for between 50% and 75% of the industry's total sales. An oligopoly composed of exactly two business firms is known as a **duopoly** (doo OP uh lee).

Differences in the Products Sold–Some oligopolies manufacture products that are undifferentiated, while others produce differentiated goods. The pe-

Because life is not a spectator sport."

Figure 8-4 Oligopoly

Oligopoly

The manufacturers of jet airliners are part of an oligopoly.

troleum industry produces an undifferentiated product. One firm's fuel oil is no different from another's. Other oligopolies, such as makers of automobiles, produce highly differentiated products.

Availability of Market Information–Because there are so many customers and only a handful of competitors, the firms that make up the oligopoly are much more secretive with their own information and spend much more time trying to gather information about their rivals than firms under perfect and imperfect competition. Each is constantly trying to determine its competitors' costs, production methods, prices, and other bits of information that will help it to gain a larger share of the market.

Control of Price–As in imperfect competition, the degree of an oligopolistic firm's control over the price of its product depends on the extent to which it can differentiate its product. Automobile makers who manufacture a distinctive car can command a higher price than they can on less differentiated models. Oligopolies that produce an undifferentiated product do not have the option of improving their product to gain more customers. For example, a small number of big producers dominate the market for oranges. If the market were left free to operate, "cutthroat competition" might result, creating tremendous bargains for customers but low profits for the producers. To avoid this problem, orange producers meet to set limits on the number of oranges each may sell, deliberately lowering the supply to keep the price high. When producers such

Corporate Spying

Keeping up with the competition is a major concern of modern oligopolies. Gaining or losing a small percentage of the market to a rival can mean millions of dollars in profits or losses. Therefore, corporations have stooped to some unorthodox means of observing the activities of their competitors in order to find ways to get a step ahead of them. While these practices are generally legal, you will notice that many in the examples below are less than ethical.

Modern businesses have been known to use the following tactics to spy on their competition:

- Taking a tour of the competitor's factory
- Using aerial photographs of factories and warehouses to analyze activities
- Sifting through the competitor's garbage
- Keeping track of the competitor's help-wanted ads
- Paying workers inside the competitor's business for information
- Analyzing the competitor's products
- Hiring employees away from the competitor to gain their information and skills
- Questioning customers and former employees of the competitor
- Studying labor contracts negotiated by the competitor
- Watching and counting goods being shipped to and from the competitor's buildings
- Obtaining information from consultants or suppliers who have worked for or done business with the competitor
- Conducting deceptive job interviews for the competitor's employees in order to gain information

as orange growers get together to affect the price of their goods, a **cartel** is said to be created.

Ease in Entering and Exiting the Industry–Barriers to entry in an oligopolistic industry usually make it very difficult to get into business. Many oligopolies have few competitors simply because of the high cost of entering the market. Imagine the expense of starting an automobile manufacturing

GNP: $246.0 billion*
Per Capita GNP: $307*
Population: 833,422,000 (1989)
Monetary Unit: rupee

India

This nation with the second largest population in the world has an economy that displays poverty and despair alongside progress and promise. After receiving independence from Britain in 1947, India charted a socialistic course for its economy by implementing government ownership and control of most of its industries. It has even used "Five-Year Plans" similar to those of the Soviet Union in its attempts to modernize and expand its controlled economy. The returns on these public ventures, however, have been low. Meanwhile, well over half of the population remains involved in small-scale farming on plots that average less than six acres each. Efforts to increase agricultural production under these conditions have made only limited progress. As a result, much of India's multiplying population remains in privation.

Despite the impediments of its industrial and agricultural base, India does have some economic bright spots. The subcontinent holds a considerable store of mineral resources, coal, and some offshore petroleum. It also boasts an abundant work force of nearly one billion to satisfy the needs of growing industries. To take advantage of these resources, India has encouraged more private business and foreign investment. Chemical and computer software companies are two of the emerging private ventures that are helping to expand the Indian economy. Growing numbers of Indians are gaining the technical skills necessary to participate in this development. The noticeable successes of these new business activities encourage India to continue cultivating more private industrial development, but that effort is made difficult by the encumbrances of the existing bureaucracy and state-controlled industries. Furthermore, economic growth has been hindered by cultural divisions, conflicts with neighboring countries, and a population that continues to grow faster than its economy. India's struggle for greater economic prosperity will continue to be arduous, and progress will depend on its ability to expand its economic opportunities at a faster pace than its population.

*figures for 1987 from the 1990 *Statistical Abstract*

company! Other oligopolistic industries have few competitors because the law has limited the number of firms. For example, the Federal Communication Commission (FCC) has limited the number of licenses it grants to firms to start new radio or television stations. Likewise, it is difficult for an oligopolistic firm to exit the industry. Oligopolistic firms such as automobile producers tend to use specialized and expensive production equipment for which there is a small market. To exit the industry would lead to tremendous losses.

Monopoly

Do you remember playing Monopoly? If you do, you will recall that success was defined as owning all four railroads, all utility companies, and all the best property, especially Boardwalk and Park Place. After placing a hotel on each piece of property, you could mercilessly drive your opponents into bankruptcy.

Number of Firms in the Industry–A **monopoly** is a form of market organization in which there is only one supplier in the industry. The word *monopoly* means ''one seller.'' The monopolist has total knowledge of all necessary information and is a price maker. It is impossible for new firms to enter the industry, and it is very difficult for the monopoly to exit. Several monopolies probably exist in your community. Your city's water, electricity, sewer, natural gas, cable television, and garbage disposal services are most probably monopolies.

Both chance and skill are involved in gaining a monopoly in the board game, but how does one gain 100% of a market in the real world? The first way a firm may gain a monopoly is by owning or controlling 100% of some resource vital to the in-

Figure 8-5 Monopoly

Monopoly

Public utility companies, such as those providing electricity, are given a legal monopoly to provide service in a particular area.

dustry, a circumstance in which the firm is said to enjoy a **natural monopoly.** When this occurs, there is a natural barrier to entry for any firm that would try to compete. Natural monopolies are becoming hard to find since very few firms have total control of a single natural resource.

A second way is the **legal monopoly,** which exists because the government has allowed the firm an exclusive right to provide the good or service. The natural gas, water, sewer, and electricity companies in your town were granted monopolies because the government decided that it would be too inconvenient or expensive to have more than one firm provide the service. For example, consider the inconvenience of having two or more companies running gas, water, or sewer lines under the ground. It is also argued that if two electric companies were allowed to compete in the same area, the customers being served would have to pay higher individual bills to pay for construction of two power plants.

Differences in the Products Sold–Since there is only one firm in the industry, only one product is available with no substitutes. Barring the threat of losing the monopoly, the firm has no incentive to innovate and improve its products or services. For example, prior to the entrance of parcel-carrying competition from United Parcel Service (UPS) and

The Breakup of "Ma Bell"

American Telephone and Telegraph (AT&T) was the largest privately owned company in the world. It was incorporated in 1885, less than ten years after Alexander Graham Bell had successfully spoken over wire for the first time. It was the parent company of the Bell System, a company that was to gain a monopoly under the protection of government regulation. With this monopoly AT&T was able to operate all long-distance telephone lines as well as most of the local telephone systems in the nation. Another one of AT&T's subsidiaries was Western Electric, a company that manufactured telephones and telephone equipment. Western Electric was not given governmental approval for a monopoly. Nonetheless, AT&T required all twenty-three of its local or regional Bell System companies to use Western Electric equipment. The high prices Western Electric charged for this equipment were simply passed to telephone customers for AT&T's profit. Customers had no alternative because they could not change to another telephone company.

The U.S. government had long noticed the problems caused by AT&T's monopoly, but effective action against the firm did not begin until the Justice Department filed an antitrust suit against AT&T in 1974 under the provisions of the Sherman Antitrust Act. In the suit, the government requested that Western Electric, Bell Labs (a research division), and all of the local and regional telephone systems separate from AT&T, the parent company. The litigation dragged on for several years while AT&T tried to deal not only with this attack but also with the new competition in long-distance service and its inability to expand into computer and data processing activities required for modern telephone services. (AT&T had agreed under the terms of an antitrust case decided in 1956 to limit its operations to the telephone business in order to keep Western Electric.)

When the case was settled and the sentence was handed down in 1982, AT&T both lost and won. It lost in its efforts to retain its local and regional telephone companies. This decision was carried out on January 1, 1984, when these subsidiaries reorganized as seven independent regional firms. However, AT&T was allowed to keep Western Electric and Bell Labs, and it was allowed to enter the new technologies of the computer information industry. Although new regional telephone companies continue to enjoy a monopoly over local telephone services, AT&T has strong competition for long-distance services, and Western Electric's telephone equipment is rivaled by that of many other manufacturers. The results of the AT&T breakup are not fully known. Competition has increased in some areas of the telephone industry, but the cost of basic service has generally risen instead of fallen. Nonetheless, AT&T emerged as a winner. Its stock is still highly prized, and its growing success in the information industry commands respect.

Federal Express, the United States Postal Service had no incentive to innovate. Indeed, complaints persist about the U.S. Postal Service's lack of service in those areas in which it still enjoys monopoly power.

*Availability of Market Information and Control of Price–*Since there is no direct competition, the monopoly has all the information possible about the industry. In addition, a monopoly is a *price setter;* that is, whatever price a monopoly sets for its product is the price that customers must pay if they want the product. Out of a fear that firms will "gouge" consumers, the government regulates the prices that many monopolistic companies charge. The fact that one firm controls the price does not necessarily mean that buyers are at the mercy of the monopoly, for when dissatisfaction sets in, an incentive is created for alternative products to be developed. If the price of electricity were to become prohibitively expensive, customers would switch to using natural gas or coal for their home heating and cooking needs. If no close substitute for a product is available, entrepreneurs in search of profits will scramble to invent a substitute. This is why consumers in a free economy need not fear so much the power of a monopolistic firm.

*Ease in Entering and Exiting the Industry–*By definition it is impossible for another firm to enter a monopolized industry. The moment another firm enters the market, it becomes an oligopoly. Also, it is very difficult for a monopolistic firm to leave the industry. Consider your electric company. Since it is the only provider of electricity, the government has made it virtually impossible for the firm to shut down. In certain cases in which strikes have threatened a shutdown of a service held by a monopoly firm, the military has been called upon to take over the operation temporarily.

Section Review

1. Describe perfect competition.
2. What is the most prevalent form of competition in America today?
3. What is a cartel?
4. Define monopoly.

III. Antitrust Policy

Let us return to the game of Monopoly. You have probably been involved in a game in which one of the players managed to get a monopoly on Boardwalk and Park Place. He then placed a hotel on each and, like a spider on its web, sat eagerly awaiting some unlucky player to fall into his trap. Eventually, one or more of the players did land on one of the dreaded properties, was forced into poverty, and had to quit the game.

Although most people enjoy playing the game, they draw the line at actually living it, especially when they are on the paying end of the transaction. Fear of a monopoly's power to charge high prices has prompted many laws prohibiting even the hint of the beginnings of an unlicensed monopoly. In the 1800s and early 1900s, Americans saw an era of tremendous growth. During this period the steel, oil, automobile production, and banking industries became oligopolies. Realizing the direction many of the oligopolistic firms were taking, and fearful of the results of monopoly power, Congress took action.

The Sherman Antitrust Act of 1890

Prior to 1890 one of big business's favorite ways of limiting competition without actually forming a monopoly was to form a trust. A **trust** was created when the head of the largest company in the industry would persuade the other firms to put their stock into a *trust account.* The manager of the trust would then look after the affairs of the larger group and would distribute the profits. To ensure that cutthroat competition would not occur and that profits would remain high, the trust manager would control the prices, promotion, and quantity of product offered by each firm.

As a response to the tremendous control of the market by the trusts, Congress enacted the Sherman Antitrust Act in 1890. The act stated that *"Every contract, combination in the form of a trust or otherwise, or conspiracy in restraint of trade"* was illegal. It was also declared illegal to *"monopolize, or attempt to monopolize, or combine or conspire to monopolize"* business. Penalties for violation of the Sherman Act are fines and imprisonment.

This 1905 anti-monopoly cartoon ridiculed trust-builder John D. Rockefeller, Jr., for a comment about sacrificing the early buds to produce a splendid American Beauty rose.

The Clayton Act of 1914

The Sherman Act led to the 1911 breakup of the Standard Oil Company and the American Tobacco Company. The American people noted, however, that because of the vagueness of the Sherman Act, many businesses were still conducting themselves in ways that hindered competition without technically monopolizing the industry or combining firms.

The Clayton Act of 1914 enumerated and clarified certain anticompetitive practices. Specifically, the Clayton Act prohibited the following practices:

1. **Interlocking directorates** Firms were skirting the Sherman Act by placing one or more directors on the boards of competing firms.
2. **Tying contracts** Some big companies, in order to secure more business for themselves, would require that smaller companies desiring to buy from them must purchase their full line of products. For example, suppose that you are the owner of a small retail store, and you wish to sell a certain manufacturer's line of shoes. However, that company forces you by contract to carry their less desirable line of costume jewelry in order to carry their shoes. In fact, many large businesses would even refuse to sell any of their products to smaller firms if those firms carried any products of a competitor.
3. **Anticompetitive takeovers** Corporations were forbidden from taking over other firms by purchasing their common stock if the effect was to limit competition significantly.
4. **Price discrimination** The Clayton Act made it unlawful for firms to sell the same good to different buyers at different prices.

Other Legislation

To promote competition further, Congress passed three additional landmark acts. The first of these was the Federal Trade Commission Act of 1914. This law provided for the establishment of the Federal Trade Commission (FTC), the agency that enforces the Clayton Act. The FTC investigates alleged violations, holds hearings, and issues "cease and desist" orders if the suspected firm is found guilty of "unfair methods of competition" or "unfair acts or practices." The Federal Trade Commission Act was later amended to protect consumers as well as competitors.

The second act was passed in 1936 and was called the Robinson-Patman Act. Small retailers were complaining that large chain stores were receiving price discounts as a result of quantity buying. The large stores were then able to sell their products at a lower price than the small retailers. The Robinson-Patman Act made it illegal for suppliers to hinder competition by selling "at unreasonably low prices."

Finally, in 1950 Congress closed another loophole by passing the Celler-Kefauver Antimerger Act. The Clayton Act of 1914 prohibited firms from buying enough of a competitor's shares of stock to control the market and lessen competion, but it made no provision to prevent one firm's purchasing the assets of another firm. Many firms skirted the spirit of the Clayton Act by purchasing a competing firm's buildings, equipment, and inventory, enabling them to control the market all the same. The Celler-Kefauver Act made this kind of quasi merger illegal.

Section Review

1. What two major laws were enacted in an attempt to break up monopolistic business activities?
2. What is a trust?

Chapter Review

Terms

market
industry
differentiated products
undifferentiated products
barrier to entry
natural barrier to entry
artificial barrier to entry
perfect competition
imperfect competition
oligopoly
tight oligopoly
loose oligopoly
duopoly
cartel
monopoly
natural monopoly
legal monopoly
trust
interlocking directorate
tying contracts
anticompetitive takeovers
price discrimination

Content Questions

1. List the five different characteristics of market organization.
2. Describe differentiated and undifferentiated products.
3. Why can a firm in a purely competitive market not slightly raise its price so that it might make a little more profit?
4. Why is it unlikely that a new firm would enter an oligopoly market?
5. What is a tying contract?
6. List the five congressional acts that were passed between 1890 and 1950 in order to preserve competition.

Application Questions

1. List the problems one might encounter when attempting to start a bank.
2. Randomly select ten business firms in your town. Describe the form of competition under which they operate.
3. Why is the oligopoly more closely associated with fierce competition than is perfect competition?

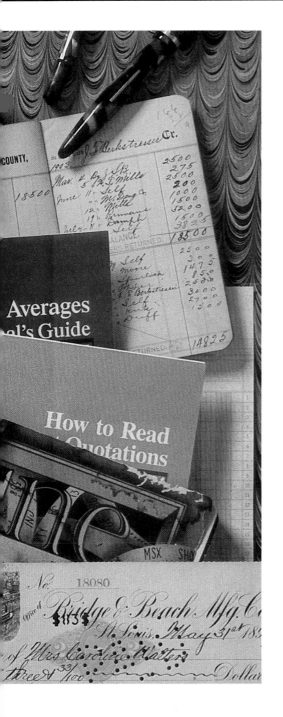

Unit IV: Economics of the Financial Market

◇ 9 Money and Banking

◇ 10 Central Banking

CHAPTER 9 _____

Money and Banking

I. Money
    A. Functions of Money
    B. Desirable Characteristics of Money
    C. Money Standards
    D. Measuring the Money Supply
    E. Creation of Money
II. Commercial Banking
    A. Dual Banking System and Regulation
    B. Functions of Commercial Banks

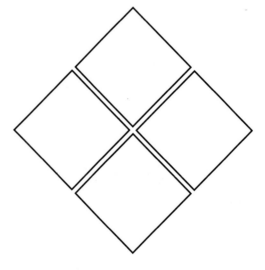

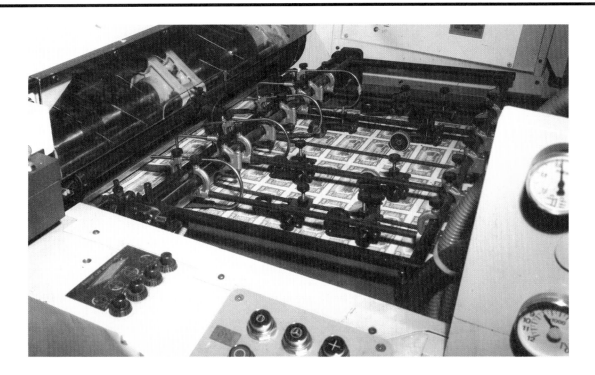

Sell that ye have, and give alms; provide yourselves bags which wax not old, a treasure in the heavens that faileth not, where no thief approacheth, neither moth corrupteth. For where your treasure is, there will your heart be also. Luke 12:33-34

I. Money

No other single object seems to have aided the economic development of mankind more than money, yet money has probably been at the heart of more problems than anything else. The desire for money has been the cause of countless wars, murders, kidnappings, broken friendships, failed businesses, treasons, thefts, and wrecked marriages. Those who believe they have too little of it may be motivated to steal, while many of those who possess much of it are inflamed to possess more. Satan deceives people into believing that their insatiable needs may be satisfied by the possession of just a little more money. Scripture warns us to avoid Satan's devices, pointing out the dismal end of the greedy:

> But they that will be rich fall into temptation and a snare, and into many foolish and hurtful lusts, which drown men in destruction and perdition. For the love of money is the root of all evil: which while some coveted after, they have erred from the faith, and pierced themselves through with many sorrows.
>
> (I Timothy 6:9-10)

Yes, money has been at the heart of many problems, but it has also been central to many benefits. The proper use of money allows man to provide for the needs of his family, to purchase clothing for the destitute, to obtain food for the hungry, to care for the sick, and to spread the gospel to the nations of the world. Christians rightly related to God perceive money as a tool to be used in His service, but to many other Christians and to most of the world, the mere possession of money is an obsession.

So far in this text we have taken money for granted. Money was introduced in the circular flow model as the key ingredient that allows an economy to function, but what exactly is this thing called money? Some may say that money is paper bills and coins; others may include checking accounts and traveler's checks. While all these things may serve as money, it has a much broader definition. **Money** is anything that is commonly used and generally accepted in payment for goods and services. Thus anything can serve as money. In the past many things have been used as money, including fur, dried fish, seashells, tobacco, human hair, shark's teeth, and a host of other items.

But to serve as money, an object must be commonly used and generally accepted. To ensure that our money is accepted by everyone in the economy, Congress has declared it **legal tender,** which means that all creditors must accept it if it is tendered (offered) by a debtor.

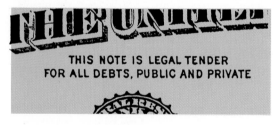

THIS NOTE IS LEGAL TENDER
FOR ALL DEBTS, PUBLIC AND PRIVATE

Functions of Money

In the minds of most people, money has but one function. Money, they believe, is something with which one buys things. Although money's primary function is to act as a means of payment for goods and services, it also acts as a measure of value and a means of storing purchasing power.

Means of Payment–By acting as a means of payment, money reduces the cost of doing business. Suppose you wanted to purchase a used car. How would you go about locating one at an acceptable price? You could stand on the street corner and ask passers-by whether they had cars to sell; you could go door to door asking the same question; or you could rent an airplane and write your message in the sky. "Ridiculous!" you might be saying to

yourself. "That would take too much time and effort and would be too costly." You are absolutely correct. Economists have found that rational people do everything possible to reduce the cost of doing business. In order to lower the cost of buying a car, a rational person uses his local newspaper's want ads, or he visits a used car lot. Likewise, a society uses money as a means of payment to reduce the cost and effort of doing business.

Consider the alternative to using money. Before using a standardized money system, primitive societies used **barter,** the exchange of one person's goods or services for another's. Barter is a very expensive and time-consuming process. For example, let us assume that you live in a barter economy and you need to have your car repaired, so you take a day off from your job as a carpenter. After spending several hours searching, you locate a mechanic. There is one problem: he does not need any carpentry work done, but he wants some steaks. So off you go in search of someone who will trade his steaks for your carpentry work so that you may in turn trade the steaks for what you desire. After a few such exchanges you would come to conclude that barter is frustrating and time-consuming. Barter is not only a frustrating way to do business, but because of the lack of a **double coincidence of wants** (both parties involved in the trade wanting what the other has to offer) it is also a very ineffi-

Some societies continue to carry on barter transactions, especially if the people have little money for purchases.

Money on Yap

Money, the medium of exchange in a society, has taken many forms throughout the centuries. Blocks of salt, beaver pelts, and cattle are just a few of the items that have served as money in the past. Among the most curious forms of money, however, is one that still exists on the Micronesian island of Yap. The traditional Yapese currency consists of large stone wheels. The island has over six thousand of these wheels, and they range from two feet to twelve feet in diameter, although most are five feet across or smaller. The limestone wheels have a hole in the center so that they may be carried by a log slipped through the opening. The larger stones may require as many as twenty men to transport them.

The stone money has been used on the island for over one thousand years. Tradition says that the first (and most valuable) stones were brought in outrigger canoes from a distant island by a warrior named Anagumang. Additional stones were brought by sailors and traders in the late nineteenth and early twentieth centuries, but their value is less,

regardless of their size, because they were transported to the island more easily. Obviously, because the large stones are difficult to carry around as pocket change, other money has also been in use. Necklaces of stone beads as well as large seashells have served in minor transactions. Today the islanders also use United States currency for many of their purchases. (The island was a part of the U.S. Trust Territories in the Pacific until it became a part of the newly independent Federated States of Micronesia.) However, the stone money is still commonly used in large transactions such as buying land, purchasing canoes, and winning permission to marry. The money also works well to settle arguments between islanders when given as a token of apology or reconciliation. When the stone money is not being used, the Yapese typically prop it up against their houses or park the stones in a village ''bank.'' One nice feature of this stone money is that its owners can have no fear of its being stolen. The big rocks are not easily carried away by thieves, and any that would be pilfered could be easily spotted and identified.

cient practice for the economy. The two or three days spent lining up multiple exchanges could have been used in producing carpentry work. Thus, barter severely hinders the development of a nation's economy. The use of money as a common means of payment, however, eliminates the multitude of time-consuming trades necessary under barter and is, therefore, less costly to the economy.

Measure of Value–What would you think if you were driving down the highway and suddenly all road signs displayed distances in kilometers? Chances are you would mentally attempt to convert distances into miles. Economics is no different. Every society must have some common and consistent measure for economic value. Therefore, a nation's money has come to be the yardstick by which its people express the value of goods and services. When you are told that a car sells for $10,000, you have a clearer idea of its value than if its worth were expressed in terms of a certain number of books, houses, cows, cookies, or seashells.

Values expressed in terms of money are easy to record and understand.

Means of Storing Purchasing Power–Another problem with barter is the difficulty of storing particular bartered goods. Milk sours, paper yellows, and furniture goes out of style, but money always keeps its face value. One could store his purchasing power by buying commodities and constantly re-selling them before they spoiled, or he could hold his purchasing power indefinitely in the form of money. Though money does retain its face value over a period of time, it is subject to a type of economic "spoilage." If the nation experiences a general rise in prices (inflation), the purchasing value of a person's savings may be reduced.

Desirable Characteristics of Money

Whether a nation's money system is determined by the government or by the society in general, certain characteristics of the object used as money are considered desirable.

Convenience and Portability–That a barter system is inconvenient and that a money standard would be far better goes without saying, but not all money standards are equally convenient and portable. The ancient Spartans used bulky slabs of iron, and many early American colonists used bales of tobacco. Today, however, some societies choose a standard such as gold, silver, or paper, which is easily carried and far more convenient.

Divisibility–A monetary standard should be divisible. That is, it should be relatively easy to divide the money into smaller denominations. The Spanish *dolár,* the monetary unit from which the dollar was derived, could actually be physically divided into eight pieces, or "bits." Each "bit" was worth 12 1/2¢. It is from this that we have come to refer to our quarter dollar as "two bits." Though our present-day currency may not be physically divisible, the amount it represents is easily divisible into smaller denominations that are more convenient for smaller transactions or for giving change.

Durability–Currency material must also be durable. Currently in the United States, a paper dollar has an average life of 18 months. Coins, on the other hand, may last several decades. In its effort to cut costs, the U.S. government has on several occasions introduced dollar coins, but to date such coins have proved unpopular.

The Eisenhower dollar and the Susan B. Anthony dollar, though durable, have not been well received by the public.

Stability–A money system should not only be convenient, portable, divisible, and durable but also keep a constant value over time. A society will not use a money standard very long if, for example, the amount it takes to buy a car will buy only a pack of gum the next day. Such is the case with the money of many nations where sound economic policies are not followed.

Money Standards

There are only three kinds of money: commodity money, representative money, and fiat money. Realizing that barter is an inefficient way of transacting business, primitive societies usually graduate to using some type of **commodity money** standard. A commodity money system is one in which some single commonly used good is selected to be the economy's medium of exchange. Anything

A Penny for Your Thoughts

In today's society penny-pinching has seemingly become futile. Why bother to stoop down to pick up a penny off the sidewalk when even ten of them would not buy a candy bar? Redeeming a jar or box full of pennies collected from pockets and purses may seem hardly worth the time it takes to wrap the coins in neat rolls of fifty. And how frustrating it is to make a purchase that totals $10.01 (or a similar odd number) and then have to fumble for that one penny. The answer to the penny problems could be simple—abolish the penny.

Some economists are now seriously advocating the abolition of the penny. Maintaining the penny supply now costs the U.S. Treasury nearly $100 million annually, and the minutes and seconds "wasted" in transactions involving pennies deprive businesses and individuals of much valuable time. The anti-penny people generally advocate that all prices and taxes be adjusted to the nearest nickel. Any inflation caused by this action

would almost certainly be offset by some lower prices. For instance, a merchant selling an item for $19.99 would probably change the price to $19.95 instead of $20.00 because of its greater psychological appeal.

The only major roadblock to abolishing the penny is its sentimental value. Americans are naturally reluctant to give up a coin that they have collected, carried, flipped, and thrown in wishing wells ever since they can remember. It remains to be seen whether pennies will ever be relegated to coin shops and chests in the attic or whether they will continue to circulate despite their apparent obsolescence.

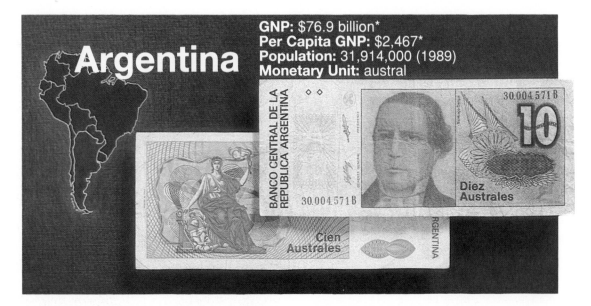

Argentina

GNP: $76.9 billion*
Per Capita GNP: $2,467*
Population: 31,914,000 (1989)
Monetary Unit: austral

BANCO CENTRAL DE LA REPÚBLICA ARGENTINA

30.004.571 B

30.004.571 B

Diez Australes

10

Cien Australes

ARGENTINA

The government of this Latin American republic has suffered many upheavals in the past, and its economic history has been turbulent in recent years as well. Such a situation seems ironic in a nation known as South America's breadbasket because of its vast wheatfields, not to mention the livestock in its extensive pasturelands. Yet a program in this century that increasingly nationalized industries and offered greater public benefits to the people has plunged Argentina into heavy debt and hyperinflation.

To finance its government-controlled industries and programs, Argentina acquired a foreign debt of over $50 billion, and as Argentinians lost faith in their currency, inflation soared. For much of the 1980s the country suffered from annual inflation rates of 1000% or higher. At times the government has been unable to print *australs* fast enough to provide the mushrooming quantity needed for exchange in Argentinian markets. This situation has discouraged both foreign and domestic capital investments in the country–investments that are urgently needed to help the troubled nation increase its productivity, stabilize its currency, and repay its debts.

*figures for 1987 from the 1990 *Statistical Abstract*

may serve as a monetary commodity, including seashells, salt, or gold, but the use of an abundant commodity has a tendency to lead to inflated prices. For example, suppose you lived on an island where seashells are used as money. Assume you go to a store to buy a coconut and the price tag says ten shells, but you have only five shells in your pocket. Do you go to work to earn more shells, or run down to the beach with a bucket? If a commodity used as money is not rare, prices will tend to skyrocket.

In our island example a coconut could rise in price to, perhaps, several thousand shells.

As societies progress, they turn to using rarer commodities that cannot be easily obtained or duplicated, such as gold or silver coins. Whenever a coin contains an amount of gold or silver equal to its face value, it is said to be a **full-bodied coin.** A coin that contains a quantity of metal less than its face value is referred to as a **token coin.** Thus a one-ounce $20 gold piece would be full bodied if the price of gold were $20 per ounce but would be a token coin if gold were worth less than $20 per ounce. All the coins commonly used in the United States today are token coins.

Representative money is money that represents some commodity held in store. In the fifteenth and sixteenth centuries Western Europeans began to deposit their gold coins with local goldsmiths out of a desire for convenience and a fear of being robbed. For a fee these early bankers would accept gold and issue receipts to their depositors. Whenever a depositor wanted to make a purchase, he would first have to go through the inconvenient and time-consuming process of redeeming his receipt for gold. Eventually, after merchants became familiar with certain goldsmiths, they began accepting the gold deposit receipts from their customers instead of actual gold.

The third kind of money, **fiat** (FEE yat) **money,** is money that is not backed by anything of value. Fiat money, which means money by government decree, came into use when governments took over the function of issuing money. Many governments confiscated their nation's gold but required businesses, through legal tender laws, to continue accepting the unbacked receipts. All money in the

Until 1934 U.S. paper currency was redeemable for gold held in the national treasury and therefore was representative money.

Figure 9-1 **M-1 Money Supply of the United States, 1989* (in billions of dollars)**

Currency and coin	$222.1
Checking accounts in commercial banks	281.2
Checkable deposits at other institutions	286.8
Traveler's checks	7.5
Total M-1	$797.6

*Source: President's Council of Economic Advisors, *Economic Report of the President* (Washington, D.C.: Government Printing Office, 1990), Table C-68

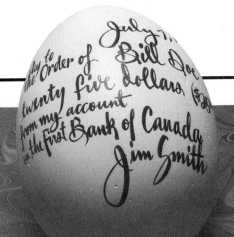

Check It Out

Just about everyone knows what a check is: an authorization to pay a designated amount of money out of an established account. But what does a check look like? The obvious answer is that it is a piece of paper, usually torn out of a booklet, and specially imprinted with the name and number of the bank and account holder involved and with blanks to fill in with other information and a final signature. Although most checks would meet this description, not all checks have been so conventional.

Unless specific laws or regulations specify otherwise, any legitimate written authorization to pay money out of an account is an acceptable check. Thus, checks have been written on newspapers, boards, handkerchiefs, and countless other unusual materials. A man in the lumber business was known for writing his checks on wooden shingles; a sailor once wrote a check with a blowtorch on a metal plate from a battleship; and a Canadian bank cashed a check written on the shell of a hard-boiled egg. The Chase Manhattan Bank Museum of Moneys of the World has a remarkable check on display. Made of solid steel and so heavy that it had to be carried by two men, this check for several thousand dollars was cashed in Cleveland in 1932. The bank promptly cancelled the check by riddling it with a submachine gun. A check can be written on anything as long as it is

1. in writing.
2. signed by the maker.
3. payable to the bearer or to the order of a specific person.
4. ordering the bank to pay a specified sum of money.
5. bearing a date no older than six months.

Figure 9-2 M-2 Money Supply of the United States, 1989* (in billions of dollars)

M-1 money supply	$ 797.6
Overnight deposits of dollars in Caribbean branches of U. S. banks	72.8
General purpose money market mutual funds	309.1
Money market deposit accounts in commercial banks	486.5
Regular passbook savings accounts	411.8
Time deposits less than $100,000	1,135.7
Total M-2	$3,213.5

*Source: President's Council of Economic Advisors, Economic Report of the President (Washington, D.C.: Government Printing Office, 1990), Tables C-68 and C-69

Figure 9-3 M-3 Money Supply of the United States, 1989* (in billions of dollars)

M-2 money supply	$3,213.5
Time deposits over $100,000	554.2
Long-term repurchase agreements	100.0
Long-term deposits of dollars in Caribbean branches of U.S. banks	83.9
Institutional money market mutual funds	102.8
Total M-3	$4,054.4

*Source: President's Council of Economic Advisors, Economic Report of the President
(Washington, D.C.: Government Printing Office, 1990), Tables C-68 and C-69

U.S. today is fiat money. Stockpiles of gold held by the government are used for some international transactions. If our dollars are not backed by gold, what, then, provides value to our money? Two things keep our current fiat money system going: the faith that others will accept the money we have accepted, and the limited quantity of money that exists.

Measuring the Money Supply

Exactly how much money exists in the United States? The answer to this question depends on how it is measured. Since money represents purchasing power, we cannot just count the paper dollars in our pockets. We must include every means of buying goods and services.

The first measure of the money supply, referred to by economists as **M-1,** attempts to measure the money Americans have available for *immediate* spending. M-1 includes paper money and coin held by the public, traveler's checks, and checkable accounts. In 1989 M-1 accounted for $797.6 billion.

A broader measure of the money supply called **M-2** represents immediately spendable M-1 money plus all money that is available to spend after a short delay. Amounting to $3,213.5 billion in 1989, M-2 comprises M-1 plus savings accounts, small time deposits, and other short-notice deposits.

Yet a third measure of the money supply is **M-3,** which is a much broader definition of money, adding up to $4,054.4 billion in 1989. M-3 includes

M-1, M-2, and longer delay deposits such as long-term time deposits at banks and other institutions.

The nation's money supply consists of more than coins and paper dollars.

The final and broadest measurement of the money supply is referred to by economists as **L.** This measure includes M-1, M-2, M-3, and other assets that may be used as investments, including commercial paper, short-term government bonds, savings bonds, and banker's acceptances. In 1989, L, which in theory represents the entire United States money supply, totaled approximately $4,838.7 billion.

Creation of Money

If a nation is using gold coins as money, the nation's money supply can grow only if its gold supply increases. If a nation is using paper money, however, it is possible to increase the money supply by merely increasing the quantity of paper bills in circulation.

This phenomenon was discovered shortly after the goldsmiths began letting customers deposit their gold in exchange for receipts. With the receipts being used as the medium of exchange, the goldsmiths found that their inventories of gold constantly increased. Realizing that the owners were not likely to redeem their receipts, the goldsmiths lent out much of their customers' gold, keeping only small emergency reserves on hand. Borrowers, not wanting to carry bulky gold coins, began requesting paper receipts instead. Thus new receipts were issued backed by the same gold that was already backing up other receipts. Through this process new money was created. Today, money is created the same way, but instead of having one piece of gold back up two or more receipts, nothing backs the U.S. dollar. The process of increasing and decreasing the United States money supply will be discussed in greater detail in Chapter 10.

Section Review

1. What three functions does money serve?
2. What means of exchange has been common in primitive societies?
3. What is a double coincidence of wants?
4. What are the three kinds of money that can circulate in an economy?
5. What is the broadest measurement of money? What does it include?

A Survey of Financial Services

Modern banking practices began as a simple but essential service amid the growing markets of the Renaissance. Italian moneychangers in sixteenth-century Florence sat in the marketplace at benches called *bancos.* This word passed with the banking trade through Western Europe and into England as "banks." Today a variety of financial institutions and services play a significant role in our nation's economy. The following list identifies the major groups of financial institutions operating in the United States today and some of their activities.

Commercial Banks: Commercial banks are often called "full-service" banks because they offer a wide range of services for both individual and business customers. These services include maintaining checking and savings accounts, granting personal and business loans, issuing credit cards, marketing government bonds, planning estates, and providing many other financial aids.

Thrifts: Three kinds of institutions were established to encourage personal saving and to provide loans to meet personal needs. Legislation in the late 1970s and early 1980s increased the allowable activities of thrifts, thereby blurring the distinction between them and commercial banks.

- **Savings and Loans (S&Ls):** Savings and loan associations have traditionally been the leading financiers of home mortgages. Their other activities were expanded to resemble those of commercial banks in the 1980s.
- **Mutual Savings Banks:** Mutual savings banks resemble savings and loans except for some technicalities of their organization. Like savings and loans, they were confined to the operation of savings accounts and mortgage loans until the 1980s. These banks are almost exclusively located in the northeastern United States.

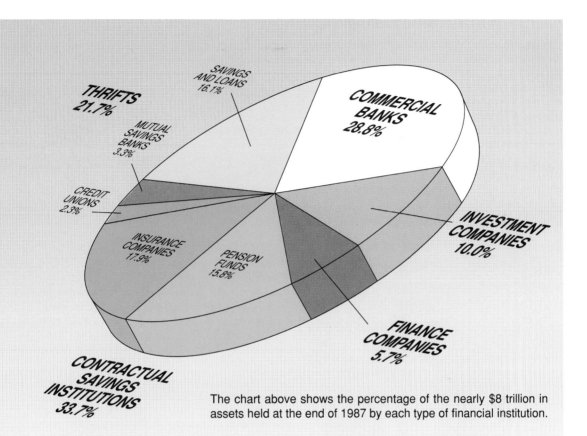

THRIFTS
21.7%

SAVINGS
AND LOANS
16.1%

MUTUAL
SAVINGS
BANKS
3.3%

CREDIT
UNIONS
2.3%

INSURANCE
COMPANIES
17.9%

PENSION
FUNDS
15.8%

COMMERCIAL
BANKS
28.8%

INVESTMENT
COMPANIES
10.0%

FINANCE
COMPANIES
5.7%

CONTRACTUAL
SAVINGS
INSTITUTIONS
33.7%

The chart above shows the percentage of the nearly $8 trillion in assets held at the end of 1987 by each type of financial institution.

- **Credit Unions:** Groups of people such as company employees, teachers, or union members formed these cooperative institutions to pool the savings of members and make consumer loans available to members. They can now make mortgage loans and offer checking accounts as well.

Contractual Savings Institutions: These institutions operate under contract to receive regular payments or premiums, invest the money, and return stipulated amounts of money under conditions prescribed by the contract. These institutions include insurance companies and pension funds.

Finance Companies: Finance companies make consumer loans for purposes such as home improvements and automobile purchases. They also lend money to small businesses. The interest rates charged by finance companies are usually higher than those of commercial banks and thrifts, largely because the finance companies take greater risks.

Investment Companies: Mutual funds and other investment companies pool resources of shareholders to buy stocks, bonds, real estate, and other investments that will return profits to the shareholders.

II. Commercial Banking

Economists speak often of the "financial market," but, of course, you cannot get into your car and drive there as you can drive to a shopping mall. The financial market is the collection of organizations that assist households in channeling their money to businesses and government. Although the financial market includes thrift institutions, insurance companies, stockbrokerage firms, and finance companies, the largest participant in the financial market is the commercial banking industry. Commercial banks account for nearly $2 trillion of the financial market's $4 trillion in assets, and they function primarily by accepting deposits from customers and making business, mortgage, and consumer loans.

Finance companies are a part of the nation's financial market.

The Savings & Loan Crisis

Savings and loan associations (financial institutions designed to collect money in interest-bearing savings accounts and then lend money primarily for home mortgages) have fulfilled a needed function for generations of Americans. However, the late 1980s saw a heavy tide of failures in these institutions, commonly known as "S&Ls" or "thrifts." As news broke that scores of other thrifts were in danger of failure, the public became aware that the industry had serious problems and that the taxpayers would eventually have to pay for the mounting debts of these failing thrifts.

How did hundreds of the approximately three thousand thrifts in the United States get into such dire financial straits? Some basic economic and political situations contributed to their demise. First, the thrifts had lost profits as they paid high interest rates on the savings deposits during the previous decade while they collected low interest rates on long-term mortgage loans made in earlier years. In addition, government regulations had eased to allow S&L owners to count "good will" as a large part of the required capital in their operations. Thus the owners had little of their own money invested in the thrifts but were often willing to take extreme risks with S&L assets in attempts to make profits. These risks resulted in defaults that caused a financial collapse. The thrifts expected the Federal Savings and Loan Insurance Corporation (FSLIC) to pay the bill. The problems went further as board members and owners used existing funds to give themselves and their friends enormous loans without requiring substantial collateral. These and other instances of widespread greed, mismanagement, and even fraud brought on growing numbers of thrift failures.

One particular example of improper S&L activity took place in Minneapolis, where the large Midwest Federal Savings and Loan Association was discovered to be insolvent in early 1989. It seems that its chairman, a well-respected local businessman, lived in luxury with a high salary while his thrift and other ventures were floundering. Midwest Federal's loans to risky ventures resulted in multi-million dollar losses and led to an FBI investigation of the thrift and its chairman for fraud, embezzlement, kickbacks, and bribery. The estimated amount needed to bail Midwest Federal out of this mess was a half billion dollars.

Some analysts have observed that the FSLIC may have inadvertently contributed to the demise of some S&Ls. Disregarding the financial stability of the institutions, savers flocked to thrifts offering high interest rates because deposits were insured. Thus custom-ers had no incentive to avoid placing their money in shaky thrifts.

When the Bush administration began to tackle the S&L problem in 1989, the prospects were bleak. The FSLIC would be able to pay only a fraction of the billions of dollars of S&L debt. The final bailout bill was $166 billion, of which the taxpayers would be obliged to pay just over $100 billion (over $400 for every man, woman, and child in the United States). Even this large public payment will not necessarily insure the health and safety of the S&L industry. New restrictions are intended to prevent fraud and gross mismanagement, but greed cannot be wiped out by laws. In addition to a loss of assets that make them less profitable, the thrifts have suffered a loss of reputation. Some analysts predict that their number will be reduced further in the future by failures, closings, and mergers.

Milton Friedman (1912-)
Monetarist

One of the leading economists in the second half of the twentieth century has been Milton Friedman, a long-time professor of economics at the University of Chicago. His views strongly support laissez-faire capitalism, roundly denouncing governmental interference in the marketplace.

As the chief spokesman for the monetarist approach, Friedman holds that the stability of the economy is tied to the supply of money in circulation. If too much money is added to the supply, inflation results. If too little money is in the supply, the economy will go into a recession. Therefore, monetarists contend that the government should seek to control the money supply, raising it slowly and steadily to facilitate economic growth. This, however, is the only intervention government should make. Business should be free to make natural adjustments to the conditions of the market through the activities of private enterprise.

The philosophy of Friedman and his associates has been termed the "Chicago school" of economics, and their ideas came to the forefront of American thought in the 1970s and 1980s. Friedman has expounded his monetary approach to economics along with the danger of government involvement in economic matters in several works including *A Monetary History of the United States, 1867-1960; Free to Choose; Capitalism and Freedom;* and *Tyranny of the Status Quo*. He was awarded the Nobel Prize for his efforts in 1976.

Dual Banking System and Regulation

A commercial bank is formally defined by the government as an institution that accepts deposits and makes commercial loans. Realizing the importance of banking in the American financial system and desiring to ensure that depositors' funds are safe, the government regulates the commercial banking industry heavily. Indeed, banks feel the heavy hand of regulation from the day that they are created. In order for a bank to open its doors, it first must receive an authorization to exist, or a **charter**. Either federal or state authorities issue charters. Federal authorization is granted by the United States Treasury's Comptroller of the Cur-

Figure 9-4 Regulators of the 12,842 U.S. Commercial Banks*

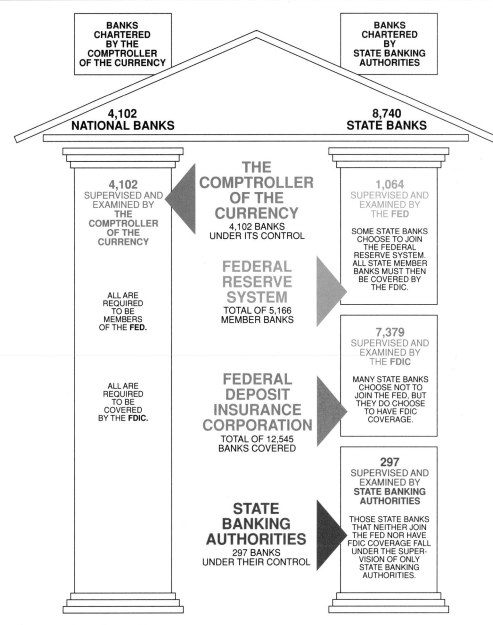

BANKS CHARTERED BY THE COMPTROLLER OF THE CURRENCY

BANKS CHARTERED BY STATE BANKING AUTHORITIES

4,102 NATIONAL BANKS

8,740 STATE BANKS

THE COMPTROLLER OF THE CURRENCY
4,102 BANKS UNDER ITS CONTROL

4,102 SUPERVISED AND EXAMINED BY THE COMPTROLLER OF THE CURRENCY

1,064 SUPERVISED AND EXAMINED BY THE FED

SOME STATE BANKS CHOOSE TO JOIN THE FEDERAL RESERVE SYSTEM. ALL STATE MEMBER BANKS MUST THEN BE COVERED BY THE FDIC.

ALL ARE REQUIRED TO BE MEMBERS OF THE **FED.**

FEDERAL RESERVE SYSTEM
TOTAL OF 5,166 MEMBER BANKS

7,379 SUPERVISED AND EXAMINED BY THE FDIC

MANY STATE BANKS CHOOSE NOT TO JOIN THE FED, BUT THEY DO CHOOSE TO HAVE FDIC COVERAGE.

ALL ARE REQUIRED TO BE COVERED BY THE **FDIC.**

FEDERAL DEPOSIT INSURANCE CORPORATION
TOTAL OF 12,545 BANKS COVERED

297 SUPERVISED AND EXAMINED BY STATE BANKING AUTHORITIES

STATE BANKING AUTHORITIES
297 BANKS UNDER THEIR CONTROL

THOSE STATE BANKS THAT NEITHER JOIN THE FED NOR HAVE FDIC COVERAGE FALL UNDER THE SUPERVISION OF ONLY STATE BANKING AUTHORITIES.

*Source: Federal Reserve Board of Governors, May 31, 1990

rency, while each state's banking commission provides state charters. Of the nation's nearly 13,000 banks, only about one-third are federally chartered.

Once a commercial bank receives its charter, it is subject to one of four regulatory authorities. First is the Comptroller of the Currency, who supervises and regulates only those banks with national charters. Second is the Federal Reserve Bank, which regulates only those state banks that have chosen to join the Federal Reserve System (FRS). If a state bank does not choose to join the FRS but desires to be insured, it is regulated by the Federal Deposit Insurance Corporation (FDIC). Finally, those state banks that are neither members of the Federal Reserve System nor insured by FDIC are supervised by their state's banking authority.

Functions of Commercial Banks

Accepting Deposits–Commercial banks fulfill three important roles in the United States financial market: accepting deposits, extending loans, and providing miscellaneous services. Accepting and guarding customer deposits, a function that began with the early goldsmiths, continues today. Not only is a bank to ensure the physical safety of deposits by maintaining strong vaults and hiring guards, but also it is to ensure the safe use of the funds by making sound investment decisions. In performing the deposit function, commercial banks have developed an array of creative deposit plans, including checking accounts, savings accounts, re-

purchase agreements, individual retirement accounts, and money market deposit accounts.

Extending Loans–The second role commercial banks perform is that of providing loans. Banks extend many types of loans, including loans to business firms for equipment and inventory, real estate loans to people for purchase of homes, and loans for automobiles. As the risk of a borrower's not repaying a loan increases, a bank will increase the interest rate that he must pay.

Provision of Miscellaneous Services–In addition to accepting deposits and extending loans, commercial banks typically provide many miscellaneous services. Most banks offer consumer services such as safe deposit boxes, traveler's checks, cashier's checks, certified checks, and wire transfers of money to virtually anywhere in the world. The trust department of commercial banks assists customers in the preparation of wills and establishment of trust accounts that will provide for family needs after the death of the client. For the business customer, banks will assist in the development of savings, investment, and pension plans for employees. Banks may also be called upon to take care of the business customer's payroll and other accounting needs.

Section Review
1. What is the financial market?
2. What is a commercial bank?
3. What four authorities regulate commercial banking?

Chapter Review

Terms
money
legal tender
barter
double coincidence of wants
commodity money
full-bodied coin
token coin
representative money
fiat money
M-1
M-2
M-3
L
charter

Content Questions
1. What is money?
2. What term refers to the fact that a merchant must accept in the payment of debts whatever the government declares to be money?
3. How does money act as a store of purchasing power?
4. What characteristics should an effective money system possess?
5. What is the name given to unbacked money when it is issued by government decree?
6. What is M-1?
7. What official authorization must a bank obtain in order to open for business? Who issues it?
8. List the functions of commercial banks.

Application Questions
1. What are some disadvantages to having a money system backed by some precious commodity such as gold or silver?
2. What would happen if the market interest rate on loans were 12% and the government, feeling the rate too high, passed laws making it illegal for banks and other institutions to lend at a rate greater than 6%? Discuss the effects on households, business firms, and the government.

CHAPTER 10

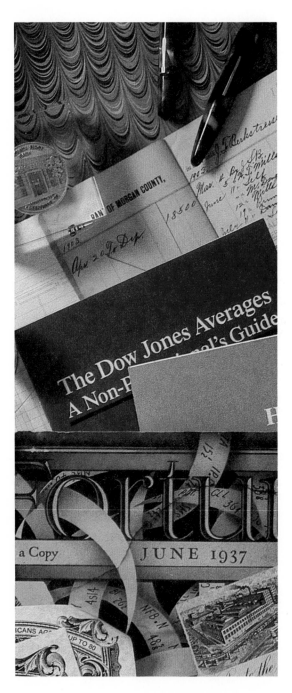

Central Banking

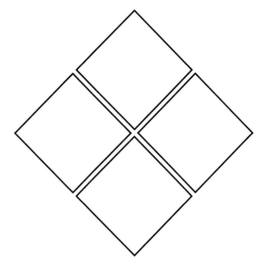

How much better is it to get wisdom than gold! and to get understanding rather to be chosen than silver! Proverbs 16:16

We saw in Chapter 9 that money is very important to the smooth functioning of an economy. Without some stable form of money, our present sophisticated economic system would not be possible. If money did not exist, people would be forced to return to barter. Because barter requires people to make numerous trades in order to obtain what they desire, they would "generalize"; that is, people would stop specializing in what they do best, choosing instead to meet as many of their own needs as possible. The effect of this "every man for himself" attitude would be very harmful to the economy.

Realizing, therefore, how vital money is to the smooth functioning of our economy, we come to the obvious question: Who creates our money? Chapter 9 briefly touched on this question when it described the creation of money by the goldsmiths of Western Europe in the 16th and 17th centuries. Today in the United States there exist three creators of money: the United States Treasury, financial institutions, and the Federal Reserve Banking Sys-tem. The U.S. Treasury creates money when it mints and sells coins to the Federal Reserve Banks. Approximately $18 billion in coin is currently in circulation, a rather small percentage of the nearly $222 billion in currency and coin. The Treasury, it should be noted, mints coins at a cost of only a fraction of their face values. It then makes a handsome profit by selling the minted coin at full face value to the Federal Reserve.

The second creator of money is the financial institutions which make up the U.S. financial market. These institutions, which include commercial banks, savings and loan associations, and credit unions, create money by lending their customers' deposits to others, who, in turn, redeposit the loaned money to be lent yet again. This process of money creation will be discussed later in this chapter.

The vast majority of new money, however, is created by the Federal Reserve Bank, the **central bank** of the United States. A central bank is established by the government to provide an elastic national currency, to serve as the nation's fiscal agent, to regulate the nation's private banks, to provide a national check-clearing mechanism, and to serve as a bank for the nation's private banks.

I. Organization of the Federal Reserve System

The **Federal Reserve Banking System,** or the "Fed," as it is known to economists, is a government institution that controls the issuance of currency, provides banking services to the nation's commercial banks, and regulates banking activity. The Fed also attempts to control prices, unemployment, and economic growth by controlling the nation's supply of money. Many nations of the world established central banks long before the United States did. The Bank of England, Britain's central bank, was founded in 1694. The Bank of France was created in 1800, and in 1882 the Bank of Japan was established. The United States introduced its central bank in 1913.

Individual Federal Reserve District Banks

In 1913 the United States was a nation of sharp contrasts. The East was the financial center; the South and Midwest were agricultural; the North was devoted to manufacturing; and the West was still considered an undeveloped frontier. Realizing that each section of the nation had diverse financial needs, and not wanting any section of the country to be at the financial mercy of another, Congress divided the nation into twelve districts, each having its own central bank. Each Federal Reserve district bank performs numerous economic tasks. For example, each Federal Reserve district bank has an operation center that sorts millions of checks per year and makes it possible for them to be sent to the banks on which they are drawn. Also, each district bank supplies currency and coin to commercial banks, enabling them to cash checks and pay out savings withdrawals.

All district banks are supervised by a nine-member board of directors composed of three bankers, three nonbank business people, and three representatives of the general public. While each Federal Reserve district bank's day-to-day affairs are still governed by the district's board of directors, they have little to do with controlling the nation's money supply. Since the mid-1930s, virtu-

The Bank of England is Britain's central bank.

ally all decisions regarding the money supply are made by the Fed's Board of Governors and the Federal Open Market Committee.

Board of Governors

The Federal Reserve Banking System is guided by a seven-member **Board of Governors.** Each board member is selected by the president of the United States and confirmed by Congress. To ensure a balanced board, no two board members may be from the same Federal Reserve district. Congress provided that one membership would become vacant every two years and that each member may serve a term of fourteen years without reappointment. Even though the maximum number of years a board member may serve is fourteen, the average term served is six years, since many board members choose to return to private business or retire before their terms have expired.

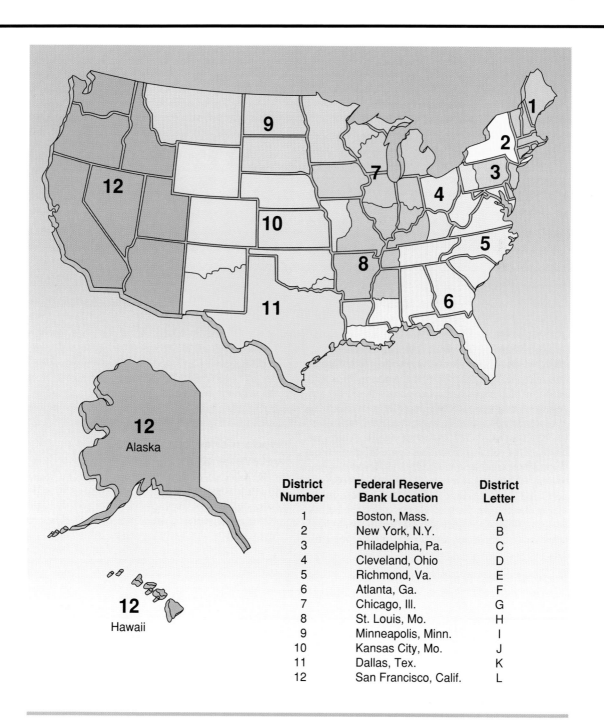

District Number	Federal Reserve Bank Location	District Letter
1	Boston, Mass.	A
2	New York, N.Y.	B
3	Philadelphia, Pa.	C
4	Cleveland, Ohio	D
5	Richmond, Va.	E
6	Atlanta, Ga.	F
7	Chicago, Ill.	G
8	St. Louis, Mo.	H
9	Minneapolis, Minn.	I
10	Kansas City, Mo.	J
11	Dallas, Tex.	K
12	San Francisco, Calif.	L

The Federal Reserve Bank of Atlanta, one of twelve district banks

The Board of Governors meets in Washington, D.C., where it has access to government officials and many economists. One of the greatest responsibilities of the Board of Governors is setting the **required reserve ratio.** Unlike the goldsmiths of 16th-century Western Europe, who had the power to lend all of their customers' gold, American banks must keep a specified percentage of their deposits on hand as dictated by the Board of Governors. Other functions of the Board include supervising and regulating commercial banks, supervising the twelve Federal Reserve district banks, and administering financial consumer protection laws such as those requiring equal credit opportunity and fair housing lending.

Federal Open Market Committee

The **Federal Open Market Committee (FOMC)** affects the money supply by buying and selling government securities such as Treasury Bills, Treasury Notes, and Treasury Bonds. This function, as you will see later in this chapter, is the Fed's most important tool in changing the quantity of money in the money supply. The FOMC is composed of twelve members, including the seven-member Board of Governors and five Federal Reserve district bank presidents. The president of the Federal Reserve Bank of New York always serves as one of the five FOMC members, because he acts as the account manager, the one who actually monitors the purchases and sales of securities in the financial market in New York City.

Independence of the Federal Reserve System

Believing that the nation needed a central bank, but fearing that such a bank might be used by self-serving politicians, Congress in its original Federal Reserve Act sought to make the Federal Reserve System independent from outside influence. The Fed is independent from outside control in three ways. First, the Fed is politically independent. With one term on the Board of Governors expiring every two years, it is difficult for one president to control the Fed for a long period of time by "packing" the Board with those whom he favors.

Second, the Fed is financially independent as a result of possessing a separate budget. Congress has learned by experience that the federal budget is a powerful force that may be used to reward cooperative agencies and punish those that do not carry out the legislature's wishes. For example, if the Federal Reserve System were under the federal budget, congressional representatives aggressively seeking re-election could threaten the Federal Reserve System with extinction if it did not create billions of dollars to be lent to banks in their districts. To avoid this problem, the framers of the Federal Reserve Act provided that the Fed would not depend on Congress for its operating funds. Instead, the Fed provides for its own needs by receiving fees on services provided to banks, selling its stock to new member banks, and collecting interest on securities and loans.

Finally, the Fed is operationally independent. Though the chairman of the Board of Governors is required to report to Congress periodically, no one may dictate actions the Federal Reserve System must take. Also, the Fed's financial records are exempt from audit by any agent or agency. No one, including the president of the United States or members of Congress, may examine the Fed's books without its permission.

This extensive independence does not mean, however, that the Federal Reserve may act irresponsibly in carrying out its duties. Two specific checks have been put in place to ensure the Fed's stability. First, members of the Fed's Board of Governors may be removed from the Board "for cause," a legal term that Congress may interpret as narrowly or as broadly as it wishes. Second, and most important, the Fed depends on Congress for its very existence. The leaders of the Fed are well aware that the Federal Reserve System was created by an act of Congress and that it could likewise be abolished by a vote of Congress at any time.

Section Review

1. Who are the three creators of money in the United States?
2. How many Federal Reserve districts are there?
3. Who selects the members of the Federal Reserve's Board of Governors? How many members are there? How long may each serve on the board?
4. What one person is specifically required to sit on the Federal Open Market Committee and serve as its account manager?

II. Functions of the Federal Reserve System

Congress passed the original Federal Reserve Act of 1913 as "an act to provide for the establishment of Federal reserve banks, to furnish an elastic currency, to afford a means of rediscounting commercial paper, to establish a more effective supervision of banking in the United States, and for other purposes." In keeping with this act, the Federal Reserve Banking System exists to furnish six national economic services: providing a uniform currency, regulating member banks, clearing checks, acting as the nation's fiscal agent, serving as the banker's bank, and creating money.

Providing a Uniform and Elastic Currency

One of the first responsibilities delegated to the Federal Reserve System was that of providing an **elastic currency.** Congress desired to possess a money supply that could be expanded as the economy grew. But, before the Federal Reserve System could even think of providing an elastic money system, it had to furnish a uniform currency that would be recognized and accepted by every person and business from coast to coast. To this end the Fed initiated the series of Federal Reserve notes that are in use today. Federal Reserve notes are not created by the Federal Reserve System but by each of the twelve Federal Reserve district banks.

Regulating Member Banks

Originally, banks that were members of the Federal Reserve System enjoyed certain benefits such as free check clearance, free currency and coin delivery, and other free services, but these banks also had to endure strict requirements in order to maintain membership. For example, the percentage the Fed required to be held on reserve against deposits was much higher than that required of nonmembers by state banking authorities. As the regulations grew more oppressive, member banks withdrew from the Federal Reserve System to adopt the less burdensome regulations of state banking authorities. The number of banks fleeing the Fed alarmed Congress. Therefore, it passed the

Ludwig von Mises
(1881-1973)
Dean of the Austrian Economists

Born in the Austro-Hungarian Empire, Ludwig von Mises studied and taught at the University of Vienna. After World War I, when Nazism was on the rise in Austria, he moved to Geneva. Then in 1940, while Europe was threatened with repression in World War II, Mises fled to America, where he gained citizenship and spent the rest of his life teaching and writing.

Although Mises is not one of the most well-known economists of the twentieth century, his contributions to the science have been very influential. He has been called the "dean" of the Austrian school of economics, a group that includes many notable economists such as Karl Menger (p. 9) and Friedrich von Hayek (p. 18). Mises's ideas greatly influenced Hayek and other economists in their support of capitalism. Among those ideas set forth by Mises were the necessity of freely derived prices to guide the market, the perils of socialism, the dangers of government manipulation of the money supply, and the desirability of private property and individual economic and political freedom. Mises's book *Human Action* has been described as the most "profound, complete [and] persuasive exposition and defense of the free market." He clearly described the inefficiencies of socialism in his 1920 book called *Socialism,* and his seventeen other books along with hundreds of articles and lectures further described the needs and dangers in modern economic thought.

Monetary Control Act of 1980, requiring *all* financial institutions to abide by the Fed's required reserve regulations. As a result, the number of banks leaving the Fed has been greatly reduced.

Clearing Checks

The twentieth century has seen an explosion in the number of checks being written. Currently checks are used for $95 of every $100 in business transactions. Each check that is written requires clearance–that is, each check must be sent to the bank that holds the original check writer's account for payment. To handle the huge volume of checks requiring clearance, the Federal Reserve System has developed an elaborate check clearance system.

Acting as Fiscal Agent

Another function of the Federal Reserve System is to serve as the nation's **fiscal agent,** another name for the government's bank. Just as a commercial bank accepts customer deposits, makes loans to borrowers, and offers financial advice to those requesting it, the Federal Reserve's job as fiscal agent is likewise threefold. First, the Federal Reserve holds the U.S. Treasury's checking account. The Internal Revenue Service (IRS), the government's tax collector, deposits all tax revenues into the government's checking account at the Fed. Out of this account, the government pays its bills. Second, the Fed makes loans to the U.S. Treasury by having the FOMC purchase government bonds. Third, through the chairman of its Board of Governors, the Fed supplies a wealth of economic information and advice to both the president and Congress.

Serving as the Banker's Bank

As mentioned in Chapter 9, currency and coin account for a relatively small portion of the total money supply, while checking accounts make up a significantly larger part. Problems arise, therefore, when a greater than expected number of people want to receive cash from their accounts. If a bank cannot meet withdrawal requests, people panic, and depositors rush to the bank to get currency. If the bank cannot supply the needed cash during such a "run on the bank," the bank may be declared insolvent and fail.

The Fed was created to prevent such panics. As the banker's bank, the Fed was designed to serve as a **lender of last resort,** creating and lending enough currency to banks to satisfy panicking depositors.

Creating Money

As a result of fulfilling its roles as the nation's fiscal agent and the banker's bank, the Fed has developed several powerful methods of expanding and contracting the money supply. The Fed relies heavily on a process called the money multiplier effect to increase the money supply.

How Checks Are Cleared

If Tom writes a $100 check on his account at First Bank to Dick, and Dick also has a checking account at First Bank, the check clears (the money is transferred) when the bank subtracts $100 from Tom's account and adds it to Dick's account. But what if Dick's account is with another local bank, or what if Tom writes the check to Harriet, who lives in a distant city? How does the check clear then? The process is not quite as direct, but it is still relatively simple.

If Tom writes the check to Dick, whose account is with either Second Bank in the same town or another bank in a nearby town, there are two possible methods of clearing the check. One is a process called **correspondent banking** in which the two banks involved have numerous regular transactions between them, and therefore they hold deposits with each other. In this situation Dick might deposit the check in Second Bank, and Second Bank would send the check on to First Bank. If First Bank finds that Tom has enough money in his account to cover the check, then the bank subtracts that amount from his account. In the midst of this process, First Bank's account with Second Bank will be decreased by the amount of the check to complete the transfer of funds from one bank to the other. Dick's account at Second Bank will be increased by the amount of the check.

The second possible method is the use of a local **clearinghouse** to handle the clearing process. A local clearinghouse is run by and for a group of local banks to help clear the checks among them. Dick's bank would send Tom's check to the clearinghouse along with many more checks from First Bank and the other banks in the group. At the clearinghouse the amounts of all the checks written to accounts in Dick's bank (including the check from Tom to Dick) will be totaled, and

also the total of all the checks drawn from Dick's bank will be tallied. The same will be done for all of the other banks in the group, and the total drawn from First Bank accounts will include the check from Tom to Dick.

Once this tallying is completed, the banks involved may have totals such as this: First Bank may need to pay out $5,000 more than it collects from the member banks; Second Bank may be able to collect $2,000 more than it pays out; Third Bank may be able to collect $3,000 more than it pays out. The banks will simply settle up by some established form of paying into the clearinghouse operation the final amount they owe or collecting the final amount they are owed by the other banks. Besides making this settlement among the banks, the checks are sent on to the banks from which they are drawn so that the amount of each check can be withdrawn from the proper account. (Thus, First Bank would receive the check Tom gave to Dick and then

subtract the amount from Tom's account.) As soon as the check is cleared by Tom's bank, the $100 will be added to Dick's account in his bank.

But what if Tom writes the $100 check to Harriet who lives in a distant town and whose bank does not do correspondent banking or participate in a local clearinghouse with Tom's bank? Then the Federal Reserve's clearinghouse operations come into play. If Tom's and Harriet's banks are in the same Federal Reserve district, Harriet's bank will send the check (along with other checks from banks in the district) to the Federal Reserve district bank. There, in an operation similar to that in the local clearinghouses, the district bank totals the amounts owed to and drawn from each bank. Using ultra-high speed electronic equipment that *reads* the magnetic ink numbers at the bottom of a check, the Federal Reserve banks are able to physically process and deliver checks to the bank on which they are drawn in a matter of days. The final amounts owed to each bank are added to their accounts with the Federal Reserve, and the amounts drawn from each bank are subtracted from their Federal Reserve accounts. When the checks are sent on to the banks from which they are drawn, Tom's account and the accounts of others who wrote checks can be reduced by the appropriate amounts. Then the check will have cleared, and Harriet's account will be increased by $100.

When Tom's bank and Harriet's bank are in different Federal Reserve districts, another step is added to this process. If Tom's bank is in the Fed district with its central bank in Richmond, Virginia, and Harriet's bank is in the Fed district served by the Kansas City, Missouri, district bank, Harriet's bank will add the amount of the check to her account and send it to the Fed at Kansas City. The Fed at Kansas City will total that check along with other checks owed to Harriet's bank and add that total to the Federal Reserve account of Harriet's bank. Then it will forward the check to the Fed at Richmond, where it will total that check with others drawn from Tom's bank, subtract the total from the Federal Reserve account of Tom's bank, and forward the check to Tom's bank so that Tom's account can be adjusted. This process results in a disparity between the district banks involved, because the amount of the check is added to a bank's Federal Reserve account in one district and subtracted from an account in another district. This problem, however, is settled by the Interdistrict Settlement Fund in Washington, D.C., which acts as a clearinghouse among the twelve Federal Reserve district banks.

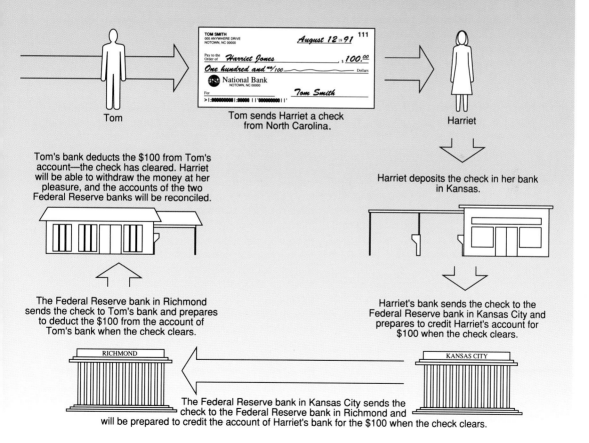

Tom

Tom sends Harriet a check from North Carolina.

Harriet

Tom's bank deducts the $100 from Tom's account—the check has cleared. Harriet will be able to withdraw the money at her pleasure, and the accounts of the two Federal Reserve banks will be reconciled.

Harriet deposits the check in her bank in Kansas.

The Federal Reserve bank in Richmond sends the check to Tom's bank and prepares to deduct the $100 from the account of Tom's bank when the check clears.

Harriet's bank sends the check to the Federal Reserve bank in Kansas City and prepares to credit Harriet's account for $100 when the check clears.

RICHMOND

KANSAS CITY

The Federal Reserve bank in Kansas City sends the check to the Federal Reserve bank in Richmond and will be prepared to credit the account of Harriet's bank for the $100 when the check clears.

The Money Multiplier Effect–The **money multiplier effect** is the expansion of the money supply as a result of commercial banks lending their depositors' money to others. Let us look at an example of how it works. Suppose Gene Merkle, an auto mechanic, deposits $10,000 cash into his checking account at the First National Bank. Assuming the Fed requires banks to hold required reserves equaling 10% of their deposits, First National must keep at least $1,000 either in its vault or on deposit with its Federal Reserve district bank. The bank may now lend the $9,000 "excess reserves" remaining. Later that day Jeff Sutton walks into the First National Bank and requests a $9,000 auto loan. The loan is granted and he takes the check to Brad's Auto Sales and purchases a car. Brad deposits the $9,000 check into his checking account at the Second National Bank. In order to meet its reserve requirement, Second National holds 10%, or $900, of the $9,000 as reserves and then lends out the excess $8,100 to another borrower, who in turn deposits the check to his account in the Third National Bank. On and on the process continues. If all deposits in excess of the required reserves are lent out and all loans are redeposited, Gene Merkle's original $10,000 will be multiplied into $100,000 worth of new deposits! The reason for this phenomenon is simple: if Gene personally lent Jeff $9,000, Gene would have relinquished ownership of the money. When his bank, however, lent his money, Gene still retained ownership of the $10,000 in his account while Jeff gained ownership of $9,000.

To determine how much the money supply may grow, one could add up all of the new deposits as depicted in Figure 10-1, or one could use a simple formula:

$$D \times \frac{1}{rr}$$

where D = initial deposit
rr = required reserve ratio

For example, by how much could the money supply grow if a $10,000 deposit is made and banks are required to hold 10% on reserve?

$$\$10,000 \times \frac{1}{.10} = \$100,000$$

Figure 10-1 The Money Multiplier Effect in Action

BANK	AMOUNT DEPOSITED −	AMOUNT HELD ON RESERVE =	AMOUNT LOANED	MONEY SUPPLY
				$10,000.00
1st National	$10,000.00 →	$1,000.00 →	$9,000.00	$19,000.00
2nd National	9,000.00 →	900.00 →	8,100.00	27,100.00
3rd National	8,100.00 →	810.00 →	7,290.00	34,390.00
4th National	7,290.00 →	729.00 →	6,561.00	40,951.00
5th National	6,561.00 →	656.10 →	5,904.90	46,855.90
6th National	5,904.90 →	590.49 →	5,314.41	52,170.31

Total Increase = $100,000.00

The factor 1/rr is called the **money multiplier,** and it represents the number of times a deposit may be multiplied. In our example, the money multiplier is 1/.10, which is equal to 10 times.

In attempting to predict changes in the money supply, the multiplier formula tends to be a poor tool. The money supply will never be fully multiplied for these two reasons. First, not all deposited money will be lent. Historically, banks have tended to hold slightly more of their depositors' money on reserve than the Fed requires. Second, not all money will be redeposited. Many people, desiring convenience or distrusting banks, choose to hold their money in the form of currency as opposed to depositing it into their checking account. Such decisions short-circuit the money multiplier, for if money is not redeposited, it cannot be reloaned. The combination of these two actions significantly reduces the money multiplier. For example, given that the average required reserve ratio in the United States today is about 6%, the multiplier should be about 16 times (1/.06). Because people choose to hold currency, and because banks do not lend all that they could, the real multiplier is approximately 2.9 times.

The Tools of Money Creation–In order to change the quantity of money in the nation's money supply, the Fed must change the amount of money subject to the multiplier effect or change the multiplier. The Fed can do this in three ways: change the discount rate, change the required reserve ratio, or buy and sell securities in the open market.

Changing the Discount Rate–The first way the Federal Reserve may increase or decrease the nation's money supply is through a process called **discounting,** or lending money to banks. When a bank borrows money from the Fed, no new money is printed, no checks are written and cleared, and no gold or silver changes hands. The Federal Reserve simply creates the money by informing the bank that the funds have been credited to its reserve account. With the extra money, the bank may now make additional loans that cause the money supply to grow via the multiplier. Just as a bank attracts more borrowers by charging a lower interest rate, the Fed attracts banks to borrow more money by lowering the **discount rate,** the interest rate it charges on loans to banks. By raising the discount rate, the Fed could discourage borrowing and cut the growth of the money supply. Although changes in the discount rate could be used as a powerful tool to change the money supply, the Federal Reserve has rarely chosen to use it for that purpose. Discounting is primarily used for its intended purpose, that of assisting banks that find themselves temporarily unable to meet large demands for withdrawals.

Changing the Reserve Requirement–The second way the Federal Reserve may affect the supply of money is by changing the reserve requirement. We saw earlier that if the reserve requirement is 10%, new deposits could potentially be multiplied by a factor of ten: $1/.10 = 10$. If the Fed wanted to increase the money supply, it could simply lower the required reserve ratio, which would have the effect of increasing the money multiplier. For example, if the required reserve ratio were lowered to 5%, the money multiplier would rise to twenty: $1/.05 = 20$. Similarly, the money supply could be decreased by raising the required reserve ratio. Be-

October 7, 1979

FEDERAL RESERVE INCREASES KEY RATE TO CURB INFLATION

DISCOUNT LEVEL A RECORD 12%

The chairman of the Federal Reserve Board, Paul A. Volcker, has anounced a new package of measures to bring inflation under control. In a rare Saturday night news conference, he said the discount rate -- the rate at which banks borrow from the Federal Reserve-- will be increased by a full percentage point to a record 12%. The move is intended to calm financial markets and bolster the dollar while it attacks inflation, which is run- at a rate of 13% for this year.

Although President Carter was not directly involved in this move, the White House has affirmed its support of the measure. In a report to the press, the President's press secretary, Jody Powell, said that the action would "help reduce inflationary expectations, contribute to a stronger United States dollar abroad and curb unhealthy speculations in commodity markets."

Mr. Powell went on to say that " the Administration believes that success in reducing inflationary pressures will lead in due course both to lower rates of price increases and to lower interest rates."

In addition to the new discount rate, Mr. Volker announced a change in the reserve requirement as measure to restrain the unhealthy expansion of bank credit. Interest rates are expected to rise because of both this action and the raising of the discount rate.

Figure 10-2   The Fed's Economic Tools

Tool	Action	Effect on the Money Supply	Impact on the Economy
discount rate	increase discount rate	reduces money supply	rising interest rates and a slowing of the economy
	decrease discount rate	increases money supply	falling interest rates and an acceleration of the economy
reserve requirement	increase reserve requirement	reduces money supply	rising interest rates and a slowing of the economy
	decrease reserve requirement	increases money supply	falling interest rates and an acceleration of the economy
open market operations	sell government securities	reduces money supply	rising interest rates and a slowing of the economy
	purchase government securities	increases money supply	falling interest rates and an acceleration of the economy

cause small changes in the reserve requirement cause dramatic changes in the money supply, the Fed has tended to be hesitant to use this method except in the most dire economic circumstances.

Using Open Market Operations–In contrast to its infrequent use of changes in the discount rate and the required reserve ratio, the Fed continually uses its **open market operations** to control the quantity of money in circulation. An open market operation is an action whereby government securities are purchased or sold by the Fed in the open market to inject money into or withdraw money from the economy. If the Federal Reserve wishes to increase the nation's money supply, it simply purchases securities in the open market. If, on the other hand, the Fed wishes to decrease the money supply, it sells securities, pulling money into itself from the general population.

Suppose that the Federal Open Market Committee (FOMC) meets and decides that the money supply needs to be $10 billion higher. Assuming a money multiplier of ten, the FOMC would direct the president of the New York Federal Reserve Bank to purchase $1 billion worth of government bonds. To pay for these bonds, the Fed would write checks totaling $1 billion to the security dealers holding the bonds. Sellers of the bonds, in turn, would deposit the money into banks, where it would be lent and borrowed again and again until the $1 billion is transformed into $10 billion by the money multiplication process. At this point one might question, "Where did the Fed get the $1 billion to buy the bonds in the first place?" Very simply, the Fed created the new money through a bookkeeping entry. Unlike ordinary customers of a bank, who must deposit money prior to writing checks, the Fed may write checks on funds created by merely adjusting its books. After all, it controls the bank.

Section Review

1. List the six functions of the Federal Reserve System.
2. What is the discount rate?
3. Which method of changing the money supply does the Fed use most often?

III. Money and the Economy

Price Stability

Now we come to the ultimate question in our discussion: What difference does it make if the Fed increases or decreases the quantity of money in circulation? One reason that was hinted earlier is price stability. As the nation produces more goods and services, the money supply must increase to the same extent so that the same quantity of dollars will purchase the same quantity of goods. If the money supply grows more quickly than the growth in production of goods and services, more dollars will be required to buy any given good, creating a general rise in prices, a situation referred to as inflation. If the money supply grows more slowly than the growth in production of goods and services, prices will generally decline and a recession may ensue because there would not be enough dollars in circulation to purchase all of the goods produced.

Control of the Interest Rate on Money

A second reason that the Fed controls the supply of money is to control the interest rate on loans. The power to control interest rates gives the Fed tremendous control over the nation's economy. In a free-market economy the price of any particular good is determined by the intersection of its demand and supply curves. The price of money–the interest rate–is determined by the intersection of the demand and supply curves for money. Figure 10-3 graphically depicts the demand for money. People and business firms will demand less and less borrowed money as interest rates rise. Why? Because as interest rates rise, it becomes less profitable for business firms to borrow money to purchase buildings and machines. The higher interest rates will reduce the firms' profits. Therefore, as interest rates rise, businesses will forego more and more projects that require the borrowing of money. On the other hand, as interest rates fall, people and business firms will want to borrow more money.

The supply ''curve'' for money as seen in Figure 10-4 is a curious vertical line. Most supply curves slope upward from left to right, illustrating

Figure 10-3

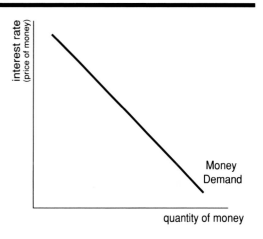

Figure 10-4

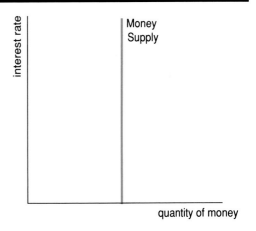

the fact that as the price of a good rises, suppliers are willing to supply more. Money, however, is created by a supplier (the Fed) which is not interested in making a profit. Because the Fed is immune to the effects of changing interest rates, the Fed's money supply line is perfectly vertical.

Figure 10-5 shows the combination of the two curves. The intersection point determines the inter-

Figure 10-5

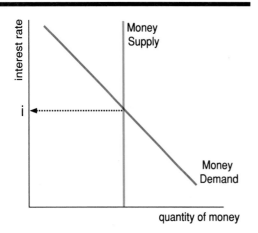

Figure 10-6

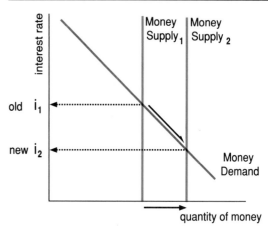

est rate. If the Federal Reserve should increase the supply of money, the vertical money supply curve will shift to the right, causing a decline in the interest rate (Figure 10-6). Conversely, if the money supply declines, the curve will shift leftward, leading to a rise in the interest rate (Figure 10-7).

But how does the ability to control interest rates give the Fed the ability to control the economy? Recall from Chapter 5 that the interest rate is the mechanism that opens and closes the financial valve which controls the flow of money to business firms. (See p. 71.) If the Fed increases the money supply, the interest rate on loans will fall, making it less costly and more profitable for businesses to borrow. The stock market will surge as people scramble to purchase stock in the now more profitable business firms. Consumers will also feel the effects of lower interest rates as houses and cars are more affordable to finance. In short, as interest rates fall, businesses will expand, consumption expenditures will rise, and, more importantly, unemployment will fall.

Dangers of Intervention by the Federal Reserve System

The obvious question many students ask at this point is, "Why does the Fed not continually print

Figure 10-7

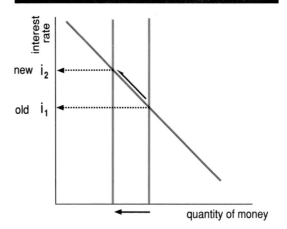

more money to stimulate the economy?'' The answer is that such activity would accelerate the economy too much. There is a point at which the economy would not be able to produce any more goods and services. At this point equipment would be running twenty-four hours a day, people would be working at full capacity, and natural resources would be stretched to their limits. If the Fed would continue to increase the money supply after the

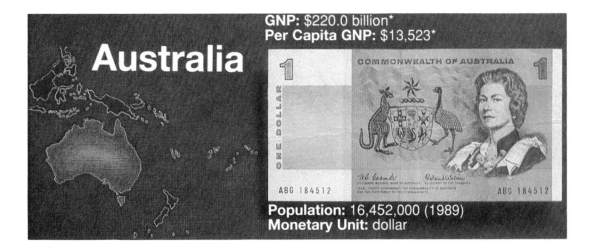

GNP: $220.0 billion*
Per Capita GNP: $13,523*

Australia

COMMONWEALTH OF AUSTRALIA

Population: 16,452,000 (1989)
Monetary Unit: dollar

Australia's land and minerals provide the nation with an immense supply of resources. Her pastures feed the sheep that have made Australia the world's largest exporter of wool. Productive mines have also made her the largest exporter of bauxite, alumina, and both coking and steam coal. In addition, Australia leads the world in the production of lead, rutile, zircon, and other minerals; and she ranks fourth among world nations as a gold producer. This great natural wealth should have helped a modern nation like Australia to become a leader in world trade and to establish a thriving economy. However, the land "down under" has come to face some serious economic problems.

Naturally, Australia came to rely heavily on the export of agricultural products and minerals for her income. When other countries of the world had high demands for Australian goods, the economy prospered. But when demand fell, Australia's export income dropped severely; the nation's farmers were hurt and many of its miners and dockworkers became unemployed. In an attempt to improve the economy, Australia erected protectionist trade barriers, but they only complicated problems. It also tried to establish new manufacturing industries that could turn Australia's raw materials into finished goods for export. However, these industries were often too expensive to operate with Australia's small work force. These and other unsuccessful economic policies led Australia into heavy foreign debt, high taxes, and sagging international trade levels. In reaction, the Australian government has begun to reform some of its economic policies by pulling down some trade barriers and encouraging economic expansion in industries that allow Australia to be competitive. Although its land and minerals will probably continue to bring in the bulk of its income, further economic reform and expansion could make Australia an economic pacesetter.
*figures for 1988 from the 1990 *World Almanac*

nation approached this point, those goods that can be produced would rise in price as they would be rationed out among the frantic buyers. When this situation occurs, economists say the economy is "overheating."

To "cool down" an overheated economy, the Fed would decrease the growth rate of the money supply, causing interest rates to rise. As interest rates rise, businesses and consumers would be discouraged from borrowing additional funds. If the

GAMBLE ©1983 The Florida Times-Union; The Register & Tribune Syndicate

"WELL, YOU LOOK GOOD! HOW WOULD YOU LIKE THE SAME OPERATION OVER AGAIN?"

Fed should decrease the money supply too much, the economy might "cool" to the point where businesses are left with idled machines and employees. To cut losses, businesses would begin laying off workers. In short, an artificial depression in the economy may closely follow an artificial expansion. This is one possible explanation for the Great Depression. After the Fed expanded the money supply throughout the 1920s perhaps causing the "Roaring '20s"–a period of unprecedented economic prosperity–business activity began to heat up. The Fed reacted by reducing the money supply from $26.5 billion in 1929 to $19.5 billion in 1933–a reduction of over 25%, which may have cooled the economy into a chilling depression.

Section Review

1. For what two major reasons does the Fed increase or decrease the money supply?
2. Why does the Fed not continually expand the money supply?

Chapter Review

Terms
central bank
Federal Reserve Banking System
Board of Governors
required reserve ratio
Federal Open Market Committee (FOMC)
elastic currency
correspondent banking
clearinghouse
fiscal agent
lender of last resort
money multiplier effect
money multiplier
discounting
discount rate
open market operations

Content Questions
1. What is a central bank?
2. Why do twelve central banks exist in the United States?
3. Who sits on the Federal Open Market Committee?
4. How is the Fed independent, and why did the framers of the Federal Reserve Act consider its independence necessary?
5. What is a fiscal agent?
6. Why is the concept of the money multiplier important?
7. What are the three ways the Federal Reserve creates money?

Application Questions
1. It has been said that the Federal Open Market Committee is more powerful than any foreign army that could march against us. Do you agree or disagree? Why?
2. If the required reserve ratio is 8% and the money supply is $500 billion, what dollar amount of government securities will the Federal Reserve need to purchase if it wants to increase the money supply by 10%?
3. Imagine you have just heard a news reporter announce the following: ''The Fed's Board of Governors announced today that it will begin pursuing a policy of 'tight' money for the next twelve months. The chairman announced that, effective immediately, the discount rate and the required reserve ratio would be increased and that the FOMC would begin selling government securities.'' Discuss the effect such a policy might have on prices, interest rates, employment, economic growth (the growth in the nation's production of actual goods and services), and the stock market.

Unit V: Economics of the Government

CHAPTER 11

Measuring the Wealth of the Nation

I. Gross National Product
   A. How GNP Is Measured
   B. Problems with GNP Measurement
II. Foreign Trade
   A. Reasons for Trade Deficits
   B. Trade Policy, Protectionism, and Free Trade

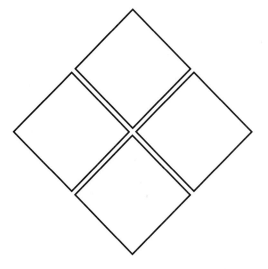

But thou shalt remember the Lord thy God: for it is he that giveth thee power to get wealth. Deuteronomy 8:18

I. Gross National Product

Just as business firms take annual accountings of how much they have produced and sold during the past year to determine whether they have been successful, nations account for their productivity by determining their **gross national product** or **GNP.** Economists make annual accountings of GNP in order to determine their nation's economic progress relative to past years and to the economic success of other nations of the world. What is GNP? Gross national product is defined as the total dollar value of all final goods and services produced by a nation in one year.

Critical to a full understanding of gross national product are three basic concepts, the first of which is **nominal GNP.** GNP is reported in current or "nominal" dollar values; therefore, this basic figure is called nominal GNP. If a washing machine cost $200 last year, $200 was included in last year's GNP. If an identical washer were sold this year for $400, $400 would be added to this year's GNP even though half of the $400 total resulted from a price increase. In 1989 nominal GNP, the total dollar value of all goods and services produced in the United States, was $5,233.2 billion.

The second important consideration is that GNP includes the sale of only **final goods and services,** goods and services that are sold to ultimate users. Nonfinal, or **intermediate goods,** are those goods that are purchased either to be immediately resold or to be incorporated into other goods. For example, a tire sold to a car owner would be considered a final good and would be included in GNP. If, however, the tire were to be sold to either an auto manufacturer or to a tire store, it would be considered an intermediate good. If GNP included intermediate goods and services as well as final goods, it would significantly over report the nation's production for the year, since the good would be counted as part of GNP not only when it was purchased by the firm but also when it was resold to the ultimate consumer.

These fan blades are intermediate goods, which will become parts of other intermediate goods–automobile engines, which will become parts of final goods–General Motors cars.

Related to the concept of final goods and services is the problem of tabulating the value of unsold inventories. What happens when a car dealership purchases a new car to resell, but the car is not sold during the year? Just as the one left standing is the loser in a game of musical chairs, whatever business firm is holding unsold inventory at the end of the year is considered to be the ultimate consumer. Therefore, in our example, the automobile dealership would be considered the *final* purchaser.

The third element in the definition is that GNP includes only goods and services that have been produced during the past calendar year. This keeps used goods such as antiques, used cars, second-hand clothing, and so on, from being included in GNP year after year. If the sale of used goods were included in GNP, a nation could be experiencing a decline in production without knowing it.

How GNP Is Measured

Totaling the dollar value of everything that has been produced in a nation is not an easy task. It is not as if the government can hire workers to go out and physically count every good and service produced in the country each year. Economists have found, however, that they can arrive at a good estimate for GNP by adding up all of the purchases made by four basic economic groups: households, businesses, government, and foreign buyers.

Household Consumption–By far, household expenditures for consumer goods and services account for the greatest portion of the nation's total purchases. In 1989 households spent a total of $3,470.3 billion on consumer durable goods, nondurable goods, and services, more than three times what the government spent in the same period, and more than four times what private business spent.

Figure 11-1 GNP and the Circular Flow

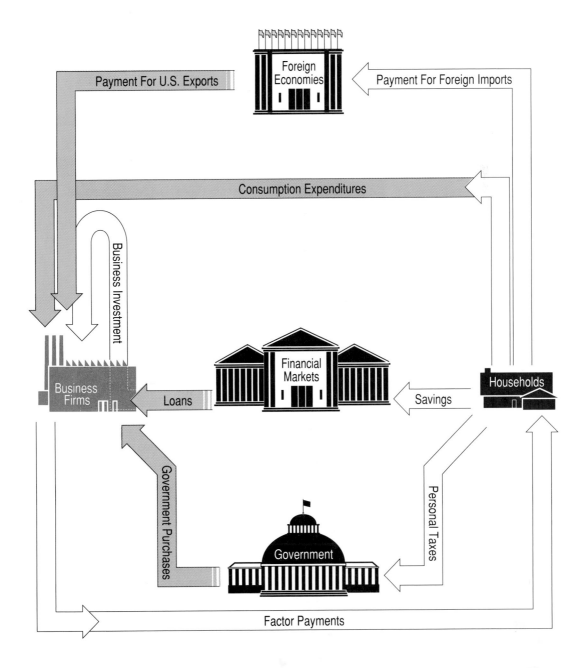

Figure 11-2 Nominal GNP by Type of Expenditure

personal consumption expenditures: 1989* (dollars in billions)

durable goods	$ 473.6
nondurable goods	1,122.6
services	1,874.1
	$3,470.3

plus gross private domestic investment:

fixed investment	$ 747.7
change in business inventories	29.4
	$ 777.1

plus government purchases of goods and services:

federal	$ 404.1
state and local	632.5
	$1,036.6

plus net exports of goods and services:

exports	$ 624.4
less imports	675.2
	$ -50.8

equals: nominal gross national product	$5,233.2

*Source: President's Council of Economic Advisors, Economic Report of the President (Washington, D.C.: Government Printing Office, 1990), Table C-1

Refrigerators and other major appliances are consumer durable goods.

In 1989 American households spent $473.6 billion on **consumer durable goods.** These are goods that have a life expectancy of more than one year. Consumer durable goods include cars, boats, furniture, and major appliances.

Consumer nondurable goods are those items that are expected to be worn out or used up within one year such as shoes, soap, and gasoline. Households spent $1,122.6 billion on nondurable goods in 1989.

The last of the three household consumption categories, **consumer services** is the largest. In 1989 consumers spent $1,874.1 billion on services. Consumer services include purchases such as haircuts, income tax preparation, and education. The reason for the great size of this category is that virtually every good sold requires some kind of economic service to accompany it.

Figure 11-3 illustrates how consumption spending as a percentage of total spending in the United States has changed. Notice how the percentage declined during World War II. During this period the U.S. government rationed many consumer goods, channeling a vast quantity of goods to military uses.

*Business Investment–*The second category of spending that economists consider when calculating GNP is **gross private domestic investment (GPDI).** GPDI, or **business investment** as it is frequently called, is the sum of all business spending on capital investment and unplanned inventories. In 1989 business firms spent $747.7 billion on capital investment, or purchases of factories and equipment. (Curiously, that amount spent on capital investment also includes purchases of newly constructed houses. Rather than including new

Figure 11-3 Household Consumption Spending as a Percentage of Nominal GNP, 1939-1989*

YEAR	NOMINAL GNP($BIL)	CONSUMPTION SPENDING ($BIL)	C. S. % GNP	YEAR	NOMINAL GNP($BIL)	CONSUMPTION SPENDING ($BIL)	C. S. % GNP
1939	$ 91.3	$ 97.0	73.4%	1965	$ 705.1	$ 440.7	62.5%
1940	100.4	71.0	70.7	1966	772.0	477.3	61.8
1941	125.5	80.8	64.4	1967	816.4	503.6	61.7
1942	159.0	88.6	55.7	1968	892.7	552.5	61.9
1943	192.7	99.5	51.6	1969	963.9	597.9	62.0
1944	211.4	108.2	51.2	1970	1,015.5	640.0	63.0
1945	213.4	119.6	56.0	1971	1,102.7	691.6	62.7
1946	212.4	143.9	67.7	1972	1,212.8	757.6	62.5
1947	235.2	161.9	68.8	1973	1,359.3	837.2	61.6
1948	261.6	174.9	66.9	1974	1,472.8	916.5	62.2
1949	260.4	178.3	68.5	1975	1,598.4	1,012.8	63.4
1950	288.3	192.1	66.6	1976	1,782.8	1,129.3	63.3
1951	333.4	208.1	62.4	1977	1,990.5	1,257.2	63.2
1952	351.6	219.1	62.3	1978	2,249.7	1,403.5	62.4
1953	371.6	232.6	62.6	1979	2,508.2	1,566.8	62.5
1954	372.5	239.8	64.4	1980	2,732.0	1,732.6	63.4
1955	405.9	257.9	63.5	1981	3,052.6	1,915.1	62.7
1956	428.2	270.6	63.2	1982	3,166.0	2,050.7	64.8
1957	451.0	285.3	63.3	1983	3,405.7	2,234.5	65.6
1958	456.8	294.6	64.5	1984	3,772.2	2,430.5	64.4
1959	495.8	316.3	63.8	1985	4,014.9	2,629.0	65.5
1960	515.3	330.7	64.2	1986	4,231.6	2,797.4	66.1
1961	533.8	341.1	63.9	1987	4,524.3	3,010.8	66.5
1962	574.6	361.9	63.0	1988	4,880.6	3,235.1	66.3
1963	606.9	381.7	62.9	1989	5,233.2	3,470.3	66.3
1964	649.8	409.3	63.0				

*Source: President's Council of Economic Advisors, Economic Report of the President (Washington, D.C.: Government Printing Office, 1990), Table C-1

houses under consumer durables, economists have chosen to consider such purchases as investments.) The second category within GPDI is investment in inventories that businesses purchased but were unable to resell by the end of the year. In 1989 unplanned inventory buildups added $29.4 billion to GPDI, bringing it to a total of $777.1 billion.

Figure 11-4 gives a historic look at gross private domestic investment. Notice that business investment, like consumer spending, fell dramatically during World War II from a prewar level of 14.6% of GNP to a low of 3.2%. This occurred as a result of several factors. First, consumer spending was limited due to rationing, making business investment in new factories and equipment unnec-

essary. Second, government was soaking up much of the nation's savings through wartime borrowing, crowding business firms out of the financial market. After the war, business investment immediately increased to an average of over 16% of GNP until 1951 in order to satisfy consumers' pent-up demands for previously rationed consumer goods.

Government Spending–Much of the goods and services produced in our country are purchased by local, state, and national governments. Indeed, in 1989, government purchases of goods and services accounted for $1,036.6 billion or nearly 20% of gross national product.

Stated differently, our federal, state, and local

Figure 11-4 Gross Private Domestic Investment as a Percentage of Nominal GNP, 1939 -1989*

YEAR	NOMINAL GNP($BIL)	GROSS PRIVATE DOMESTIC INVESTMENT ($BIL)	G. P. D. I. % GNP	YEAR	NOMINAL GNP($BIL)	GROSS PRIVATE DOMESTIC INVESTMENT ($BIL)	G. P. D. I. % GNP
1939	$ 91.3	$ 9.5	10.4 %	1965	$ 705.1	$ 116.2	16.5 %
1940	100.4	13.4	13.3	1966	772.0	128.6	16.7
1941	125.5	18.3	14.6	1967	816.4	125.7	15.4
1942	159.0	10.3	6.5	1968	892.7	137.0	15.3
1943	192.7	6.2	3.2	1969	963.9	153.2	15.9
1944	211.4	7.7	3.6	1970	1,015.5	148.8	14.7
1945	213.4	11.3	5.3	1971	1,102.7	172.5	15.6
1946	212.4	31.5	14.8	1972	1,212.8	202.0	16.7
1947	235.2	35.0	14.9	1973	1,359.3	238.8	17.6
1948	261.6	47.1	18.0	1974	1,472.8	240.8	16.3
1949	260.4	36.5	14.0	1975	1,598.4	219.6	13.7
1950	288.3	55.1	19.1	1976	1,782.8	277.7	15.6
1951	333.4	60.5	18.1	1977	1,990.5	344.1	17.3
1952	351.6	53.5	15.2	1978	2,249.7	416.8	18.5
1953	371.6	54.9	14.8	1979	2,508.2	454.8	18.1
1954	372.5	54.1	14.5	1980	2,732.0	437.0	16.0
1955	405.9	69.7	17.2	1981	3,052.6	515.5	16.9
1956	428.2	72.7	17.0	1982	3,166.0	447.3	14.1
1957	451.0	71.1	15.8	1983	3,405.7	502.3	14.7
1958	456.8	63.6	13.9	1984	3,772.2	664.8	17.6
1959	495.8	80.2	16.2	1985	4,014.9	643.1	16.0
1960	515.3	78.2	15.2	1986	4,231.6	659.4	15.6
1961	533.8	77.1	14.4	1987	4,524.3	699.9	15.5
1962	574.6	87.6	15.2	1988	4,880.6	750.3	15.4
1963	606.9	93.1	15.3	1989	5,233.2	777.1	14.8
1964	649.8	99.6	15.3				

*Source: President's Council of Economic Advisors, Economic Report of the President (Washington, D.C.: Government Printing Office, 1990), Table C-1

governments currently purchase about one of every five dollar's worth of products and services made in this country. Historically, government purchases have been rather small until the twentieth century. Government purchases reached an all-time high in 1943 (during World War II), when they accounted for 46% of GNP.

Net Exports–The final component needed to tabulate GNP involves the amount of goods sold to foreign nations. **Net exports** is the difference between the dollar amount a nation takes in from the sale of exports and the dollars which left the nation for the purchase of imports. If GNP calculations did not take net exports into account, the goods we would buy from other nations would be counted as part of our production when sold to the final con-

sumers. Subtracting imports, therefore, helps us determine a more accurate accounting for gross national product. In 1989 the United States experienced a trade balance of –$50.8 billion. That is, we purchased $50.8 billion more in goods from other nations than we sold abroad. Net exports added to household consumption, business investment, and government spending, accounted for all spending in a nation. Thus, GNP has been calculated. In 1989 GNP totaled $5,233.2 billion. The subject of exports and international trade will be further discussed later in this chapter.

Problems with GNP Measurement

GNP figures are supposed to tell economists and government officials how productive the U.S.

Figure 11-5 Government Purchases as a Percentage of Nominal GNP, 1939-1989*

YEAR	NOMINAL GNP($BIL)	GOVERNMENT PURCHASES ($BIL)	G. P. % GNP	YEAR	NOMINAL GNP($BIL)	GOVERNMENT PURCHASES ($BIL)	G. P. % GNP
1939	$ 91.3	$ 13.6	14.9 %	1965	$ 705.1	$138.6	19.7 %
1940	100.4	14.2	14.1	1966	772.0	158.6	20.5
1941	125.5	25.0	19.9	1967	816.4	179.7	22.0
1942	159.0	59.9	37.7	1968	892.7	197.7	22.1
1943	192.7	88.9	46.1	1969	963.9	207.3	21.5
1944	211.4	97.1	45.9	1970	1,015.5	218.2	21.5
1945	213.4	83.0	38.9	1971	1,102.7	232.4	21.1
1946	212.4	29.1	13.7	1972	1,212.8	250.0	20.6
1947	235.2	26.4	11.2	1973	1,359.3	266.5	19.6
1948	261.6	32.6	12.5	1974	1,472.8	299.1	20.3
1949	260.4	39.0	15.0	1975	1,598.4	335.0	21.0
1950	288.3	38.8	13.5	1976	1,782.8	356.9	20.0
1951	333.4	60.4	18.1	1977	1,990.5	387.3	19.5
1952	351.6	75.8	21.6	1978	2,249.7	425.2	18.9
1953	371.6	82.8	22.3	1979	2,508.2	467.8	18.7
1954	372.5	76.0	20.4	1980	2,732.0	530.3	19.4
1955	405.9	75.3	18.6	1981	3,052.6	388.1	19.3
1956	428.2	79.7	18.6	1982	3,166.0	641.7	20.3
1957	451.0	87.3	19.4	1983	3,405.7	675.0	19.8
1958	456.8	95.4	20.9	1984	3,772.2	735.9	19.5
1959	495.8	97.9	19.7	1985	4,014.9	820.8	20.4
1960	515.3	100.6	19.5	1986	4,231.6	872.2	20.6
1961	533.8	108.4	20.3	1987	4,524.3	926.1	20.5
1962	574.6	118.2	20.6	1988	4,880.6	968.9	19.9
1963	606.9	123.8	20.4	1989	5,233.2	1,036.6	19.8
1964	649.8	130.0	20.0				

*Source: President's Council of Economic Advisors, Economic Report of the President (Washington, D.C.: Government Printing Office, 1990), Table C-1

economy has been at any given time. That information helps them to make decisions concerning national economic policy. Economists have found, however, that GNP is not as precise a measuring tool as they hoped it would be.

Unrecorded Transactions–One of the reasons GNP does not perfectly measure the total wealth of the nation is that, contrary to its definition, it does not account for all final goods and services produced in the nation over the past year. Many goods and services produced in the country are not recorded because they were not sold for money, instead their transaction involved barter. A barter transaction is one in which goods or services are traded for other goods or services.

Some transactions go unrecorded because they are "do-it-yourself" activities. Obviously, if one owns a lawn-care business, the service provided to homeowners is counted as part of gross national product, but when a homeowner cuts his own grass rather than paying someone else to do it, the work is not counted as a part of GNP. The homeowner's services are just as real as those of the professional, but since no market transaction took place and no money changed hands, the services are not recorded in the national figures. Each year hundreds of millions of activities go unrecorded in the GNP figures as a result of productive home activities such as haircutting, housecleaning, painting, washing cars, and raising vegetables in a family garden.

Other unaccounted-for transactions include the production and sale of illegal goods and services.

Figure 11-6 Real GNP, 1939-1989*

YEAR	NOMINAL GNP($BIL)	GNP IMPLICIT PRICE DEFLATOR (1982=100)	REAL GNP ($BIL)	REAL GNP GROWTH	YEAR	NOMINAL GNP($BIL)	GNP IMPLICIT PRICE DEFLATOR (1982=100)	REAL GNP ($BIL)	REAL GNP GROWTH
1939	$ 91.3	12.74%	$ 716.6		1965	$ 705.1	33.78%	2,087.6	5.8%
1940	100.4	12.99	772.9	7.9%	1966	772.0	34.96	2,208.3	5.8
1941	125.5	13.80	909.4	17.7	1967	816.4	35.94	2,271.4	2.9
1942	159.0	14.72	1,080.3	18.8	1968	892.7	37.74	2,365.6	4.1
1943	192.7	15.10	1,276.2	18.1	1969	963.9	39.78	2,423.3	2.4
1944	211.4	15.31	1,380.6	8.2	1970	1,015.5	42.03	2,416.2	-0.3
1945	213.4	15.75	1,354.8	-1.9	1971	1,102.7	44.38	2,484.8	2.8
1946	212.4	19.36	1,096.9	-19.0	1972	1,212.8	46.49	2,608.5	5.0
1947	235.2	22.05	1,066.7	-2.8	1973	1,359.3	49.54	2,744.1	5.2
1948	261.6	23.60	1,108.7	3.9	1974	1,472.8	54.96	2,729.3	-0.5
1949	260.4	23.48	1,109.0	0.0	1975	1,598.4	59.31	2,695.0	-1.3
1950	288.3	23.95	1,203.7	8.5	1976	1,782.8	63.07	2,826.7	4.9
1951	333.4	25.10	1,328.2	10.3	1977	1,990.5	67.28	2,958.6	4.7
1952	351.6	25.48	1,380.0	3.9	1978	2,249.7	72.22	3,115.2	5.3
1953	371.6	25.89	1,435.3	4.0	1979	2,508.2	78.57	3,192.4	2.5
1954	372.5	26.30	1,416.2	-1.3	1980	2,732.0	85.72	3,187.1	-0.2
1955	405.9	27.15	1,494.9	5.6	1981	3,052.6	93.96	3,248.8	1.9
1956	428.2	28.07	1,525.6	2.1	1982	3,166.0	100.00	3,166.0	-2.5
1957	451.0	29.08	1,551.1	1.7	1983	3,405.7	103.86	3,279.1	3.6
1958	456.8	29.68	1,539.2	-0.8	1984	3,772.2	107.73	3,501.4	6.8
1959	495.8	30.43	1,629.1	5.8	1985	4,014.9	110.95	3,618.7	3.4
1960	515.3	30.94	1,665.3	2.2	1986	4,231.6	113.82	3,717.9	2.7
1961	533.8	31.24	1,708.7	2.6	1987	4,524.3	117.40	3,853.7	3.7
1962	574.6	31.93	1,799.4	5.3	1988	4,880.6	121.28	4,024.4	4.4
1963	606.9	32.40	1,873.3	4.1	1989	5,233.2	126.33	4,142.6	2.9
1964	649.8	32.93	1,973.3	5.3					

*Source: President's Council of Economic Advisors, Economic Report of the President (Washington, D.C.: Government Printing Office, 1990), Table C-1

Some transactions are left out of GNP figures because reporting them would invite arrest and imprisonment. Transactions of this type include drug trafficking, illegal gambling, blackmail, extortion, and the sale of illegal liquor.

Counterproductive Items—Besides many productive transactions or "goods" not added to GNP, there are also counterproductive items or "bads" that have not been subtracted from GNP. Bads are undesirable products or services such as water pollution, air pollution, and noise pollution. Many economists believe that when a firm produces a $100 good at the expense of $200 worth in damage to the environment, the nation's GNP should be *reduced* by $100. The problem with subtracting "bads" from GNP, however, is one of accurately measuring such environmental damages.

Inflation—Besides some goods and bads not being counted, inflation distorts GNP so that it does not reflect the true dollar value of the nation's production. Inflation is a situation in which virtually all prices are rising. Suppose you lived in a very small country that produced only shoes. Last year your nation produced and sold 1,000,000 pairs at $10 per pair. GNP therefore totaled $10,000,000. This year your country again produced 1,000,000 pairs, but inflation drove the price up to $20 per pair. GNP therefore will be reported as $20,000,000. To the casual observer GNP doubled, but to the economist GNP did not grow at all since no more actual goods were produced this year than last.

Economists have developed a way to factor in-

Figure 11-7 Per Capita Real GNP, 1939-1989

YEAR	REAL GNP($BIL)	POPULATION (THOUSANDS)	PER CAPITA REAL GNP ($BIL)	PER CAPITA REAL GNP GROWTH	YEAR	REAL GNP($BIL)	POPULATION (THOUSANDS)	PER CAPITA REAL GNP ($BIL)	PER CAPITA REAL GNP GROWTH
1939	$ 716.6	130,880	$ 5,475.20		1965	$2,087.6	194,303	$10,744.04	4.5 %
1940	772.9	132,122	5,849.90	6.8 %	1966	2,208.3	196,560	11,234.74	4.6
1941	909.4	133,402	6,816.99	16.5	1967	2,271.4	198,712	11,430.61	1.7
1942	1,080.3	134,860	8,010.53	17.5	1968	2,365.6	200,706	11,786.39	3.1
1943	1,276.2	136,739	9,333.11	16.5	1969	2,423.3	202,677	11,956.46	1.4
1944	1,380.6	138,397	9,975.65	6.9	1970	2,416.2	205,052	11,783.35	-1.4
1945	1,354.8	139,928	9,682.12	-2.9	1971	2,484.8	207,661	11,965.66	1.5
1946	1,096.9	141,389	7,758.03	-19.9	1972	2,608.5	209,896	12,427.58	3.9
1947	1,066.7	144,126	7,401.16	-4.6	1973	2,744.1	211,909	12,949.43	4.2
1948	1,108.7	146,631	7,561.16	2.2	1974	2,729.3	213,854	12,762.45	-1.4
1949	1,109.0	149,188	7,433.57	-1.7	1975	2,695.0	215,973	12,478.41	-2.2
1950	1,203.7	152,271	7,904.99	6.3	1976	2,826.7	218,035	12,964.43	3.9
1951	1,328.2	154,878	8,575.78	8.5	1977	2,958.6	220,239	13,433.59	3.6
1952	1,380.0	157,553	8,758.96	2.1	1978	3,115.2	222,585	13,995.55	4.2
1953	1,435.3	160,184	8,960.32	2.3	1979	3,192.4	225.055	14,184.98	1.4
1954	1,416.2	163,026	8,686.96	-3.1	1980	3,187.1	227,757	13,993.42	-1.4
1955	1,494.9	165,931	9,009.17	3.7	1981	3,248.8	230,138	14,116.75	0.9
1956	1,525.6	168,903	9,032.40	0.3	1982	3,166.0	232,520	13,616.03	-3.5
1957	1,551.1	171,984	9,018.86	-0.1	1983	3,279.1	234,799	13,965.56	2.6
1958	1,539.2	174,882	8,801.36	-2.4	1984	3,501.4	237,001	14,773.78	5.8
1959	1,629.1	177,830	9,161.00	4.1	1985	3,618.7	239,279	15,123.35	2.4
1960	1,665.3	180,671	9,217.31	0.6	1986	3,717.9	241,625	15,387.06	1.7
1961	1,708.7	183,691	9,302.03	0.9	1987	3,853.7	243,934	15,798.13	2.7
1962	1,799.4	186,538	9,646.29	3.7	1988	4,024.4	246,329	16,337.50	3.4
1963	1,873.3	189,242	9,898.97	2.6	1989	4,142.6	248,777	16,651.86	1.9
1964	1,973.3	191,889	10,283.55	3.9					

flation out of GNP in order to determine the true production of the economy. They divide nominal gross national product (GNP in today's dollars) by a factor called the **gross national product implicit price deflator** (GNP deflator). The GNP deflator is a price index that rises as the price of all goods and services rises. The result of this adjustment is a figure called **real GNP.** Figure 11-6 compares the nominal GNP to the real production of goods and services from 1939 through 1989.

To calculate the GNP deflator, government economists begin by choosing a base year in which a dollar is said to buy a dollar's worth of that year's goods. (In the case of Figure 11-6, the base year is 1982.) After the base year, surveyors are sent out to check the prices of all goods and services to see

if prices have generally risen or fallen. For example, in 1983 goods and services cost 3.86% more than in 1982 as indicated by 1983's deflator of 103.86%. Likewise, prices in 1988 were 21.28% higher than 1982's prices.

Changes in Population–By calculating real GNP, economists have developed a fairly accurate measure of the wealth of a nation, but the true measure of a nation's wealth is the nation's wealth per person. The United States economy may have produced 2.9% more goods and services in 1989 than in 1988, but if the American population increased by 3%, then the nation's *wealth per person* or **per capita real GNP** would actually have fallen.

Per capita real GNP is found by dividing the

Air pollution produced by industries is not a "good" but a "bad."

nation's real gross national product by its total population. Figure 11-7 gives a historical perspective of growth in per capita real GNP.

Section Review

1. What is nominal GNP?
2. What four economic groups determine a nation's GNP?
3. Household consumption involves what three kinds of purchases?
4. What kinds of transactions are not recorded as a part of GNP?

II. Foreign Trade

In 1989 the United States exported $624.4 billion but imported $675.2 billion in goods and services from foreign nations. The resulting $50.8 billion difference was carried on the U.S. books as a **trade deficit** or a "negative balance of trade." Had the United States sold $675.2 billion in goods and services while purchasing $624.4 billion worth, it would have had a "positive balance of trade" in the form of a $50.8 billion **trade surplus.**

From 1929 until 1983 the United States had only three years of trade deficits. Between 1983 and 1989, however, the United States experienced continual trade deficits, reaching a peak in 1987 at $123 billion. Though net exports currently account for a relatively low drain on total GNP, the trade deficit has been featured in news headlines for two reasons. First, when dollars flow out of the United States due to trade deficits, foreign jobs are increased at the expense of American jobs. Second, it is a blow to American prestige in the world to imagine another nation besides America able to produce either a better or a less costly product. Over the years it has become accepted to assume that the United States would dominate all meaningful markets, but as other nations of the world have progressed economically, they have been able to produce many goods more cheaply or of better quality. Americans, therefore, have become alarmed by the increase in international competition and the continuance of trade deficits.

Reasons for Trade Deficits

Foreign trade is a very sensitive issue in the United States. Some Americans argue that a trade deficit is damaging to the nation, while others believe that a negative trade balance helps the economy. Before examining philosophies of trade, it would help to look at the reasons that trade imbalances exist. What exactly causes positive or negative balances of trade? In other words, what causes someone to buy more from his neighbor than he sells to him? There are six main causes of trade imbalances:

Figure 11-8 Net Export's Percentage of Nominal GNP, 1939-1989*

YEAR	NOMINAL GNP($BIL)	NET EXPORTS ($BIL)	N. X. % GNP	YEAR	NOMINAL GNP($BIL)	NET EXPORTS ($BIL)	N. X. % GNP
1939	$ 91.3	$ 1.2	1.3%	1965	$ 705.1	$ 9.7	1.4 %
1940	100.4	1.8	1.8	1966	772.0	7.5	1.0
1941	125.5	1.5	1.2	1967	816.4	7.4	0.9
1942	159.0	0.2	0.1	1968	892.7	5.5	0.6
1943	192.7	-1.9	-1.0	1969	963.9	5.6	0.6
1944	211.4	-1.7	-0.8	1970	1,015.5	8.5	0.8
1945	213.4	-0.5	-0.2	1971	1,102.7	6.3	0.6
1946	212.4	7.8	3.7	1972	1,212.8	3.2	0.3
1947	235.2	11.9	5.1	1973	1,359.3	16.8	1.2
1948	261.6	7.0	2.7	1974	1,472.8	16.3	1.1
1949	260.4	6.5	2.5	1975	1,598.4	31.1	1.9
1950	288.3	2.2	0.8	1976	1,782.8	18.8	1.1
1951	333.4	4.5	1.3	1977	1,990.5	1.9	0.1
1952	351.6	3.2	0.9	1978	2,249.7	4.1	0.2
1953	371.6	1.3	0.3	1979	2,508.2	18.8	0.7
1954	372.5	2.6	0.7	1980	2,732.0	32.1	1.2
1955	405.9	3.0	0.7	1981	3,052.6	33.9	1.1
1956	428.2	5.3	1.2	1982	3,166.0	26.3	0.8
1957	451.0	7.3	1.6	1983	3,405.7	-6.1	-0.2
1958	456.8	3.3	0.7	1984	3,772.2	-58.9	-1.6
1959	495.8	1.5	0.3	1985	4,014.9	-78.0	-1.9
1960	515.3	5.9	1.1	1986	4,231.6	- 97.4	-2.3
1961	533.8	7.2	1.3	1987	4,524.3	-112.6	-2.5
1962	574.6	6.9	1.2	1988	4,880.6	- 73.7	-1.5
1963	606.9	8.2	1.4	1989	5,233.2	- 50.8	-1.0
1964	649.8	10.9	1.7				

*Source: President's Council of Economic Advisors, Economic Report of the President (Washington, D.C.: Government Printing Office, 1990), Table C-1

1. Domestic Inability to Produce

America has been forced to import certain products as a result of an inability to produce the same goods in any meaningful quantity. For example, since American businesses find it difficult to produce bananas, diamonds, coffee, and teakwood, America has become an importer of these goods.

2. Better Quality of Foreign Goods

Although domestic firms can manufacture an acceptable product, buyers may believe that, dollar for dollar, the competing foreign product is of higher quality. Consumers will therefore shun the domestically produced goods.

UNITED STATES OF AMERICA

3. Cheaper Foreign Materials

Some foreign producers, since they have a source of lower-cost raw materials, are able to manufacture and sell a product for a lower price than domestic competitors.

4. Lower Foreign Wages

Foreign competitors may be able to sell their products at lower prices because their nation's workers receive lower wages than do American workers. Foreign firms then pass along this savings to their international customers.

5. Lower Foreign Capital Costs

The governments of some foreign nations may attempt to foster the growth of certain industries through the provision of low-interest-rate loans and tax breaks to firms in those industries. This encouragement is referred to as **national industrial policy.** When a government engages in national industrial policy, it is enabling some business firms to purchase capital equipment at a lower overall cost, resulting in a lower-priced product that can compete more effectively in the world market.

6. Foreign Government Subsidies

Finally, some foreign competitors are able to sell their products at lower prices because their government taxes its citizens and pays the company a subsidy. That is, the nation's taxpayers make up for the lost profits a business firm experiences when it charges a price in America that is lower than the price the American producers charge.

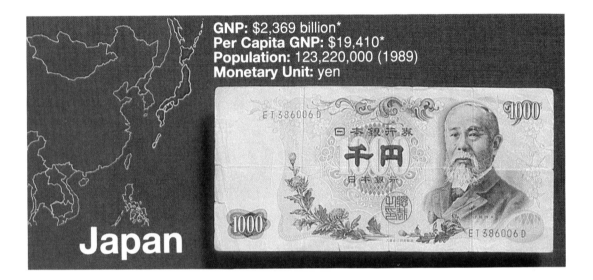

GNP: $2,369 billion*
Per Capita GNP: $19,410*
Population: 123,220,000 (1989)
Monetary Unit: yen

Japan

After Japan's defeat in World War II, Americans may have expected the island nation to develop into a smaller version of the United States with the same kind of democratic government and free capitalistic economy. However, modern Japan has definitely added some features of its own to become a leading, independent economic power. The government's Ministry of International Trade and Industry (MITI) has persistently promoted a national industrial policy that fosters the growth of large industries and foreign trade while also protecting small businessmen from foreign competition. Large Japanese businesses follow a system called "corporate paternalism" that allows them to demand long hours and unswerving loyalty from employees in return for modest but secure rewards. The concerted push for peak production, high quality, and heavy trade has made Japanese industry extremely prosperous.

The Japanese people have contributed to economic prosperity by their industriousness and their penchant for saving. With an average household savings rate of 18.3%, the Japanese save nearly three times as much of their incomes as do Americans. The Japanese generally live in cramped housing with minimal comforts, but their savings provide capital for Japanese businesses to flourish. Also, the Japanese persistently seek new technology and new markets abroad in efforts to expand their industries further.

In recent years the rise of Japanese economic influence and the growth of large trade deficits with Japan have made Americans uneasy. Some believe that governmental support for Japanese industry and trade has given the Japanese an unfair advantage in the marketplace. Others contend that Americans simply have not learned to work as efficiently, save as faithfully, or seek new markets as effectively as do their Japanese counterparts. This unsettled debate over Japanese-American trade remains a prominent economic problem.

*figures for 1987 from the 1990 *Statistical Abstract*

John Stuart Mill (1806-1873)
Economic Philosopher

Commonly regarded as the greatest economist of his day, John Stuart Mill had an extraordinary upbringing. His father, James Mill, a notable British historian and philosopher, became the child's teacher and exposed him to a broad education. At age three John began to learn Greek, and by the time he was seven he had read much classical Greek literature. At eight, Mill began his studies in Latin, and by age twelve he had studied most of the Roman classics. In addition, he had studied geometry, algebra, calculus, and logic. The next year he took up the study of political economy, devouring all that had been written on the subject up to that time. These studies were supplemented as the youth sat in on many conversations with the friends of Mill's father. These friends included the eminent economists and philosophers of that day such as David Ricardo and Jeremy Bentham.

Mill analyzed contemporary economic thought and, while upholding most classical theories, advanced the idea that society did not have the ability to alter its economic production capabilities, but it did have the ability to alter the way it distributed its economic products. In his major economic work, *The Principles of Political Economy,* Mill detailed the principles that governments should follow to control the distribution of wealth. Mill also argued in support of individual freedom and advocated social reforms such as shorter working hours and tax reform. Although many of Mill's specific economic prescriptions have been outdated by the changes of the last century, his work served as a foundation for many of the advances of later economists.

Trade Policy, Protectionism, and Free Trade

In the area of foreign trade, two distinct groups have appeared on the American scene: **protectionists** and those who advocate **free trade.**

Protectionists believe that trade deficits lead to a decrease in the number of American jobs; so they wish to protect those jobs through trade legislation. First, they support limitations on the quantity of

A Petition

Frederic Bastiat (1801-1850) was a Frenchman whose writings attacked the growth of socialistic thought in nineteenth-century France. As an economist and statesman, he argued against policies of protectionism and other increased governmental controls of the economy. The following excerpt from one of his works views the protectionist-free trade debate with a satire that continues to be apropos.

From the Manufacturers of Candles, Tapers, Lanterns, Candlesticks, Street Lamps, Snuffers, and Extinguishers, and from the producers of Tallow, Oil, Resin, Alcohol, and Generally of Everything Connected with Lighting.

To the Honorable Members of the Chamber of Deputies.

We are suffering from the ruinous competition of a foreign rival who apparently works under conditions so far superior to our own for the production of light that he is flooding the domestic market with it at an incredibly low price; for the moment he appears, our sales cease, all the consumers turn to him, and a branch of French industry whose ramifications are innumerable is all at once reduced to complete stagnation. This rival, which is none other than the sun, is waging war on us so mercilessly that we suspect he is being stirred up against us. . . .

We ask you to be so good as to pass a law requiring the closing of all windows, dormers, skylights, inside and outside shutters, curtains, casements, bull's-eyes, deadlights, and blinds—in short, all openings, holes, chinks, and fissures through which the light of the sun is wont to enter houses, to the detriment of the fair industries with which, we are proud to say, we have endowed the country, a country that cannot, without betraying ingratitude, abandon us today to so unequal a combat. . . .

When a product—coal, iron, wheat, or textiles—comes to us from abroad, and when we can acquire it for less labor than if we produced it ourselves, the difference is a *gratuitous gift* that is conferred upon us. The size of this gift is proportionate to the extent of this difference. It is a quarter, a half, or three-quarters of the value of the product if the foreigner asks of us only three-quarters, one-half, or one-quarter as high a price. It is as complete as it can be when the donor, like the sun in providing us with light, asks nothing from us. The question, and we pose it formally, is whether what you desire for France is the benefit of consumption free of charge or the alleged advantages of onerous production. Make your choice, but be logical; for as long as you ban, as you do, foreign coal, iron, wheat, and textiles, *in proportion* as their price approaches *zero,* how inconsistent it would be to admit the light of the sun, whose price is zero all day long!

Source: Frederic Bastiat, *Economic Sophisms,* Irvington-on-Hudson (New York: The Foundation for Economic Education, Inc., 1964)

certain goods that foreign nations may import into the United States. To use a simple example, suppose Americans purchase 1 million motorcycles per year and American motorcycle manufacturers are able to produce only 100,000; then protectionists would support legislation to limit the number of imported motorcycles to 900,000. Protectionists believe that by limiting the number of imported motorcycles, jobs at American manufacturing plants would be saved and the American unemployment rate would not rise. Second, many protectionists support using the power of taxation to limit imports. If an American motorcycle costs $2,500 while a foreign model of equal quality costs $2,000, many protectionists would support a tax greater than $500 on each imported unit. The American product, which was formerly undesirable because of its relatively higher price, would become relatively less costly and would therefore become the purchaser's first choice.

Those who believe in free trade, on the other hand, believe that the consumer, not the producer, is of paramount importance and that trade deficits do not automatically lead to higher levels of unemployment. Free traders believe that protectionism is a thinly disguised return to the mercantilist policies of the seventeenth and eighteenth centuries. Under mercantilism the wealth of a nation was believed to be increased if it sold more goods than it purchased. Free traders agree that protectionist legislation would, in our example, increase employment in the American motorcycle manufacturing industry, but a decrease in the *overall* American unemployment rate would not necessarily follow. For example, advocates of free trade point out that if laws were passed limiting the quantity of imported foreign motorcycles, many American dockworkers would become unemployed, since fewer motorcycles would need to be offloaded from foreign ships. American salesmen and service technicians who sell and service the foreign product in the United States would lose their jobs as well. In addition, if Americans cease buying foreign goods, foreigners will not acquire the dollars they need to purchase American goods, purchases that increase employment in the United States.

Free traders believe that increasing taxes on imports, the protectionist's second method of attack, will have the same effect. Previously, when Americans purchased the less expensive foreign motorcycles, they had more money left over to purchase other products. Making the foreign product more expensive in order to force Americans to buy the American motorcycles would eliminate the jobs supported by those dollars that were previously left over. Free traders believe that in the long run, protectionist legislation passed by Congress has a tendency to save jobs in targeted industries only by redistributing the unemployment to other industries.

The issue of foreign trade is and will always be one which stirs up great emotion, for it strikes at the pride of a nation. Whether, therefore, a nation should undertake protectionist trade policies or allow the free market to rule will be a subject for debate decades from now. What, then, is the correct policy? As you recall, the science of economics is the science of making choices; so it is important for us to make the wisest choice regarding trade. Other things being equal, free trade tends to be the better alternative since free trade tends to be the policy which lends itself to the lowest prices to consumers.

1. Those domestic industries that are not competitive with their foreign rivals will be the ones that experience unemployment. Under protectionism innocent industries are the ones that suffer.
2. Buyers are free to make choices based on unpolluted information. Although some protectionists argue that high taxes on foreign goods are helpful, they are, nevertheless, arguing in favor of *forcing* buyers to act in a manner contrary to their own best interests.

Section Review

1. What is a trade deficit?
2. Why might a nation experience a trade deficit?
3. What two groups have differing opinions on the subject of international trade?

Chapter Review

Terms

gross national product (GNP)
nominal GNP
final goods and services
intermediate goods
consumer durable goods
consumer nondurable goods
consumer services
gross private domestic investment (GPDI)
business investment
net exports
GNP implicit price deflator (GNP deflator)
real GNP
per capita real GNP
trade deficit
trade surplus
national industrial policy
protectionists
free trade

Content Questions

1. Define gross national product.
2. What is the difference between a final good and an intermediate good?
3. Why are used goods that are resold in a later year not included in GNP for that year?
4. What is GPDI?
5. What are the four complications that lead to inaccuracies in GNP figures?
6. What two methods do protectionists advocate for reducing trade deficits?
7. Why do those who advocate free trade believe protectionism to be ineffective or harmful to the economy?

Application Questions

1. What are some reasons that the gross national product tends to increase each year?
2. Can you think of any ways in which the government or business firms may use gross national product information?
3. Given the following figures from 1980 (in billions of dollars), compute the real per capita GNP for that year.

Purchases of consumer durables	$219.3
Purchases of consumer nondurables	681.4
Purchases of consumer services	831.9
Capital investment	445.3
Inventory investment	−8.3
Government purchases	530.3
Exports	351.0
Imports	318.9
GNP deflator	85.7%
U.S. population	222,757,000
	(0.222757 billion)

4. If you worked for an American car company, how would you react to news that Congress was passing protectionist legislation in behalf of American automobile manufacturers? What would you expect to be the ramifications of this action? Explain your answers.

CHAPTER 12 _____

The Business Cycle and Unemployment

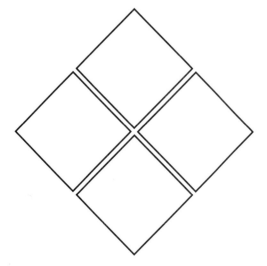

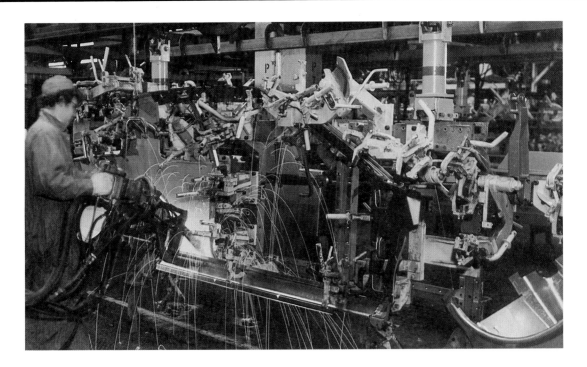

Put not your trust in princes, nor in the son of man, in whom there is no help.

Psalm 146:3

I. The Business Cycle

Because of current earthshaking economic events most people tend to think that the U.S. economy has been relatively stable until recent years. In actuality our economy has been consistently volatile, experiencing periodic ups and downs in business activity. This **business cycle,** as it is called, consists of alternating periods of rising and falling real GNP known as expansion, peak, recession, and trough.

Phases of the Business Cycle

Expansion and Peak Phases–During the **expansion phase** of the business cycle, the nation's gross national product rises, the number of available jobs grows, the unemployment rate falls, and national income expands.

Another characteristic of the expansion phase is an increase in credit purchases because people feel more financially secure and self-satisfied. God warns his people that during times of economic expansion and financial prosperity they should be careful to give God the glory.

Lest when thou hast eaten and art full, and hast built goodly houses, and dwelt therein; And when thy herds and thy flocks multiply, and thy silver and thy gold is multiplied, and all that thou hast is multiplied; Then thine heart be lifted up, and thou forget the Lord thy God, which brought thee forth out of the land of Egypt, from the house of bondage. And thou say in thine heart, My power and the might of mine hand hath gotten me this wealth.   (Deuteronomy 8:12-14, 17)

Eventually, after running its expansionary course, the economy will reach its **peak phase,** which signals a halt to rapid expansion. A nation's economy cannot continually boom. While it is possible for a particular country's GNP to increase year after year, it is not possible to sustain the rapid *rate of growth* the economy achieves during the expansion. Three factors act as a ceiling, preventing further rapid growth: limited raw materials, limited labor, and limited financial capital.

First, as the economy expands, sales of virtually all goods hit record levels. To replenish their inventories, stores flood factories with more orders than can be filled. Factories then ration their limited products by raising their prices. Stores in turn are forced to pass along these higher prices to their customers.

Second, the expanding economy causes the price of labor to rise. To meet the demand for additional products, firms must enter the labor market to hire more employees. Because prior economic expansion has lowered the unemployment rate, firms are forced to lure workers from competing companies with promises of larger paychecks. As the firms increase the wages they pay, they are forced to push the price of their goods even higher.

A third factor putting upward pressure on consumer prices is an increase in the costs businesses must pay to borrow money. As demand for goods and services continues to rise, banks are flooded with demands from businesses for loans. Fast-food restaurants need new equipment, steel companies desperately need new factories, and retail firms are frantic to build new store buildings. The pressure on the limited amount of lendable funds eventually forces banks to charge a higher interest rate to ration the scarce funds.

The peak of the business cycle is therefore characterized by shortages in natural resources, high wages, low unemployment, and rising interest rates, all of which combine to create higher prices for consumers.

Recession and Trough Phases–Eventually prices of goods and services rise to a point where consumers are no longer willing to purchase greater and greater quantities. This change in consumer attitude is the turning point in the economy and the beginning of the **recessionary phase.** During a recession consumers gradually adjust their spending habits.

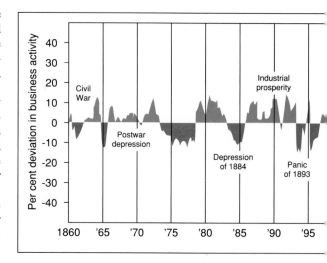

The first type of purchase to decline is that of "big ticket" consumer durable goods such as new homes, automobiles, and major appliances. Consumers demand fewer of these because they are usually purchased on credit. With buyers becoming uncertain of their future ability to repay loans, they decide to wait until the future looks brighter to purchase these more expensive goods. As sales of such items decline, suppliers cut their prices to sell excess inventory. Factory owners, finding their

Figure 12-2 Business Cycle

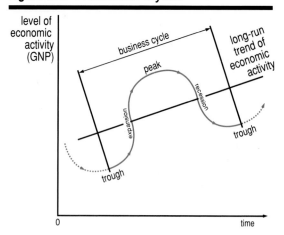

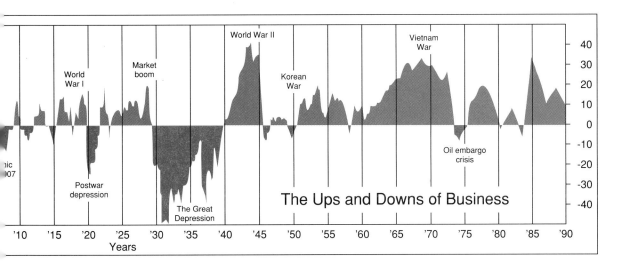

The Ups and Downs of Business

World War II

Vietnam War

World War I

Market boom

Korean War

Postwar depression

The Great Depression

Oil embargo crisis

ıic 907

40
30
20
10
0
-10
-20
-30
-40

'10 '15 '20 '25 '30 '35 '40 '45 '50 '55 '60 '65 '70 '75 '80 '85 '90

Years

warehouses full of unwanted inventory, see little need to continue producing more and are forced to lay off workers.

As floating survivors of a sinking ship are pulled under by the suction of a sinking vessel, virtually all businesses are caught in the whirlpool caused by a declining durable goods market. As fewer new homes are sold, the sales of furniture, carpet, lumber, glass, electricity, cookware, stereo systems, paint, and even light bulbs will decline. This decline puts even more people on the unemployment line. Eventually a downward spiral develops; those who find themselves unemployed reduce their spending, causing even greater unemployment.

Eventually the bottom of the cycle is reached. If economic conditions are especially bad and prolonged, this **trough phase** is called a **depression.** The trough phase is characterized by low prices, a high unemployment rate, and depressed incomes.

Causes of the Business Cycle

Economists know that the economy moves in cycles, but they do not fully understand why. Many believe that if they could determine why the cycles exist, they might be able to smooth them out by eliminating the frantic peaks and miserable troughs.

An economic decline can bring industrial expansion to a grinding halt.

When the bottom of the recession phase is severe, as it was in the 1930s, it is referred to as a depression.

Sunspot Theory–One of the first and most bizarre explanations of the business cycle was put forth by William Jevons. In 1875, after years of observations, Jevons, the discoverer of the principle of diminishing marginal utility, became convinced that sunspots had a significant impact on the business activity of England. He noted that with remarkable regularity, shortly after sunspots appeared, business activity tended to fall. While at first Jevons's sunspot theory seemed laughable, it actually had some logical basis. Jevons reasoned that sunspots, which are violent nuclear explosions on the surface of the sun, alter earth's weather patterns, causing changes in agricultural yields, dramatically affecting the economies of nations heavily oriented toward agriculture.

Psychological Theory–As time progressed and reliance upon agriculture diminished, a better explanation for business cycles was needed. Economists abandoned the search for physical causes, choosing instead to look for psychological reasons. Many of us know what it is like to have a bad day on the basketball court, golf green, tennis court, or baseball diamond. Once a player loses confidence in his abilities, problems begin to compound, further affecting his performance. Likewise, the psychological theory of business cycles attributes cyclical economic behavior to the degree of confidence people have in their economy. According to this theory, the people of a nation feel that when the economy is at its peak, prosperity cannot continue indefinitely. Upon the first hint of economic decline, they postpone major purchases out of fear for their future economic security. This action profoundly affects the economy by causing sales, profits, and income to tumble and setting in motion a downward spiral as unstoppable as a roller coaster in its first plunge. When incomes and prices finally hit bottom, the consumer decides that things cannot become worse. At this point people begin to make purchases, which in turn raises national income and employment.

Monetary Theory–A third, and possibly most logical, explanation for the business cycle regards the effect that changes in the money supply have on prices and interest rates. According to the monetary theory, the expansion phase is fueled by increases in the money supply. As the growth of the money supply outstrips the growth of the nation's production of goods and services, prices rise as products are rationed by the market. Since demand for goods is increasing, business firms are desperate to borrow additional money to build new factories and stores. The financial market accommodates this need since, as you may recall from Chapter 10, increases in the money supply push interest rates down to deceptively low levels. (See p. 159.) Prices continue to soar as demand exceeds the limits of natural resources and labor markets. Eventually the explosive growth in the money supply is halted, leaving prices high. Unable to sell the higher priced goods, the economy begins to stall, soon to plunge into the recessionary spiral.

Proponents of the monetary explanation of business cycles point to examples in U.S. history, examples including the Panic of 1837, a severe recession that followed the Bank Credit Land Boom of 1835. The 1849 California gold rush prosperity was followed by the Panic of 1857. The money-expanding Silver Purchase Act of 1872 was followed by a prolonged depression lasting from 1873 until 1878. The ''easy'' money period of the Gold Resumption of 1878 was followed by a depression in 1884. In the mid 1920s, the Fed fueled inflation, only to apply the monetary brakes in 1929, leading to the financial panic of October 1929, which heralded the Great Depression.

Section Review

1. What is the business cycle?
2. What are the four phases of the business cycle?
3. What occurs when the economy reaches the peak of its business cycle?
4. What three theories attempt to explain the business cycle?

The hardships of the Great Depression sent many desperate Americans to the West in search of employment.

II. Unemployment

Historically the two major swings in the business cycle are associated with two major economic problems. Recessionary downswings in the economy are associated with growing unemployment while upswings in business activity are equated with inflation's rising prices. The remainder of this chapter will examine the problem of unemployment, and Chapter 13 will then take a closer look at inflation.

I have six little children to take care of. I have been out of work for over a year and a half.

Am back almost thirteen months and the landlord says if I don't pay up before the 1 of 1932 out I must go, and where am I to go in the cold winter with my children? If you can help me please for God's sake and the children's sakes and like please do what you can and send me some help, will you, I cannot find any work. I am willing to take any kind of work if I could get it now. Thanksgiving dinner was black coffee and bread and was very glad to get it. My wife is in the hospital now. We have no shoes to were [sic]; no clothes hardly. Oh what will I do I sure will thank you.

Source: Milton Meltzer, *Brother, Can You Spare a Dime? The Great Depression 1929-1933* (Alfred A. Knopf, Inc., 1969), p. 103.

The foremost problem associated with the downside of the business cycle is an increase in unemployment. This fact is sharply illustrated by the above passage, taken from a letter written by an unemployed worker to the governor of Pennsylvania. Perhaps one of the greatest blessings God gave mankind was the ability to work.

Every man also to whom God hath given riches and wealth, and hath given him power to eat thereof, and to take his portion, and to rejoice in his labour; this is the gift of God.

(Ecclesiastes 5:19)

When a person is not able to take advantage of God's gift of laboring, the results can be tragic; but when an entire nation experiences high levels of joblessness, the consequences can be truly devastating. As nations experience long periods of joblessness, economists have noted sharp increases in spouse and child abuse, suicides, heart attacks, divorces, homicides, and psychological disorders. Unemployment can also have other tragic long-term effects. The longer a person remains unemployed, the greater is his loss of future productivity as his skills deteriorate, reducing his employability further. As unemployment continues, savings accounts that were set up for retirement are depleted for present consumption, leaving a generation of senior citizens to face the specter of hunger and deprivation in their old age. Because of these and many other reasons, economists seek methods to lower the unemployment rate.

Thomas Sowell (1930-)
Controversial Economist

A high school dropout raised in North Carolina and the Harlem ghetto, Thomas Sowell succeeded in "pulling himself up by his bootstraps." He eventually joined the marines, and after his enlistment was up, Sowell used the provisions of the GI Bill to help him go to Harvard, Columbia, and the University of Chicago to earn a Ph.D. in economics. Meanwhile, Sowell's economic philosophy took an about-face from an espousal of Marxist thought to a firm support for capitalism.

Sowell began a prolific writing career in 1971 that resulted in books not only on economics but also on education, law, and racial issues. His writings won the admiration of many of his fellow economists and political philosophers. His most noted and most controversial work dealt with race and economics. Sowell believes that government civil rights activities in recent decades have led to policies that are harmful to American blacks. Sowell thinks that affirmative action and other governmental meddling in the social process has simply made blacks dependent on government and has discouraged personal improvement. Sowell has taken much criticism from black leaders who want increased government aid and protection for the interests of their community. Nonetheless, Thomas Sowell can point to the hard work that took him from the ghetto to academic accomplishment without preferential treatment because of his color.

The Unemployment Rate

Before the unemployment rate can be controlled, it must be measured. The **unemployment rate** is the percentage of the labor force that is not employed but is looking for work. To calculate the unemployment rate, the United States Bureau of Labor Statistics separates the population into two groups. The first is made up of those who are under sixteen or over sixty-four years of age, those who are in the armed forces, and those who are institutionalized in schools, prisons, or asylums. These people are not counted in labor statistics.

The second group comprises the majority of the U.S. population and commands the attention of economists. This group is made up of those between sixteen and sixty-four years of age who are

Figure 12-3

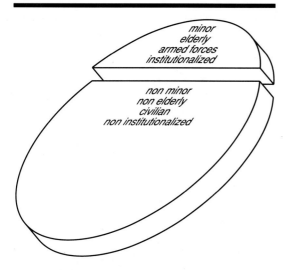

Figure 12-4

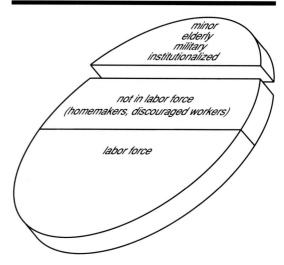

neither in the armed forces nor institutionalized. This major segment of the population is itself composed of two subgroups: those in the labor force and those not in the labor force.

The **labor force** is composed of the employed, those persons who are working, and the unemployed, those who are actively looking for a job. Those people who are not in the labor force are there for one of two reasons. First, some are there by choice, such as homemakers who have chosen not to work outside the home. Second, some people have been out of work for six months or longer, and the government assumes they have stopped looking for work. These chronically unemployed people are called **discouraged workers.**

The *unemployment rate,* therefore, is the number of unemployed people divided by the total number of those in the labor force. According to Figure 12-6, the unemployment rate in 1989 was roughly 5.3% of the labor force.

The unemployment rate is a very important number to economists and politicians. Increases in the unemployment rate create concern that the United States is slipping into recession, while declines in the unemployment rate may indicate upswings in the economy.

Figure 12-5

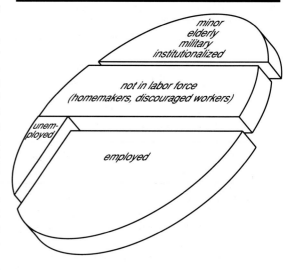

Flaws in Unemployment Statistics

Because government spending policies are based on unemployment information provided by

Figure 12-6 U.S. Unemployment Statistics, 1989*

total U.S. population (in thousands)	248,777
less: military, institutionalized, or those less than 16 years of age	62,384
equals: civilian noninstitutionalized adult population	186,393
less: those not in the labor force	62,524
equals: labor force	123,869
less: those employed	117,342
equals: those unemployed	6,527
divided by: labor force	123,869
equals: unemployed rate	5.26%

*Source: President's Council of Economic Advisors, Economic Report of the President (Washington, D.C.: Government Printing Office, 1990), Table C-32

Figure 12-7a

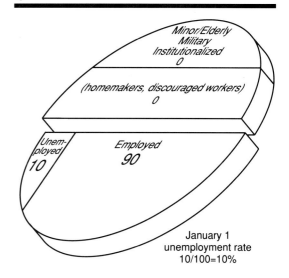

January 1
unemployment rate
10/100=10%

Figure 12-7b

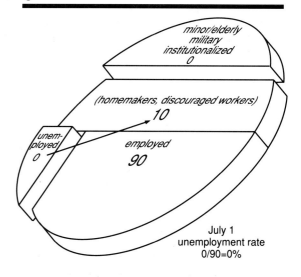

July 1
unemployment rate
0/90=0%

the Bureau of Labor Statistics, it is very important that unemployment figures be accurate. Unfortunately, the following discrepencies in unemployment statistics paint a faulty picture of joblessness in the United States.

1. **Many people work but are not counted as being employed.** If a person is a homemaker, is in the armed forces, is a student working his way through school, or is a prisoner on work release, he is not counted in employment statistics.

2. **Some people do not work and are not included in unemployment statistics.** Even though discouraged workers are not working, they are not counted as unemployed. This omission tends to give the casual observer a false impression of the state of the economy. For example, look at Figures 12-7 and notice that in our hypothetical economy the unemployment rate is 10%. Let us assume that all of those who are unemployed lost their jobs on January 1. Let us further assume that all of those unemployed persons are unsuccessful in finding jobs. On July 1 these unemployed persons will all be labeled discouraged workers. This new labelling causes the unemployment

rate to fall to a deceptively low 0%, since all of those now in the labor force are working.

3. **Some people are counted as being employed but are actually underemployed.** The government considers someone employed if he works without pay fifteen hours per week in a family-owned business or at least one hour per week for pay. It is possible for someone earning a wage of $4.25 per hour to be counted as employed while working only fifty-two hours per year. At that rate the person would earn an annual income of less than $225!

4. **Some who are counted as unemployed do have jobs.** If one has been laid off his job for a very short period of time or has signed a contract to go to work but has not yet begun, he is still counted as being unemployed.

Returning now to our original question of what is unemployment, we can see that unemployment is very narrowly defined by the government as something that happens only to persons between the ages of sixteen and sixty-four: these persons are neither in the armed forces nor institutionalized in schools, prisons, or asylums, have not been without work longer than six months, and are actively looking for work.

Types of Unemployment

Why are people unemployed? Economists have sought to answer this question in the hope that some solution may be found to the problem of unemployment and the economic problems that are associated with joblessness.

Frictional Unemployment–Many are unemployed simply because they are temporarily between jobs. These people experience what is known as **frictional unemployment.** Some have voluntarily left a previous job to seek one that pays more money or that better suits their desires. Others have been laid off or fired. Each month about one out of every twenty employees will quit his job, be laid off, or be fired. Whatever the reason, it takes time to locate another job, time during which the person is unemployed.

Is frictional unemployment bad for an economy? Not necessarily. Frictional unemployment demonstrates that the labor market is competitive. It is evidence that workers have the freedom to leave a job if they think they are not being paid what their skills are worth. Likewise, it shows that employers have the freedom to replace employees with more productive workers. Some socialist nations have boasted of having a 0% unemploy-

Industrial plant workers laid off during an economic downturn are listed among the unemployed.

ment rate. If such claims were true, then every worker must have been satisfied with his job and would not leave it to find another, the workers were not allowed to quit and change jobs, or those who reported the statistics were not telling the truth.

Structural Unemployment–**Structural unemployment** occurs when a worker's skills do not match available jobs. Structural unemployment may occur for at least two reasons. First, change in industrial needs may make certain job skills obsolete. For example, blacksmiths in the early part of this century found themselves structurally unemployed when the automobile came into use. A second reason for structural unemployment is that some people have never developed the skills necessary for existing jobs. This group may include unskilled people such as high school dropouts. Of course, some employers provide training for unskilled new employees, but in many cases the cost of training new workers exceeds the revenue the employee could bring into the firm.

Seasonal Unemployment–A certain number of those in the unemployment lines of America are out of jobs because of seasonal factors. As the seasons change, certain jobs are created while others are eliminated. Many construction workers lose their jobs at the onset of winter, while jobs involving the sales of winter products such as snow tires, Christmas decorations, and winter clothing are created. Another type of **seasonal unemployment** is created when the labor force is seasonally decreased, as when students over sixteen years of age leave the work force after the summer to return to school. Seasonal unemployment in one sector tends to balance seasonal employment in another, so that overall seasonal unemployment tends to be negligible.

Cyclical unemployment–The down side of the business cycle causes **cyclical unemployment**. As the economy slides into a recession, sales decline, leading to layoffs of workers nationwide.

Unemployment and the Government

The United States Congress, noting the recessions that followed previous wartime expansions and fearing that the soldiers returning from combat in World War II would be coming home to a life of unemployment, passed the Employment Act of 1946. This legislation declared that it

is the continuing policy and responsibility of the Federal Government to use all practicable means consistent with its needs and obligations and other essential considerations of national policy, with assistance and cooperation of industry, agriculture, labor and State and local governments, to coordinate and utilize all its plans, functions, and resources for the purpose of creating and maintaining in a manner calculated to foster free and competitive enterprise and the general welfare, conditions under which there will be afforded useful employment opportunities, including self-employment, for those able, willing, and seeking to work and to promote maximum employment, production, and purchasing power.

In other words, Congress declared that the federal government's number one priority was maximum employment. The Employment Act of 1946 lacked clear goals; therefore, three decades later, Congress, fearing a fresh bout of recession, passed the Full Employment and Balanced Growth Act of 1978 as an amendment to its previous legislation. The Humphrey-Hawkins Act, as it was later called, proposed specific goals for government control of unemployment and inflation. For example, Congress decreed that by 1983 the unemployment rate should be 4% of the labor force, and the inflation rate should be 3%. (They were actually 9.6 % and 3.8%, respectively, that year.) Congress further declared that the inflation rate should be 0% by 1988.

Realizing that both national and local governments desire to prevent joblessness, what can the government actually do to reduce the rate of unemployment? The answer, unfortunately, is "not much." Frictional unemployment–unemployment experienced by persons temporarily between jobs–theoretically could be reduced by the development of more efficient procedures for bringing job seekers and employers together. Attempts have been made to do this through the establishment of local

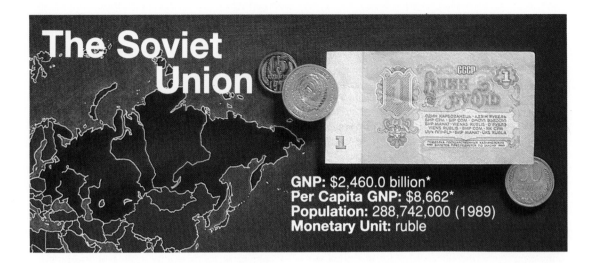

The Soviet Union

GNP: $2,460.0 billion*
Per Capita GNP: $8,662*
Population: 288,742,000 (1989)
Monetary Unit: ruble

Vladimir Lenin and his new Communist dictatorship imposed socialism on Russia following the 1917 revolution. The civil war strife combined with the lack of incentive for production soon brought severe shortages to the nation and pressured Lenin to reinstate some capitalistic measures in his "New Economic Policy" (NEP). Lenin's successor, Joseph Stalin, quickly eradicated most capitalistic practices and erected a strictly planned socialist economy. State-controlled production was based on government-decreed five-year plans. The Soviet government continued this regimented economy, diverting large amounts of resources to military and industrial build-up while neglecting the production of adequate amounts of consumer goods.

Faced with continual shortages, long lines in the marketplace, and discontent among consumers, Mikhail Gorbachev instituted economic reforms after his rise to power in 1985. His *perestroika* or "restructuring" of the Soviet economy once again introduced some capitalistic incentives to boost efficiency in production. By 1990 the changes occurring in Eastern Europe and the continued problems of the Soviet Union prompted Gorbachev to take even more dramatic steps. The proposed acceptance of private property and dissolution of one-party rule may have opened the way

for further economic reforms that may bring profound change to the nation.

Traditionally, socialists condemned capitalist countries for allowing unemployment to occur. The Soviets often boasted of their zero unemployment level, which supposedly insured that all Soviet workers were employed, regardless of other economic consequences. By the late 1980s changing economic and political conditions opened some of the Soviet Union to Western scrutiny, and these glimpses revealed that their land was not free of the scourge of unemployment. In fact, conditions in the troubled Soviet republic of Uzbekistan had reached a point where as many as 1.5 million people in that region alone were unemployed. Denying that unemployment existed, the Soviet government was not equipped to handle the problem through relief measures, and neither could the unemployed Soviets simply pack up and move to areas where more jobs existed. Government controls made such movement virtually impossible. As a result, the Soviet government faced a growing problem of joblessness in addition to the other economic and political woes that beset the troubled Communist regime.

*figures for 1987 from the 1990 *Statistical Abstract*

Government employment offices seek to reduce frictional unemployment.

employment security commission offices, which act as central clearinghouses of job information and financial assistance. Though such programs may be helpful, most jobs are located by the jobless themselves without governmental assistance.

The government has attacked structural unemployment–unemployment due to a lack of job skills–by providing job training and creating programs that pay all or part of an employee's salary during the unproductive phase of his training in a private business. Two major economic problems, however, plague government job training programs. First, government can spend only the money which it taxes or borrows from its citizens. In setting up job training programs or paying salaries of trainees while they are learning a skill, the government must appropriate taxpayers' money that would otherwise be spent on other goods. When the government taxes its citizens to set up job training programs, it decreases the taxpayers' ability to buy things such as cars, houses, appliances, and thousands of other products and services. This decrease in spending causes jobs to be lost in the manufacturing, sales, and service sectors of the economy. Therefore, the jobs gained through government job training programs are partially, if not totally, offset by jobs lost in other sectors where spending has been diminished. A second problem with government job training programs is a lack of information. In many cases by the time the government perceives a need, recruits trainees, and then provides training, the need for those specific skills may have disappeared, rendering the training program of little effect. For example, according to the the U.S. Department of Labor, fewer than 40% of the young people receiving training under the Job Training Partnership Act (JTPA) receive a job, even for one day.

Government can do little or nothing about seasonal unemployment except to suggest that companies that produce seasonal goods spread their work over the course of the year. Nonseasonal production can be very expensive for some firms, however, as they produce goods that must sit idle until the big selling period begins.

Cyclical unemployment was shown to be related to the economy's position in the business cycle. Besides trying to control the business cycle itself, the government also tries to combat cyclical unemployment by penalizing firms with a higher incidence of cyclical unemployment. Businesses hardest hit by downturns in the business cycle may be required to make higher contributions to unemployment compensation programs as their layoffs increase. As a result the financial loss involved in keeping seasonally unneeded workers becomes somewhat less painful than the financial loss involved in paying higher unemployment compensation insurance. One undesired effect of the graduated unemployment compensation contributions is that when business finally picks up, employers are reluctant to hire new workers out of a fear that they may later have to lay them off, thus incurring financial penalties.

Unemployment and the Market

Earlier in this chapter we saw that there are several types of unemployment, including frictional, structural, seasonal, and cyclical. Free-market economics holds that the latter three of these cat-

Minimum Wage Laws and Unemployment

When Americans hear that Congress has approved an increase in the minimum wage, the general reaction seems to be one of rejoicing. While workers in low-paying jobs have visions of fatter paychecks, economists recognize that the effects of such a mandatory increase in the cost of labor are not totally beneficial. In fact, such an increase actually encourages unemployment. The following example may help us understand how this effect occurs.

Suppose that a business firm has a demand curve for workers like the one in Figure A. Given the demand curve for labor, the firm will want to hire one hundred workers at $20 per hour, two thousand workers at $1 per hour, or other numbers of workers at various wages as shown. Now, assume that there are five hundred workers available to work for

this firm. Therefore, the graph clearly shows that, in a situation in which wages are the only consideration, the market would be in equilibrium if the workers were paid $4 per hour. At that price all five hundred workers would have jobs, and the firm would have the number of employees it needed.

What would happen if a minimum wage law were enacted, setting wages at $10 per hour? Figure B shows that at that level, there would still be five hundred workers available, but the firm would demand only two hundred employees. Therefore, three hundred of the workers would be unemployed. Such are the laws of supply and demand. Whenever the price of anything–shoes, jewelry, or workers–is higher than its equilibrium price, there will always be a surplus. And in the labor market, a surplus of employees means higher unemployment.

An additional problem economists find with minimum wage laws is that they tend to

Figure A

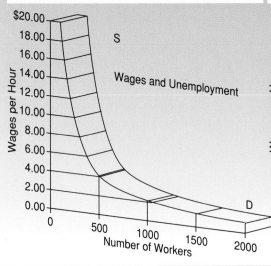

Figure B

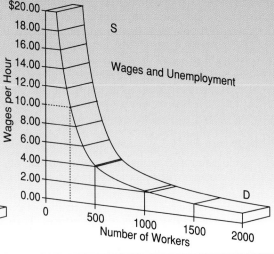

hurt the very people they are intended to help. Because most jobs requiring skilled workers pay well above the minimum wage, the law has little effect on their situation. However, unskilled workers with low incomes have the most to lose from a minimum wage higher than the market level. Many of them will be in danger of losing their jobs because employers will not consider their work worth the increased wages. Fast-food restaurants and other businesses that hire unskilled employees will keep their most valuable help in the face of the increased wage costs, while laying off those that they can no longer afford to pay. Thus many teenagers, high school drop-outs, and other hard-to-employ people will be left without jobs entirely. Currently, unemployment among teenagers is 15.9% compared to 5.3% for the general population of the United States.

Figure 12-9

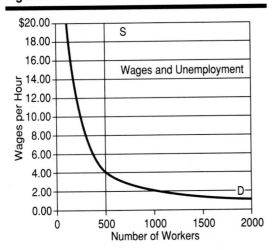

egories are related to a single cause: a difference between the price sellers of labor are asking and the price buyers are willing to pay for that labor. Chapter 4, you will remember, revealed that the laws of supply and demand are the basis for all economic decisions. You saw that if there is a buildup of inventories of a product, it was not due to the fact that irrational people were unwilling to pay an obviously just price. Rather, you discovered that rational buyers realized that the benefits they would enjoy would be overshadowed by the price they would have to pay. The same case holds true with labor. If the amount charged by the supplier of labor (the worker) exceeds what the buyer (the employer) is willing to pay, there will be a buildup of unused labor, and unemployment will result. Therefore, the market's solution to unemployment is to allow wages to adjust with supply and demand conditions.

Section Review

1. What two major economic problems are associated with downturns and upswings in the business cycle?
2. What is the labor force?
3. How is it that some people who are not working are not counted as unemployed when the unemployment rate is tabulated?
4. Name the four kinds of unemployment.
5. What is the market solution to unemployment?

Chapter Review

Terms

business cycle
expansion phase
peak phase
recessionary phase
trough phase
depression
unemployment rate
labor force
discouraged workers
frictional unemployment
structural unemployment
seasonal unemployment
cyclical unemployment

Content Questions

1. Describe the expansion and recession phases of the business cycle.
2. Explain the three theories that attempt to explain the existence of business cycles.
3. Suppose there is an announcement on the evening news that the unemployment rate is 6%. Does this number accurately reflect the number of people out of work? Why or why not?

4. What is a discouraged worker?
5. Is frictional unemployment undesirable in a nation's economy? Explain your answer.
6. What has government done to try to eliminate structural unemployment? What is the hidden cost of its efforts?
7. How does the free market explain the existence of unemployment?

Application Questions

1. Describe why some business firms actually do well in periods of recession and depression.
2. How does unemployment hurt those who are not themselves out of a job?
3. List several characteristics that you believe would increase your chances of being unemployed.
4. What do think would be the short- and long-term results if the government, in its effort to reduce structural unemployment, simply required businesses to hire a certain percentage of unskilled workers?

CHAPTER 13 _____

Inflation

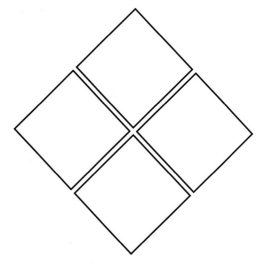

One indication of inflation has been an ongoing rise in the price of postage stamps.

Wilt thou set thine eyes upon that which is not? for riches certainly make themselves wings; they fly away as an eagle toward heaven.

Proverbs 23:5

I. What Is Inflation?

It seems that there is an unchangeable law of the universe which states that just after your employer gives you a raise in salary, prices must go up by the same degree, leaving you in the same financial position as before. Though this statement is humorous, it is a fact that prices have been going up almost every year for several decades, and it appears that price increases are going to be around for many years to come. **Inflation** is the term economists use to describe a sustained rise in the average price level.

The existence of inflation does not necessarily mean that the price of every good is rising. Even when most prices are rising, some prices fall. For example, though the general price level rose by 311% between 1967 and 1984, the price of electronic calculators and computers actually declined.

During the same period, however, the price of energy rose faster than the general price level, going up by over 423%. Though some prices may fall, overall prices, generally speaking, increase during a period of inflation. To be sure, the inflation we have experienced in the United States has been burdensome, but our inflation fades to insignificance when compared to the very rapid inflation, or hyperinflation, experienced by other nations.

Inflation: Who Wins and Who Loses?

Inflation has many victims, but those hardest hit by inflation are those who live on fixed incomes, such as the elderly. Older citizens, many of whom are living on fixed retirement pensions that were granted before payments were automatically adjusted to take inflation into account, find it increasingly difficult to survive year after year. As prices go up, those on fixed incomes find that their dollars purchase fewer and fewer goods, and thus they are forced to dig deeper into their modest but precious savings. Currently many employers take future inflation into consideration when developing their

Hyperinflation

After World War I, Germany's economic troubles led to one of the worst cases of hyperinflation in history. The inflation was fueled as the German government, known as the Weimar Republic, desperately tried to meet the reparations payments that the Allied victors had imposed upon the nation. Because of Germany's defeat in the war, its industries and trade were stifled. The government printed more and more marks to meet expenses, causing the German people to soon lose all confidence in the mark, Germany's unit of currency. The result of the increase in the money supply was a tremendous fall in the value of the mark. The inflation devastated life savings and created a panic that helped pave the way for the rise of Adolf Hitler.

Date		Number of marks equal to one dollar (monthly average)
July	1914	4.2
Jan.	1919	8.9
Jan.	1921	64.9
Jan.	1922	191.8
July	1922	493.2
Jan.	1923	17,972
July	1923	353,412
Aug.	1923	4,620,455
Sept.	1923	98,869,000
Oct.	1923	25,260,208,000
Nov.	1923	4,200,000,000,000

During the post-World War I period, the German mark became virtually worthless. These notes for millions of marks lost almost all value during the hyperinflation period.

Although the most famous case of hyperinflation was that in post-World War I Germany, the worst case of modern inflation occurred in Hungary during World War II. Prior to the war, it took about six Hungarian pengos to purchase a dollar's worth of goods. By the end of the war it required nearly 6,300,000,000,000,000,000,000,000,000,000 (6.3 quintrillion) to make the same purchase.

pension plans, agreeing to make **cost of living adjustments (COLAs),** which adjust payments upward as inflation causes prices to rise.

Creditors are also hurt by inflation. Those who have lent money to others are injured as they receive fixed loan repayments during periods when their costs are rising. If inflation becomes too severe, credit markets may collapse entirely, making it impossible for businesses or consumers to receive loans. Bolivia, a nation that until mid-1985 was running an annual inflation rate of over 25,000%, saw a near disintegration of its financial markets. After all, why would a creditor wish to lend money to someone for the purchase of a luxury car, only to have the future loan repayment equal the value of a bottle of aspirin!

To remedy this inflationary problem, many lenders incorporate inflation-fighting clauses into loan contracts, tying the interest rate of the loan to the inflation rate. Such floating-rate loans require higher payments as the general price level rises and lower payments as deflation, a fall in prices, occurs. If inflation occurs very rapidly, it becomes impossible for creditors to adjust their records as lenders suffer from a kind of information overload.

Savers, a third group hurt by inflation, are penalized severely when prices rise. If prices increase at a rate greater than the interest rate offered on savings, it becomes foolish to save money. For example, imagine that you have $10,000, and you need to purchase a car. You believe that you can drive your old car for one more year and save your money at a 6% interest rate. You reason that at the end of the year you can purchase the $10,000 car and pocket $600 interest. If the nation is experiencing a 10% inflation rate, however, you stand to lose money by saving. The car's price next year will be $11,000 ($10,000 + 10%), while your savings account would grow to only $10,600 ($10,000 + 6%). Obviously, in this case it would be foolish

for you to save your money. Logically, therefore, the upshot of inflation is for consumers to spend their money more quickly so that they will beat future price increases.

Inflation causes an almost pathological fear of lost savings. As a result, the economy suffers two major blows. First, when personal savings decline, business firms will find less money available to borrow from the financial market. This decline in available money will result in businesses' being unable to borrow money to repair old factories or buy new ones and, therefore, unable to produce goods for tomorrow's needs. Second, as savings decline and consumer spending rises, a heavier burden is placed on the nation's already inadequate factories, equipment, and personnel.

A fourth group that loses to inflation is consumers. Some economists believe that a little inflation, around 2% to 3% per year, can be a good stimulant to the nation's "economic bloodstream." They

claim that the rising prices that accompany inflation act like the proverbial carrot on a stick, encouraging business firms to invest more money in factories, equipment, and employees. Such is not the case. Whenever the average consumer's income does not rise as fast as prices, inflation robs him of the purchasing power he has earned and acts like a hidden tax on his income.

Are there any winners during inflation? Actually, for almost every loser there is a corresponding winner. In the case of those living on fixed pensions, the winner is the former employer or fund holder. By virtue of the massive size of the pension fund, the fund manager is not subject to the inflationary plight of the small saver. By investing in government securities, fund managers are able to earn a return greater than the inflation rate. While gathering profits from those investments, he is required to pay out only the low fixed pensions to the retirees.

While creditors lose to inflation, borrowers tend to be the winners. As inflation progresses, the incomes of borrowers rise, but payments on fixed-rate loans remain the same.

Finally, while savers lose by keeping their money in low-yielding bank accounts, financial institutions, not unlike big pension fund managers, are able to use the relatively inexpensive funds for more profitable investments.

It appears that inflation is not really a problem as long as one ensures that he is on the winning side of business transactions. In reality, however, even the apparent winners are part of a general loss; for when inflation envelops a country, the entire nation loses confidence in its economic system. When inflation takes hold of a nation, governmental leadership is despised, the work ethic is ignored, thrift is spurned, current consumption becomes paramount, and each individual takes on an attitude of ''everybody for himself.''

How Is Inflation Measured?

Because of the harmful effects of inflation, economists must have some device to detect its existence, to measure its growth, and to make adjustments in order to dampen its effects. Econo-

mists have developed two tools for this purpose: the gross national product implicit price deflator (GNP deflator) and the consumer price index (CPI).

GNP Deflator–Chapter 11 introduced you to the ultimate inflation-measuring device: the GNP deflator. Computed by comparing the prices of all goods and services from year to year, the GNP deflator is able to measure the changes in prices of everything from hot dogs to battleships. Once economists have an idea of the rise in general prices, adjusting loan contracts and wages is a simple task. The problem with using the GNP deflator as a COLA factor is that it measures changes in the prices of *all* goods in the nation. If the price of military hardware rises while prices on everything else remain level, the GNP deflator would still rise. Would it be economically sound, however, to increase wages paid to construction workers as a result of an increase in the GNP deflator in this instance? Obviously not. Economists recognized this problem and developed a way to measure changes in the prices that household consumers pay. They call it the **consumer price index** or **CPI.**

Consumer Price Index–The consumer price index is used by government economists to measure the changes in the prices that affect a selected market basket of goods and services. To calculate the CPI, economists repeatedly measure the prices of approximately four hundred goods and services purchased by an average urban household. The prices of these goods and services in the initial period of the survey, or **base period,** serve as a benchmark against which future prices are compared. The most recent base period used is that of the years 1982 through 1984. Figure 13-1 lists CPI figures from the years 1960 through 1989. The figure indicates that a basket of goods which cost the average urban household $100.00 during the base period (1982-1984) cost only $29.60 in 1960 and $124.00 in 1989.

Uses of CPI–One of the major uses of the consumer price index is the calculation of inflation rates. It is possible to calculate the rate of inflation for the interval between any two CPI figures by

GNP: $25.9 billion*
Per Capita GNP: $6,194*

50

בנק ישראל

50

5481797643

50

5481797643

BANK OF ISRAEL

Israel

Population: 4,371,000 (1989)
Monetary Unit: shekel

Since its birth in 1948, the modern nation of Israel has experienced a dramatic economic rise and fall. With the hope of reclaiming their ancient homeland, Jews from around the world began moving to Palestine following World War I, and this migration has continued throughout the twentieth century. When the nation was formed, the problems faced by a new people settling and developing the land were tackled by extensive governmental economic planning. The Israeli government developed public railroads, utilities, and other vital industries, and it undertook a monumental agricultural program intended to ''make the desert bloom.'' The hard work of new settlers committed to building their nation brought great advances eventually. Private as well as public industries grew to make Israel the most industrialized nation in the Middle East. Farmland was allocated to collective farms called *kibbutzim* and farmers' cooperatives called *moshavim,* which implemented extensive irrigation systems and modern agricultural techniques. Israeli farmers were able to make part of their desolate land bring forth enough fruits, vegetables, cotton, and some other crops both to supply Israel and to use in trade for other agricultural needs.

Israel enjoyed great economic growth from the late 1950s until the mid-1970s. Then stagnation set in, combining high inflation with virtually no growth in the economy. An obvious reason for the economic downturn has been the growing military expenses Israel has incurred during persistent conflicts with its Arab neighbors. However, Israel's plight undoubtedly stems from the economic controls that have stifled growth. Among these burdensome controls are high taxes, subsidies to aid unprofitable industries, price controls, and widespread demands and regulations of the Histadrut, Israel's General Confederation of Labor, which imposes its desires on Israeli industry with little regard to their effect on economic development. In the midst of political turmoil, Israeli leaders have had to turn some of their attention to the evident economic difficulties of the nation. The government has attempted to trim some of its heavy expenditures for domestic programs in order to bring down inflation, but it has yet to decrease significantly the controls that discourage private industrial growth. If Israel does not take action soon, its economic ruin may become a reality.

*figures for 1987 from the 1990 *World Almanac*

Figure 13-1 Consumer Price Index, 1960-1989*

YEAR	CPI	YEAR	CPI
1960	29.6	1971	40.5
1961	29.9	1972	41.8
1962	30.2	1973	44.4
1963	30.6	1974	49.3
1964	31.0	1975	53.8
1965	31.5	1976	56.9
1966	32.4	1977	60.6
1967	33.4	1978	65.2
1968	34.8	1979	72.6
1969	36.7	1980	82.4
1970	38.8	1981	90.9

YEAR	CPI	
1982	96.5	⎫
1983	99.6	⎬ (96.5 + 99.6 + 103.9) / 3 = 100
1984	103.9	⎭
1985	107.6	
1986	109.6	
1987	113.6	
1988	118.3	
1989	124.0	

*Source: President's Council of Economic Advisors, Economic Report of the President (Washington, D.C.: Government Printing Office, 1990), Table C-58

Figure 13-2 Inflation Rates, 1961-1989*

YEAR	INFLATION RATE	YEAR	INFLATION RATE
1961	1.01 %	1976	5.76 %
1962	1.00	1977	6.50
1963	1.32	1978	7.59
1964	1.31	1979	11.35
1965	1.61	1980	13.50
1966	2.86	1981	10.32
1967	3.09	1982	6.16
1968	4.19	1983	3.21
1969	4.60	1984	4.32
1970	5.72	1985	3.56
1971	4.38	1986	1.86
1972	3.21	1987	3.65
1973	6.22	1988	4.14
1974	11.04	1989	4.82
1975	9.13		

using the following formula:

$$\frac{Recent\ CPI - Earlier\ CPI}{Earlier\ CPI} \times 100$$

For example, let us calculate the inflation rate that occurred between 1986 and 1987:

$$\frac{113.6 - 109.6}{109.6} \times 100 = 3.649$$

Based on these calculations, the inflation rate for 1987 was 3.649%. That is, a good which cost $100 in 1986 cost $103.65 in 1987 (Figure 13-2).

In addition to using the CPI to determine rates of inflation, it is also used to determine one's purchasing power. Using the CPI to compare current and past purchasing power is quite easy. For example, let us assume that a person earned $12,500 in 1967, $24,000 in 1976, and $37,000 in 1986. Obviously, his nominal income went up, but was he able to purchase more with those added dollars? To determine one's real earning power relative to the CPI, one must divide nominal earnings by the CPI for that year. (Remember, the CPI figures are percentages; so 100% really equals 1.00 CPI.) As you can see, between 1967 and 1976 his purchasing power relative to the CPI's market basket of goods rose, but it fell between 1976 and 1986.

1967: $12,500/.334 = $37,425
1976: $24,000/.569 = $42,179
1986: $37,000/1.096 = $33,759.12

Many individuals and business firms alike have recognized the eroding influence of inflation on purchasing power and have, therefore, accepted the CPI as the primary tool to index or adjust wages, prices, and interest rates. **Indexing** is a process of tying present wages and prices to some adjustment figure so that real wages and real prices are maintained. A building contractor may include an inflation clause in his bid that would tie his price to the CPI, allowing him to raise his price to keep pace with the rising costs he must pay. Workers, realizing how the purchasing power of fixed wages and pensions can be eroded by inflation, often include cost-of-living clauses in their job contracts and pension plans, tying their wages and retirement benefits to the CPI.

Limitations of CPI–For all of its benefits, the CPI is not a perfect measure of changes in living costs but is only a good approximation. There are at least three major reasons that the CPI does not provide exact information on changes in the cost of living. First, the CPI assumes that all urban households consistently purchase, month after month, the same market basket of goods and services, while in reality buying preferences change.

A second limitation of the CPI is the problem of adjusting price changes to quality changes. We are fond of thinking that the quality of goods manufactured in the past was significantly better than the quality of today's products. While such may be the case for some items, most goods today are more efficient, reliable, and productive. Hence, today's products are generally more valuable, but economists do not adjust the higher prices of today's goods with respect to their higher quality. For example, if a washing machine cost $250 ten years ago, and today one costs $500, the CPI would report that the price has doubled. But what if the quality of today's washing machine is such that it will last four times longer? Would it not be wiser to say that the new machine *actually* costs $125 (500/4)? Because quality is not taken into account, the CPI tends to overstate the rate of inflation.

A third problem with the CPI is that it tends to ignore the law of demand. As the price of a good rises, other things being held constant, people will tend to demand less of the good and will purchase a less expensive substitute. As the price of housing rises, people tend to rent rather than buy. As new automobiles become too expensive, consumers tend to hold on to their old cars longer, choosing to repair rather than replace them. The CPI, however, assumes that no matter how high the price a good in the market basket rises, consumers will continually purchase the same quantity. To allow a true picture of the cost of living, the CPI's market basket should constantly reflect change in the quantities consumers buy as prices change.

Section Review

1. What is hyperinflation?
2. Who is generally hurt by inflation?
3. Who receives some benefits from inflation?
4. What are the two tools used to measure inflation?
5. How is the consumer price index tabulated?

II. Inflation: Causes and Cures

One of the most disturbing problems with inflation is its tendency to accelerate. The inflationary experiences of many South American nations have demonstrated this sad fact. A nation's inflation rate may begin at a modest 2% or 3% per year, but it has a frightening tendency to accelerate to the point where prices double or triple on a daily basis. When this occurs, a nation's financial system grinds to a halt, panic becomes commonplace, industries shut down as workers strike for higher and higher wages, and there is a serious threat to national security.

Causes of Inflation

To better understand the causes of inflation, recall the lesson of Chapter 3 which first introduced the concept of price. Remember that the two key variables in determining the price of every good and service are supply and demand. As Figure 13-3 illustrates, the price of a good is determined by the intersection of its supply and demand curves.

Figure 13-3

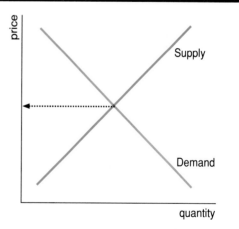

Since the price of a good is determined by the intersection of the supply and demand curves, only two situations can cause a price increase: a shift of the supply curve to the left, or a shift of the demand curve to the right. A shift left of a supply curve

Figure 13-4

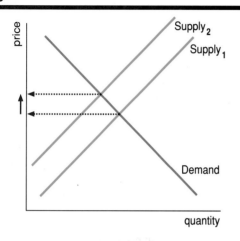
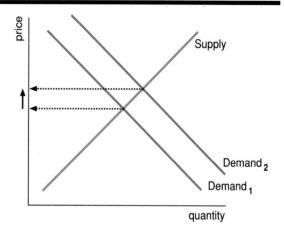

indicates that the producer is producing less of the good, while a shift right of the demand curve indicates that buyers are suddenly demanding more.

Likewise, the overall price level in the country is determined by the intersection of what we might call the total demand and total supply curves (Figure 13-5). Instead of a graph showing the price of

Figure 13-5

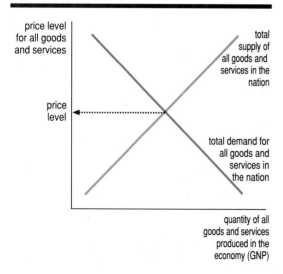

a single good relative to its quantity, the total supply and demand curves use a graph with the *price level* on one axis and Gross National Product on the other. Why GNP? Because GNP is the *quantity* of all goods sold in the country.

Since the nation's price level is determined by the intersection of the total supply and the total demand curves, there can be only two possible explanations for inflation: a decrease in the nation's supply of goods and services (represented by a shift left in the total supply curve), or an increase in the nation's demand for goods and services (represented by a shift right in the total demand curve). Economists have labeled these two explanations "cost-push inflation" and "demand-pull inflation," respectively.

Cost-Push Inflation–Many economists believe that inflation is triggered when a nation's businesses raise their prices, either to pass along higher costs of materials or labor or to accumulate higher profits. Consumers, unable to pay the higher prices, demand higher wages of their employers. It is from this cycle of higher costs pushing up prices, causing an increase in wages, further pushing up prices that the name **cost-push inflation** originates.

According to the cost-push theory, business firms begin the inflationary process by charging

Figure 13-6

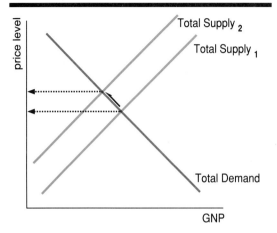

Figure 13-7

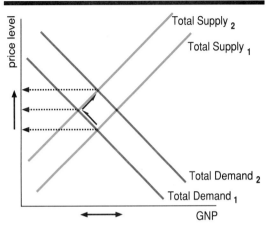

higher prices, an action that shifts the total supply curve to the left (Figure 13-6).

As prices soar, consumers become unhappy because they are unable to buy as many goods and services with their normal incomes. They complain to their employers (or take more drastic action) to gain pay increases. Employers, either out of sympathy to their employees' plight or out of fear of a strike, grant their employees larger paychecks. As employees receive larger paychecks, consumer income rises, causing the total demand curve to shift to the right (Figure 13-7).

As a result of these two shifts, GNP is right back where it was before, but notice that the price level has risen. This is not the end of the story, however. Where will these compassionate businesses get more money to pay their workers higher salaries? They will get it by increasing prices and shifting the supply curve to the left again, prompting workers to again demand higher wages. Thus, the cost-push inflationary spiral continues: rising prices lead to rising wages, which again lead to rising prices, etc.

This cost-push inflation theory is attractive both to business firms and labor unions. Big business firms claim that the demands of labor unions for higher wages trigger the cost-push spiral while union leaders claim that the seeds of inflation are

planted when business firms raise their prices to glean higher profits. As appealing as the cost-push theory may be, it fails to explain the cause of *sustained* inflation. There is one basic variable in the inflationary spiral for which the cost-push believers do not account: money.

If the prices of all goods and services are rising, and the paychecks of all workers are increasing as well, the supply of dollars must also increase; otherwise, inflation could not continue its upward spiral.

Follow this logic: an individual business firm attempts to recover its higher costs by hiking its prices. Consumers now have a choice. Either they may buy less expensive substitutes or they may continue to buy the now higher-priced good but will have to forego buying some other good. Either one of these two actions will cause the sales of some goods to suffer, and unemployment will result. The only way all firms could charge higher prices and pay workers more is if there is more money to do so. If additional money is not created, employers would not be able to pay their workers higher salaries, and unemployment would result.

Demand-Pull Inflation—Cost-push inflation holds that the inflationary spiral begins with a shift left in the supply curve as a result of businesses passing along higher costs. **Demand-pull inflation,** on the other hand, maintains that the inflationary trend begins with an increase in demand. According to demand-pull inflation, consumers, for some reason, begin demanding more of everything: cars, houses, washing machines, and millions of other products. According to the theory, this shift right in the demand curve causes the price level to rise. As prices rise, businesses are forced either to increase the workers' wages or else watch their employees depart for higher paying jobs. When the business firms pass on these higher payroll costs as higher consumer prices, the total supply curve shifts to the left. Consumers unable to buy the now more expensive goods demand still higher wages. When higher wages are paid, the consumers' total demand curve shifts to the right. On and on the spiral continues, much like cost-push inflation (Figure 13-8).

Money Growth: The Root Cause of Inflation – The argument between the proponents of cost-push and demand-pull inflation is purely academic. It really does not matter what *triggered* the inflationary episode. The important thing is recognizing that a continual increase in the money supply keeps the price level going up.

The definition of inflation given at the beginning of this chapter, though in keeping with the official definition, is still somewhat inaccurate. Traditionally, economists have defined inflation as a situation in which prices of virtually everything in the nation are rising. In reality a rising price level is merely a *symptom* of inflation. Consider the following illustration: if you were to fill a car's tires with air, you would see the car rise. In the strictest sense of the word, the *action* of the rising car is not inflation. Inflation is actually that which caused the car to rise, specifically the addition of more air into the tires. The lifting of the car is merely a logical result. Likewise, price increases are but a logical result of the infusion of more money into the economy. If new money is not injected into the economy, business firms would be unable to pay higher wages and consumers would be unable to pay higher prices.

Cures for Inflation

Wage-Price Controls – Those who view inflation as

Figure 13-8

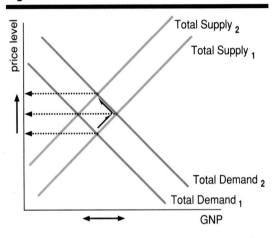

a price phenomenon have a rather simple solution: simply make it illegal for business firms to raise the prices of their products or the wages of their workers. In a sense they advocate "freezing" the total supply and total demand curves in place. The problem with wage and price controls, however, is that they cannot work if the government continues inflating the money supply. Imagine the foolishness of inflating a car's tires but putting a barrier above the car that will not allow it to rise. If the inflation continues for too long, the car will be damaged and the tires will explode.

Likewise, if the government imposes wage and price controls while continuing to inflate the money supply, demand for goods and services will continue to grow while business firms will have neither the ability to produce more nor the power to increase the prices of existing products. The store shelves of law-abiding merchants will be picked clean as buyers snatch up scarce goods at bargain prices. Afterwards, the producers of those goods will be unable and unwilling to supply more because to continue to sell goods may mean incurring losses. Elsewhere, other producers will continue to produce, selling their products on the black market at the profitable but illegal market price.

Wage and price controls are not a new idea. Attempts to hold down prices and wages artificially date back to around 1800 B.C., when a ruler of

Robert Lucas (1937-)
Expositor of the Rational Expectation Hypothesis

Robert Lucas, a professor at the University of Chicago, takes a different approach to economic theory from the monetarists at that school, such as Milton Friedman. Lucas has advanced the rational expectation hypothesis, which says that people act rationally when they foresee economic changes, and their actions in turn affect the results of the changes.

For example, if the government announces that it will increase the money supply in an attempt to solve an unemployment problem, the people will recognize that the increase will probably bring inflation. Therefore, they take precautions to minimize their losses and seek wage increases to compensate for the expected inflation. When this occurs, the money that the government intended to be used by businesses hiring new workers instead must go for higher wages and costs. The unemployment problem is left unsolved because the people's ''rational expectations'' naturally led them to divert the money from its intended purpose.

Lucas contends that publicly announced measures to change the money supply or alter other economic features will often result in failure. People are concerned about the impact of national economic adjustments on their own personal finances, and their reaction to discretionary measures tends to shift the outcome of any governmental economic action away from its desired end.

Babylonia threatened death by drowning to anyone who violated his wage and price freeze. The Roman emperor Diocletian issued an edict in A.D. 301 called *commanded cheapness,* in which he set a maximum price on beef, clothing, and other commodities. In addition he set maximum wage rates for doctors, lawyers, and other workers. (Those who violated the edict were to be slain.) In A.D. 314 Lactantius wrote of the harmful effects of price controls, lamenting that there was

> much bloodshed upon very slight and trifling accounts; and the people brought provisions no more to market, since they could not get a reasonable price for them; and this increased the dearth [famine] so much that after many had died by it, the law itself was laid aside.

Limitation of Money Creation–If, on the other hand, one believes that inflation is caused by an excessive demand for goods and services created by increases in the money supply, the obvious solution is to limit the quantity of money being created. In 1985 Bolivia was experiencing an annual inflation rate of over 25,000%: prices were changing by the minute, workers were taking managers hostage, and the nation's third biggest import was currency. In August of 1985 Bolivia's president announced that the government would stop creating money to pay its bills and would spend only that money which was received as tax revenues. Up to that point the government was creating 85¢ of each dollar spent. Within two months, inflation was down to an annual rate of 20%.

Section Review

1. What is a situation in which a rise in prices set by businesses for their products is followed by a rise in workers' wages?
2. What is the root cause of inflation?
3. Why are wage and price controls usually ineffective?

Chapter Review

Terms
inflation
cost of living adjustment (COLA)
consumer price index (CPI)
base period
indexing
cost-push inflation
demand-pull inflation

Content Questions
1. What is the official or traditional definition of inflation?
2. What is a COLA, and how does it work?
3. Why is it unprofitable for people to save during periods when the inflation rate is high?
4. How is the consumer price index different from the GNP deflator?
5. Describe the limitations involved in the CPI.

6. What is the difference between cost-push and demand-pull inflation?
7. What are the two possible means of curing inflation? Which is better? Why?

Application Questions
1. A worker's income in 1979 was $12,500. In 1986 his income was $19,000. If these figures were adjusted for inflation (according to the CPI statistics in Figure 13-1), would his income have increased or decreased during the seven-year period? If his earnings of $12,500 in 1979 were strictly tied to the CPI, what would have been his equivalent earnings in 1986?

2. Given the CPI data found in Figure 13-1, calculate the rate of inflation between 1976 and 1983.

CHAPTER 14

Fiscal Policy

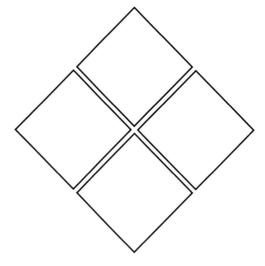

The Lord maketh poor, and maketh rich: he bringeth low, and lifteth up.   I Samuel 2:7

A revolution of sorts occurred in the United States in the early 1930s. It was a quiet revolution, consisting not of violent explosions and nightly news headlines. The revolution was one of attitude, and the battlefield was within the mind of each American. Having once believed that the only province of government should be to maintain military and police forces and to provide a limited number of public goods, Americans began to demand that the government pull the nation out of the economic morass in which it lay.

This outcry, born of the deepest economic depression experienced by the United States, was the beginning of the extensive use of fiscal policy. **Fiscal policy** refers to the actions the government takes to affect output (gross national product) and employment through the way it spends its money, taxes its citizens, and borrows.

Understanding fiscal policy requires understanding the concept of the business cycle–the perpetual increase and decrease in real GNP, which was introduced in Chapter 12. Obviously, periods of economic decline are undesirable because they are characterized by reductions in national income, increases in unemployment, and declines in standards of living. Likewise, periods of economic prosperity are fraught with peril. If real GNP grows too quickly, the economy may "overheat." That is, the nation's ability to purchase goods and services may outstrip its ability to produce them, resulting in spiraling inflation. Fiscal policy attempts, then, to keep in check this cycle of economic decline and prosperity.

In 1936 British economist John Maynard Keynes (KANES) developed the basic idea of fiscal policy in his book *The General Theory of Employment Interest and Money.* Keynes's ideas, later dubbed **Keynesian Economics,** all hinge on the premise that peaks and troughs in the business cycle are caused by alternating periods of excessive and insufficient demand for the nation's production. Therefore, according to Keynes, the govern-

Figure 14-1

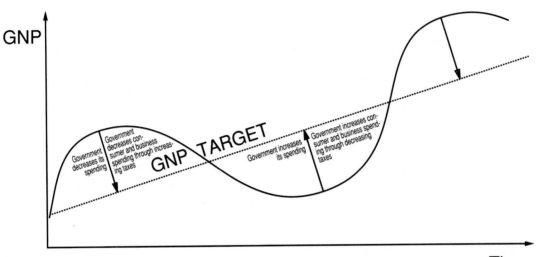

ment should intervene in the economy to regulate demand. During periods of economic expansion (periods of heavy demand for goods), the government should cut national demand by reducing its own purchases of goods and services. It also should increase taxes, making it difficult for consumers to demand more and more goods.

The reduction of government spending, combined with an increase in taxes, would lead to a federal budget surplus–money to be held in store against the day of economic decline. Then, according to Keynes, during these periods of economic decline the government should "reverse gears" by increasing its spending while reducing taxes to encourage consumers to boost their spending.

I. Government Spending

It is the highest impertinence and presumption of kings and ministers, to pretend to watch over the economy of private people, and to restrain their expense, either by sumptuary laws, or by prohibiting the importation of foreign luxuries. They are themselves always, and without any exception, the greatest spendthrifts in the society. Let them look well after their own expense, and they may safely trust private people with theirs. If their own extravagance does not ruin the state, that of their subjects never will. (Adam Smith: *An Inquiry into the Nature and Causes of the Wealth of Nations,* 1776.)

The first tool the government may use in its effort to control the economy is the management of its own spending. How does the government spend its money? Obviously, the government must purchase goods and services to continue operating. Congress must buy everything from french fries to fighter aircraft, and it must pay for the services of its employees. Its payroll reaches down to congressional elevator operators and extends as high as the White House.

In addition to purchasing goods and services, the government pays out money for transfer payments–payments of money for which the government receives nothing in exchange. Transfer payments include food stamps, expenditures on social security benefits, Aid to Families with Dependent Children (AFDC), unemployment compensation, and farm subsidies. Whenever a discussion about government spending arises, three issues invariably dominate the conversation: the size of the national budget, the programs that the government supports, and the way the dollars flow through the economy after they leave the government's hands.

Size of the National Budget

Currently, total federal and state government spending on purchases of goods and services accounts for nearly $1 of every $5 spent in the United States. Although total government spending has never been higher in terms of absolute dollars, the over $1 trillion spent by both federal and state governments in 1989 is a far smaller percentage of the 1989 GNP than that spent out of the 1943 GNP.

In that World War II year, combined federal and state purchases of goods and services reached a peak of nearly 46% of the GNP compared to only 20% in 1989.

The staggering figure of $404 billion spent on purchases of goods and services in 1989 appears small, however, when compared to *all* federal spending, including income transfer programs. The federal government spent over $1.14 trillion, including transfer payments for which expenditures are incurred but no goods or services are received.

How did our federal government spend such a vast amount of money, an amount that comes to over $36,000 of spending *per second?* Though many believe that the largest item on the federal budget is military spending, such is not the case.

Figure 14-2

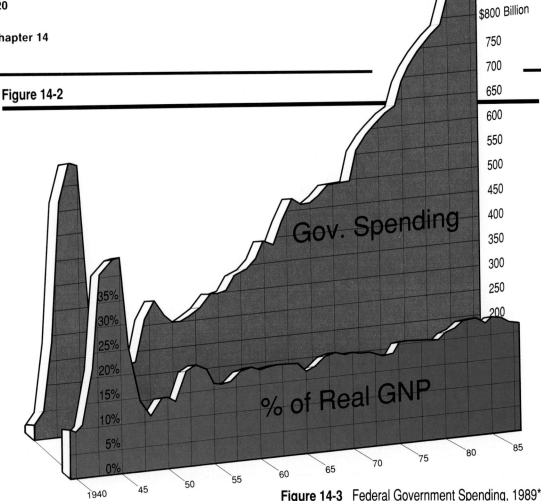

Gov. Spending

% of Real GNP

Figure 14-3 Federal Government Spending, 1989*

Congress spent $303.6 billion on national defense in 1989, whereas it paid out over $368 billion, or over 32% of its budget, on income security programs such as social security, welfare, unemployment compensation, and other transfer payments.

The third largest, and perhaps the most frightening, item on the federal budget is interest on the national debt. Just as consumers must pay banks for the use of borrowed money, so the government must pay those from whom it has borrowed. In 1989 the federal government paid out over $169 billion in interest, or $5,300 per second. Economists are concerned about the growth of this figure since it represents a real expenditure which the government must pay without receiving anything tangible in return.

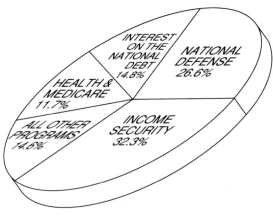

INTEREST ON THE NATIONAL DEBT 14.8%

NATIONAL DEFENSE 26.6%

HEALTH & MEDICARE 11.7%

ALL OTHER PROGRAMS 14.6%

INCOME SECURITY 32.3%

*Source: President's Council of Economic Advisors, Economic Report of the President (Washington, D.C.: Government Printing Office, 1990), Table C-77

CATEGORY	$ SPENT (MILLIONS)	% OF TOTAL GOV'T BUDGET
Income Security: Social Security and Other Income Security	368,573	32.3 %
National Defense	303,559	26.6
Interest on the National Debt	169,137	14.8
Health and Medicare	133,354	11.7
Social Services, Education, Training, and Employment	36,684	3.2
Veterans Benefits and Services	30,066	2.6
Commerce and Housing Credit	27,719	2.4
Transportation	27,608	2.4
Agriculture	16,948	1.5
Natural Resources and Environment	16,182	1.4
General Science, Space, and Technology	12,838	1.1
International Affairs	9,574	.8
Administration of Justice	9,422	.8
General Government	9,124	.8
Community and Regional Development	5,361	.5
Energy	3,702	.3
Offsetting Receipts, Fees, etc.	‹37,008›	‹3.2›
Total	1,142,643	100 %

*Source: President's Council of Economic Advisors, Economic Report of the President (Washington, D.C.: Government Printing Office, 1990), Table C-77

The Effects of Spending on the Economy: The Expenditure Multiplier

Chapter 10 explained how the money multiplier acts in such a way that dollars deposited into financial institutions are constantly lent and redeposited, with each round increasing the money supply a little more. A similar situation occurs with spending on goods and services. A dollar spent has a tendency to become more than a dollar's worth of income in the overall economy. After receiving their paychecks, people tend to save a little of their income and spend the rest. Merchants who subsequently receive consumers' dollars tend to do the same; that is, they save a little and spend the rest. On and on the process continues, providing income and jobs.

The portion of each dollar that the average individual chooses to spend is called the **marginal**

Figure 14-4 The Expenditure Multiplier in Action

NAME	DOLLARS RECEIVED (increases in national income)	_ DOLLARS SAVED	_ DOLLARS SPENT	NATIONAL INCOME
Amy	$100.00	$10.00	$90.00	$100.00
Davina	90.00	9.00	81.00	190.00
Pam	81.00	8.10	72.90	271.00
Bob	72.90	7.29	65.61	343.90

Total Increase = $1,000.00

propensity to consume or **MPC**. If the average person spends 85% of his income, his MPC is 0.85. On the other hand, the percentage of each dollar that the average consumer saves is known as the **marginal propensity to save** or **MPS**. MPS will always be 1 – MPC. If the average person spends 85% of his income, then by definition he is saving 1 – 0.85 or 15%. MPC makes the income multiplication process possible. Let us assume, for example, that the nation's MPC is 0.90. Amy, a bright high school senior, recently won an essay contest and received a $100 prize. Figure 14-4 illustrates how, upon Amy's receipt of the check, the nation's income initially increased by $100. In keeping with the national MPC of 0.90, Amy purchased $90 in goods from Davina, the owner of a clothing store. After the sale, Davina's income went up by $90; hence national income rose by an additional $90. Davina later spent $81 (90% of $90) and saved $9. Eventually this process created income for many people. This cycle has come to be known by economists as the **expenditure multiplier.**

Notice how Amy's $100 prize actually turned into $1000 of income for the nation as a whole. If one wanted to find out how a given amount affected national income without having to go through each cycle, one could use the expenditure multiplier formula:

$$\textit{Amount initially received} \times \frac{1}{1 - MPC}$$

Fleecing the Nation

Americans watched as government expenditures doubled in the 1980s to over $1 trillion per year and budget deficits skyrocketed. The growing national debt strikes fear in the heart of American taxpayers as well as stifles business expansion in the economy. Somehow the deficits must be erased if America's economic prosperity is to be preserved, but how? Some advocate raising taxes. Others propose cutting back government programs. A seemingly painless way is to cut out government waste and inefficiency, but on further examination this naturally appealing method does not appear so easy.

In 1975 Senator William Proxmire of Wisconsin began issuing what he called "Golden Fleece Awards," monthly recognitions of the most ridiculous government expenditures. The first award went to the National Science Foundation for using $84,000 in federal funds for a study of why people fall in love. The Reagan administration began an attempt to cut waste in 1982 by appointing a group of private businessmen to study federal finances and find ways to save money. The group, known as the Grace Commission (because of its chairman, J. Peter Grace), reported two years later that "the government is run horribly." They cited such instances as the Pentagon's having paid $91 for screws that could have been bought at any hardware store for a few cents, as well as having spent enormous sums for inexpensive spare parts. They noted many instances of inefficiency, including the processing of a letter in one cabinet department that took 47 days and 55 to 60 people to produce. Also, they pointed out many instances of the continuance of unneeded expenses. These included funds for maintaining obsolete military bases, post offices in very small towns, and Veterans Administration's health facilities that cost two or three times as much as similar private facilities. A final major recommendation was that pensions for retired government employees, which are often far more generous than those in the private sector, be pared down to reasonable levels.

Action to eliminate such abundant government waste should be swift, but it is not. For one thing, the bureaucratic trappings of government make corrective measures such as getting rid of expensive screws and slowly produced, labor-intensive letters difficult. For another, congressmen are not about to refuse legislation that offers federal funding benefiting their constituents. Congressmen, for example, regularly block military base closings in their states or districts, and they regularly supply funds for ridiculous programs in order to win votes. Some recent "pork barrel" legislation appropriating $60,000 for a Belgian Endive Research Center at the University of Massachusetts was introduced by a congressman from that state. Also, a North Dakota senator recently supported a provision to require the government to buy $10 million worth of sunflower oil. These absurd requests and many like them are logrolled through Congress and can become law when attached as a "rider" to an important bill. The president must either pass the entire bill or veto the important legislation along with the riders.

Although some policies can possibly prevent bureaucratic waste and implement greater efficiency and accountability, there seems to be little hope of significant improvement. The following are two possible remedies that can prevent the excesses of Congress's pork-barrel legislation. First, the president can be given the "line-item veto,"–the ability to accept some parts of a piece of legislation while rejecting other parts, especially pork-barrel riders. The second remedy requires that all appropriations be passed as separate bills, thus eliminating the "lard-filled" riders.

In Amy's case:

$$\$100 \times \frac{1}{1 - .90} =$$

$$\$100 \times \frac{1}{.10} =$$

$$\$100 \times 10 = \$1,000$$

The Government and the Expenditure Multiplier

The expenditure multiplier is of great importance to the government in its attempts to level out the business cycle. The government may either pull the nation out of a recession or put a damper on an overheating economy by increasing or decreasing its own spending. A government recession-fighting scenario would look something like this:

Government economists notice that the nation's GNP is $100 billion lower than they think it should be. If the nation's MPC is 0.90, Congress would need to spend only $10 billion to raise the GNP by the desired $100 billion. You may be asking yourself how the government would spend the $10 billion. Since the purpose of the spending is to boost national income and GNP by $100 billion, it would not really matter how the $10 billion enters the system. Chances are, however, that liberal members of Congress would want the funds spent on social programs, while conservatives would advocate earmarking the money for additional defense spending.

Conversely, should the economy be hurtling headlong into runaway inflation, the government would attempt to use the expenditure multiplier process in reverse. Congress, estimating that national income needs to decline by $100 billion, would decrease its spending by $10 billion.

Problems with Using Government Spending as a Tool of Fiscal Policy

During the early 1930s Keynesian economic theory seemed to be a refreshing change from Adam Smith's free market. During periods of national economic distress, free-market capitalism could promise that the economy would stabilize itself only if given enough time. But with Keynes's ideas it appeared, rather, that a quick cure to the economy-wrenching business cycle had been found. If the economy began sliding into a recession, Congress would need only to increase spending slightly, letting the expenditure multiplier work its magic. If, on the other hand, Congress got too carried away and over-expanded the economy, it would need only to reduce spending.

When Keynesian policies failed to pull the nation out of the Great Depression and later were unable to cure even mild recessions and inflations, it was clear that something was wrong with Keynes's "new economics." Economists have identified four critical problems which make it difficult for the government to control the economy.

Problem #1: Time Lags–Congress frequently puts off many fiscal policy issues or spends so much time debating solutions that the solution, when finally reached, no longer matches the problem. Time lags caused by debate, political maneuvering, and compromise often render useless many decisions on fiscal policy.

Congress uses its spending power both to provide necessary goods and services and to control the economy.

Politicians are quick to support heavy government spending, such as that for Johnson's "Great Society" programs in the 1960s, even though the spending fuels inflation.

Problem #2: Politics–Theoretically, the cure for recession is for government to reduce taxes and increase spending, while its inflationary counterpart calls for an increase in taxes and a cut in government expenditures. Such theory works well in university classrooms but fails miserably in political reality. Whereas most politicians are only too happy to cut taxes and boost spending on government programs to battle recession, they shrink with horror at the politically suicidal prospect of raising taxes and cutting government spending during inflationary periods. On the contrary, political success requires that politicians constantly increase spending and reduce taxes regardless of the economic conditions.

Problem #3: An Uncertain Multiplier–According to Keynesian theory, the expenditure multiplier enables Congress to stimulate the economy to a greater degree than its original spending would do. Likewise, if Congress wished to cool down an overheated economy, it would need to reduce its spending to a fraction of the total decrease deemed necessary. Keynesian theory fails, however, because it is not possible for government economists to gauge the multiplier with any great precision, and without that knowledge it is impossible to predict with any degree of accuracy the effect of an increase or reduction in government spending.

Problem #4: The Source of Additional Spending–Americans have a distressing tendency to believe that the government can spend money, create jobs, and expand the economy at no cost. In reality, Congress only can spend money that has been received in taxes, that has been borrowed, or that has been created through its monetary policies. (See Chapter 10.) Because excessive use of monetary policy causes inflation, taxation and borrowing must be its chief sources.

Let us assume that the MPC is 0.90 and that the government, in its attempt to expand the economy, spent $10 billion, which, via the expenditure multiplier, became $100 billion. Such a move would have created millions of jobs. Without a doubt the government would have been praised for its action, but what about the opportunity cost? Jobs cannot be created by magic. Where did the job-creating money come from? If the government had to increase personal taxes by $10 billion, then consumers would become $10 billion poorer, and the economy as a whole would have $100 billion less in income. The two actions of taxing and spending would have offset each other. Therefore, in reality government created no new employment; it merely redistributed it.

If Congress taxes business firms instead of the public for the $10 billion, then firms will have that much less money with which to pay employees and purchase new machines, inventory, and buildings. Again, the increase in GNP caused by government spending will be offset by a decrease in business investment. In short, Congress may be able to create some jobs, but it will destroy others in the process. Taxation, then, cannot create more jobs for the economy as a whole. It will destroy other jobs in the process. Borrowing, the alternative to taxation, has detrimental effects as well, and will be further discussed later in this chapter.

Section Review

1. Who was the British economist that developed the concept of fiscal policy?
2. According to the proponents of fiscal policy, what two steps should be taken in periods of economic decline?
3. The largest portion of the federal budget is spent for what?
4. What economic term refers to the portion of each dollar that the average individual chooses to spend?
5. What four problems are associated with using government spending as a tool of fiscal policy?

Real GNP: $87.6 billion*
Per Capita GNP: $8,260*

Hungary

Population: 10,567,000 (1989)
Monetary Unit: forint

For more than forty years after World War II, communism and its command-economy operations had maintained a stranglehold on Eastern Europe and many other parts of the globe. In 1989, however, the free world became encouraged as several nations began to throw off communist entrapments and reach for economic freedom. One of the countries that spearheaded these amazing developments was Hungary. That nation helped to lead the way for other Eastern European nations that were struggling to establish new, more capitalistic economies. The question now is whether these nations can make successful economic changes that will help to provide their needs and open their countries to more political freedom.

Hungary had gradually allowed greater private enterprise for its people following the introduction of the "new economic mechanism" in 1968. However, an overall system of central economic planning and control kept progress minimal until gigantic steps were taken in 1989 to reduce communist authority and open the economy. The Hungarians dramatized this change by literally tearing down the barbed-wire "Iron Curtain" between Hungary and Austria as a clear symbol of their desire for an opening of trade with the West. Hungary's success in moving toward capitalism hinges on the ability of the nation to adapt quickly to the unfamiliar workings of the free market and to build private industries. Foreign trade and aid will assist this process, but the Hungarians must also be determined to endure the difficulties they will meet on the road to capitalism.

*figures for 1987 from the 1990 *Statistical Abstract*

II. Taxation

"There is no art which one government sooner learns of another than that of draining money from the pockets of the people." (Adam Smith: *An Inquiry into the Nature and Causes of the Wealth of Nations,* 1776.)

Immediately after a governing authority is established to rule a people, a system of taxation is established to cover the expenses the government incurs in fulfilling its role. Since the 1930s, however, the U.S. government has used its powers of taxation as a tool of fiscal policy.

Sources of Tax Revenues

In 1989 the U.S. government received over $990 billion in tax receipts. Figure 14-5 illustrates the size and importance of various sources. Personal income taxes constitute the greatest source of tax revenue for the federal government. Most personal income taxes are deducted from a worker's income before he receives his paycheck.

Social security taxes are also required by the **Federal Insurance Contribution Act (FICA)** and are likewise deducted from paychecks before workers receive them, but on a slightly different basis. Employees pay a percentage of their income (up to a certain maximum income) which is then matched by the employer and sent to the government. Although not designed to be a complete retirement program, social security taxes provide retirement benefits for older Americans and disability income for survivors of employees who have contributed to the system.

Corporations also must pay taxes on their income, but these taxes are taken out of the firms' profits after all other expenses have been paid. Many business firms are able to minimize their tax burden by planning expenses in such a way as to reduce reported profits. In 1989 business firms paid out over $103 billion in corporate taxes.

A final source, excise taxes, are taxes levied on

© 1988 CARLSON—MILWAUKEE SENTINEL

Figure 14-5 Federal Tax Revenue Sources, 1989*

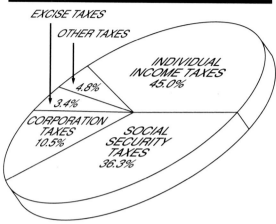

CATEGORY	TOTAL (MILLIONS)	% OF RECEIPTS
Individual Income Taxes	$445,690	45.0%
Social Security Contributions	359,416	36.3
Corporation Income Taxes	103,583	10.5
Excise Taxes	34,084	3.4
Deposits of Excess Fed Earnings	19,604	2.0
Customs Duties	16,334	1.6
Estate and Gift Taxes	8,745	.9
All Others	3,235	.3
Total	$990,691	100%

*Source: President's Council of Economic Advisors, *Economic Report of the President* (Washington, D.C.: Government Printing Office, 1990), Table C-77

the sale of certain targeted consumer goods, such as gasoline, alcoholic beverages, and cigarettes.

Types of Taxes

Not all taxes are meant to apply equally to all people. Taxes are classified rather by what proportion of a person's or a business firm's income the government takes as that income rises.

Proportional Taxes–A **proportional tax** is one in which all people, no matter how great or small their income, pay the same percentage of their earnings. For example, if income tax were proportioned at a rate of 10%, one would have to pay $1,000 on an income of $10,000, while a wealthy person would have to pay $1 million on an income of $10 million.

Progressive Taxes–A **progressive tax** is one that takes a greater percentage of a person's income as his income increases. A progressive tax is used, for example, if one had to pay $1,000 on an income of $10,000 (10%) while his rich neighbor paid $3 million on an income of $10 million (30%). The personal income tax in the United States is an example of a progressive tax and is based on a philosophy called the **ability-to-pay principle.** The ability-to-pay principle defines a tax as being fair if it is levied on those who have the ability to pay, whether or not benefits received are proportionate to the amount paid.

As was shown earlier, Keynesian economic theory holds that government can smooth the business cycle by reducing its spending during periods of national economic overexpansion and increasing its spending when the economy slips into recession. Another tool of the government, according to Keynes, is its ability to tax. The theory claims that the government should tax away consumers' greater purchasing power during periods of economic expansion. Conversely, as consumers' incomes decline during periods of recession, the government should decrease the tax rate.

It is in this regard that the personal income tax is said to be an "automatic stabilizer." As the economy expands and prices rise, increasing paychecks cause additional upward pressure on prices. To relieve this pressure, the progressive feature of the personal income tax allows the government to take a higher percentage out of each additional dollar received. On the other hand, as incomes decline during recession, the government allows people to keep more of their incomes by lowering personal tax rates.

Regressive Taxes–A **regressive tax** is one that takes a smaller percentage of a person's income as his income rises. For example, the tax on gasoline is a regressive tax. While at first glance it looks like a proportional tax–with everyone, regardless of income, paying the same amount of tax per gallon–it actually takes a smaller percentage of a buyer's income as his income rises. Why? People do not increase their purchases of gasoline to the same

John Maynard Keynes (1883-1946)
The Economic Influence of the Twentieth Century

Coming from a well-educated family and receiving his advanced instruction at Eton and King's College, Cambridge, the British economist John Maynard Keynes developed a quick, analytical mind and a sharp tongue. He was swift to condemn economists and politicians for actions that he believed would hurt the economy. One such open criticism appeared in 1919 when he wrote *The Economic Consequences of the Peace,* an attack on the reparations agreements made at Versailles at the end of World War I. Though Keynes was chided for his rebuke of eminent world leaders on this matter, his economic views soon gained prominence as many of his insights proved correct.

In contrast to the economists of the past, who had maintained that in the long run the basic principles of economics would lead the market to adjust naturally to an equilibrium, Keynes was concerned with making immediate economic progress during times of economic imbalance. Keynes observed that in the long run "we are all dead," and therefore something should be done to improve the situation now. The economic problems of the Great Depression of the 1930s gave Keynes the opportunity to advance his new approach. He set forth a macroeconomic view of the situation, noting that the major problem of the economy at that time was that more was being produced than was being bought. The key to solving the problem, then, would be increasing spending to a level at which demand would rise to meet the supply. Keynes then prescribed ways in which government could increase the flow of spending by increasing governmental expenditures and encouraging consumers to spend their money. Keynes's work, *The General Theory of Employment, Interest, and Money,* published in 1936, elaborated on his view.

The idea that government should get involved with trying to fine tune the economy flew in the face of traditional laissez-faire thought. Nonetheless, the hardships and despair of the Depression brought popular support for measures that might help alleviate the economic difficulties. Thus many of the New Deal measures introduced by Franklin Roosevelt were the outgrowth of Keynesian thought. And though flaws and shortcomings have since been revealed in Keynesian economics, the government has continued to embrace an active role in the economy since the Depression.

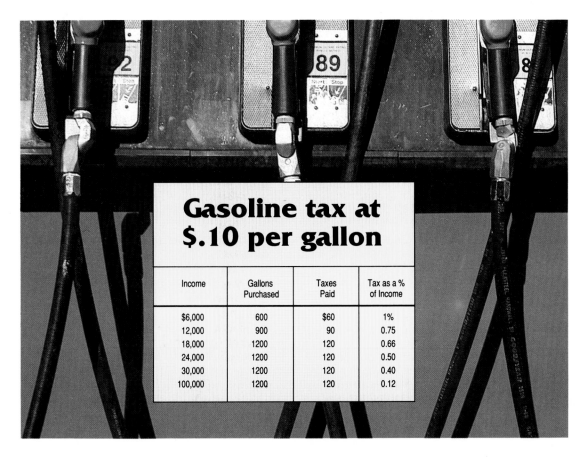

Gasoline tax at $.10 per gallon

Income	Gallons Purchased	Taxes Paid	Tax as a % of Income
$6,000	600	$60	1%
12,000	900	90	0.75
18,000	1200	120	0.66
24,000	1200	120	0.50
30,000	1200	120	0.40
100,000	1200	120	0.12

degree that their incomes rise. If the gasoline tax were 10¢ per gallon, the example above would show typical results.

Problems with Using Taxation as a Tool of Fiscal Policy

Obviously, the use of taxation as a means of affecting the economy presents many of the same problems that plague government spending. Taxation suffers from the time lags, politics, and effects of an uncertain multiplier; but taxation poses two additional unique problems.

Problem #1: Effect on the National Work Ethic– The traditional work ethic in the United States holds that work is morally good and that if one works hard enough, is frugal in his spending habits, and saves his money, he can enjoy a progressively higher standard of living. Fiscal policy, with its short-run solutions, may have the undesired effect of nullifying this ethic. There exists an obvious disincentive to work harder and produce more when one realizes that he will receive progressively lower percentages of his earnings. Sweden, with a heavy progressive personal income tax, takes between 50% to 60% of the average Swede's income in taxes. A decrease in incentive increases part-time employment, decreases productivity, and increases the use of barter to avoid reporting income-producing transactions.

Tax incentives in the 1970s encouraged farmers to buy too much equipment on credit.

Problem #2: Confusion in the Marketplace–Business firms base many financial decisions on their effect on the firms' tax burden. In the 1970s farmland values were high. Tax incentives, coupled with low-interest government loans, influenced farmers to borrow heavily to purchase agricultural equipment. After a few years, farmers, ready to trade in their used equipment, found that it commanded an attractive price. They could have used the income from the sale of their old equipment to pay for a majority of their new higher-priced equipment, but the tax incentives made it alluring for farmers to borrow the money again. Then 1981 saw an end to these tax incentives. Between 1981 and 1984 exports of grain and soybeans plummeted, commodity prices fell, interest rates escalated, and land values declined by 25%. Many farmers were forced to refinance their loans at higher interest rates as their debts matured. Other farmers, whose land value had declined, were denied refinancing altogether because of insufficient collateral, and as a result, many were forced into bankruptcy.

Other taxes that confuse the market are those levied on gains from savings and investment. In its attempt to boost the nation's marginal propensity to consume, the government has systematically penalized investing in capital assets such as stocks, bonds, and homes through high "capital gains" taxes, taxes on the profit realized on the sale of such property. However, the "profit" may be only an increase in the selling price caused by an increase in inflation, such as the sale of a home after several years of inflation. When the tax penalty for such a sale is greater than the reward, households shift their dollars from investing to buying consumer goods, thereby reducing the pool of borrowable funds available for business expansion.

Section Review

1. What is the greatest source of tax revenue for the federal government?
2. What are excise taxes?
3. What are proportional taxes, progressive taxes, and regressive taxes?
4. What are the two major problems with using taxation as a tool of fiscal policy?

III. Government Borrowing

It seems almost impossible to stimulate the economy without dampening it to the same degree. If the government wants to spend more, taxpayers will have to spend less, offsetting in the long run any gains the additional government spending brought about. Keynesian economists developed what they thought to be the answer to this problem by forging the third link in the fiscal policy chain–government borrowing. They reasoned that through borrowing, the government could increase its spending without taxing consumers or businesses.

"Pump Priming"

Keynesians believe that during a recession the government could borrow money and spend it. The expenditure would boost national income via the expenditure multiplier, and the momentum of the economy would keep GNP rising. The government would later raise taxes when the economy became prosperous and would use the increased revenue to retire the debt.

Thus, according to a famous Keynesian analogy, government may use debt to "prime" the economy, much as the old-time farmer "primed" a water pump with a bucket of water. After the pump began working, the bucket was refilled and set aside. In a similar fashion, Keynesians expected the economy to repay the debt when it began expanding and prospering.

Problems with Using Government Borrowing as a Tool of Fiscal Policy

The analogy of government borrowing to priming a quaint hand pump may be attractive and nostalgic, but it is seriously flawed.

Problem #1: There Is No Bucket of Idle Money Sitting on Reserve–According to Keynesian economic thought, the idle funds waiting to prime the economic pump are those dollars that households save. Keynesians believe that savings are wasted money, since the savings are not used to purchase job-creating goods and services. By borrowing the funds from the financial market, the government is believed to be liberating those captive, idle dollars

by putting them back into service.

The fallacy becomes obvious when one realizes that banks and other financial intermediaries do not accept deposits only to let them sit idle. Rather, they use deposited funds to make loans to business firms to purchase plants and equipment that will later generate enough income to pay off the loans and provide a profit. If the government channels these funds to itself, the economy will of course be stimulated through increased government spending. However, in the long run the economy will also be dampened to the same degree by the reduction in business investment.

Problem #2: Government Borrowing Becomes Addictive–Keynesian theory states that government should borrow in order to smooth the business cycle by pulling the economy out of recession, and later retire the debt when the economy has expanded. Politicians, on the other hand, desire to constantly stimulate the economy in order to produce jobs for the voting public. This attitude has led to federal budget deficits and government borrowing for 43 out of the 50 budgets between 1939 and 1989. As part of his 1984 presidential bid, Senator Walter Mondale of Minnesota campaigned under the Keynesian banner of increasing taxes to retire the tremendous deficit incurred in earlier years. He argued that the economy had sufficiently recovered and it was time to pay the debt. Voters showed their disdain for this part of Keynesian theory by their 49-state support of the Republican candidate, Ronald Reagan. No longer is fiscal overspending reserved for economic emergencies; it has become a way of life.

Problem #3: Government Borrowing Destroys a Nation's Future Productivity–In Chapter 1 you were introduced to the idea of opportunity cost. In that chapter it was emphasized that *every* decision provides both an opportunity benefit and a hidden opportunity cost. The opportunity benefits of government borrowing are immediate and obvious: jobs for the unemployed, food for the poor, shelter for the homeless, and clothing for the destitute. Less obvious but far more important is the opportunity cost. What does a nation forego when its government chooses to borrow from the financial market? For what would the money have otherwise been used? Had the government not borrowed the money, business firms would have borrowed the funds to build larger factories and purchase more efficient equipment. They too would have created jobs and income for the hungry, homeless, and destitute; however, the result would be less immediate since it requires time for new factories to be built.

The short-run benefits of government borrowing are deceptively attractive, but the long-run effects are truly debilitating. When the money which the government borrowed runs out, the government job is terminated, the food supply ceases, the shelter is closed, and the clothing disappears. Business firms, on the other hand, use the funds to create *permanent* jobs. By buying factories and equipment, they create products that will generate revenues sufficient to pay off the loan *and* provide further employment.

By borrowing from the financial markets, the government succumbs to short-run opportunity benefits that are eventually overshadowed by a far greater opportunity cost–the loss of future national productivity.

Section Review

1. How did Keynesians expect government borrowing to stimulate the economy?
2. What are the three problems associated with using government borrowing as a tool of fiscal policy?

Chapter Review

Terms

fiscal policy
Keynesian economics
marginal propensity to consume (MPC)
marginal propensity to save (MPS)
expenditure multiplier
Federal Insurance Contribution Act (FICA)
proportional tax
progressive tax
ability-to-pay principle
regressive tax

Content Questions

1. What are the three tools of fiscal policy?

2. List the three largest expenditures in the federal budget.
3. What is the expenditure multiplier?
4. What are the three largest sources of federal tax revenues?
5. What does the phrase "pump priming" mean?

Application Questions

1. List several examples of proportional and regressive taxes.
2. Analyze the current economic climate in the nation. What conditions suggest that the government is following Keynesian economic policies? Note any examples of laissez-faire policies.

Unit VI: Economics of the Household

CHAPTER 15

Budgeting and Buying

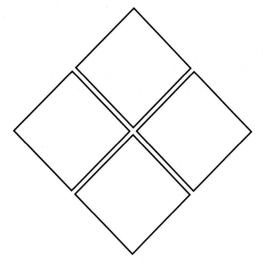

For the love of money is the root of all evil: which while some coveted after, they have erred from the faith, and pierced themselves through with many sorrows.

I Timothy 6:10

One sunny Monday morning a trainee arrived at his new place of work eager to make a good impression and looking forward to all of the new experiences that were awaiting him. Shortly after he arrived, he was ushered into the dark mahogany-paneled office of the president of the company. The silver-haired gentleman looked quite distinguished as he peered through his reading glasses at the young man's resume. "Son," the president's pause was punctuated by the deep tick-tock of the grandfather clock in the corner, "we run a tight business here. There is no room for slip-ups in this organization. You are coming to work for a store which buys and sells a commodity unlike that sold in any other store. This is a bank, and the commodity with

which we deal is held in higher esteem in the average American family than God Himself: Money."

At first glance this true story makes one uneasy. As Christians we are offended that even an unsaved bank president could be that callous. The sad fact, however, is that the bank president's observation is, for the most part, true. How do Americans demonstrate their high esteem for money? The average American spends more time, energy, and resources in his quest for financial security than he does in his quest for God. Out of contempt for this money-grabbing attitude, some believers unfortunately attempt to divorce themselves from all money issues. Some Christians believe that money itself is evil rather than the *love* of money. Therefore, they avoid budgeting, sound investing, and wise financial planning. As a result, they live from month to month and from crisis to crisis bringing grief upon themselves and reproach upon the name of Christ. While consistently warning against covetousness and greed, Jesus Christ also preached about financial preparation.

> For which of you, intending to build a tower, sitteth not down first, and counteth the cost, whether he have sufficient to finish it? Lest haply, after he hath laid the foundation, and is not able to finish it, all that behold it begin to mock him, Saying, This man began to build, and was not able to finish.
>
> (Luke 14:28-30)

Perhaps nowhere is financial preparation more important than in the home. In this chapter we will examine how to develop an effective budget for the home; then we will consider some principles involved in being a wise Christian consumer.

I. The Household Budget

A **budget** is a tabulation of income and planned expenditures. For centuries business firms and governments have used budgets to attempt to get the most for their money. Likewise, families and individuals may use household budgets to allocate their scarce funds to their greatest possible use.

THE IMPULSE BUYER'S DREAM COME TRUE...

WOW! I COULD USE A MINI TV!!

...TOUCHTONE SHOPPING!

Benefits of Budgeting

Why develop a personal or family budget? After all, it takes quite a bit of time to sit down and think through where all of your money is coming from and where it is going. Consider the following reasons:

First, a budget identifies spending priorities. Chapter 1 of this book pointed out that all of us live in a world in which we cannot have everything we want. Therefore, we are pulled between insatiability on one hand and scarcity on the other. As a result, we must make choices about what we do with our finite time, how we allocate our limited effort, and how we spend our scarce money. One way or another, choices will be made. In the area of our spending, if we do not create a budget which provides a systematic plan for future spending, we will live from moment to moment buying those things which strike our fancy. Such unplanned purchases or **impulse buying** may force us later to forego purchasing some things which are truly im-

portant. Developing a budget allows us to set our priorities ahead of time, permitting us to make our own choices as opposed to having choices dictated to us as circumstances develop.

Second, a budget prevents potential conflicts with loved ones. When a husband and wife prepare a household budget in which family priorities are addressed, many future tensions are avoided. A family that spends without regard to priorities can easily make purchases beyond its income, forcing the family either to forego purchasing some necessities or to rely on credit. When this occurs, the seeds of resentment and disharmony find fertile soil. On the other hand, as a husband and wife plan their budget together, their relationship is strengthened. Each now has a financial stake in the relationship, each must compromise personal needs and wants for the good of each other and the family, and each is inclined to be more willing to sacrifice in the future if their jointly-created budget needs adjustment.

Third, a budget is a big first step toward a successful, comprehensive **financial plan.** By developing a budget, a family can balance not only their present needs and wants, but also plan toward the purchase of certain necessary items such as automobiles or houses with a minimum of debt. A budget allows the family to provide insurance for emergencies, savings for their children's college expense, and provision for retirement.

Finally, the budget allows the Christian to properly exercise his role as a steward. Do you recall the origin of the word economics? Chapter 1 noted that the word "economics" is actually derived from two Greek words which mean "rule of the house." In the truest sense of the word, therefore, economics begins in the home, with the home's finances ruled by an effective budget. By developing a Christ-centered family budget, a family can provide for the Lord's work through Scriptural giving, meet the physical needs of family members, and assist others as well.

A HOUSEHOLD BUDGET . . .

1. **IDENTIFIES SPENDING PRIORITIES**

2. **PREVENTS POTENTIAL CONFLICTS WITH LOVED ONES**

3. **AIDS THE DEVELOPMENT OF A FINANCIAL PLAN**

4. **ENCOURAGES GOOD STEWARDSHIP**

By developing a budget, a family can allocate their scarce funds to the greatest possible use.

Creating a Budget

Budget Categories–The first step in creating an effective budget is the identification of priorities. Generally speaking, there are fifteen spending categories with which the family must deal.

1. **Scriptural Giving and Other Contributions and Gifts** The first item on the Christian's budget should be systematic Scriptural giving, because giving is commanded by God.

> Honour the Lord with thy substance, and with the firstfruits of all thine increase: So shall thy barns be filled with plenty, and thy presses shall burst out with new wine.
> (Proverbs 3:9-10)

> Upon the first day of the week let every one of you lay by him in store, as God hath prospered him, that there be no gatherings when I come.
> (I Corinthians 16:2)

Besides providing for the financial needs of one's local church and other worthy Christian ministries, one must budget any other giving which he wishes to make. This category includes gifts to other charitable organizations, birthday, Christmas, anniversary, wedding, and graduation gifts.

2. **Saving** In the decade of the 1970s the average American family saved nearly 8% of its income while its Japanese counterpart saved nearly 20%. During the decade of the 1980s, American savings fell to about 5% while the Japanese figure declined only to 17%. It is no

wonder that personal savings in the United States has been dropping so dramatically, given the fact that most families give it last place in their budgets. Many Americans believe that savings should come from money left over after all purchases have been made. When we consider that desires for purchases are unlimited, it is a miracle that American families can save anything at all. In order to save meaningful amounts, savings must become systematic. Saving becomes much easier if a family purposes that saving is important and specifically budgets a certain dollar amount or percentage of its income to be deposited each month. Many financial planners suggest that families set aside at least 10% of their incomes toward savings, but this may be too difficult a goal to set at first. As a family gradually reduces its unnecessary spending it may gradually increase its savings. Keeping in mind that families also "save" by investing in the purchase of a home, contributing to private and business retirement plans, and purchasing investment-type insurance policies, this 10% figure may be adjusted to suit the family's situation. Specific methods of saving will be discussed in greater detail in Chapter 17.

3. **Food** When families budget for their food needs, they have a tendency to include only the expense of foods prepared at home. This category should also include the purchase of school lunches, coffee break money, and the purchase of food in restaurants.

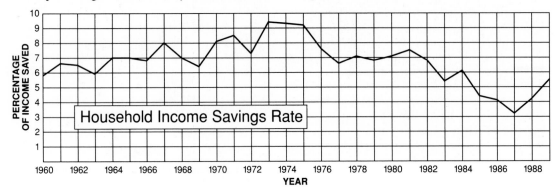

4. Housing   Housing includes mortgage payments, property taxes, homeowner's insurance, and rent. Many lending institutions will provide for a home buyer's property taxes and property insurance to be paid through what is known as an **escrow account.** The lender will determine the total of the buyer's annual obligation for property taxes and property insurance, will divide the amount by twelve months, and will increase the borrower's monthly payment. The additional money will be held in the escrow account until the tax collector and the property insurance company send the lending institution a bill. Escrow accounts permit homeowners to avoid the inconvenience of having to make large lump-sum payments every six months or year. Also included in the housing category are the costs of routine maintenance and repairs, such as paint and wallpaper, and of furnishings such as carpets, furniture, appliances, etc.

5. Utilities   The utility budget should include expenses for electricity, heating oil, natural gas, telephone, water, sewage disposal or septic tank service, and garbage pickup (if not paid for by property taxes).

6. Transportation   The transportation budget includes payments on automobile loans, license renewal charges, license fees, vehicle inspection charges, automobile insurance, gasoline, oil, other maintenance expenses, and parking expenses such as change for parking meters and fees for parking garages. Also included are other transportation charges such as car rentals, and airplane, bus, train, and subway tickets.

7. Clothing   The clothing budget includes not only the purchase of garments but also items

A family's budget should include provisions for common needs such as clothing, food, and transportation.

Insuring Your Home and Auto

Ownership of a house or car entails many financial responsibilities such as taxes, utility bills, and maintenance expenses. Because of the ever-present danger of accidents, theft, or damage to these expensive possessions, insurance may also be a wise purchase. Because insurance policies vary in coverage and in price, and because not all insurance companies and agents have the same reputation for dealing promptly and fairly with claims, the consumer should shop carefully for the insurance purchase that best suits his needs.

Homeowner's Insurance

Homeowner's insurance usually includes both liability coverage and a comprehensive policy. Homeowner's liability insurance will pay for bodily injury and property damage incurred by any visitor on the insured person's property (for instance, if a delivery man trips on the steps and breaks his leg). Comprehensive coverage protects the homeowner from heavy loss due to a number of possible misfortunes, generally including fire, theft, windstorms, hail, and lightning damage. When buying such a policy, the consumer should make sure that the most likely dam-

ages and losses will be covered by the comprehensive insurance. Homeowners in certain areas of the country may want to add special coverage for disastrous events such as earthquakes and floods to their basic comprehensive coverage. The amount of money for which a home should be insured should be at least 80% of the replacement cost of the house, and preferably 100%. Periodic adjustments should be made for increased value because of inflation.

A beneficial feature of a homeowner's comprehensive policy is that it covers not only the house and other buildings on the property but also the policyholder's personal property, such as furniture, clothing, and appliances, from damage or loss because of covered misfortunes. This coverage extends to losses away from the property as well (for instance, if a suitcase is stolen out of his car). For those who do not own their own home but have valuable personal property, renter's insurance provides a similar coverage. Because a landlord's insurance does not cover a renter's personal property losses, this kind of insurance is often advantageous.

Automobile Insurance

There are several kinds of automobile insurance coverage, and of these, three of the most common are liability, collision, and comprehensive. Most states require car owners to carry liability insurance, which covers the costs of bodily injury and property damage to others caused by the insured car or driver. On a liability policy the limits of coverage will usually appear something like this: 100/300/50. In this example the insurance company would pay up to $100,000 for each person injured in a mishap up to a total of $300,000 for all personal injuries, and it would pay up to $50,000 for damage to property. In determining how much coverage the consumer should buy in each of these categories, he should consider the average court costs and settlements for accidents in his area of the country.

Collision insurance will pay for the repair or replacement of the policyholder's car. This coverage is generally required if there is a mortgage on the vehicle, and it is otherwise practical if the car has significant value. If, however, the car is more than a few years old and of no classic value, collision insurance is usually unnecessary and not cost-effective.

Comprehensive automobile insurance covers damage and loss to the vehicle by means other than traffic accidents. It generally includes protection against theft, vandalism, hail damage, glass breakage, and other misfortunes. This comprehensive insurance, along with collision insurance and homeowner's comprehensive insurance, usually stipulates a "deductible." A deductible is the amount the policyholder must pay before the insurance policy will cover the remainder. The deductible on a typical comprehensive automobile insurance policy could be $200. In this case, for example, when a $500 claim is filed for hail damage, the insurance company will deduct the $200 from that claim and pay the policyholder

$300. In this way insurance companies avoid paying for many minor mishaps altogether, such as nicks in the car paint or the theft of a battery. Generally speaking, the higher the deductible, the lower the cost of the insurance policy.

Another kind of automobile coverage is medical payments insurance. This pays for the medical expenses of the policyholder and his family in the event of an accident. Because many health insurance policies already cover these expenses, this coverage is often unnecessary. Uninsured motorist insurance pays for damage incurred in an accident that was the fault of another driver who does not have liability insurance.

No-fault insurance is another kind of coverage that is required in a few states. This insurance pays the policyholder for damage and injury in any accident, regardless of who was at fault. The intent of this kind of insurance is to limit costly litigation in accident cases and provide speedy payment of claims.

The costs of automobile insurance vary widely not only with the type of coverage but also with the kind of car and driver to be insured and conditions in the state in which the driving will be done. Insurance companies keep many statistics to determine the probability of accidents involving various kinds of cars and drivers. As a result, high-performance sports cars are usually much more expensive to insure than compact economy cars. Because they tend to have far more accidents, young single men aged 16 to 25 are more expensive to insure as drivers than are women and married or older men. However, drivers can often reduce their costs if their insurance company allows discounts for a good driving record, taking a driver-training course, or maintaining good grades in school.

such as hats, purses, shoes, billfolds, dry cleaning bills, laundry expenses, sewing notions, patterns, and material.

 8. **Health** All health insurance should be budgeted under this category including hospital, medical, dental, and life insurance. Also included should be prescription drugs.

 9. **Personal** The personal budget includes sundries such as soaps, hair care items, toothpaste, make-up, and self-medications including bandages, over-the-counter allergy medications, aspirin, and foot powder.

10. **Entertainment and Recreation** This part of the budget should include all planned expenses related to vacations, hobbies, sporting events, cameras and film, babysitting fees, and other related expenses.

11. **Education** The education budget should include all items of a personal improvement nature. Such expenses consist of school tuition and fees, books, newspaper and magazine subscriptions, office equipment used in the home, dictionaries, encyclopedias and other reference books, and the bookshelves to hold them.

12. **Work** Some families incur expenses which are directly related to employment including charges for uniforms, safety items such as shoes, gloves, or glasses, work related tools, and office equipment.

13. **Allowances** Many families provide small allowances for children (and adults as well!) for which the use is not specifically budgeted.

14. **Miscellaneous** The miscellaneous category includes expenses which are so small or so infrequent that a separate category for each is impractical. Miscellaneous expenses may include bank service charges, watch batteries, and photocopying charges.

15. **Contingencies** A **contingency** is an uncertain event. It is unlikely that all expenses will be accurately predicted; therefore, it would be wise to create a contingent category in one's budget. Contingency expenses may include those which are a result of unforeseen damage to one's house, higher costs related to unexpected guests, and **deductibles,** amounts not covered by insurance policies.

Fixed Versus Variable Expenses–The obvious purpose of a budget is to determine where money has been going in the past and how to best allocate it in the future. When creating a family budget, consider that there exist two kinds of expenses. First, **fixed expenses** are those expenses which do not rise or fall as the family's income increases in the short run. Fixed expenses cannot be changed immediately without disrupting the family's financial situation. Examples of fixed expenses include rent or mortgage payments, minimum food expenses, minimum utilities, property taxes, and essential transportation costs.

Variable expenses, on the other hand, are those costs which rise and fall as the family's income changes. If the family experiences a cut in income, variable expenses may be reduced without significantly harming the family's financial situation. Examples of variable expenses include vacation expenses, gifts, entertainment expenses, new clothing purchases, and allowances.

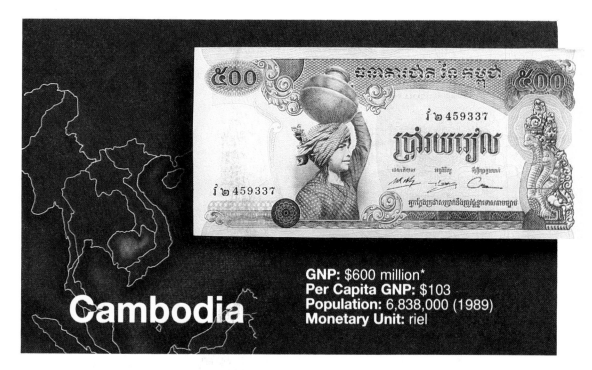

Cambodia

GNP: $600 million*
Per Capita GNP: $103
Population: 6,838,000 (1989)
Monetary Unit: riel

The economy of the small agricultural country of Cambodia (also known as Kampuchea) has been in disarray since the Vietnam War spilled into the land. Though never a rich country, Cambodia had developed a simple economic system in which fishermen and farmers provided all the fish and rice the people needed, and the nation was able to export some rice, rubber, and black pepper. The Communist advance in Southeast Asia, however, brought upheaval to the land of the Cambodians.

In the early 1970s the anti-Communist government struggled to fight off the rising tide of communism. Communists called the Khmer Rouge overthrew the government in 1975 and established a harsh totalitarian state. The Khmer Rouge isolated Cambodia from the world economy and even abolished the nation's currency. Agriculture was collectivized, and people were driven from the cities to raise crops on the organized farms. In the process, over one million Cambodians

were killed. This adversity was followed by further fighting as Vietnamese Communist troops poured into the country in 1979 to set up their own regime. Though pushed out of power, the Khmer Rouge moved into the countryside to carry on guerrilla warfare. In addition, non-Communist leaders sought to regain control of land. Constant conflict drove many Cambodians off the land and into refugee camps and totally disrupted the nation's agricultural and business activity. International relief efforts were necessary to save large numbers from starvation.

Although Vietnamese troops left Cambodia in 1989, the political turmoil continued. Currency has been reintroduced, but the rebuilding of the Cambodian economy will require a significantly more stable government than the Cambodians have experienced in some time.

*figure for 1981 from *Clement's Encyclopedia of World Governments*

Stretching the Family Budget

Most families who consider their budget agree that they could benefit from a decrease in some of their expenses. Decreases are usually possible if a family is determined to use available opportunities to save money, but where should they begin? Numerous possibilities exist in almost every household for successfully "cutting corners" to reduce spending. Some may be obvious; others may require some ingenuity. Here are a few suggestions that could help a family economize.
• When possible, buy groceries that are on sale, and use coupons for further reductions.
• Prepare more meals at home from scratch instead of buying more expensive prepared foods.
• Consolidate business and shopping errands into fewer driving trips, and walk when possible.
• Buy conservative and versatile clothing instead of faddish garments and accessories that must be replaced frequently.

• Do not hesitate to buy only sale-priced items in a store without buying additional merchandise.
• Play games at home or visit local parks and museums instead of pursuing more expensive entertainment.
• Conserve energy by turning out all unneeded lights, running only full loads in the dishwasher and washing machine, and setting the thermostat up or down a degree or two to cut the use of the air conditioner or furnace.
• Buy "day-old" bakery goods and outlet merchandise at a discount, when possible, rather than paying full price for needed items.
• Buy more breakfast foods, which are less expensive, and cut back on evening meals.
• Take snacks from home instead of buying candy and drinks from vending machines or convenience stores.

Putting Your Budget in Writing–Probably the biggest reason most people refuse to budget their money is that they believe the process is too time consuming. The process can be made much easier, however, if the family makes up its own budget sheet and uses it as a guide in the budgeting process. The budget preparation sheet should have three columns. The first column is for the family to write down all *current* expenditures being made for each of the fifteen categories. Rather than simply using last month's expense figures, it might be more accurate to use an average of the amounts spent in each category over the past three months. These figures should be a good starting point in determining the amounts which are to be included in the budget. The second column provides for planned adjustments to current spending. This is the column over which considerable thought must be given. To get all members of the family involved, parents may wish to assign their children certain research projects to detect methods of reducing costs.

The third column, then, is simply column one minus column two. This column represents the actual amount budgeted for the month. In theory the figures in column three are the maximum amounts the family may spend for each category. As the amount spent gets closer to the maximum amount, the family may be forced to slow spending in that category or else "rob" a different category. Keep in mind that the budget is a tool; as emergencies and unforeseen circumstances develop, the budget may be modified. Many families make the mistake of creating a budget which is very difficult to achieve, become discouraged, and give up.

Consider the case of John and Joanne Carter in Figure 15-1. He is forty-one years of age and she is forty. Mr. Carter works full-time in his own heating and air-conditioning business, bringing home $2,000 per month after taxes. Mrs. Carter works part-time as a substitute teacher, and she brings home $619 per month after taxes. Their combined monthly after-tax income, therefore, is $2,619. Because their only child recently left for college, Mr. and Mrs. Carter are concerned that their spending is out of line with their income; so they had a meeting to plan their budget. After computing their actual spending, they discovered that over the last three months they spent an average of $47 more than their monthly income. After discussing each category of spending, they came to the conclusion that they could decrease some of their variable costs and increase their monthly savings by $94 per month for a total of $244 per month. Their desire is to build up a sizeable account balance in order to assist their son in school and plan for their re-

Figure 15-1

	Actual Spending (month)	Proposed Adjustments (month)	New Amount Budgeted
Contributions:			
Scriptural Giving	300	—	300
Rescue Mission	25	—	25
Heart Fund	10	—	10
Savings:			
	150	+94	244
Food:			
Groceries	286	-36	250
Eating Out	40	-10	30
Housing:			
Mortgage Payment	382	—	382
Home Owner's Ins.	25	—	25
Property Tax	20	—	20
Maintenance	28	—	28
Utilities:			
Electricity	77	-17	60
Natural Gas	27	—	27
Telephone	33	-5	28
Water	23	—	23
Transportation:			
Auto Payment	114	—	114
Auto Insurance	23	—	23
Gas & Oil	42	—	42
Maintenance	18	—	18
Parking Garage	10	-10	0

	Actual Spending (month)	Proposed Adjustments (month)	New Amount Budgeted
Clothing:			
New Purchases	64	-14	50
Dry Cleaning/Laundry	11	—	11
Health:			
Health Insurance	64	—	64
Medicine	20	—	20
Doctor Bills	33	—	33
Dental Care	12	—	12
Personal:	87	-27	60
Entertainment/Rec.:	35	—	35
Education:			
Christian College Pmt.	400	—	400
Books	100	—	100
Work:	0	—	0
Allowances:	50	-10	40
Miscellaneous:	82	-12	70
Contingencies:	75	—	75
Total	2666	-91	2619
Income	2619		2619
Difference	<47>		0

tirement which they hope to commence when Mr. Carter turns 60. Upon retirement, the Carters, out of a deep desire to serve the Lord, wish to purchase a motor home and spend ten years traveling throughout the United States and Canada visiting and assisting missionaries and pastors.

Monitoring Your Budget

A budget is of no value if it is put on a shelf and forgotten immediately after it is created. It should be constantly referred to as the family tries to get its spending in line with its income. A budget is like a speedometer. It is a gauge to show if the family's money is going out faster or slower than had been projected. Therefore, it is of great importance to monitor actual monthly spending relative to what was budgeted. Figure 15-2 is the Carter's second statement listing their actual monthly spending for each category relative to what they had budgeted. Column one shows their budgeted amounts, column two lists their actual spending, column three is the variance, or difference between columns one and two, and column four provides a space for explanations of differences.

One month after their first budget meeting Mr. and Mrs. Carter met to determine if they were keeping in line with their new budget. They were generally pleased with their results. They saved some money by not eating out, but they paid out more for transportation because they had to have new brakes installed on their car. They spent a little more than anticipated on entertainment and recreation by taking the pastor and his wife out for her birthday, and their kitchen sink plumbing developed a leak leading to higher-than-anticipated contingency spending. All things being considered, they were very pleased with their first month, but they promised to try a little harder next month.

Section Review

1. What is a budget?
2. What are the four benefits of budgeting?
3. What should be the first category in the Christian's budget? Why?
4. How may a budget be used after purchases have already been made?

Figure 15-2

	Monthly Budgeted Amount	Actual Spending	Variance	Reason
Contributions:				
Scriptural Giving	300	300	0	
Rescue Mission	25	25	0	
Heart Fund	10	10	0	
Savings:	244	244	0	
Food:				
Groceries	250	269	<19>	
Eating Out	30	0	30	Didn't eat out
Housing:				
Mortgage Payment	382	382	0	
Home Owner's Ins.	25	25	0	
Property Tax	20	20	0	
Maintenance	28	28	0	
Utilities:				
Electricity	60	74	<14>	
Natural Gas	27	32	<5>	
Telephone	28	24	4	
Water	23	25	<2>	
Transportation:				
Auto Payment	114	114	0	
Auto Insurance	23	23	0	
Gas & Oil	42	33	9	
Maintenance	18	65	<47>	New brakes needed
Parking Garage	0	0	0	

	Monthly Budgeted Amount	Actual Spending	Variance	Reason
Clothing:				
New Purchases	50	40	10	
Dry Cleaning/Laundry	11	15	<4>	
Health:				
Health Insurance	64	64	0	
Medicine	20	16	4	
Doctor Bills	33	0	33	
Dental Care	12	19	<7>	
Personal:	60	72	<12>	
Entertainment/Rec.:	35	50	<15>	Took Pastor and wife out for dinner
Education:				
Christian College Pmt.	400	400	0	
Books	100	120	<20>	
Work:	0	0	0	
Allowances:	40	40	0	
Miscellaneous:	70	43	27	
Contingencies:	75	100	<25>	Replaced plumbing under kitchen sink
Total	2679	2672	<53>	
Income				
Difference				

II. Wise Purchasing

Principles of Purchasing

Proverbs 31:16 and 18 describe the virtuous woman as one who is a wise consumer, a consumer who *thinks* about what she is about to purchase:

> She considereth a field, and buyeth it: with the fruit of her hands she planteth a vineyard. . . . She perceiveth that her merchandise is good: her candle goeth not out by night.

Likewise, all Christians, whether male or female, should be wise stewards of the money the Lord has entrusted into their care. Therefore when a believer enters the marketplace, it is important for him to keep in mind eight principles of wise purchasing.

Principle #1–Purpose to Honor God with Your Purchases: What is your motive for purchasing a product? Before making a purchase ask yourself if the use of it will honor or dishonor God.

> Whether therefore ye eat, or drink, or whatsoever ye do, do all to the glory of God.
>
> (I Corinthians 10:31)

Principle #2–Shop with Knowledge: Before you go shopping, especially for major purchases, check the product's features and reliability with consumer product publications. Does the manufacturer guarantee the product? Will the manufacturer provide good service after the sale? In addition to checking published reports, investigate the dealer or store from which you are buying. Consult the

Getting Information Before You Buy

A wise consumer is an informed consumer. Major purchases that take a significant bite out of the family income should not be made without knowledge about the product and the company that sells it. Several sources of helpful information for consumers are readily available, and their use may prevent an unwise purchase and the increased expense that it entails. Many consumers use the following three organizations to help them be wise and informed purchasers.

Consumers Union

Consumers Union, founded in 1936, is a nonprofit organization that tests common products for their safety, defects, economy, and other advantages and disadvantages. After comparing the products of several manufacturers, Consumers Union publishes its analysis and comparisons in a publication called *Consumer Reports.* Consumers Union buys the products it tests and it accepts no advertising in its magazine so that it may publish an objective report for the consumer. *Consumer Reports* gives information on the most common brands of many products from automobiles and insurance to walking shoes and refrigerators.

Consumer Research, Inc.

Consumer Research is an organization similar to Consumers Union that publishes its own findings on products in *Consumers' Research Magazine.* Consumer Research sometimes rents or borrows expensive products for testing rather than buying them independently, but even so it strives to give a fair and objective appraisal of the items it surveys.

Better Business Bureaus

The National Better Business Bureau was organized in 1916, and it has offices in all major cities and counties around the nation. Businesses support this organization because it benefits an honest business's own reputation and discourages unscrupulous competitors. It not only provides consumers with information about the products and business practices of local businesses before a purchase but also helps consumers get redress for legitimate complaints against goods and services after they have bought them.

Better Business Bureau to see if the firm has a history of dissatisfied customers.

Principle #3–Shop with a Plan: Before you shop for anything, know exactly what you need to buy and what questions to ask. For example, when you shop for groceries, shop with a list of items you need for the coming week. Of course, it takes time to "do your homework" before you shop, but if you do so without a plan, you will have a greater tendency to make impulse purchases. Without a plan you will be unsure of what questions to ask salespeople.

Principle #4–Carry Only the Necessary Amount of Money: As the police are often fond of saying "Motive plus Opportunity equals Crime," likewise, a shopper's momentary desire fueled by the opportunity provided by having ready cash or credit cards may very easily equal an unwise purchase.

Principle #5–Look Carefully at the Price Tag and Receipt: Do not be fooled by "sales." In some cases merchants will mark an item with a much higher price only to "mark it down" to a price which is still higher than one should pay. Also, pay attention to **unit pricing.** Unit pricing is the price per measure unit of the product. For example, when deciding between bags of potato chips of equal quality, do not look at the price tag on the bags as the determining factor; look at the price per ounce. One brand may sell a slightly smaller bag in order to display a smaller overall price while at the same time charging a higher price per ounce. If the store does not display unit prices, take along an electronic pocket calculator and determine unit prices for yourself. After you shop, compare the price you were charged with the actual price of the item. If your store uses cashiers who manually enter prices into a cash register, errors may occur out of carelessness. On the other hand, if your store uses electronic scanners which scan the UPC bar codes, there is a chance that prices were programmed incorrectly or that sale prices were not entered to override the original higher price.

Principle #6–Consider the Total Cost: Remember that the "cost" of an item not only includes its price tag, but all of the costs associated with it throughout its life. For example, assume that you find a "terrific buy" on a popular sports car. Instead of costing its normal price of $30,000, it can be purchased for only $12,000. But do not stop there. Check for other costs. Is the dealer charging a preparation fee? How about taxes and registration fees? Consider insurance; the cost of insuring a sports car may be prohibitively expensive.

Principle #7–Ask for Advice: When making a major purchase such as a house, an automobile, or a major appliance, it would be wise to have an expert provide counsel. For example, have a reputable auto mechanic look over a used car before making a commitment to purchase it. It may cost a few dollars, but it will be a few dollars well spent. He may be able to spot hidden costly problems which you would not have noticed until after a contract was signed.

Principle #8–Do Not Be fooled: Some salespeople prey upon the vanity or ignorance of shoppers by using deceitful advertising or fraudulent sales methods. Be aware of the techniques they might employ.

CHEEZY CHIPS
9 OZ   0109672
$1.89
UNIT PRICE
21.1¢
PER OUNCE
273-217
DIRECT

CHEDDAR CHIPS
10 OZ   0004673
$1.99
UNIT PRICE
19.9¢
PER OUNCE
289-217
DIRECT

Fraud and Deception

There exists an old Latin maxim *caveat emptor* "let the buyer beware!" which means that it is the buyer's responsibility to ensure that he is not being deceived. While government regulation does protect consumers to a greater degree than it did a century ago, fraudulent business practices have not yet ceased to exist, and the buyer must still beware.

It would be nice if consumers could always trust salespersons and advertisements to be totally honest about the products they are attempting to sell. Unfortunately, however, the depravity of man is all too evident in many cases. One common advertising deception is known as a **bait-and-switch.** In this type of dishonesty a company advertises a product, say a refrigerator or some carpeting. The advertisement makes the product seem fine and offers it at a very low price. That is the "bait" that draws customers into the store, but when they arrive, they find that the product they came to buy is somehow undesirable or unobtainable. The refrigerator may be scratched and dented, or the advertised product may be "sold out" (although it probably never was available for sale). The carpet may be of an obviously inferior quality. A salesman then explains that what the customer really needs is a larger refrigerator with more features or a higher quality carpet–items that are priced significantly higher.

Other forms of deceptive advertising include bogus contests and giveaways. A customer is told that he has won some prize or can have something absolutely free. Whether it be a new television or wonderful vacation package, there is likely to be some kind of catch. Usually the "winner" must buy something else at a high price to receive his prize.

Fraud occurs when someone is deliberately dishonest in order to make his sale. He may give false information about a competing product or claim that his product can do something that it cannot do. He may trick a customer into signing a contract or charge for extra parts or services that he does not include. In a land scam he may sell a "beautiful lot in a plush resort area" that turns out to be a small piece of unusable swampland. In a sly telemarketing scheme, he may sell get-rich-quick investments to people gullible enough to give their credit card number or send a check for the impossible deal before he disappears with the money.

Ingenious swindlers and unethical businesspersons are constantly finding ways to dupe unwary consumers into unwise purchases. While advertising deception and fraud are illegal, innocent people who succumb to them are often too embarrassed to make the wrong known. Even if they do press charges, the inconveniences and expense of the ordeal are dismaying. Therefore, it is always best to remember *caveat emptor!*

The Government and the Consumer

In addition to the things that a customer can do to protect himself from making unwise purchases, he may recognize the government regulations ensuring many of his rights. These regulations and the regulatory agencies designed to implement them may prove helpful if the consumer suffers from unfair business practices.

Consumer Rights–Because of an explosion of fraudulent business practices during the first half of the twentieth century and the courts' *caveat emptor* attitude at that time, American consumers rose up and demanded that the government protect them. The era of **consumerism,** the drive for the enforcement of consumer rights, was born in 1962 when President John Kennedy sent a bill to Congress which would guarantee four fundamental consumer rights:

1. *The right to safety*–American consumers should have the right to be confident that the product they purchase will not be dangerous to their lives or to their health.
2. *The right to be informed*–Americans should have the right to expect that business will provide enough information to assist consumers in making informed choices.
3. *The right to choose*–American consumers should not be held at the mercy of monopoly companies. The government should guarantee free competition, for where competition exists, there also exists a greater number of product choices at lower prices.
4. *The right to be heard*–When the government is making policy decisions, consumers should have the right to effectively express their concerns.

Since 1962 other presidents have added to President Kennedy's list:

5. *The right to an environment free of pollution.*
6. *The right to education on consumer issues*–American consumers have a right to be educated by the government about consumer issues.
7. *The right to fight back*–If a consumer suffers as a result of buying a defective product or service, he should have the right to **redress;** that is, he should have the right to be heard in court and receive reasonable compensation.

Enforcement of Consumer Rights–In order to enforce the consumer rights proposed by President Kennedy and those who followed him, a number of federal agencies were created. These agencies were given the power to enact laws and subsequently to punish offenders.

Food and Drug Administration In keeping with the first of President Kennedy's consumer rights, the Food and Drug Administration (FDA), which was created in 1906, was empowered in 1962 to test all new drugs before they could be admitted to the marketplace. Additionally, that same year, the FDA was given the power to require that drugs not only be safe, but also "effective."

Federal Trade Commission The Federal Trade Commission (FTC), created in 1914, today ensures that the second of President Kennedy's consumer rights is maintained, the right to be informed. It is the FTC which monitors advertising, labeling, and deceptive practices, and reviews applications for complaints. If the FTC discovers a deceptive practice, it may either issue a **cease and desist order** which prohibits a firm from continuing a deceptive practice, or it may require **counteradvertising.** Counteradvertising is advertising that a firm must produce, at its own expense, for the purpose of correcting any false claims which its earlier advertising promoted.

Consumer Product Safety Commission In response to a growing number of unsafe consumer products that did not fall under the administration of the FDA, the Consumer Product Safety Commission (CPSC) was created in 1972 by the passage of the Consumer Product Safety Act. The CPSC has broad powers to detect and regulate potentially hazardous consumer products. The CPSC has the power to devise safety standards for consumer products and may forbid sales of products considered hazardous. For example, the CPSC has forced some toy manufacturers to recall products possessing parts that might be easily swallowed by small children.

Ralph Nader (1934-)
Spokesman for Consumerism

This lawyer and son of Lebanese immigrants, Ralph Nader, rose to become America's first and foremost consumer advocate. From his youth he was deeply concerned about matters regarding public safety and corporate power, and he dreamed of becoming a "people's lawyer." As he attended Princeton and earned a law degree from Harvard, his extracurricular activities reflected his intense concerns. In the 1960s he began a crusade to dramatize one of these concerns, the issue of auto safety, and to gain federal regulation.

Ralph Nader wrote a book, published in 1965, called *Unsafe at Any Speed*. The work condemned the automobile industry (and especially General Motors in its production of the Chevrolet Corvair) for allegedly sacrificing safety in its attempt to achieve a popular style. Nader carried on his attack by testifying before a Senate subcommittee. When it was later learned that General Motors had been harassing Nader for his pursuit of the issue, passage of the Traffic and Motor Vehicle Safety Act of 1966 was assured. Seatbelts appeared in all new cars, and Nader won his reputation as a consumer advocate.

Nader did not limit his political action to matters of automobile safety, however. He built a network of organizations under the banner of Public Citizen, Incorporated, to investigate corporate abuse of consumers and to lobby government for regulative action. This work resulted in many federal laws involving everything from air and water pollution to meat and poultry inspection.

Nader was a popular hero for several years because he had generally fought for the rights of the common man. Even so, by the mid-1970s Nader's popularity began to wane as he voiced stronger pleas for government regulation of America's private businesses and even the nationalization of industry. A growing public concern for maintaining free-enterprise capitalism caused people to reject such socialistic ideas and to abandon Nader as a controversial voice proclaiming his dangerous brand of consumerism.

In addition to these three agencies, other government agencies exist to further ensure consumer rights. These agencies include the Department of Health and Human Services, the Environmental Protection Agency, and a number of state agencies. Several private "watchdog" organizations, including the Consumers Union and the Better Business Bureau (BBB), also exist to aid consumers.

Your Responsibilities as a Consumer

Much is being made today of the responsibilities of business firms to consumers, but what, if any, responsibilities do consumers have toward business firms? While not codified into laws, there exist some common courtesies which should be extended by all Christian consumers.

1. *Courteous treatment*–Many times it is the consumer demanding courteous service who is rude in his dealings with business people. If we expect sympathetic and courteous treatment as customers, we should likewise be sympathetic and courteous in our dealings with businesses. Remember, when placing an order or delivering a complaint you may be dealing with a business firm, but a living, breathing person is across the desk or at the end of the telephone line.

2. *Prompt and fair returns*–When customers purchase products, they expect them to perform as advertised. If a product is unsatisfactory, the customer should return it immediately for an exchange or a refund. Although some consumers soon realize that a product is slightly defective, they use it for days, weeks, or even months before returning it and still expect a full refund. Had the item been returned immediately, it might have been easily repaired and resold, but because of a long delay the firm may suffer a financial loss. Also, if after a purchase a customer realizes that he really cannot afford the product, or that he does not like the style, he should return it without using it.

3. *Prompt payment*–While most consumers would be incensed at having to wait two months to receive an order, many have no problem withholding payment from a business for several months or years. It is usually reasoned that the money is being withheld from a "big company" that really does not need the money too badly. Remember, if a business firm experiences a problem with its cash flow, the consumer will ultimately feel the adverse effects. As the bills the company owes become past due, its suppliers will withhold shipments of raw materials delaying production and shipment. If a customer cannot pay his obligation immediately, the least he should do is contact the firm, explain the situation, and work out a payment plan.

4. *Common sense on the part of the customer*– Because of a proliferation of lawsuits, businesses have had to write longer and longer instruction manuals in their attempt to cover every possible problem. One manufacturer of a portable television set which may be plugged into a car's cigarette lighter was forced to print the following caution in large, bold letters: *Warning: Do not attempt to watch this television while operating your vehicle.* While such warnings appear frivolous, they are included by the firm with great seriousness in order to avoid lawsuits for damages that are the result of the customer's own lack of forethought.

5. *Consideration of other consumers' needs*–An example of how some consumers selfishly harm fellow consumers by unjust business practices may be found in the airline industry. A common practice, which has frustrated many airline passengers, is that of deliberate overbooking–allowing more reservations to be made for a flight than the airplane has seats. The reason this practice came into being, however, was that airlines found a high probability that a percentage of booked passengers would not show up. Studies commissioned by the airline industry found that the reason for the predictable number of "no shows" was that some passengers were booking reservations under several names in order to ensure that they would receive a seat, regardless of the effect on the airlines and the travel plans of other passengers. Such actions have resulted in the inconvenience of many air travelers. These and other inconveniences could often be avoided if consumers would simply consider the effect of their actions on other customers.

Section Review

1. What are the eight principles of wise purchasing?
2. Describe the four basic consumer rights as outlined by President Kennedy in 1962.
3. What does the CPSC do?

Chapter Review

Terms
budget
impulse buying
financial plan
escrow account
contingency
deductibles
fixed expenses
variable expenses
Better Business Bureau
unit pricing
caveat emptor
bait-and-switch
consumerism
redress
cease and desist order
counteradvertising

Content Questions
1. What is a budget?
2. How does a budget allow a Christian to exercise his role as a steward?
3. What is the current average savings rate in the United States?
4. What are utilities?
5. What is the difference between a fixed expense and a variable expense?
6. What are the steps involved in creating a written budget?
7. What is unit pricing?
8. What is consumerism?
9. What are the key responsibilities of the Food and Drug Administration?

Application Questions
1. Many people argue that to live under a budget places one under bondage. Do you agree or disagree? Discuss.
2. Why is Scriptural giving so important to God? Why does He need your money? Discuss.
3. Some believe that educational costs are an expense while others hold that they are an investment. What do you believe?
4. Besides checking with consumer publications and the Better Business Bureau, how might a consumer shop more knowledgeably?
5. Former President Ronald Reagan instituted a series of deregulation efforts which many hailed as the end of consumerism. Is consumerism dead?
6. Do you believe that consumer protection agencies are doing too little, too much, or the right amount in order to protect consumers? Discuss.
7. Provide some Scriptural justification for some of the five courtesies that business firms should be able to expect from consumers.

CHAPTER 16

Consumer Credit

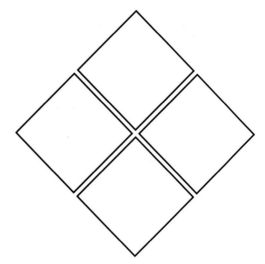

The rich ruleth over the poor, and the borrower is servant to the lender.

Proverbs 22:7

I. The Christian and Debt

Christian Debt Philosophies

Perhaps there is no other topic in personal economics as sensitive as the use of consumer credit. The issue of debt has polarized Christians into two groups: those who totally oppose its use, and those who believe that debt may be used wisely but cautiously. Opponents to consumer borrowing declare all debt to be immoral and un-Scriptural citing such verses as Deuteronomy 15:6 and Romans 13:8:

> For the Lord thy God blesseth thee, as he promised thee: and thou shalt lend unto many nations, but thou shalt not borrow; and thou shalt reign over many nations, but they shall not reign over thee.

Owe no man any thing, but to love one another: for he that loveth another hath fulfilled the law.

There is a second group, on the other hand, which maintains that debt is neither immoral nor un-Scriptural, but is like fire: useful, but extremely dangerous. First, they point out that debt is a fact of life for everyone, even for the most conscientious debt-avoiding Christian. Whenever one receives anything for which he has not yet paid, such as electricity, gas, or water, he is in fact a **debtor,** or borrower, until his monthly statement is paid. They then ask what the difference is, therefore, between paying one's electric bill on time or paying for a credit card purchase at the end of the month without incurring an interest charge.

Second, this group argues that debt is not absolutely forbidden by God as evidenced by Scripture's treatment of lending. Obviously, if borrowing is a sin, then lending would be considered equally sinful since it would be pandering to another's sinful habits. To argue otherwise, this group believes, would be like condemning drunkenness as sin while applauding one who sells alcohol. Indeed, if lending is sinful, then even the most conscientious debt-avoider would be sinning by depositing money in a bank since bank deposits are, in fact, loans to institutions which in turn lend to individuals and businesses. What, therefore, does the Bible say about lending? Instead of condemning the practice of lending, Scripture places restrictions upon it and even, at times, encourages the practice:

> And if thy brother be waxen poor, and fallen in decay with thee; then thou shalt relieve him: yea, though he be a stranger, or a sojourner; that he may live with thee. Take thou no usury (loan interest) of him, or increase: but fear thy God; that thy brother may live with thee. (Leviticus 25:35-36)

> Give to him that asketh thee, and from him that would borrow of thee turn not thou away. (Matthew 5:42)

> Wherefore then gavest not thou my money into the bank, that at my coming I might have required mine own with usury? (Luke 19:23)

Biblical Cautions

Those Christians who do not condemn borrowing do not, however, believe it is something in which to engage without restraint. Rather, they believe it may be useful in some situations, but the Christian should keep in mind certain dangers and Biblical cautions:

1. Debt is associated with bondage. No matter the reason one may have for borrowing money, the fact remains: the borrower is dependent upon the lender. A debt contract is designed to bind a borrower to repay a given sum of money. In that way, a Christian debtor is "bound" to a creditor. In the words of Solomon "the borrower is servant to the lender" (Prov. 22:7). While debtor's prisons have gone the way of the horse and buggy, and modern debt contracts severely limit the hold a **creditor** (or lender) has over a borrower, the lender still has

some power over the borrower. The lender has a hold over the borrower's income by requiring the borrower to make periodic payments. Oftentimes the lender has power to **garnish** the borrower's wages (have his employer pay the debt out of the borrower's earned wages prior to receiving his paycheck) in case of **default** (failure to pay on time). In some cases the lender also has a hold over the use of the item which was purchased with the borrowed money.

2. The use of debt may prevent a Christian's mobility. Closely associated with the idea that debt is a form of bondage is the fact that debt may limit the mobility of a Christian and bind him to his job and his current geographical location. Imagine that a Christian businessman and his family receive the call of God to leave his present career in order to serve the Lord on the mission field. If they are bound by debt contracts on automobiles, boats, and credit cards, it may be years before they are able to obey the call. However, if a Christian is debt-free, he may be able to move much more quickly. It is therefore important for believers to allow the Holy Spirit to guide them when contemplating financial activities which would be potentially binding. In the words of Timothy,

> No man that warreth entangleth himself with the affairs of this life; that he may please him who hath chosen him to be a soldier. (II Timothy 2:4)

3. Debt presumes upon an uncertain future. Rather than patiently making periodic deposits to a savings account, allowing the funds to accumulate interest over a period of time and later withdrawing the funds to make a purchase, debtors choose to "save in reverse." That is, they first borrow money from the bank and "deposit" it later with interest. The problem with this arrangement is that the borrower presumes he will be able to repay the loan. Whenever a lender examines an applicant's ability to repay, he takes into account such factors as the likelihood that the borrower will continue to live in the area, that he will remain employed during the period of the loan, that his

Impracticalities of Credit

An estimated 80% of all conversations between a husband and wife concern money. The pressures of money are a leading cause in divorce, heart attacks, suicide, and crime. Life has enough problems without the added weight of credit.

First is the emotional toll of credit. The trauma of unexpected bills–medical needs, broken appliances, etc.–is enough to sap a paycheck. If a person borrows, he takes away money that could be used to meet these problematic expenses; then an unexpected need can create a crisis in the home. The head of a household bears the weight of monthly bills, which are oblivious to changing circumstances. The added burden of credit drains a worker's energy, making him less effective at work and more susceptible to illness, anger, and sin.

Second, credit actually lessens a consumer's buying power. A person who relies on credit may pay high interest rates. A young married couple with good credit might be able to buy quality furniture, an expensive entertainment system, appliances, and many other amenities now for their new home, but they will still be making payments when these things begin to break down and wear out. Over the same period a wise couple that makes due with less will earn interest on their savings and pay cash for even better things later. Take one simple illustration. A credit-hungry couple sees a $400 stereo for $15 a month, and they buy it. When their stereo is paid off, four years and much wear later, another couple in the same circumstances who did without will have saved enough money to buy a new, advanced model with $400 to spare! If these two couples continue with their separate philosophies, the one will have old and worn-out possessions later in life, while the other will have new possessions and money to spare for gifts, vacations, hobbies, etc.

Third is the temptation to abuse credit. Advertisements beg consumers to "buy now and pay later." A person with good credit will find his mailbox stuffed with "pre-approved" credit cards and "pre-approved" loans. Those with little self-discipline use these as an opportunity to buy what they want rather than what they can afford.

In its worst form, abuse of credit will leave the consumer "overextended." When credit payments (excluding mortgage debt) demand more than 20% of take-home pay, the consumer begins to experience the horrors of overextended credit. Signs include late payment of bills, minimum payment on credit cards, loans for basics (such as food and gas), and new, higher loans to pay off old loans. Every unexpected expense becomes a crisis. Credit companies no longer extend new credit; in its extreme form, over-extended credit leads to bankruptcy. "Credit-happy" Americans have been turning more and more to bankruptcy court to "solve" the problems of their buying binges. Widespread debt causes excessive financial strain, as is evidenced by the fact that each year approximately 1 million Americans declare bankruptcy, 3 million are on the verge, and 24 million are in serious financial trouble.

income either will remain constant or increase, that his health will remain good, and that his other expenses will not increase beyond his income. While such assumptions may be commonplace with the unsaved, the child of God must not fail to take into account the fact that the Lord may have different plans for his residence, employment, income, health, and expenses.

> Boast not thyself of to morrow; for thou knowest not what a day may bring forth.
> (Proverbs 27:1)

> Go to now, ye that say, To day or to morrow we will go into such a city, and continue there a year, and buy and sell, and get gain: Whereas ye know not what shall be on the morrow. For what is your life? It is even a vapour, that appeareth for a little time, and then vanisheth away. (James 4:13-14)

Many a church has gone into debt to finance a big building project assuming that the membership would grow and offerings would continue to increase. Later, to their chagrin, the church finds that

Truth in Lending Act

Because borrowers were often unaware of the interest rates, finance charges, and other conditions of their loans, Congress passed the Consumer Credit Protection Act. More commonly known as the Truth in Lending Act, this legislation first took effect in 1969 and has since been amended several times.

The law requires that creditors disclose the annual percentage rate of interest charged, the dollar amount of all finance charges, and all other conditions of the loan. The act also requires regulations for the advertising of credit terms by lending institutions, and it provides some legal guidelines for credit card issuing companies. The Federal Trade Commission holds the most responsibility for enforcing these and other provisions of the Truth in Lending Act.

its assumptions were faulty, its ability to repay the debt has disappeared, and the name of Christ has been sullied in the community.

4. The use of debt may interfere with the Lord's provision or protection. Several cases in Scripture record the Lord using someone's poverty as an opportunity to show Himself strong either through the working of a miracle or through the benevolence of other believers. By using credit to meet a financial need, one either may miss the blessing of seeing the Lord work on his behalf or may rob another saint of the blessing which would come as a result of assisting a brother in need.

> For the eyes of the Lord run to and fro throughout the whole earth, to shew himself strong in the behalf of them whose heart is perfect toward him. (II Chronicles 16:9)

> But my God shall supply all your need according to his riches in glory by Christ Jesus.
> (Philippians 4:19)

The Lord may also use a lack of finances to prevent someone from purchasing something or involving himself in an activity contrary to His will. Through the unwise use of credit, believers may surmount barriers which the Lord has placed before them to protect them from unwise purchases. Today, by using debt financing, more Christians than ever before are able to purchase material possessions that were unaffordable to believers in the past. As a result of this expansion of their purchasing power, many have fallen for the oldest of Satan's deceptions: that one can serve himself and Jesus Christ at the same time.

> Ye ask, and receive not, because ye ask amiss, that ye may consume it upon your lusts. (James 4:3)

Section Review
1. What is a debtor and a creditor?
2. How is debt associated with bondage?
3. How does debt presume upon the future?
4. Why might God want a person to be in a position where a lack of finances might prevent him from purchasing something?

II. The Consumer and Debt

Most Americans are oblivious to the debate between the two Christian groups. Indeed, the majority of people in the United States take a very careless attitude toward the use of consumer debt. Figure 16-1 illustrates the fact that going into debt is almost a national pastime. In 1989 American consumers had over $776 billion outstanding in consumer debt while having only about $538 billion in savings.

Whatever a person's belief about the propriety of debt, one thing is certain. A complete understanding of economics is not possible until one understands consumer credit. We will spend the rest of this chapter examining the reasons Americans choose to use debt, the types of debt which people use, sources of credit, and the criteria lenders use in determining who may and may not receive credit.

Before we look at the mechanics of debt, it would be useful to examine why people borrow money. There are only two reasons borrowing takes place. People borrow either for current consumption or for the purchase of investments.

Consumption Borrowing

Many purchases are made as a result of **consumption borrowing.** That is, some people use debt to purchase goods which will be consumed almost immediately. Examples of consumption borrowing include using a credit card to pay for dinner at a restaurant, buying automobile tires from an auto parts store using their in-house credit, or borrowing money from a finance company to take a long summer vacation. The problem with consumption borrowing is that one is obligating future income to pay for goods which provide pleasure today. Many people become trapped in the web of consumption borrowing as they borrow against in-

Figure 16-1 U.S. Consumer Credit Versus Personal Savings, 1950-1989* (in billions of dollars)

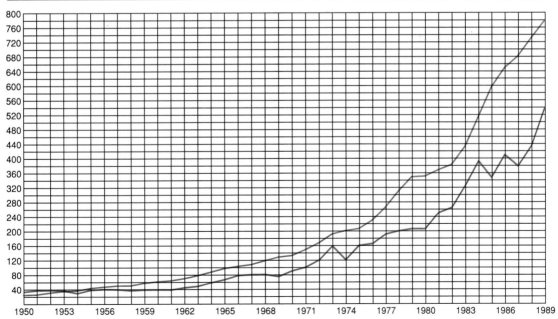

Key: Consumer Credit Outstanding (red)   Personal Savings (blue)

*Source: President's Council of Economic Advisors, Economic Report of the President (Washington, D.C.: Government Printing Office, 1990), Tables C-29 and C-75

come further and further into the future to pay for momentary desires. Before they realize what has happened, they find themselves hopelessly in debt with nothing but memories of past pleasures. Scripture maintains that those who only live for the moment are not wise.

> He that loveth pleasure shall be a poor man:
> he that loveth wine and oil shall not be rich.
> (Proverbs 21:17)

Much of today's consumption borrowing is a result of either covetousness or a lack of financial planning. Covetousness is a strong desire to possess something which one does not have. A person sees something which he wants to buy and, lacking the money to pay for it, he obligates his future income by using credit. Scripture continually admonishes the believer to beware of covetousness (Luke 12:15) and to be content with such things as he has (Heb. 13:5). Rather than obligating tomorrow's income to pay for today's purchases Scripture maintains that the child of God should trust the Lord to meet his current needs (Luke 12:27).

Others may not be covetous, but their borrowing is a result of poor planning. For example, one may save all of the money necessary to purchase an automobile but fail to take into account all of the other expenses incidental to car ownership such as property taxes, insurance, and maintenance.

While most borrowing for current consumption is patently un-Scriptural, many Christians believe there exist some circumstances when this kind of debt may be not only acceptable, but actually may be good stewardship. The first exception arises when the price of a good is rising faster than the cost of debt used to purchase it. If the price of an automobile, for example, is rising at a rate of 30% per year and the interest rate on debt is 20%, it would actually be profitable for a consumer to purchase the car today with borrowed money. Figure 16-2 illustrates this idea. If a buyer was planning on purchasing a certain automobile at the end of the year which today costs $10,000, he will have to pay 30% more, or $13,000. However, if he purchased the car today with borrowed funds, repaying the loan at the end of the year with a single pay-

Figure 16-2

	PURCHASED TODAY WITH BORROWED MONEY	PURCHASED AT END OF YEAR
Price of automobile	$10,000.00	$13,000.00
Cost of loan (20%)	2,000.00	0.00
Total cost of automobile	$12,000.00	$13,000.00

ment, he would pay a total of only $12,000.

Many believe that the use of interest-free loans constitutes a second possible exception to the prohibition on consumption borrowing. For example, let us assume that a consumer named Marvin has been saving to buy a new piano. He has accumulated $2,000 in a savings account yielding 6% interest per year. Instead of withdrawing the cash to make the purchase, he uses the store's "90 days same as cash" terms. That is, he is allowed to owe

An interest-free loan may actually allow a consumer to save money on a major purchase.

the store the $2,000 for three months, paying the price in full at the end of the period with no interest charges. At the end of 90 days, Marvin withdraws the cash and pays the bill in full. During the 90 days which transpired between the purchase of the piano and the savings withdrawal, Marvin *earned* over $29 in interest on his deposited funds, interest which would have been lost had he chosen to forego using debt.

Certainly there may be isolated cases in which consumption borrowing is more profitable than paying cash for purchases, but exceptions to the rule are few, the profits are usually inconsequential, and the temptation to borrow can be overwhelming. Christians would be well advised to avoid consumption borrowing unless an exception is thoroughly justified.

Investment Borrowing

While consumption borrowing is associated with the impulsive use of tomorrow's income to receive present enjoyment, **investment borrowing** is the calculated use of debt to purchase goods which will increase in value, produce income in the future, or reduce expenses.

One type of investment borrowing is the use of debt to purchase **appreciating assets,** or goods which increase in value over time. Examples of appreciating assets might include real estate, art, and diamonds. Obviously if the price of an object rises faster than the cost of the borrowed money with which it was purchased, the borrower will experience a profit. The problem is, however, determining what is and is not an appreciating asset. Many believe that real estate is always an appreciating asset, but such may not be the case. Many areas in the United States have experienced a severe depression in housing prices at times. The believer needs to be very careful when purchasing appreciating assets; they just might not appreciate!

The second type of investment borrowing is the use of borrowed money to purchase goods which will increase a person's income. For example, some people borrow money to purchase tools which are needed to earn an income which would not be otherwise possible. This concept was alluded to in

Fair Credit Billing Act

The Fair Credit Billing Act went into effect in 1975 to help people deal with disputed credit card bills. Under this law a person who disputes his bill must notify the creditor within 60 days of receiving the bill. The creditor then must acknowledge the notification and settle the dispute within 90 days. Provisions of the law keep the creditor from retaliating for the dispute by passing along misleading information about the situation to a credit bureau and thereby damaging the credit cardholder's credit rating.

Additionally the law requires that creditors mail bills to cardholders at least fourteen days before payments are due. It also gives cardholders the right under certain conditions to withhold payment for defective items purchased with a credit card within the cardholder's home state (or within 100 miles of his home). This feature makes creditors responsible for helping to find a settlement between the businesses involved and the dissatisfied customers.

Chapters 4 and 5 where business firms borrow money to purchase their tools of production. An extension of this idea is the use of credit to purchase an automobile to transport the borrower to a higher-paying job. Some even hold that the use of debt to finance a college education is a legitimate reason to borrow money since the loan is preparing one to be employed in a higher-paying career.

A third category of investment borrowing is the use of borrowed funds to reduce expenses. When a business firm purchases insulation to go in the ceiling of a factory it is not purchasing an asset which will appreciate in value, and it certainly will not generate additional sales; management justifies its use of credit by pointing to the fact that the insulation is reducing its energy costs. The purchase of the insulation could reduce the firm's electric bill by $2,000 per year while the annual cost of the loan's interest is only $1,500. Likewise, many homeowners use debt to purchase cost-reducing goods for their homes.

Robert Morris
(1734-1806)
Financier of the American Revolution

After emigrating from England in 1747, Robert Morris learned the responsibilities of business in a mercantile firm in Philadelphia. His industry and integrity propelled him into a very successful partnership in the import-export business. When the American colonies began their struggle for independence, Morris represented Pennsylvania in the Continental Congress; and he was one of only two men who signed all three of the nation's early and notable documents: the Declaration of Independence, the Articles of Confederation, and the Constitution.

During the Revolution, Morris devoted his efforts to financing the costly maintenance of the Continental Army during its prolonged struggle. For a while he served as chairman of the Secret Committee of Trade, organizing the importation of vital military supplies. Then from 1781 to 1784, with the nation's financial problems intensifying, the Continental Congress called upon him to serve as superintendent of finance. In that office Morris displayed remarkable skill and self-sacrifice as he steered the almost-penniless government through a continuous financial crisis. In this effort Morris used his own reputation and credit to secure precious funds and patience from increasingly skeptical creditors. Morris thus earned the widespread appreciation and admiration that later sent him to the Constitutional Convention and to the Senate for one term.

After the war, Morris's success in renewed business interests added to his fortunes, and he determined to increase his wealth further by land speculation. Morris and two partners bought millions of acres of western lands and thousands of lots in the rising capital, Washington, D.C., incurring heavy debts in the process. When economic decline in Europe and other problems frustrated the finance and sale of these lands, Morris began to face his own financial crisis. Soon he was beset by angry creditors seeking promised payments. "I am latterly become so fully convinced that much wealth does not increase happiness that I cannot help regretting that so much of my time has been spent in the pursuit of it," he lamented, "and I would this moment give up a great deal of what I possess if by such a cession I could at once close the scene of business and become master at will of my time." And on another occasion he vowed, "If I can once get square, I will never contract another debt."

Morris saw the grand mansion he was building in Philadelphia stand unfinished because of his distress, and eventually his unpaid debts of $3 million brought full legal consequences. The frustrated financier spent three years, from 1798 to 1801, in the Prune Street debtors' prison in Philadelphia. Though George Washington and other men of prominence visited him in prison and continued to offer friendship, they could not extricate him from the financial pit into which he had fallen. Morris spent the last five years of his life humbly living on the support of his family and friends. The renowned financier of the Revolution died a pauper.

Types of Consumer Credit

While there are many motives for borrowing money, there are only two types of credit: installment credit and open-end credit.

Installment Credit–When a borrower signs a contract agreeing to pay for a purchase by making periodic payments, he is said to be using **installment credit.** Some installment loans are referred to as **single-payment loans.** As its name implies, a single payment loan is an installment loan with only one installment. Most installment credit involves paying a specified amount of money each month for a given **term,** or number of months. Figure 16-3 is an example of the payments required for a $100 installment loan for various terms and different interest rates. By using this table one can determine close approximations of the payments required for even longer loans. For example, to determine the payment required for a $1,000 loan at 18% for one year (12 months), multiply $9.168 (the payment required for a $100 loan with those characteristics) by 10 (since the amount of the loan is 10 times $100). Hence, the monthly payment would be approximately $91.68.

While not readily apparent, each payment of an installment loan consists of two parts, principal and interest. **Principal** is the original amount borrowed, and **interest** is the additional charge a creditor requires of the borrower to cover the cost of making the loan and to provide a profit. Because the principal amount is greatest at the beginning of the loan's term, the interest portion of the payment is at its highest for the first payment and declines as more principal is paid. Figure 16-4 illustrates this principle by presenting an **amortization schedule** for a $1,000 loan at 18% to be paid in 12 monthly installments. An amortization schedule is a table which breaks down each payment into its principal and interest components.

When one adds the principal and interest payments, one will find that the total amount repaid is $1,100.16 which is the same as multiplying $91.69 times 12.

Amortization schedules can be truly revealing, especially to one who borrows money for a long period of time. If a person borrows $80,000 for 25 years at 10% to purchase a house, his monthly payments will be $726.96. Out of his first month's

Figure 16-3 Monthly Installment Payment (Principal and Interest) Required to Repay $100

NUMBER OF MONTHLY PAYMENTS	ANNUAL PERCENTAGE RATE									
	12%	13%	14%	15%	16%	17%	18%	19%	20%	21%
12	8.885	8.932	8.979	9.026	9.073	9.120	9.168	9.216	9.263	9.311
24	4.707	4.754	4.801	4.849	4.896	4.944	4.992	5.041	5.090	5.139
36	3.321	3.369	3.418	3.467	3.516	3.565	3.615	3.666	3.716	3.768
48	2.633	2.683	2.733	2.783	2.834	2.886	2.937	2.990	3.043	3.097
60	2.224	2.275	2.327	2.379	2.432	2.485	2.539	2.594	2.649	2.705
72	1.955	2.007	2.061	2.115	2.169	2.225	2.281	2.338	2.395	2.454

*Round each payment to the nearest cent.

payment only $60.29 will be applied toward the reduction of the principal balance while $666.67 will go toward the payment of interest. The $80,000 that the home buyer originally borrowed will actually cost him ($726.96 × 300 payments) $218,088.00! In most cases a borrower may reduce his total interest cost by paying a little more per month than the loan agreement stipulates. All money in excess of the regular payment is applied toward the principal balance, thus reducing the total interest one must pay.

After signing an installment loan contract, the borrower usually makes repayment in one of three ways. The first method of repayment is the use of coupons. After receiving loans many borrowers receive booklets filled with coupons. Each month the borrower tears one of the perforated coupons out of the booklet and mails it to the creditor along with his payment. When all of the coupons have been used, the debt is paid in full. A second method of paying an installment loan is the use of a statement. Instead of using coupon booklets, which may be lost or misplaced, some creditors mail bills to borrowers each month. With the advent of high technology, a third method of payment has been introduced, the automatic draft. After receiving permission from the debtor, a creditor may electronically withdraw the payment from the borrow-

Figure 16-4   Amortization Schedule for $1,000 Loan at 18% for 12 Months

PAYMENT NUMBER	PAYMENT AMOUNT	PRINCIPAL	INTEREST	PRINCIPAL BALANCE AFTER THIS PAYMENT
1	$91.68	$76.68	$15.00	$923.32
2	91.68	77.83	13.85	845.49
3	91.68	79.00	12.68	766.49
4	91.68	80.18	11.50	686.31
5	91.68	81.39	10.29	604.92
6	91.68	82.61	9.07	522.32
7	91.68	83.85	7.83	438.47
8	91.68	85.10	6.58	353.37
9	91.68	86.38	5.30	266.99
10	91.68	87.68	4.00	179.32
11	91.68	88.99	2.69	90.33
12	91.68	90.33	1.35	0.00
TOTAL	$1,100.16	$1,000.00	$100.16	

er's bank account on a particular day each month.

An installment loan may either be secured or unsecured. A **secured loan** is one which is "backed" by **collateral,** valuable goods which may be taken by the lender and resold in case the borrower does not repay the loan. An **unsecured loan,** on the other hand, is one for which there is no collateral behind the loan. Unsecured loans tend to carry more risk for creditors; therefore, lenders often have both higher standards which an applicant must meet to qualify for a loan and higher interest rates than on secured loans.

Open-End Credit–The second type of credit is known as **open-end credit.** Also known as "revolving credit," an open-end account is one from which a debtor may continually draw more and

more money. These accounts are not truly open-ended since each account usually has a predetermined **credit limit** which is the maximum amount a given borrower may draw. Credit limits are usually determined by such things as the borrower's

Consumer Loan Clauses

Out of a desire to protect themselves, lenders often include several clauses in the "fine print" of loan contracts. Some of the following may be standard, but they can be frightening and may cause trouble for a borrower who does not understand their ramifications before he signs on a dotted line.

Acceleration clause: This provision makes the entire debt due immediately if the borrower is late on one payment, thereby making repossession more likely.

Add-on clause: When a borrower makes two separate purchases at different times on credit from the same business and the first purchase is not completely paid for before the second is made, an add-on clause consolidates both loans into one. If the borrower then defaults, he loses both purchases to repossession, even if the first was subsequently paid for.

Balloon clause: This clause stipulates that the borrower makes only interest payments or other small payments on a loan until the last payment, at which time all the principal or some other large sum is required.

Prepayment penalty: Many loan contracts stipulate that the borrower pays most of the interest on a loan when he pays off early. This penalty is commonly based on the "rule of 78s." According to this rule 12/78 of the year's interest is to be paid for the first month, 11/78 for the second month, 10/78 for the third, etc., for what would be a twelve-month total of 78/78 of the year's interest. Thus, if a borrower were paying 10% interest on a $1,000 loan, which he paid off after six months, instead of owing $50 of the annual interest of $100, he would owe 57/78 of $100 or $73 in interest.

Repossession: If a borrower defaults on his loan payments, the creditor can physically seize the security for the loan according to the contract's stipulations and the state's legal procedures. Some laws and agreements may make repossession relatively simple for the creditor.

Garnishment: Although federal law limits the garnishment of an indebted person's wages to approximately one-fourth of his take-home pay, a creditor may make provision in a contract to use this legal provision to withhold wages until the debt is paid.

Credit Card Fraud

If trends continue, Americans will lose $1 billion *every year* from credit card swindles. The losses now exceed $700 million each year. Common-sense precautions by alert card holders would stop most of these schemes.

First, when dealing with cashiers make sure that 1) the slip shows the exact amount you purchased, 2) no extra slips are made, 3) the card is not taken out of your sight (no honest cashier needs to go to a back room with your credit card), 4) the card is returned to you immediately, and 5) the carbon copy with your credit card number and expiration date is destroyed.

Second, do not trust strangers who call you on the phone requesting credit information. Do not, for any reason, give them your social security number or your credit card number. They may claim that you have won a prize "with proper verification," make you a "fabulous one-time offer you can't refuse," conduct a "credit card survey," or claim to be a bank representative trying to clear up confusion about an account "with a number similar to yours." Any information you give may enable crooks to use your numbers to make purchases directly or to apply for credit cards in your name (true-name fraud). Victims across the country tell horror

stories about how their lives were almost wrecked by credit card crooks.

Third, do not trust the trash collector. Destroy unused and expired credit cards, old bills, and receipts.

Fourth, carry only the credit cards you will be needing. People often carry every credit card they possess at all times, and when their wallets and purses are lost or stolen, their headaches are multiplied.

As a further precaution, keep a list of your cards and numbers to call if a card is lost or stolen. Also, compare the items on your monthly statement with your sales slips. Report any discrepancies immediately.

The simple believeth every word: but the prudent man looketh well to his going.
(Proverbs 14:15)

income, length of residence, and past credit experience. Examples of revolving accounts include bank credit cards (also known as bankcards) such as Mastercard and Visa, department store credit cards, and some oil company credit cards. Since the principal amount may vary from month to month the monthly payment may likewise vary. When his monthly statement arrives, the open-end credit borrower has the option either to pay the entire balance, the minimum payment due, or any amount in between. Nearly all revolving accounts are unsecured.

Section Review

1. What are the only two possible motives for borrowing money?
2. What is an appreciating asset?
3. What is the difference between a secured loan and an unsecured loan?
4. Which type of credit involves a credit limit?

Commercial banks are a common source of consumer credit.

III. The Creditor

Sources of Consumer Credit

There exists a host of organizations more than willing to grant credit to American consumers, but the majority of credit granted in the United States is accomplished through three major sources. They include banks, thrift institutions, and finance companies.

Commercial Banks–The first source of credit which comes to almost everyone's mind is the commercial bank. Commercial banks offer a wide range of loan options both to consumers and business firms. They offer installment loans both on secured and unsecured bases. Because it offers the best protection to the bank, one of the least expensive types of secured installment bank loans is the **savings assignment.** A savings assignment is a loan with the borrower's savings account serving as collateral. The bank places a "hold" on the account so that the funds may be withdrawn to the degree that the loan principal has been reduced. If the borrower defaults on the loan, the bank merely pays for the loan using the funds remaining on hold. Since banks bear virtually no risk of loss on savings assignment loans, the interest rate tends to be much lower than that for other types of installment loans. Most banks charge an interest rate of only 2% to 3% above the rate being paid on the deposit. Thus, if one is earning 5% on a regular passbook savings account, he may only have to pay around 7% or 8% for a savings assignment loan. In addition to savings accounts, commercial banks also accept other major forms of collateral for installment loans including vehicles, real estate, stocks, and bonds. Banks also grant unsecured installment loans, but because of the higher risk of loss, banks usually limit this type of loan to only the most creditworthy customers.

Open-end loans in the form of revolving charge accounts are another method of borrowing from a commercial bank. One of the most popular types of open-end bank loans was created to keep checking account holders from experiencing "overdraft" charges. As a result of bad bookkeeping or carelessness, many checking account holders accidentally "bounce" checks (write checks for more than is in their checking accounts). Because of the costs involved in returning checks through the national check clearance system, most banks charge an overdraft charge of $15 or more per overdrawn check. In addition, many merchants who receive overdrawn checks also levy a service charge of $10 or more per returned check. As you can see, it could become very costly for a consumer to accidentally write ten to fifteen overdrawn checks before he discovers his error.

To protect their customers as well as to provide interest income, many commercial banks offer an open-end line of credit which serves as **overdraft protection.** This service ensures that deposits are automatically made to a customer's account, up to a predetermined credit limit, whenever his checking account balance falls below zero. While this service may be a financial help, consumers need to inquire about the terms and conditions which a bank places on its overdraft protection loans. While some banks deposit only the exact amount needed to cover an overdraft, others deposit fixed increments such as $100, leading a customer to pay more interest than necessary. Another item customers should question is the rate of interest. Overdraft protection interest rates usually range between 15% and 21%.

A second type of open-end bank credit is the bank credit card. Many commercial banks issue plastic credit cards which may be used to purchase merchandise from thousands of retailers. In addition to offering customers the ability to charge merchandise, bank credit cards also may have a **cash advance** feature. This feature enables a bank cardholder to enter virtually any bank and receive cash against his account. Often the interest rate is higher on purchases of merchandise than on cash advances, but interest on cash advances begins being charged the day of the advance. Interest charges on purchases, on the other hand, usually do not begin until approximately twenty-five days after the credit card bill is issued to the customer. Typically, interest rates on bank cards range from 16% to 21%. Many bank cards also require the holder to pay an annual fee of $20 to $50.

Thrift Institutions–Thrift institutions include savings and loan associations (S&Ls) and credit unions. Savings and loan associations appeared in the United States in the late 1800s and were created to

help those with modest incomes to purchase homes.

Home loans typically take one of two forms. A **first mortgage** is the type of loan used to initially purchase a home. A first mortgage is secured by using the property as collateral. A **second mortgage** is a loan which is made using the **equity** one has in his house as collateral. For example, Ted and Betty Jones purchased their first home in California in 1975 for $40,000. After putting $4,000 of their own money down, they signed a $36,000, 20 year, 7% first mortgage loan with payments of $279 per month. In 1985 their children persuaded them to install an in-ground swimming pool, which cost $10,000. Not having $10,000 in savings, Ted and Betty went to their savings and loan association for a loan. The loan officer noted that the value of

their home had risen to $90,000 and the principal balance on their first mortgage was only $24,000. The difference between the value of the home and the amount owed on the first mortgage, therefore, was $66,000. This $66,000 represents the amount of equity the Joneses have accumulated in their home and is the maximum amount a savings and loan association would be willing to lend.

Up until the mid-1970s, savings and loan associations continued the tradition of merely accepting savings deposits and extending first and second mortgage home loans, but after that time they began to aggressively market new services in order to increase their profitability. To encourage second mortgage lending, many savings and loan associations began to offer their version of overdraft protection. Acting much the same as a commercial bank's overdraft service, savings and loan associations offered their customers far greater credit limits by basing their lines of credit on the equity borrowers had in their homes.

Credit Cards Versus Debit Cards

The bank just gave you a MasterCard II. It has the same logo as a MasterCard, and you use it much the same way—to pay for goods at the store when you forget your checkbook or do not have any cash. But it is not a credit card. It is a *debit card*. When a cashier rings up a purchase on a debit card, the amount is subtracted directly from your checking account. You may as well be giving the merchant a check, except you are saved from the bookkeeping hassles.

The primary advantage of this new type of plastic card is that the cardholder can draw on a bank's services at an automatic teller 24 hours a day—cash withdrawals, deposits, and inquiries, even on weekends. Because you are not borrowing from the bank, the card is usually free for your convenience.

Yet there are some obvious—and not so obvious—disadvantages. The cardholder can easily forget to record a card purchase and suddenly be overdrawn. Furthermore, if he loses his card or it is stolen, he is protected by the weaker Electronic Funds Transfer Act, not the consumer credit acts. He can be liable for up to $500 if he fails to inform the bank within two days, and his liability is unlimited if he forgets to inform the bank sixty days after his last bank statement. He also has fewer options if he purchases a defective product or finds a billing error.

A home equity loan could provide the credit a family needs to remodel a kitchen or to make other home improvements.

Credit unions, the second type of thrift institution, also provide a source of credit for potential borrowers. Instead of ''depositing'' money into one's savings account, credit union members purchase shares of ownership in their credit union as they add money to their accounts. From this pool of funds other members may borrow. When a member is in need of a loan, a voluntary committee of members reviews his application. When a loan is granted, the credit union typically arranges for payments to be deducted from the borrower's paycheck. Since they are nonprofit organizations and they incur very low overhead expenses as a result of using volunteer managers, loans from credit unions usually carry a lower interest rate than loans granted by commercial banks or savings and loan associations.

Finance Companies–Finance companies are private companies which exist to extend loans to the general public. Two types of finance companies

exist: consumer finance companies and sales finance companies. **Consumer finance companies** are finance companies which make secured and unsecured personal loans and debt consolidation loans to the general public. A **personal loan** is one which is used to pay for vacations, education expenses, or to cover personal temporary cash deficits. Without thinking, many consumers use their credit cards, credit lines, and installment loans to the point where they cannot manage their burden of debt. In order to relieve some of the pressure caused by an abundance of debt, a borrower may seek a **debt consolidation loan**. A debt consolidation loan combines all outstanding debts into one loan which carries a single monthly payment which is lower than the combined payments of the previous debts. Financial advisors warn those who are considering a debt consolidation loan to carefully examine the costs involved. While the monthly payment may be lower, it is usually because the loan is stretched over a longer period of time, a factor which may significantly increase the amount one pays in interest.

Two well-known examples of consumer finance companies are the Household Finance and the Beneficial Finance Corporations. In addition to the large nationally known consumer finance companies, most cities have local versions with lower lending abilities. State laws usually regulate the maximum amount which consumer finance companies may lend and the maximum interest rate they may charge. Typically consumer finance companies are permitted to make loans of up to $5,000. In addition to setting lending limits, state laws usually mandate that the interest rate which is charged must decline as the size of a loan increases. For example, some states permit a maximum interest rate of 48% on loans of $500 or less while borrowers may be charged 24% on loans over $2,000.

While many borrowers might complain that the interest rates charged by consumer finance companies are excessive, it should be noted that they make loans of a much smaller size and with considerably greater risk than those made by thrift institutions. Loans with a higher risk of default require the consumer finance company to spend greater amounts in investigating applicants' creditworthiness and in collecting those which have gone into default. In addition, the source of the funds which consumer finance companies lend is not low-interest savings and checking deposits; rather, they must borrow the funds they need from commercial banks and thrift institutions.

Unlike consumer finance companies, the purpose of **sales finance companies** is not to meet the personal or debt consolidation needs of the general public. Rather, they are usually subsidiary companies created by larger corporations for the purpose of financing purchases of their products. For example the General Motors Acceptance Corporation (GMAC) provides loans which enable buyers to purchase General Motors products. The interest rate on loans from sales finance companies tends to be lower than that charged by consumer finance companies for two reasons. First, sales finance companies do not make the high-risk loans associated with consumer finance companies. Sales finance companies tend to screen loan applicants, choosing only the best credit risks. Second, firms the size of GMAC and Ford Motor Credit do not have to borrow their funds from financial institutions; rather, they can issue their own bonds to the general public at a much lower interest rate.

Other Sources of Credit–Besides thrift institutions and finance companies, several other sources exist which, by themselves, play a relatively minor role in the extension of credit, but combined they are responsible for a great deal of credit in the United States. One source of credit is life insurance companies. If policyholders have life insurance policies which have an optional investment feature, they may borrow from the insurance company using their accumulated cash values as collateral. A second source of credit is companies which specialize in making loans by mail. Other than the facts that they do not have physical offices and that they make loans of even higher risk, these firms are virtually indistinguishable from consumer finance companies.

A third source of funds is educational loan companies. Borrowers who wish to finance their education borrow money from government and private educational loan services. Usually these loans are granted to borrowers on the basis of their financial need and their academic achievement.

Pawnbrokers are a fourth source of credit. Pawnbrokers provide loans which usually must be repaid in one single payment within six months of the loan. The pawnbroker usually accepts as collateral some item of value such as jewelry or stereo equipment. Rather than signing a formal note, the borrower simply receives a "pawn ticket" and cash in exchange for the collateral. If the loan is not repaid by the date specified, the pawnbroker has legal authority to sell the collateral. This type of borrowing is strongly discouraged by credit counsellors because the amounts loaned are usually significantly less than the value of the property and interest rates on pawnbroker loans may sometimes be as high as 100%.

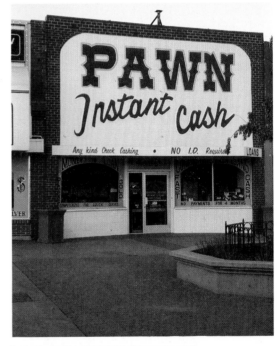

A pawnbroker is a poor source of consumer credit.

GNP: $1137.6 billion*
Per Capita GNP: $13,940*
Population: 9,888,000 (1989)
Monetary Unit: franc

As one of Western Europe's highly industrialized countries, Belgium has demonstrated its ability to import raw materials and unfinished goods, manufacture finished products, and then export them at a profit. Examples of the country's products include Belgian lace and linen made from imported fibers and steel made with imported minerals and fuels. Because of its industrial production and the ability to sell its products abroad, Belgium is one of the highest per capita exporters in the world. The country's successful foreign trade is aided by Belgian membership in several economic alliances, most notably the European Economic Community (Common Market) and the Belgium-Netherlands-Luxembourg Economic Union (Benelux).

Belgium's economy is largely one of free-enterprise capitalism, but like most of its neighboring countries, its government does own and manage much of the land's public transportation and communication networks, and it does provide socialized medical care for its people. Some of the nation's food is imported because Belgian agriculture employs only 5% of the work force and its farms are small and not particularly efficient. Many Belgian farmers were still using horses instead of tractors until the 1960s. Belgium's industrialized economy, however, adequately provides its people with a comfortable standard of living.

*figures for 1987 from the 1990 *Statistical Abstract*

Finally, some borrow from family or friends in order to avoid the impersonal commercial aspects of borrowing and also to avoid high interest rates. In many situations loans from family members tend to be thinly disguised gifts. Those who wish for family or friends to take personal loans seriously should design the loan to be as businesslike as possible by drawing up an informal written promise to repay which details the terms and conditions of the loan.

Creditworthiness

The word "credit" was derived from the Latin word "creditum," which means to entrust something into someone's care. Much has been said so far in this chapter about "creditworthiness" and its effect on a person's ability to receive a loan and the interest rate which he must pay, but how does a lender determine who is worthy of credit? Most professional lenders first require applicants to complete a credit application. Figure 16-5 is an example of such an application.

Figure 16-5

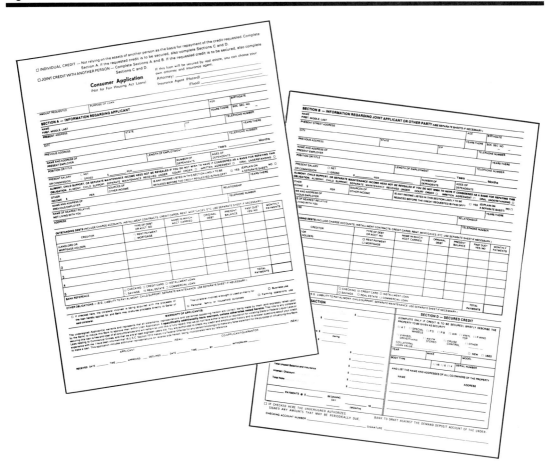

By carefully scrutinizing a potential borrower's loan application and other sources of information, the lender is able to determine what is popularly known as the "five C's of credit": the borrower's character, capacity, capital, collateral, and conditions.

Character–If a friend were to ask to borrow $100, one of the first questions you would ask yourself would be, "Will this person pay me back?" Likewise, the first area a potential creditor examines is the character of the applicant, or his honesty and reliability. While determining character may be a fairly easy task for the one who is considering a loan to his friend, it is very difficult for lenders who are not acquainted with the applicant. To determine an applicant's character, a lender examines the applicant's history of repaying loans by checking the records of a **credit bureau.**

Major lenders periodically report to credit bureaus the performance of those to whom they have lent money. Credit bureaus in turn act as central warehouses storing information on borrowers

Fair Credit Reporting Act

The Fair Credit Reporting Act, passed in 1971, protects consumers from the effects of inaccurate credit reports. Creditors gain information from credit bureaus about one's credit record before extending a loan. Information about any unpaid bills or bankruptcy proceedings in these reports often influences a creditor to reject a loan application. However, credit bureaus sometimes receive inaccurate or incomplete credit information from businesses or make errors in the recording of the information. For instance, people with the same name as someone else in the community may find that credit records of the other person are included in their own credit reports. If the other "John Smith" has a poor credit record, the results could be damaging to a person with a commendable credit history. To protect consumers from such unfair damage to their credit ratings, Congress established several regulations in the Fair Credit Reporting Act.

The law decrees that credit reports must be recent, relevant, and accurate. Therefore, credit files are to be retained only seven years (ten years in cases of bankruptcy). If a company turns down a credit application or increases credit costs because of a bad credit report, the company must disclose the name and address of the reporting agency to the consumer. If a consumer suspects errors in his credit report, he has the right to demand a copy of the record, to have incorrect information changed, and to include his version of any dispute in the report. To insure that unauthorized people do not gain copies of a consumer's credit record, the law also established guidelines to be followed by credit bureaus when reports are requested.

Smith John A 322 G
Smith John A 4 Len
Smith John A 99 Ha
Smith John A Surry
Smith John A 7242
Smith John A 2113
Smith John A 362

for seven years (information about personal bankruptcy is retained for ten years) subsequently charging lenders for examining the files of particular applicants. A credit file includes the names of lenders, the amounts of loans previously granted, the term of the loans, any outstanding balances, and the borrower's performance in repaying the loans. If an applicant's lack of credit experience is evidenced by insufficient information in his credit file or if the information points to the fact that he cannot be trusted with a loan, the lender may decline to make a loan and must notify the applicant in writing.

Capacity–While a potential borrower's character is the most important consideration in the credit decision, it is also important to examine one's *ability* to repay. Even though the friend who asked you for a $100 loan may have exceptional character, you might be reluctant to make him the loan if he has no job or other source of income. Banks and other commercial creditors must likewise be assured that an applicant has the capacity to repay a loan; therefore, they require that potential borrowers disclose all sources of income.

Capital–When a banker or other lender mentions the word "capital," he is speaking of the borrower's net worth. The **net worth** of a borrower is what he owns minus what he owes. In other words, the financial net worth of someone is what he would have left if he sold everything he owned and paid off all his debts. A person who has $4 million in houses and other assets may be considered a wealthy and prosperous man to his friends, but he may actually be a poor loan risk if he owes creditors $3,990,000. To determine an applicant's capital, lenders sometimes require a borrower to complete a personal financial statement which lists all of his assets and all of his liabilities (debts).

Collateral–If an applicant's character is good, his capacity to repay is sufficient, and his capital is adequate, a lender next examines the collateral which the applicant will use to secure the loan. Lenders must ask themselves if the collateral would

Fair Debt Collection Practices Act

Because debt collectors sometimes harrassed consumers to pay their bills, Congress passed the Fair Debt Collection Practices Act in 1977 to protect consumers from possible abusive and unfair practices. Some of the unreasonable practices targeted by this legislation were threats, abusive language, repeated phone calls and phone calls at odd hours, and false claims by the debt collector to be someone he is not (a lawyer, public official, etc.) in order to gain access or information.

To prohibit such harsh and unjust practices, the Fair Debt Collection Practices Act set procedures for how a debt collector is to contact the credit user. The act outlawed deception and harassment and established other guidelines limiting the debt collector's ability to seize payment.

be sufficient to repay the loan should the borrower be unable to do so. Contrary to popular belief, lenders, such as bankers, are not in business to repossess collateral. Taking possession of collateral is an expensive, time consuming, and often emotional experience. The sole aim of a bank's repossession of collateral is the protection of its depositors' funds. Bankers and other lenders, therefore, are reluctant to make a loan solely on the basis of good collateral.

Conditions–The final "C" of credit is "conditions," which refers to general economic conditions. If the economy is healthy and much money is available for lending, many loans will be made, even some marginal loans which otherwise would be denied. If conditions are poor, however, some loans, even those to very good customers, might be denied.

Cosigning

Occasionally if a lender is impressed with a potential borrower's character, but his income is

Dangers of Cosigning

Jerry and Eddie were brothers. Jerry was single, a big talker, lazy, and irresponsible. Eddie was married, a hard worker, and concerned about his brother. When Jerry mentioned he needed an amplifier for his new music teaching career, Eddie was skeptical. Jerry said he could not get a loan without a cosigner. When he begged his brother and said that the responsibility of a loan was just what he needed to change his ways and become "an honest citizen," Eddie gave in. He told Jerry to get a loan larger than he needed, putting the extra money in the bank in case he could not make a payment. Eddie figured he had no risks.

Jerry made the first payment without any problem, and Eddie forgot about the matter. Then Eddie got a call from the bank concerning an overdue payment. Noticeably upset, he called Jerry. His brother apologized profusely and explained that he was a little late, but he would take care of the payment immediately. Jerry kept his word, but soon Eddie received another call, threatening his own credit record and loans. Eddie again called Jerry, and he found out that Jerry had spent his savings. Eddie heard new apologies and assurances, but the process continued. The ugly matter disrupted Eddie's life for months until the debt was finally paid.

Besides the Biblical cautions against cosigning (Prov. 6:1-2, 11:15, 17:18, 22:26-27), there are numerous practical concerns. Here is a sample warning that banks give cosigners, under new laws: "The bank can collect from you without first trying to collect from the borrower. You may be sued for payment although the person who receives the loan is able to pay. If this debt is ever in default, that fact may become part of your credit record."

The dangers of cosigning are obvious. No matter how well the cosigner knows the person with whom he is cosigning, the fact remains that the borrower is a poor credit risk. (Otherwise he would not need a cosigner!) The cosigner is *not* simply vouching for the character of the borrower. He promises to pay the debt as well as any late penalties or collection fees. The bank does not have to inform the cosigner about any problems until it may be too late.

No matter how well-intentioned the borrower may be, he cannot be sure of his future income. Should he default, or even be late on a payment, the cosigner can become caught up in an embarrassing, frustrating hassle that could prove devastating to his reputation and wallet. Such an experience also ruptures most relationships–a risk not worth taking.

less than adequate, his capital is small, or his collateral is weak, he may "qualify the loan," that is, he may promise to grant the loan if another more creditworthy person will also sign the note promising to pay if the original borrower cannot. This practice is known as **cosigning.**

Section Review

1. What is a savings assignment?
2. How is a second mortgage connected to the concept of equity?
3. What are the two types of finance companies?
4. What are the five C's of credit?

Chapter Review

Terms
debtor
creditor
garnish
default
consumption borrowing
investment borrowing
appreciating assets
installment credit
single payment loans
term
principal
interest
amortization schedule
secured loan
collateral ·
unsecured loan
open-end credit
credit limit
savings assignment
overdraft protection
cash advance
first mortgage
second mortgage
equity
consumer finance companies
personal loan
debt consolidation loan
sales finance companies
pawnbrokers
credit bureau
net worth
cosigning

Content Questions
1. What are the two philosophies of debt over which Christians tend to differ?
2. What are the four Biblical cautions regarding debt?

3. What is the difference between consumption borrowing and investment borrowing?
4. What are the three ways people may engage in investment borrowing?
5. Why is more interest paid out of the first payment of an installment loan than out of the last payment?
6. What kind of credit is extended when a person uses a credit card?
7. Why do commercial banks consider savings assignment loans virtually risk-free loans?
8. What kind of loans do sales finance companies provide?
9. How do lenders investigate the character of potential borrowers?
10. When a lender speaks of a borrower's "capacity," to what is he referring?

Application Questions
1. Is there any difference between credit and debt?
2. What factors would cause interest rates to differ from one loan to another and from one lender to another?
3. Do you believe that interest rates on loans should be regulated by law to prevent lenders from overcharging borrowers?
4. During the early 1980s the interest rates on loans were lower than the rate of inflation. Discuss the consequences of this situation from the standpoints of borrowers and lenders.
5. Do you believe lenders should have access to the credit histories of potential borrowers? Should credit-reporting agencies keep information in their files for a longer or shorter period than is done currently?
6. What does the Bible say about cosigning for the debts of others? Cite specific references and examples.

CHAPTER 17

Cash Management and Saving

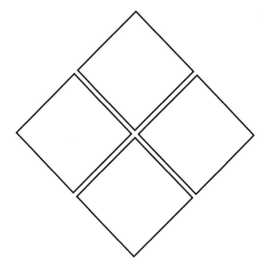

Lay not up for yourselves treasures upon earth, where moth and rust doth corrupt, and where thieves break through and steal: But lay up for yourselves treasures in heaven, where neither moth nor rust doth corrupt, and where thieves do not break through nor steal: For where your treasure is, there will your heart be also.   Matthew 6:19-21

I. Cash Management

The Christian and Wealth

Most people entertain brief fantasies of what it would be like to be wealthy. Some daydream about a life devoid of work in which their hours are filled with nothing but pleasure. Others conjure images of themselves living in enormous homes, extravagantly entertaining hundreds of equally wealthy friends. Still others fantasize about calling their stockbrokers from their personal jets in order to buy or sell an enormous amount of stock. As fanciful as these daydreams might be, Christians must remember that their goal in life is to glorify Jesus Christ, a goal which is far more important than the mere accumulation of dollars and the things they can buy.

There is perhaps no greater force used by Satan to prevent unsaved men and women from coming to Jesus Christ than the desire to acquire and retain wealth. A poignant example is provided in the gospel of Mark. A rich young man came to Jesus Christ asking what he might do to gain eternal life. Realizing the young man's concealed devotion to riches, the Lord pointed to the fact that salvation is demonstrated by a single-minded devotion to God.

> Then Jesus beholding him loved him, and said unto him, One thing thou lackest: go thy way, sell whatsoever thou hast, and give to the poor, and thou shalt have treasure in heaven: and come, take up the cross, and follow me. And he was sad at that saying, and went away grieved: for he had great possessions. And Jesus looked round about, and saith unto his disciples, How hardly shall they that have riches enter into the kingdom of God! And

the disciples were astonished at his words. But Jesus answereth again, and saith unto them, Children, how hard it is for them that trust in riches to enter into the kingdom of God! It is easier for a camel to go through the eye of a needle, than for a rich man to enter into the kingdom of God.

(Mark 10:21-25)

Not only does Satan use the desire for wealth to prevent the unsaved from coming to God, he also uses the pursuit of money to distract the child of God from his Master's service. Like children mindlessly lured by colorful toys and brightly wrapped candy, Christians all too often wander from the path of God's service in their desire to acquire riches which do not satisfy.

Ye have sown much, and bring in little; ye eat, but ye have not enough; ye drink, but ye are not filled with drink; ye clothe you, but there is none warm; and he that earneth wages earneth wages to put it into a bag with holes.

(Haggai 1:6)

Knowing, therefore, what God thinks about the pursuit of riches, many students may be wondering why a chapter on personal money management is included in this text. The answer may be found in one word: stewardship. The goal of this chapter is not to provide a ''how-to'' manual for those who wish to accumulate wealth. Rather it is to present information which will assist Spirit-filled believers in their exercise of financial stewardship. Whether the Lord has provided one with great wealth or with just enough money to meet his basic needs, He demands that His provision be used wisely.

Successful personal financial stewardship is the result of correctly handling one's money on each of three levels. The first level is the proper control of one's cash in the short run. Whereas Chapter 15 deals with the wise use of cash to make purchases, this chapter discusses the *management* of the cash itself over a period of days and weeks. The second level is the wise handling of one's wealth in the intermediate run. As opposed to managing one's cash today or next week, the intermediate period is characterized by wise saving over a period of months. Chapter 18 will discuss retirement, the fi-

nal phase of personal financial management which involves the long-run storage of excess funds.

Purpose for Holding Cash

Cash management is the activity of accounting for cash inflows, storing short-term cash balances in ways that will be most profitable, and the timely payment of one's financial obligations. Many individuals, business firms, churches, and Christian schools might not be suffering great financial losses as a result of poor cash management, but they could be serving the Lord better by taking a more serious approach to the handling of their day-to-day cash transactions. For example, the principal of a Christian school recently noticed that thousands of dollars were sitting idle each month between the first of the month when tuition payments were made and the middle and end of the month when payroll checks were distributed to the faculty. He decided to open an interest-bearing account for the school to which he deposited all tuition payments. Whenever a payroll was due, the exact amount of money was withdrawn, leaving the rest to draw interest. At the end of the year the school had earned over $3,000 in interest. Because of this principal's wise cash management, the church was able to provide the faculty a modest salary increase without having to raise students' tuition.

Before we examine how one might better handle his money, it would be wise to determine why people need to hold cash balances. People desire to hold cash for three reasons: to pay for routine transactions, to pay for unexpected emergencies, and to act as a store of value.

To Pay for Routine Transactions–Each day practically everyone engages in transactions for which he needs to pay money. Perhaps already today you have been involved in some routine transactions. You may have carried a specific amount of cash with you to pay for a trip on a city bus, you may have spent a predetermined amount for lunch at school, or you may have spent some money at a pay telephone calling your parents for a ride home from basketball practice. Most adults hold cash for the same reason, only on a larger scale. After being paid, they in turn pay certain bills which arrive in their mailboxes like clockwork–bills such as monthly house payments, electricity and water bills, and insurance premium payments. Usually the amounts of each of these transactions is fairly predictable; therefore, people plan on holding a certain amount of their income in cash to meet these routine obligations.

To Pay for Unexpected Emergencies–The second reason people hold cash is to be prepared for "rainy days." If everyone kept only enough cash to pay for his routine transactions, he would soon find himself in trouble. If an emergency should arise and one is not able to secure enough cash, he may be forced to draw from the funds normally used to pay routine obligations; when those bills come due, he may be forced to sell something to generate enough cash to stay current with his creditors.

The amount of money one should hold to meet unexpected needs depends on the income of the person and the amount of other resources he has at his disposal. First, economists have found that

Unexpected car expenses can create a financial emergency.

those with relatively high incomes tend to have "rainier" days than those with lower paychecks. Whereas a student may need to keep only a few dollars on reserve against some unforeseen emergency, a homeowner with three children and a car might need to hold a greater amount of cash.

The amount one needs to hold in reserve against a future financial emergency also depends on the amount of other available resources. For example, a person with disability insurance may not need to hold as much money on reserve against the threat of a short-term incapacitation as others since his policy will continue to pay his salary while he is convalescing from an injury or illness. Many financial consultants believe that it is wise for a person to keep three to four months of income on reserve to meet unexpected emergencies.

To Act as a Store of Value–The final reason people wish to hold cash is to store it for some predetermined future use. One possible reason is to save for some major purchase such as an automobile or home appliance. A second reason many wish to store cash is to accumulate funds until they have enough to invest in some income producing or appreciating asset.

Ways of Holding Cash

Paper Bills and Coin–Obviously, the primary way one can hold cash is by holding actual paper money and coin. We have all heard stories of a rich eccentric who, out of a distrust of banks, buried money in his yard or stashed it in the walls of his home. Upon his death neighbors or relatives ransacked his home searching for the hidden treasure. Two specific dangers present themselves when one holds money in the form of paper money and coins. First is a danger of losing the money because of carelessness or theft. Whenever one holds great amounts of money in currency, he becomes a target for thieves. The second danger is the threat of loss because of inflation. If a person buried $10,000 in 1929 and dug it up at the end of 1991 he would still have $10,000 in cash; however, he would still have lost a tremendous amount of money since a dollar in 1929 could have purchased nearly seven times more goods than a dollar can buy today.

Instant Cash

Walk up to a bank at any time of the day or night, punch a few buttons, and–presto!–cash drops into your hand. The *automatic teller machine* (ATM), which was first installed in 1969, has revolutionized banking to meet the demands of today's fast-paced society.

ATMs mean convenience. They are located anywhere people need fast cash–banks, shopping centers, malls, airports. Customers can avoid long lines and perform routine business after hours, activities such as deposits, withdrawals, transfers between accounts, instant cash loans, and loan payments. To use the ATM, the customer simply inserts a plastic *debit card* into the machine, punches in his secret *personal identification number* (PIN), and completes his transaction.

Even if you go out of town or overseas, your bank's debit card may help you get ready cash. Many of the 100,000 + ATMs in the United States belong to a network, and the numbers are growing daily. The Cirrus cash card network has over 26,000 ATMs in North America, and the Plus System has almost as many. With more than 50,000 ATMs overseas in over 21 countries, even when you are traveling abroad, you can easily withdraw yen or pounds at the best rates without carrying traveler's checks, taking a loan, or paying commissions. For example, after punching in your request for £20 at a Plus ATM in London, the computer converts the amount to dollars and calls the main Plus office in Denver, which then relays the request to your home bank. Provided that your account has the money, the Denver office will approve your instant cash within 15 seconds. The money is withdrawn directly from your home bank account.

Along with the advantages of the ATM comes a disadvantage: the opportunity for a new form of crime. In one instance, computer criminals got some codes from the phone lines with the help of a GTE consultant and planned to steal $14 million. Fortunately, they were caught. Another individual used a Security Pacific National Bank ATM master card, which can enter any account, to take $237,000. Smalltime crooks sometimes hide near ATMs to attack customers who have just withdrawn cash.

Although crooks can break any code or barrier, the industry has taken extreme precautions. Random code systems are being developed that make it impossible even for someone who knows the system to eavesdrop on your computer line. The customer should take some obvious precautions as well–never give your card or PIN number to anyone, avoid out-of-the-way ATMs, take a friend, and beware of someone suspiciously loitering around an ATM. The law says that you are liable for only $50 if you report the loss of your card within two days, and liable for $500 if you wait longer. Your losses can be unlimited if you do not notify the bank within sixty days of an unauthorized withdrawal on your bank statement.

Transaction Accounts–For buying goods from vending machines and for making other small purchases most people use currency or coin, but for larger purchases, they prefer to use transaction accounts. A **transaction account** is an account at a financial institution against which one may write a note ordering the institution to pay a specific sum of money to the one named on the note. The most popular transaction account, the **checking account,** is offered by commercial banks. By law only commercial banks are permitted to offer checking accounts, but also by law they are forbidden from paying interest on checking accounts. To bypass these laws, commercial banks and savings and loan associations devised a second type of transaction account, a savings account called a **negotiable order of withdrawal (NOW) account** against which withdrawal slips may be written and transferred to others. A negotiable order of withdrawal is virtually indistinguishable from a check; the only difference is that a NOW account pays interest, whereas most checking accounts do not. Most banks and savings and loan associations require

NOW account holders to maintain a minimum monthly balance of perhaps $1,000 in order to be eligible for receipt of interest. Many banks and S&Ls offer the third type of transaction account, the **super NOW account.** It pays a higher rate of interest, but also requires the depositor to maintain a significantly higher balance in his account.

Since credit unions are forbidden from offering checking accounts, and since they do not offer savings accounts against which negotiable orders of withdrawals may be written, they offer a fourth type of transaction account called the share draft account. It was pointed out in Chapter 16 that whenever a member of a credit union deposits money to his account, technically he is purchasing shares of ownership in that credit union. The **share draft account (SDA)** is an account upon which a credit union member can write check-like instruments called share drafts. Instead of ordering the credit union to draw money from a checking or savings account, the share draft orders the credit union to liquidate a portion of the member's ownership account.

A share draft from a credit union, a check from a commercial bank, and a negotiable order of withdrawal from a savings and loan association

Opening and Maintaining a Transaction Account

Opening a Transaction Account–The requirements for opening a transaction account are very simple. One must be of legal age, and one must fill out a signature card. The signature card both authorizes the institution to maintain an account and serves as a security device to permit the institution to verify the account-holder's signature. If an account is shared by two or more people, a **joint account** is said to exist. When opening a joint account, applicants should consider the laws of survivorship. For example, if a husband and wife wish to open an account which would ensure that upon the death of one the funds would become the property of the other, they should open a joint account with **right of survivorship.** If, on the other hand, two people want to open a joint account without right of survivorship, they should ask for a joint account as **tenants in common.**

Writing Checks–After a new transaction account is opened, the institution's customer service representative may provide the new account holder with a small packet of blank checks to be used until the customer's printed checks arrive. Writing checks is a very simple process. The example on the next page illustrates what is involved. First, the account holder must date the check. One must be careful in filling out the date, because a check cannot be cashed if it is postdated or staledated.

A **postdated** check is one which bears a future date. It is not good practice to write postdated checks since they often clear the bank undetected. For example, a couple wrote a postdated check to their landlord because their apartment rent was going to be due while they were on vacation. They gave him strict instructions not to deposit the check until the normal due date since their paychecks would not be automatically deposited until that time. The landlord forgot his promise and deposited the check a few days later. The postdated check slipped through the bank's operation center undetected and caused several of the couple's other checks to bounce.

A check is considered **staledated** if it bears a

An application for opening a transaction account

date more than six months old. One couple devised a unique way of saving to purchase a new car: they lived off his paycheck and each week placed her paycheck into their safe deposit box. Three years later they were stunned to discover that the bank could only cash the most recent six months' worth of the over 150 weekly paychecks they had accu-

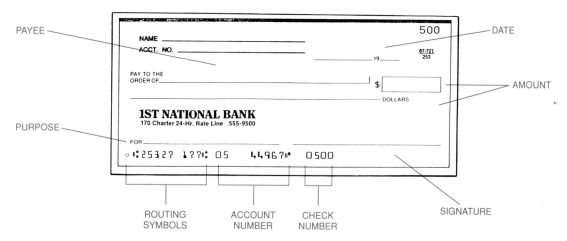

mulated. They were relieved, however, when her employer agreed to redeem the checks.

The second step in writing a check is filling in the name of the **payee,** the one receiving the check. Be sure to write legibly, and do not leave blank the payee line on a check. If the payee line is left blank and the check is stolen, the thief could fill in his own name and cash the check.

Writing the amount of the check is the third step. For safety's sake, printed checks provide two places for the check amount to be filled in. One line requires the check writer to write out the amount in words whereas the other must be written in numerals. In case the two amounts disagree, the amount in words is accepted as the legally correct figure. Each time a check is written, the account holder should immediately subtract the amount of the check from his previous account balance to avoid overdrawing his account.

In order to present a blameless testimony in the community and to avoid possible criminal charges, a Christian should never overdraw his transaction account. One's account is overdrawn if a check is presented to a bank for which sufficient funds are not on deposit. Most checks which are overdrawn are done out of carelessness, but a great number are written with full intent to defraud a merchant. Should a checkwriter make an error in completing a check, such as entering the wrong date or writing it for an incorrect amount, he should draw a line through the incorrect entry, write the correct date or amount above it, and initial the change.

The final step in completing a written check is for the account holder to sign the check. Each check should be signed exactly the same way as one's signature appears on the account's signature card. It is important for an account holder to guard his checks from being lost or stolen. If a checkbook is stolen, an account holder should contact the institution immediately so that the account may be closed. At the same time the old account is closed, a new account may be opened from which legitimate checks written on the old account will be paid.

Making Deposits to a Transaction Account—Making deposits to a transaction account is a fairly simple process. First one must enter the correct amount of currency and coin on the deposit slip. Second, each check to be deposited should be listed individually along with its routing number to help the bank trace the deposit in the event a check is lost during processing.

When depositing or cashing checks, a depositor must first endorse each check. To **endorse** a check is to acknowledge receipt of the amount written on the front of the check. After endorsing the check, the payee may receive cash from a bank, make a deposit to his account, or transfer the check to a person to whom *he* owes money. Checks may be endorsed in four ways. First is the blank endorse-

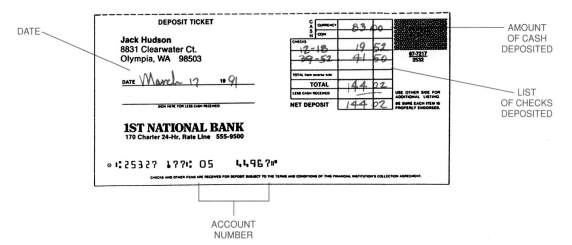

DATE

DEPOSIT TICKET

Jack Hudson
8831 Clearwater Ct.
Olympia, WA 98503

DATE March 17   19 91

SIGN HERE FOR LESS CASH RECEIVED

1ST NATIONAL BANK
170 Charter 24-Hr. Rate Line 555-9500

⊙ ⑈:25327 ⑈77⑈: 05   44967⑈

CHECKS AND OTHER ITEMS ARE RECEIVED FOR DEPOSIT SUBJECT TO THE TERMS AND CONDITIONS OF THIS FINANCIAL INSTITUTION'S COLLECTION AGREEMENT.

CASH CURRENCY 83 00
      COIN
CHECKS
12-18   19 52
39-52   41 50

67-7217
2532

TOTAL from reverse side
      TOTAL   144 02
LESS CASH RECEIVED
NET DEPOSIT   144 02

USE OTHER SIDE FOR ADDITIONAL LISTING.
BE SURE EACH ITEM IS PROPERLY ENDORSED.

AMOUNT
OF CASH
DEPOSITED

LIST
OF CHECKS
DEPOSITED

ACCOUNT
NUMBER

ment. A **blank endorsement** of a check simply consists of the signature of the payee on the back of the check. Blank endorsements can be dangerous. If on his way to the bank a depositor should lose a check which contained a blank endorsement, any person could sign his name under the first name as if he had been given the check by the original payee and cash the check.

A **special endorsement** is used when the recipient of a check wishes to use the check to pay someone else. For example, assume that your dentist, Dr. William U. Drillwell, billed you $500 for dental work. When you submitted the bill to your dental insurance company, it wrote a check payable to you. You could deposit the check into your personal account and then write a personal check to the dentist, or you could simply mail the insurance company's check directly to the dentist after writing the following endorsement: ''Pay to the order of Dr. William U. Drillwell'' followed by your signature. Financial advisors caution against using

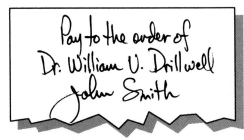

this type of endorsement. When a check is presented to the checkwriter's bank it is paid, canceled (marked paid), and sent to the one who wrote the check (in our example the insurance company) to act as evidence that the bill was paid and payment was accepted. The person who merely transfers the check to another will not receive a canceled check to act as evidence that a bill was paid.

Rather than using a blank endorsement for checks to be deposited or special endorsements to sign a check over to another person, the restrictive endorsement tends to be a safer method of endorsing checks for either of these two purposes. A **restrictive endorsement** restricts the use of an endorsed check by using the word ''only.'' Instead of using a blank endorsement to endorse a check to be deposited, a depositor can ensure that the check will not be put to any unauthorized use by endorsing the check ''For deposit only to the account of'' followed by his signature. A special en-

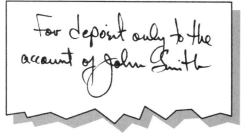

dorsement allows a check holder to sign a check over to another party; however, once he signs the check over and the other party signs the check, the second party in turn may sign the check over to yet another party. If a check holder wishes for only a certain party to cash or deposit the check, he may make a restrictive endorsement out of a special endorsement by adding the word "only." The new endorsement will read "Pay to the order of Dr. William U. Drillwell only," followed by your signature.

A **conditional endorsement** is the final type of endorsement. It stipulates the conditions under which a check may be cashed. For example, if you were to contract someone to build a garage for your house, you could endorse the check "Pay to the order of Chuck Naildriver only upon completion of garage construction" followed by your signature. This type of endorsement is not advised, for it places the bank in a position of deciding if work was completed. Many institutions refuse to honor checks endorsed with conditional endorsements.

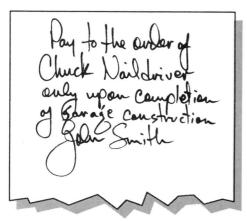

***Stopping Payment on a Check*–**Occasionally check writers do not wish for their banks to cash checks which they have written. This situation occurs most often when a customer finds that a product which he purchased is defective or incomplete. To ensure that a check will not be paid, one may go to his bank and issue a **stop payment order.** If the check has not yet been cashed, the bank will guarantee that for the next six months it will not honor the check; rather it will return the check to the payee notifying him that payment was stopped by the account holder. After the six month period, the check will be considered staledated and non-negotiable. Fees for issuing a stop payment order usually range from $3 to $10.

Stopping payment on a check can be a very serious matter. If a merchant sells a customer some goods, and the customer stops payment on his check, it would be very easy for a merchant to believe that the customer is a thief: he has goods in his possession for which he has not paid. To avoid such charges and to present a spotless testimony in the community, a Christian needs to return all goods for which payment has been stopped along with an explanation as to why a stop payment order was necessary.

***Reconciling a Transaction Account*–**One of the biggest responsibilities in maintaining a transaction account is ensuring that one's checkbook balance is correct. Each month most banks send a statement to each checking account customer listing all deposits which have been made, all checks which have been presented for payment, and the customer's final account balance. In many cases, financial institutions provide the courtesy of sending the account holder all of the canceled checks which have cleared his account. (Institutions usually make a microfilm record of each check for their files.) The end-of-the-month account balance on the bank's monthly statement rarely agrees with the balance in the customer's checkbook register for one or more of four reasons. First, there may be deposits in the mail which the account holder has already added to his balance but which the bank has not yet received. Second, there may be checks

Cashing Checks

Many people become angry at banks for not cashing a check they have presented. When one puts himself in the banker's shoes, so to speak, it is understandable why the banker is reluctant to cash some checks. Imagine that you received a check drawn on the First National Bank for $4,000 from the sale of a car to John Smith, a man completely unknown to you until he responded to your classified advertisement in the newspaper. You do not have a checking account at any bank, so you stroll down to the bank nearest your house, the Second National Bank, and request that they give you $4,000 for the check. Most banks would refuse to cash your check for two reasons: first, they do not know you. How is a banker to know that you did not steal the check from the original recipient of the check and are now trying to cash it fraudulently? If you show proper identification confirming that you are the one listed as the payee, how is the banker to know that you did not alter a legitimate $40 check to be $4,000? Or, maybe you have a printing press and you just printed up a few hundred checks and are going from bank to bank collecting a harvest of $4,000 at each stop.

Second, the banker does not know the check writer. Because the Second National Bank is not the bank on which the check is drawn, it has no way of knowing if the real Mr. Smith is the one who wrote you the check, if there are sufficient funds in the account at the First National Bank to pay the check, or even that such an account really exists. Surely the Second National Bank could call the First National Bank and confirm that there are sufficient funds at the moment, but who is to say that the funds will still be there in a few days when the bank ultimately presents the check for payment?

In the words of one banker, "the unknown check casher has everything to gain while the bank has everything to lose." The Second National Bank is in business to make a profit, and there is nothing profitable about cashing a potentially fraudulent check written by one stranger of the bank to another stranger of the bank. How, therefore, could this check in our story be cashed? Very simply, you may take the check to the bank on which the check is drawn. If the payee can identify himself and the bank can confirm that the check was written by the account holder, then the bank must cash the check. Verifying that the account holder wrote the check may involve checking the account holder's signature and, in the case of checks involving large amounts of money, calling the depositor to verify that he did indeed write the check. But what can one do, you might ask, if the First National Bank is on the other side of the country? In order to cash an out-of-town check, you may take the check to any bank, and for a small fee, it will send the check to the bank on which the check is drawn. The out-of-town bank will then send a cashier's check which can be cashed by the in-town bank with no risk of loss. Or, more simply, a person may send the check himself via registered and insured mail to the out-of-town bank and request a cashier's check.

Figure 17-1

DATE	CHECK NUMBER	CHECKS ISSUED TO OR DEPOSIT RECEIVED FROM	AMOUNT OF DEPOSIT	✓ T	AMOUNT OF CHECK	BALANCE 0 00
2 9		Initial Deposit	500 00	✓		500 00
2 10	101	Handy Food Store		✓	87 50	412 50
2 10	102	Brad's Auto Parts		✓	47 94	364 56
2 12	103	City Water Service			24 00	340 56
2 14	104	City Electric Company		✓	88 84	251 72
2 15		Deposit	819 25			1 070 97
2 15	105	Fidelity Mortgage Company			428 16	642 81
2 16	106	Exxon			21 12	621 69
2 17	107	Fairview Bible Church			125 00	496 69
		Service Charge		✓	3 45	493 24

19____   BE SURE TO DEDUCT ANY PER CHECK CHARGES OR MAINTENANCE CHARGES THAT MAY APPLY.

which have been written by the account holder and subtracted from his check register which have not yet been presented to the bank. Third, the account holder may have added a deposit or subtracted a check in his register incorrectly. And fourth, the bank may have made an error in adding the customer's deposits or subtracting his checks. By **reconciling** one's transaction account, one may determine if the bank's balance and his check register balance are correct.

To illustrate a proper reconciliation let us look at the account of Scott Case, as seen in Figures 17-1, 17-2, and 17-3, which show both the front and back of the bank's monthly account statement and Scott's check register. Notice first Scott's check register. He opened his account with a deposit of $500, and between the date he opened the account and the statement closing date, he made one additional deposit of $819.25 and wrote seven checks totaling $822.56. His check register balance was $496.69. After receiving his monthly checking account statement, Scott was a little confused. His

check register stated that he had a balance of $496.69, but the bank said he had only $272.27 in his account. Turning the account statement over he noticed that the bank provided a form to help him reconcile his checking account. After he completed the final step in the reconciliation process, he was satisfied that his balance and the bank's balance were in agreement. The only difference between the two balances was that the bank had not yet credited one of his deposits, and several checks had not yet been presented for payment.

One mistake made by many checking account holders is the failure to record in their check registers all checks written. When they believe that they may be nearing the end of their funds, they call the bank's bookkeeping department and inquire about their checking account balance. The bookkeeping department provides customers with the balance on the bank's records, but with the possibility of checks having not yet cleared the bank, this balance may be overstating the available amount in the customers' account. Encouraged by

Figure 17-2 Bank Statement and Check Register

MONTHLY CHECKING ACCOUNT STATEMENT							

SCOTT CASE
6936 BETTYHILL DRIVE
SAN ANDREAS, CA 91185

ACCOUNT NUMBER
43 69 2125 1
STATEMENT PERIOD
01/14/91 through 02/14/91

ACCOUNT SUMMARY							
PREVIOUS BALANCE	DEPOSITS & CREDITS		CHECKS & DEBITS		INTEREST	SERVICE CHARGE	CURRENT BALANCE
	NUMBER	AMOUNT	NUMBER	AMOUNT			
$0	1	$500.00	4	$227.73	$0	$3.45	$272.27

DETAILED MONTHLY ACTIVITY					
DAY	AMOUNT	CHECK NO. OR DESCRIPTION	DAY	AMOUNT	CHECK NO. OR DESCRIPTION
09	$500.00	DEPOSIT			
11	47.94	102			
12	87.50	101			
14	88.84	104			
14	3.45	SERVICE CHARGE			

the bank's higher balance, customers begin writing more checks on their accounts, only to be surprised at receiving several overdraft notices.

Guaranteed Checks

Certainly most payments are made in cash or by using a transaction account, but what is a buyer to do when he cannot use either of these two means of payment? Occasionally a transaction is so large that it would be impractical to use cash. At the same time, the merchant is unfamiliar with the buyer and refuses to accept a personal check. In such cases customers may purchase checks which guarantee payment. That is, by accepting a **guaranteed check**, the merchant has 100% assurance that he will receive the funds when the check is cashed.

There are four types of guaranteed checks: certified checks, cashier's checks, money orders, and traveler's checks.

Certified Checks–A **certified check** is a customer's personal check which a bank or other financial institution guarantees to pay upon presentation. To have a check certified, one must completely fill out a personal check listing the payee and the check amount. The bank then places a hold on the funds to ensure that when the check is ultimately presented, the exact amount of money will be in the depositor's account for payment. After placing a hold on the funds, the bank imprints the word *certified* on the face of the check, and the certification is signed by an officer of the bank. This certifica-

Figure 17-3

TO RECONCILE YOUR CHECKING ACCOUNT BALANCE, FOLLOW THESE SIX SIMPLE STEPS:

1. Subtract from your check register all service charges, check printing charges, and any other miscellaneous charges which we have deducted from your account as shown on the front of this statement.

2. Add to your check register all credits, service charge refunds, NOW account interest, and any other miscellaneous additions which we have made to your account as shown on the front of this statement.

3. Compare the checks shown on this statement to your check register and indicate checks which have cleared by placing a check mark (✔) beside them in your check register.

4. List all checks which have not yet cleared the bank:

CHECKS OUTSTANDING	
CHECK NUMBER	CHECK AMOUNT
103	24.00
105	428.16
106	21.12
107	125.00
TOTAL	598.28

5. Enter the ending balance as shown on the front of this statement: $ 272.27

 Add deposits made after the statement closing date: + 819.25

 TOTAL: =$ 1,091.52

 Subtract the total of your outstanding checks: − 598.28

6. This figure should agree with the balance shown in your check register: =$ 493.24

tion notifies the payee that the bank guarantees payment upon presentation. Fees for check certification usually range between $1 and $5.

Cashier's Checks–Another form of guaranteed check is the **cashier's check.** Whereas a certified check is paid out of funds frozen in the depositor's checking account, a cashier's check is one which is drawn on the bank itself and paid out of an account held by the bank. Since the bank is selling a check which is guaranteed to be paid upon presentation, it will accept only guaranteed funds for its purchase. For this reason, banks and other financial institutions will sell a cashier's check only upon presentation of cash, a checking or savings withdrawal drawn on the bank itself, or a guaranteed check from another institution. After receiving the guaranteed funds, the bank completes the cashier's check. The name of the payee is affixed, and the amount of the check is imprinted in such a way that alteration is virtually impossible. A bank offi-

cer signs the check. All cashier's checks are numbered, enabling the bank to record the details of the check for future reference. Like the charge for a certified check, the fee for purchasing a cashier's check usually ranges between $1 and $5.

Money Orders–A **money order** is another form of guaranteed check and operates much the same as a cashier's check. Unlike cashier's checks–usually used for large transactions such as purchasing an automobile or a major appliance–money orders generally are sold to people who do not have checking accounts to pay for routine small transactions such as utility bills and car payments. Money orders may be purchased from a variety of sources ranging from commercial banks and other financial institutions to branches of the U.S. Post Office and convenience stores. The fee charged is based upon the amount of the money order and may vary from 50¢ to $5.00.

Traveler's Checks–When going on vacation or on a business trip, it is nearly impossible to get a merchant to accept an out-of-town personal check, but carrying a sizable amount of cash would be foolhardy. Since the face amount of certified checks, cashiers checks, and money orders must be specified at the time of purchase, they are likewise impossible to use. **Traveler's checks,** on the other hand, may be purchased in denominations of $10, $20, $50, and $100 and are accepted by nearly every merchant. Issuers of traveler's checks include major financial institutions such as Citicorp, and major credit card companies such as VISA and American Express. Traveler's checks are usually sold by financial institutions which charge about 1% of the face amount of the checks. The bank, in turn, typically keeps 90% of the fee and remits 10% to the issuer of the traveler's checks. Thus, if a purchaser was to buy $1,000 worth of traveler's checks, he would pay a fee of about $10. The bank would keep $9 of the fee and send $1 to the traveler's check company. At the time of purchase, the buyer must sign each of the traveler's checks in the presence of a bank officer. Later, when goods are purchased with a traveler's check, the user must countersign the check next to the original signature. If the signatures match, the merchant accepts the check just as he would accept cash, even providing change if the purchase is less than the face amount of the traveler's check. In order to guarantee their acceptance, most traveler's check companies ensure merchants that they will redeem all traveler's checks, even if they later prove to be stolen or counterfeit, as long as, according to the judgment of the merchant, the signatures match.

Section Review

1. What are the three areas which must be addressed for successful personal financial stewardship?
2. Why do people hold cash?
3. What is a joint account with right of survivorship?
4. What does it mean to endorse a check, and what are the four types of endorsement?
5. How does a certified check operate?

II. Saving

The second step in the three step process of good financial stewardship is the proper handling of one's money in the intermediate run. Many families complain that their expenses are so great that they cannot afford to save. The first problem with which this section will deal is one of finding enough money to save; second, investigating how compound interest works; third, examining how and where to save.

Generating Money to Save

"We can't afford to save, we can barely keep our heads above water as it is. It seems as if there is always too much month left over at the end of the money!" This is a common complaint of many individuals and families, but with diligence and a little creativity, some money can be saved. There are actually two phases to saving. The first phase is the reduction of expenditures, that is, not spending more money than is necessary. Chapter 15 discusses this phase of developing a family budget and sticking to it. The second phase is setting aside specific amounts of money before one has a chance to spend it. Clearly, it is not the person who occasionally puts away a nickel here and a dime there who accumulates a sizable savings account, but rather by one who develops and maintains a disciplined systematic savings schedule. Obviously one's first financial responsibility is that of Scriptural giving, and after that, his second goal should be saving a fixed portion of his income. Most financial planners advocate saving 10% of one's paycheck each month. An individual has a few options that can help him to generate savings by setting aside a specified portion of income.

Automatic Payroll Deduction–Many employers provide a service whereby a given percentage of one's paycheck is automatically deposited to a savings account. By having the funds deducted from one's check before receiving the check, it is a little easier to live on what is left as opposed to personally making a deposit. A deduction of only $50 per month when deposited at a 5.5% interest rate will grow to nearly $3,500 in five years; in ten years

Families find many ways to generate savings that may be tucked away for safety in a bank or in other secure investments.

this figure will rise to nearly $8,000; in twenty years it will reach over $21,000. By adopting a payroll deduction plan early in one's career, not only will one accumulate a sizable balance over a period of years, but he will begin a savings habit which will last for a lifetime.

***Employer Savings Plans*–**Closely related to the payroll deduction is the employer-sponsored savings plan. To encourage savings, provide an added employee benefit, and on occasion encourage ownership of the company's stock, many business firms provide plans whereby they will contribute a predetermined amount of money toward a savings and investment plan for each dollar an employee contributes, up to a maximum amount. For example, one company contributes 50¢ for each dollar an employee contributes to the company savings and investment plan up to a maximum employee contribution of $2,000 per year. This means that if an employee contributes the maximum $2,000, the employer will contribute an additional $1,000 for a total account value of $3,000, that is a 50% return on one's savings *before interest!* Employers offering such plans occasionally provide several savings and investment options from which the employee

may choose. For example, the employer in the above scenario allows his employees to contribute to a fund of different common stocks, a regular interest bearing account with rates competitive to those offered by commercial banks, or a fund of the company's stock. Besides restricting the amount of the contribution, most firms require the money to be on deposit for a minimum period of time (perhaps three to five years) before the employee may withdraw the employer's portion of the contribution as well as his own. Without such restrictions employees could make contributions and withdraw their funds immediately after the employer makes his contribution.

***Claim Fewer Exemptions*–**When one begins working for an employer, he is required to complete a form for the Internal Revenue Service (IRS) called a W-4. On the W-4 a new employee declares the number of dependents for which he is responsible. On the basis of this number, the government calculates the amount of income tax it will withhold from the employee's paycheck. If, at the end of the year, the government has not withheld enough income tax, the employee must send the IRS a check for the balance due. If, on the other hand, the tax-

Electronic Money

Imagine a world in which you no longer carry cash, coins, or even checks. Computers make this futuristic vision technically possible. Americans find themselves making more and more financial transactions without ever seeing their money by using electronic funds transfer systems (EFTS).

For example, EFTS enable banks to deposit payroll and social security checks directly into a bank account. Banks also pay loan installments, mortgages, insurance premiums, electricity bills, and even credit card bills for you automatically. You simply give the bank a signed authorization slip, and the bank does the rest. Automatic bill payment saves time, money, and the embarrassment of late payments. You receive a warning statement 10 to 14 days prior to the transaction, and you can revoke your authorization at any time.

Many transactions that once required a visit to the bank (or an automatic teller machine) can now be done with a home banking system (HB). By linking home computers or "intelligent" phones to certain banks over the phone, customers can analyze their bank accounts, pay bills using a telephone bill-paying system (TBP), request investment advice, purchase products from on-screen retail-store catalogues, and obtain other miscellaneous information (telephone numbers, weather reports, airline reservations, etc.).

Banks have long used wire transfers (WTs) to transfer more than half a billion dollars each day between banks. Although the ATM is still the most popular place where private electronic fund transfers occur, customers now use their debit cards at retail stores and gas stations to transfer money from their personal account to the merchant's

account (called a point-of-sale system, or POS). One drawback to EFTS is the possibility of privacy violations. An account holder's financial transactions are open to anyone who can tap into the computer system.

Electronic money does not prevent bank robberies, however. In one famous case, thieves claiming to be from the Central Bank of Nigeria requested a wire transfer from a New York bank for $21 million. The money was placed in some overseas accounts and withdrawn before the bank knew what was happening. A programmer at another bank altered the computer's software to siphon off over half a million dollars. The legal system is only now beginning to understand and confront these new forms of crime.

payer has had too much income tax withheld, the government will refund the overpayment. The greater the number of dependents claimed on the W-4, the less the government will withhold in tax; the lower the number of dependents the taxpayer claims, the greater the amount it will deduct from the employee's paycheck. By claiming fewer exemptions than one is entitled, one may actually overpay his taxes, thereby increasing the amount of an end-of-the-year income tax refund. Thus, some employees deliberately claim fewer dependents than allowed, using the U.S. Treasury as a personal savings account.

Some people argue that this is a poor way to save money since the government is getting interest-free use of one's money for an entire year. While it may not be the most cost-effective method of saving money, it can be a way to force one to save if he cannot bring himself to actively make deposits to his personal savings account.

Automatic Transfers from Checking to Savings– For those with both checking and savings accounts in the same institution, another simple way of saving is to use the automatic transfer service which many institutions offer. Most banks provide a service whereby on a specific day of each month a prearranged amount of money is transferred from a depositor's checking account to his savings account. This can be a useful way of saving as long

as the depositor makes sure to specify a day of the month when he knows sufficient funds will be in his account, such as the day after each payday. Those using automatic transfer services must also remember to deduct the amount of the withdrawal from their checking accounts lest they accidentally overdraw their account.

*Save Unexpected Windfalls–*In the past, during the apple harvest season, growers had to pay workers to go out into the fields to physically hand-pick each apple. Occasionally they were fortunate to have a strong gust of wind come and blow down a great deal of their crop, thus reducing their expenses and increasing their profits. Today, when any unexpected profit comes someone's way, he is said to enjoy a ''windfall.'' Rather than spending all financial windfalls, such as income tax refunds, inheritances, cash prizes, or purchase rebates, financial advisors suggest that the recipient save 75% of the windfall and spend 25%, thus providing a great deal of savings while at the same time allowing current use of some of the funds. By saving windfalls, a substantial savings account can be accumulated over a relatively short period of time.

*Adopt a ''Frugal Month''–*Just as a runner sees the finish line and puts on a last-minute burst of

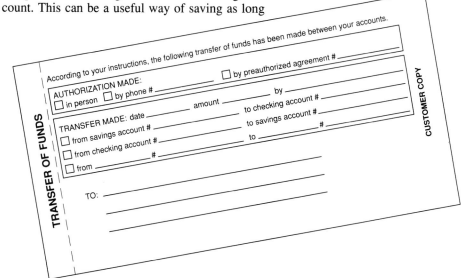

speed, some people can accumulate extra savings by putting on one burst of savings each year in the form of a "frugal month." During the frugal month the family reduces every expense as much as possible. Rather than having the frugal month simply be a month of lean living, a family can have some fun turning it into a challenge. During the month each family member takes his lunch to work or school, and no money is spent on clothing, furniture, or entertainment. During the month each member of the family tries to come up with the best money saving tips. Be prepared because some of the suggestions may appear rather bizarre, such as using bath water to water the lawn or wash the cars, burning candles instead of lightbulbs, or living on bread and water! Advisors suggest that the frugal month either be in the spring or in the fall when utility bills are low and when no significant holidays will interfere with expenses.

Continue Installment Payments When a Debt Is Paid–Whenever someone has been making an installment payment on a debt over a long period of time, his lifestyle adjusts to living on the lower consumption spending. A golden opportunity for savings, therefore, presents itself every time an installment loan is paid off. Rather than spending the extra income each month on new obligations, the former debtor could continue to write checks for the amount of the installment payment and deposit them into his savings account.

Save Your Raise–As people become more experienced and productive in their work, or as the cost of living increases, many employers give raises to their employees. Since the worker has been living on less, it might be relatively easy for him to "bank" all or part of his raise.

Stashing Cash–One final method of saving money is the actual hoarding of cash. Some people keep a jar in which they deposit all loose change at the end of the day. Another useful, but sometimes dangerous method of stashing cash is collecting high denomination pieces of currency. For example, one man has a habit of accumulating one hundred dollar bills. Whenever he accumulates enough currency, he goes to the bank and has it converted to hun-

Loose change may provide additional savings, but it should be collected periodically and added to an interest-bearing account.

dreds. Within two years he had accumulated twenty-one one hundred dollar bills. Granted, they are not earning interest, but at least it is $2,100 more in savings than he had before! Savers are advised to be careful when saving money in this manner, though, since it is easier to have the money lost or stolen. Also, since the money sits without earning interest, this method of saving is considered to be wise only if the cash is frequently collected and added to some interest-bearing investment.

Understanding How Interest Works

One of the most important principles of money management is never to let money sit idle; rather, when money is not being used, it ought to be loaned to others who are willing to pay interest for its use. In Matthew 25 the Lord presented a parable in which this principle was assumed. A master gave each of his servants some money to manage in his absence. Upon his return he commended those servants who received a profit but condemned the steward who let his money sit idle.

Sylvia Porter (1913-)
Economic Reporter and Tutor for the Masses

After her widowed mother lost most of their family savings in the stock market crash of 1929, Sylvia Porter decided to change her major at Hunter College from English literature to economics. In the midst of the economic difficulties the nation was beginning to experience, she was curious to find out how the economy did or did not work. That curiosity and a talent for writing about the technicalities of economics in a clear and simple manner soon led her into an impressive career in economic reporting. After her graduation (magna cum laude) in 1932, Porter gained work experience at several brokerage firms while taking graduate courses at New York University. Her writing career took off when in 1935 she began to write a regular financial column for the *New York Post*. She also contributed articles to many popular magazines and in 1939 wrote her first book: *How to Make Money in Government Bonds*. By the end of the decade she was called "the girl wonder of Wall Street."

At first the young writer used the name of S.F. Porter to conceal the fact that she was a woman capable of comprehending the male-dominated realm of economics. However, the merit of her work soon brought respect to the lady economist, and she changed the name of her syndicated financial column to simply "Sylvia Porter."

Many of Porter's major book titles reflect the practical nature of her writing. Among them are *How to Live Within Your Income* (1948) and *How to Get More for Your Money* (1961). Also, beginning in 1960, Porter published *Sylvia Porter's Income Tax Guide* annually.

She updated her 1975 best-seller, *Sylvia Porter's Money Book: How to Earn It, Spend It, Invest It, Borrow It, and Use It to Better Your Life*, with a new version "for the 80's" in 1979 that also became a best-seller. In these writings she admirably attempted to eradicate "economic ignorance" with down-to-earth economic instruction and practical advice for the general public.

His Lord answered and said unto him, Thou wicked and slothful servant, thou knowest that I reap where I sowed not, and gather where I have not strawed: Thou oughtest therefore to have put my money to the exchangers, and then at my coming I should have received mine own with usury. Take therefore the talent from him, and give it unto him which hath ten talents.

(Matthew 25:26-28)

Therefore, the most important consideration when saving money is the rate of interest paid on the deposit. Consider the following example cited by financial analysts to emphasize the importance of interest. Many a history student has balked at the injustice of the colonists for paying the Indians a mere $24 for the purchase of the island of Manhattan in 1626. But think a little further. Had the Indians taken the $24 and deposited it into a savings account paying 6% interest, their account balance would now stand at $39 *billion!* Such is the effect of compound interest. **Compound interest** is the calculation of interest on reinvested interest as well as on the original principal. For example, assume that on January 1, 1992 you deposited $100 in a savings account which pays 6% interest. At the end of 1992 your account balance would be $106.00, an increase of $6, or 6% of your original $100. At the end of 1993 your account would increase by an additional $6.36 to a new total of $112.36 because 6% interest was not only being paid on the original $100, but an additional 6% was being paid on the previous year's $6 interest which was added to the account. Therefore, the next year the account would earn 6% on $112.36, and so on. The amount a deposit grows, or is compounded, is a result of three factors: the nominal rate of interest, the frequency of compounding, and the length of time the deposit remains on deposit.

Nominal Interest Rate–The first factor to consider when one saves is the nominal rate of interest. The **nominal interest rate** is the rate of interest which a financial institution *says* it will pay for your deposit. The nominal interest rate an institution is willing to pay depends on the size of the deposit and the length of time one is willing to commit his funds for deposit. As one is willing to deposit greater amounts of money, institutions become more willing to pay a higher nominal rate of interest. The reason for this is simple: as borrowers seek larger loans, the pool of funds becomes smaller so that they become willing to pay a higher rate of interest. In order to attract big deposits, financial institutions in turn offer savers a greater nominal interest rate.

Financial institutions are also willing to pay a higher nominal interest rate on savings as depositors commit their funds for greater periods of time. Again, borrowers are willing to pay a higher rate of interest for loans with a longer term. Statistically speaking, a borrower who signs a note to repay a loan in 30 days has a lower chance of defaulting than someone who signs a note for 30 years. Because the risk of default is greater on longer term loans, financial institutions are reluctant to make them at the same interest rate which is charged on short-term loans. Borrowers who wish to secure long-term loans, therefore, are willing to pay a higher rate of interest. In order to attract long-term deposits to cover the higher interest paying long-term loans, lenders offer savers a higher nominal rate of interest for committing their funds for longer periods of time.

Effective Interest Rate–As a Christmas gift from their parents, two brothers each received $1,000 with instructions that it was to be saved for college. They devised a little savings contest, and on January 1 each set out to earn the greatest one-year return possible. The first brother had never taken an economics class and, therefore, did not realize that he ought to be concerned with the nominal interest rate offered by savings institutions. When he saw the big blue sign in the window of the First National Bank promising 5.75% interest, he immediately went in and made his deposit. His brother secretly laughed at his sibling's ignorance as he deposited his own $1,000 in an account at the Second National Bank advertising a 5.80% nominal interest rate. At the end of the year when the two brothers withdrew their funds, the second brother was smug as he pocketed his $1,058 in principle and interest. His self-satisfaction was turned to

Haiti

GNP: $1.8 billion*
Per Capita GNP: $296
Population: 6,322,000 (1989)
Monetary Unit: gorde

The poorest nation in the Western Hemisphere, Haiti suffers from seemingly inescapable economic ills. Added to the fact that the nation lacks well-developed industries, most of its people attempt to make their living by farming small plots (usually about two acres) of poor, mountainous land. Workers in Haitian towns make about $3 per day; farm workers make less, and many of the people remain unemployed.

In the past, Haiti's major sources of income have been foreign aid and investment as well as tourism. Unfortunately for this poor country, even these means of support have been disrupted by recent political and social developments. The nation's government escaped the thirty-year dictatorial control of the Duvalier family in 1986 only to be passed back and forth between ineffective civilian leaders and military dictatorships. The political unrest has discouraged foreign aid and investment and, along with a widespread AIDS epidemic, has caused the tourist industry to decline dramatically.

Haitian farmers sell crops of coffee, cacao, sisal, and sugar cane. The only major industries are a few processing mills for these products. Many of this small Caribbean nation's people make and sell handicrafts, such as woven baskets and carved wooden objects, in the local markets. But the uncertainties of Haiti's political climate have encouraged a continuing decline in the nation's total per capita productivity. Unless Haiti gains some political stability, prospects for economic improvement are grim.

*figures for 1986 from the 1990 *World Almanac*

shock and confusion as his less astute brother withdrew $1,059.18! How could this be possible? With a curt little smile the first brother simply said "you chose the highest nominal interest rate; I chose the highest effective interest rate."

The **effective interest rate** is the true rate of interest an account earns: a combination of the nominal rate of interest and the frequency of compounding. We saw earlier that $100 at 6% interest will earn $6 over a one-year period. The unspoken assumption of that example was that the interest was compounded annually; that is, interest was calculated once, at the end of the year. Such interest is referred to as **simple interest.** What would happen if interest were calculated semiannually (twice each year)? Instead of calculating 6% interest at the end of the year, 3% would be added to the account in the middle of the year and another 3% would be added to the account at the end. If in the middle of the year one-half of the interest is added to the account, the account balance would become $103 by the end of June. At the end of the year when the second half of the interest is compounded, 3% interest would be calculated on $103 bringing the end of the year balance to $106.09. Interest may be compounded as many times per year as one wishes. Interest may be compounded annually, semiannually, quarterly, monthly, weekly, daily, hourly, or each minute. In the case of the two brothers, the First National Bank compounded their interest every day; that is, 1/365 of 5.75% was calculated on and added to each previous day's balance. As Figure 17-4 illustrates, if a $100 deposit is being paid a 6% nominal rate of interest, the end of the year balance of the account rises as the frequency of compounding increases.

The effective interest rate on a deposit is the actual one-year percentage gain the deposit earned. Note the balance of the final month in Figure 17-4. The effective interest rate of 6% compounded annually is 6%; if it is compounded semiannually it is 6.09%, quarterly–6.14%, and monthly–6.17%. Thus the effective interest rate of a deposit increases as the frequency of compounding increases.

Figure 17-4 Simple and Compound Interest

MONTH	BALANCE AT END OF EACH COMPOUNDING PERIOD			
	ANNUALLY	SEMIANNUALLY	QUARTERLY	MONTHLY
1	—	—	—	$100.50
2	—	—	—	101.00
3	—	—	$101.50	101.51
4	—	—	—	102.03
5	—	—	—	102.53
6	—	$103.00	103.02	103.04
7	—	—	—	103.55
8	—	—	—	104.07
9	—	—	104.57	104.59
10	—	—	—	105.11
11	—	—	—	105.64
12	$106.00	106.09	106.14	106.17

How to Calculate the Effective Rate of Interest

The effective rate of interest on a deposit is a combination of the nominal interest rate and the frequency of compounding. The formula for calculating the effective interest rate is

$$Y = 100 \times \{[1 + (i / n)]^n - 1\}$$

Y = The effective rate of interest
i = the nominal rate of interest
n = the number of times interest is compounded per year

Here is a simple example: what would be the effective interest rate on a 6% deposit compounded semiannually?

$$Y = 100 \times \{[1 + (.06/2)]^2 - 1\}$$
$$= 100 \times [(1 + .03)^2 - 1]$$
$$= 100 \times (1.0609 - 1)$$
$$= 100 \times .0609$$
$$= 6.09\%$$

The calculations become difficult as the number of times the account is compounded each year increase. For example, if the 6% deposit was compounded each minute, the formula would be

$$Y = 100 \times \{[1 + (.06 / 525,600)]^{525,600} - 1\}$$

In order to work this kind of formula one would need a calculator which calculates powers. By the way, the effective interest rate in this case is 6.183919326%!

Had the Manhattan Island Indians taken the $24 which they received in 1626 and invested it at 6%, they would have $39 billion today. This figure was derived by using simple interest (annual compounding). If their account was compounded monthly, that figure would now be $69 billion! Recalling that the first principle of money management is never to let money sit idle, the second is always to have money compounding as frequently as possible.

Two important footnotes to compounding are in order. First, all savers need to realize that the compounding of interest and the posting of interest to one's account are not necessarily accomplished at the same time. That is, for the bank's bookkeeping purposes, interest may be compounded monthly, but it might not be posted to a saver's account until later. For example, assume that interest on the deposit in Figure 17-5 is compounded monthly but *posted semiannually*. If a depositor wished to withdraw his money, in the month of November he would receive only $103.04 since that would be the amount in his account at the last semiannual posting. Theoretically, interest could be compounded each minute, but if interest was posted annually, the saver would receive no interest were he to withdraw his funds the day before it was posted. Therefore, in addition to looking for high effective rates and frequent compounding, savers should also find out *when* interest is posted.

The second footnote has to do with the length of time one may keep idle money on deposit. To prevent financial institutions from having to pay interest on money which has been deposited and forgotten, each state has passed laws of escheat. **Escheat laws** dictate that if accounts are left dormant for lengthy periods of time (usually around five years), then the financial institution must turn the funds over to the state. An account holder usually may keep his money from going into escheat by conducting some activity with the account every few years, activities such as making a deposit or a withdrawal. Before opening an account, savers are advised to consult with the savings institution about their particular state's escheat laws.

Duration of the Deposit–Whereas the effective interest rate is a result of the combination of the nominal interest rate and the frequency of compounding, the ultimate dollar amount earned is a result of the effective interest rate and the length of time one keeps his money on deposit. It is important for savers to avoid the constant temptation to withdraw from their savings accounts to pay for current consumption. Setting a specific dollar goal for the account is one way to ensure that money will remain untouched in that account. For example, a couple may have as their goal the purchase of a house. If the house will cost $90,000 and a lender requires a 20% down payment, the couple should not withdraw any funds until the account reaches $18,000.

Other savers may not have a specific dollar goal in mind, rather their goal might be to keep their money on deposit until it doubles. A rule of thumb used by financial analysts to determine approximately how long money must be on deposit in order to double is called the rule of 72. The **Rule of 72** states that the product of the approximate number of years required for doubling a deposit amount with accruing interest multiplied by the interest rate should equal 72. For example, approximately how long should it take to double a $1,000 deposit earning 6% interest? The formula should look like this:

$$Number\ of\ Years \times Interest\ Rate = 72$$
$$N \times 6 = 72$$
$$N = 72/6$$
$$N = 12\ years$$

The rule of 72 may also be used to calculate the approximate rate of interest a saver must receive in order to have his money double over a specific number of years. For example, if a saver wishes to double his money over a three-year period, he would need to receive an approximate rate of interest of 24% (72/3 years).

Savings Instruments

Now that you have seen how to accumulate money to save and how to evaluate the interest which a savings instrument pays, take a look at some specific ways in which to save. Generally

Is Your Money Safe?

When more than 8,000 banks failed during the Great Depression, Americans grew wary about depositing their savings in financial institutions. The failures resulted in heavy losses for some depositors and created in others a fear that they might lose all of their life savings in a future bank failure. To restore the reputation of the nation's banks, Congress created the Federal Deposit Insurance Corporation (FDIC) in 1933. This federal agency began insuring the bank deposits of the nation in return for a flat fee collected from all participating banks. Originally each depositor was insured for $5,000, but through the years that amount was increased to $100,000. Depositors can increase that amount by dividing larger sums into a mixture of individual, joint, and trust accounts. In addition to the FDIC, similar insurance programs were developed for savings and loan institutions and credit unions: the Federal Savings and Loan Insurance Corporation (FSLIC) and the National Credit Union Administration (NCUA).

The trust inspired by insured deposits stabilized the banking industry for several decades, but underlying weaknesses began to surface in the 1980s. Large numbers of savings and loans began to turn up insolvent, and many banks were also in serious trouble. The FSLIC's resources were soon depleted with the many failures, and the FDIC was in danger of a similar plight. This crisis prompted Congress to provide over $100 billion to bail out, at taxpayers' expense, the failed S&Ls. It also dissolved the FSLIC and placed the remaining insured S&Ls under the FDIC's protection. However, the potential for future problems remained high because the basic insurance system was left intact.

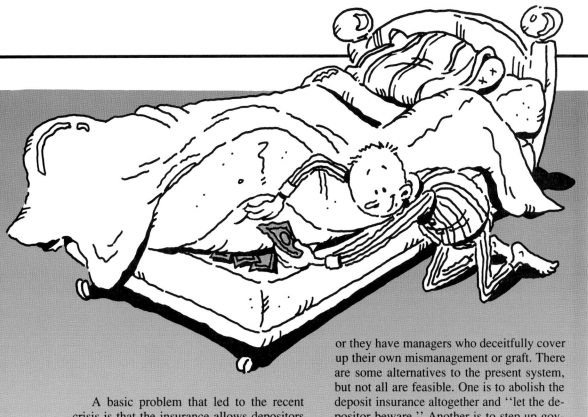

A basic problem that led to the recent crisis is that the insurance allows depositors to be unconcerned with the integrity of their financial institution, and it allows the management of the banks and S&Ls to be irresponsible with their institution's funds without personal risk. Whatever happens, the depositor is guaranteed not to lose his money. The failure of S&Ls usually resulted from their policies of making many risky high-interest loans. When those loans went into default in the 1980s, the S&Ls lost the assets that were tied up in them. With their assets depleted, the thrifts were soon insolvent, and taxpayers were left to make good on the government's promises.

The FDIC tries to examine banks and keep them out of serious financial troubles, but government regulation is difficult. Many institutions have been able to portray themselves as sound and responsible; yet they have too many assets tied up in risky ventures

or they have managers who deceitfully cover up their own mismanagement or graft. There are some alternatives to the present system, but not all are feasible. One is to abolish the deposit insurance altogether and ''let the depositor beware.'' Another is to step up governmental regulation of financial institutions, but that would require more government bureaucracy and hamper the operation of good banks and S&Ls. A third is to allow private deposit insurance companies to replace the FDIC. Private companies would naturally demand that the institutions they insure were worthy of their backing, and the amounts they charge for the insurance could increase with the risks presented by each bank or thrift. The financial institutions would have an incentive to manage their assets wisely in order to maintain their own reputations and lower rates with the insurance agencies. If they did not act responsibly, they would lose their insurance and with it their depositors. None of these options is without drawbacks, but if no action is taken, more S&L and bank failures will undoubtedly result in a mounting need for further bailouts.

speaking, there exist three outlets for savings: floating-rate accounts, time deposits, and government securities.

Floating-Rate Accounts–As its name implies, a **floating-rate account** is a short-term savings instrument for which the interest rate may fluctuate as economic conditions change. The most popular of the floating-rate accounts are NOW, Super NOW, and credit union share draft accounts which were discussed earlier in this chapter. These federally insured accounts provide a floating rate of interest competitive with regular savings accounts, but which also offer the saver the opportunity to write an unlimited number of checks. Another popular floating-rate account is the money market account. **Money market deposit accounts (MMDAs)** are insured accounts offered by commercial banks and thrift institutions which pay a rate of interest based on the market's demand for short-term loans. Depositors are usually allowed to make as many deposits as they wish but are limited in the number of withdrawals which may be made. Most institutions require a minimum initial dollar investment of $500 to $1,000 to open a money market account. Stock brokerage firms offer similar accounts called **money market mutual fund accounts (MMMFs).** These accounts pay the same, if not a slightly higher, rate of interest than financial institutions; however, brokerage firms' accounts are not insured by the federal government.

Time Deposits–Unlike the floating-accounts which have fluctuating interest rates, **time deposits** are savings accounts which earn fixed rates of interest as they remain on deposit. Time deposits are so named because either they may require a specific amount of time between the request for a withdrawal and the actual withdrawal of the funds, or they may carry a specific maturity date. Those time deposits which require notification of withdrawal include passbook accounts, club accounts, and restricted passbook accounts. On the other hand, those time deposits with fixed maturity dates are called certificates of deposit.

Passbook accounts are time deposits which are offered by commercial banks and thrift institutions

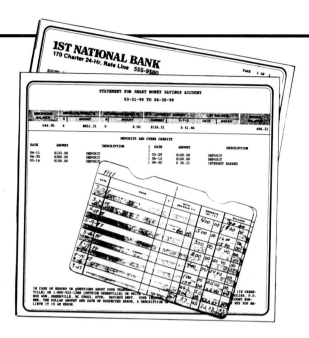

to savers with relatively small amounts of money (usually less than $2,500) or to those who need to have ready access to their money. Passbook accounts were given their name because many years ago, when a customer opened a small savings account, he was given an actual passbook–a booklet within which a teller would record all deposits, withdrawals, and interest payments. Today, however, most banks no longer rely on passbooks since the books tend to be inconvenient and can easily be stolen or misplaced. Instead, most institutions allow deposits and withdrawals to be made without a passbook. Instead of using the passbook to itemize deposits, withdrawals, and interest payments, institutions simply mail their customers monthly or quarterly statements detailing their transactions. People do not usually identify passbook accounts with time deposits because they are able to access their money immediately. What they are not aware of is that most financial institutions reserve the right to require prior notice (usually 10 days) before funds may be withdrawn. Because passbook accounts tend to be small with virtually immediate availability of funds, they pay a relatively low rate of interest. Most passbook accounts currently pay approximately $5\frac{1}{2}\%$ interest.

One of the biggest drains of cash on the average family is the expense of holidays and vacations. Instead of preparing for these events by saving, many people incur tremendous debts which last well into the next year. To prevent consumers from going on a debt-incurring binge for holiday and vacation spending, many financial institutions offer Christmas, Hanukkah, and vacation club accounts to provide a means for orderly saving. Club account deposits are typically quite small–$5 to $10 per week, and the rate of interest is usually the same or less than that offered on passbook accounts.

Offering $\frac{1}{4}$ to $\frac{1}{2}$% greater interest is the restricted passbook account. Virtually identical to the passbook account, the restricted passbook account is one for which withdrawals are limited. For example some permit withdrawals only during the first ten days of each calendar quarter, while others require 90 days notice before a penalty-free withdrawal may be made.

Certificates of deposit (CDs) are time deposits which carry with them a specific maturity date and yield a higher rate of interest than those paid on passbook or club accounts. Financial institutions usually offer an assortment of CDs with maturity dates as early as seven days and as long as five years. CDs with longer maturity dates usually pay higher rates of interest. Depositors who choose the longer maturity CDs must be willing to leave their money on deposit, for the penalties for early withdrawal can be substantial. For example, the penalty for early redemption of a CD with a maturity greater than one year is six month's worth of interest. If a depositor purchases a two-year certificate of deposit today and tomorrow changes his mind and redeems the CD, he will receive his principal, less the equivalent of six months worth of interest. Savers should purchase CDs only if they are willing to hold them to maturity, but they can plan ahead for emergencies. For example, you have $10,000 and you wish to purchase a two-year certificate of deposit. Instead of purchasing one large CD, you might wish to purchase ten $1,000 CDs so that in the event you would need some of your money, all of your principal would not be penalized.

Most certificates of deposit are sold for a minimum of $500, but depositors usually may purchase a CD in any odd amount as long as it is greater than the minimum required. When shopping for a certificate of deposit, be sure to determine if the institution compounds its interest or if it pays simple interest. If a one-year, $10,000 CD is paying 8% interest, the depositor will receive $800 in interest if simple interest is paid. If, on the other hand, interest is compounded quarterly, the depositor will earn $24.32 more.

Government Securities–In its need to finance the national debt, the federal government provides some of the safest and most profitable savings instruments available today. The most popular types of short-term government securities are U.S. Savings Bonds and U.S. Treasury Securities.

U.S. Savings Bonds are considered by financial advisors to be risk-free investments because they are backed by the full faith and credit of the United States Government. U.S. Savings Bonds come in two versions–Series EE and Series HH.

Series EE Bonds are those of which most people think when they hear the term U.S. Savings Bonds. EEs may be purchased in denominations which range from $50 to $10,000 and are purchased at a discount, that is, at one-half of their face value. As interest accrues, the value of the bond approaches the amount stated on the front of the bond. As a result of the interest being the difference between the value of the bond and the price for which it was purchased, no periodic interest is paid directly to the bondholder. EEs may be purchased directly from the Treasury Department or through payroll deduction plans set up by employers. They may be redeemed beginning six months after they are purchased. Bonds held less than five years pay a guaranteed rate of 6% interest compounded semiannually. If one holds an EE bond longer than five years, the rate of interest paid is the greater of either 6% or 85% of the latest six-month average rate paid on five-year U.S. Treasury Securities. EEs may be held up to forty years, after which time interest will stop accruing.

Not only is the interest rate on Series EE Bonds

attractive, but other benefits should be considered as well. First, interest on EEs is not considered to be taxable income until the bonds are redeemed. If one purchases, for example, a five-year CD, he might not receive his interest until the end of the five year period; however, he must pay income tax on the interest as it accrues each year. Second, interest on EEs is not subject to state and local income taxes. Third, for those with incomes less than $60,000, the federal government will not tax the interest as income at all if the interest will be used to pay for educational expenses of the bond-holder or his dependents.

Series HH Bonds are similar to Series EE Bonds, but they differ in three ways. First, Series HH Bonds are purchased for full face value. Second, Series HH Bonds may not be bought with cash; they may only be purchased by "rolling over" (redeeming) Series EE Bonds. Third, interest on HHs are paid via treasury checks to bondholders. Just like EE bonds, the interest on HH bonds is exempt from state and local taxes. Federal income tax on HH interest is not due until the bond matures.

The final type of government savings instruments discussed here are U.S. Treasury Securities.

Whereas a relatively small portion of the nearly $4 trillion national debt is financed by U.S. Savings Bonds, the majority is financed through the sales of Treasury Bills (T-Bills), Treasury Notes (T-Notes), and Treasury Bonds (T-Bonds). Since the majority of the budget deficit is financed with Treasury Bills, we will examine only T-Bills here. **Treasury Bills** may be purchased with maturities as short as 90 days or as long as one year. Treasury Bills may be purchased in one of two ways. First, they may be purchased directly from the U.S. Treasury through any main office or branch of the Federal Reserve Bank. Second, for a fee one may purchase a Treasury Bill through a commercial bank or stockbrokerage firm. Interest rates on T-Bills are very competitive with the best short-term savings instruments offered on the market.

Section Review
1. How may a person or a family generate enough money to save?
2. What is compound interest?
3. What is the difference between a floating rate account and a time deposit?
4. List a few of the characteristics of Series EE U.S. Savings Bonds.

Chapter Review

Terms

cash management
transaction account
checking account
negotiable order of withdrawal (NOW) account
super NOW account
share draft account (SDA)
joint account
right of survivorship
tenants in common
postdated
staledated
payee
endorse
blank endorsement
special endorsement
restrictive endorsement
conditional endorsement
stop payment order
reconciling
guaranteed check
certified check
cashier's check
money order
traveler's checks
compound interest
nominal interest rate
effective interest rate
simple interest
escheat laws
Rule of 72
floating-rate account
money market deposit accounts (MMDAs)
money market mutual fund accounts (MMMFs)
time deposits
passbook accounts
certificates of deposit (CDs)
U.S. Savings Bonds
Series EE Bonds
Series HH Bonds
Treasury Bills

Content Questions

1. What is cash management?
2. Which of the three motives for holding money prompts people to hold money for ''rainy days''?
3. What is an SDA?
4. On a check, two places are provided to fill in the amount of the check. Why? What will the bank do if the two written amounts disagree?
5. What is a conditional endorsement?
6. What is a W-4?
7. What is the formula for calculating the effective rate of interest being paid on a deposit?
8. Why is it important to determine when interest is posted to a savings account?
9. What is the Rule of 72?
10. What are two of the types of floating-rate accounts?

Application Questions

1. How might interest rates affect the amounts of money people would wish to hold for transactions, emergency, and store of value purpose?
2. Should minors (those under 18) be allowed to open individual checking accounts? What are the advantages and disadvantages both for the minor and for the bank?
3. Why use a check when one can pay cash?
4. Why would a merchant want a guaranteed check?
5. What is the effective rate of interest on an 8% savings account which is compounded quarterly?

CHAPTER 18 _____

Financial Planning

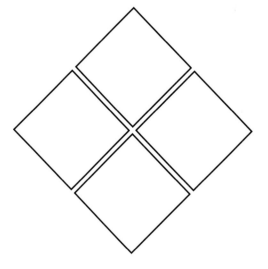

But if any provide not for his own, and specially for those of his own house, he hath denied the faith, and is worse than an infidel.
I Timothy 5:8

I. Financial Planning: Considerations

The Christian and Financial Planning

***The Necessity of Financial Planning for the Christian*–Financial planning** is the process of developing and implementing plans in order to achieve financial objectives. Typically, one's financial objectives have both short-term and long-term perspectives. The short-term provisions generally include the preparation of a will, the purchase of life and health insurance, and the establishment of a short-term emergency savings account. A family's financial stability could be devastated without these preparations for emergencies. The long-term perspective includes building up retirement accounts and making secure long-term investments. Whereas financial planning is normally regarded as a common-sense activity for unbelievers, financial planning for Christians has been fraught with controversy. Many Christians believe that a man is evidencing a lack of faith in God's provision when he plans for the present and future financial security of his family. On the other hand, to ignore financial planning may be to ignore God's admonition to prepare for the future.

George Mueller, the great pioneer of faith and prayer, believed that financial planning was indicative of a lack of faith. In *George Mueller of Bristol* Mueller is quoted as saying, "Let no one profess to trust God and yet lay up for future wants, otherwise the Lord will send him to the hoard he has amassed, before he can answer the prayer for more." Because of his strong personal faith in God's provision, he consistently refused to accept contributions for his own personal financial needs. In the words of biographer A. T. Pierson, Mueller

George Mueller

had settled the matter beyond raising the question again, that he would live from day to day upon the Lord's bounty, and would make but *one investment,* namely, using whatever means God gave, to supply the necessities of the poor, depending on God richly to repay him in the hour of his own need, according to the promise: 'He that hath pity upon the poor lendeth to the Lord, and that which he hath given will He pay him again' (Proverbs 19:17).

The great faith of George Mueller was based on Biblical convictions which he lived by and which the Lord honored. Scripture consistently implies that faith such as George Mueller's, while admirable, is neither required nor recommended of all Christians. On the contrary, one of the main themes of the Bible is preparation: preparation for one's eternal destiny, preparation of one's heart for the leading of God, and judicious preparation for one's present and future financial needs.

Scripture admonishes the child of God to prepare both for short-term and long-term financial needs. For example, in the familiar passage found in Luke 14:28-31, Jesus indicated that it is not wise to leave short-term planning undone. In His example of the man building a tower, our Lord was very clear in his condemnation of poor preparation.

Scripture points out that financial planning is not to be isolated to the short run. Proverbs 6:6-8 indicates a need for long-range financial planning as well:

> Go to the ant, thou sluggard; consider her ways, and be wise: Which having no guide, overseer, or ruler, provideth her meat in the summer, and gathereth her food in the harvest.

The Beneficiaries of the Christian's Financial Planning—As far as the unsaved world is concerned, the main goal of financial planning is to ensure that one is financially secure, that he will encounter no hardships should he become sick or injured and that he will enjoy a life filled with pleasure in his old age. Obviously, as has been indicated in previous chapters, provision for one's present and future selfish desires should not be the goal of the Spirit-filled child of God. If, therefore, financial planning should not primarily benefit the planner, who should be the beneficiary of the Christian's financial plans?

The first beneficiary of a Christian's financial plans should be his Lord, Jesus Christ. One of the most important reasons that financial planning is required of Christians is that the unbelieving world is carefully watching for occasion to ridicule. It behooves believers, therefore, to ensure that the name and reputation of the Lord are not sullied in the world through accusations of financial carelessness or mismanagement.

The second beneficiary of the Christian's financial plans should be his own family. This chapter's opening verse quoted, ''But if any provide not for his own, and specially for those of his own house, he hath denied the faith, and is worse than an infidel'' (I Tim. 5:8). In other words, if a Christian does not plan for and meet the needs of his own family, he has denied the tenets of his faith in the eyes of the world. To meet his family's financial needs, a believer should create a financial plan which meets the needs of his children, his spouse, and, as many frequently neglect to do, his parents in their old age.

Need Help Developing a Financial Plan?

If, like millions of other Americans, you find the intricacies of financial planning mind-boggling, you can turn in a number of directions to find help. The first is to enlist the services of a qualified financial counselor. Lawyers and public accountants often provide useful assistance, but many Americans turn instead to people who specialize in financial planning. These professionals may or may not have college degrees in financial counseling, but they probably will exhibit some credentials such as those of a Certified Financial Planner (CFP), Chartered Financial Consultant (CFC), or Registered Financial Planner (RFP). Various schools and associations establish the qualifications for these and other labels, but beware of placing your finances in the hands of any planner without checking his reputation carefully. Scams involving the fraudulent schemes of dishonest financial counselors have victimized all too many unwary Americans.

A second source of information for financial planning is a library of helpful books and magazines. By reading widely in this area and purchasing a good collection of these materials for continued reference, you can find most of the information you need to plan for yourself, or at least confer with your financial advisor more intelligently. Remember that tax laws, financial markets, and other pertinent conditions are constantly changing, and so you will need to keep yourself updated with current information.

One more tool that has become common as an aid in financial planning is the personal computer. Software is available for portfolio management, investment analysis, and other tasks associated with financial planning. Caution is necessary when selecting financial software, however, because many programs on the market are of limited use. Carefully investigate the capabilities of the software packages you choose before you purchase them, and also consider the use of an electronic spreadsheet package that you can modify to meet your own financial planning needs. Although a computer can be a useful tool for helping you create and maintain your own financial plan, remember that it will take some time to enter needed information. Also, you will need to read to keep abreast of current financial information in order to use the software to your best advantage.

Elements of a Financial Plan

To the unsaved world a financial plan is a roadmap which one develops to assist him in his pursuit of a better life. When asked why they believe a financial plan is necessary, most people respond with, ''I want to make sure that if I'm disabled I'll have enough money on which to live,'' ''I want to retire when I'm fifty years old and spend the rest of my days enjoying the 'good life','' or ''I want to be rich.'' Instead of being a roadmap to security and riches, a Christian's financial plan should be a blueprint which assists him in building his life and the lives of his family into monuments which glorify Jesus Christ.

To be of maximum effectiveness, the Christian's financial plan should be in writing and should address two specific financial issues. The first aspect that the plan should cover is the family's short-run financial needs. This short-term perspective should address a few specific questions. First, if the family's income earners should die, how would those remaining be provided for? If the income earners of the family should become unable to work because of illness or injury, how would the financial needs of the disabled member and his family be met? The second area deals with a family's long-run needs and answers the question of how the family will be provided for when the income earners retire.

Section Review

1. What are the short-term and long-term objectives of financial planning?
2. Why is financial planning not un-Scriptural?
3. Who are the beneficiaries of the Christian's financial plan?

II. Short-Term Financial Planning: Elements

The first area to be covered in a Christian's financial plan is the preparation for events which could occur at any time, especially death and disability. While there are not many things of which we can be absolutely sure, it is sure that unless the Lord returns first to take us to be with Him, we will all die. Since financial planning deals with preparing for the future, it is of utmost importance to prepare for death by establishing a last will and testament and by providing life insurance to meet the financial needs of dependents who will be left behind. Another event for which we must all prepare is the possibility of becoming temporarily or permanently disabled through an accident or illness. One may prepare for such an occurrence through the purchase of health care insurance and disability insurance and the establishment of an emergency cash reserve.

Estate Planning

The Necessity of a Will–Most people have the impression that only the wealthy need a will. On the contrary, each adult Christian needs to establish a **last will and testament,** for it represents one's final legal opportunity to ensure that what he leaves behind will be disposed of according to his wishes and in a manner which would be glorifying to God. What a person leaves behind is known as his **estate** and includes both assets and liabilities. For example, on the asset side, a person's estate may consist of all of his cash (including his portion of joint accounts which have right of survivorship), jewelry, stocks, bonds, other investments, life insurance, his portion of any jointly held real estate, and any other possessions which would be considered valuable. On the other hand, a person's estate also includes his liabilities, that is, what he owes. When a person dies his debts must be paid, and a will provides for an orderly payment of all obligations.

Many Christians refuse to write a will because of its close association with death. However, by completing a will a Christian is fulfilling an essential part of his role as a Christian steward. Not only

is a steward responsible to wisely handle his wealth in life, but at the end of his life he must pass along his wealth in a way that is honoring to God. Any person who is over 18 years of age and of sound mind may write a will. Currently over 75% of the adult United States population has never written a will. If a person dies without a will, the state in which the person lived will use a predetermined formula to divide his property among his relatives. State laws take no consideration of what the deceased "would have wanted." There is no provision in state laws for the charitable contribution of money or property to ministries which the deceased held dear. Likewise, the courts care nothing about how the relatives will spend the money once it is distributed. In many cases the formula for dividing an estate is so strict that family heirlooms must be sold at a public auction so that each recipient will receive the exact share to which he is entitled.

Good stewardship dictates that every adult Christian have a will, for by executing a will, the child of God can specify where the money and goods God has provided him may go and for what purposes they may be used (Prov. 13:22). In his will a Christian may specify that a portion of his estate go to a Christian ministry such as a local church or Christian school. In addition to specifying where one's assets are to go, a will also allows a Christian to avoid the high fees which come of the state's appointing a stranger to administer his estate.

Perhaps the most compelling reason for a Christian to execute a will is to ensure that his minor children will be cared for in a way which would be pleasing to Christ. If a Christian couple were to die without a will leaving several young children, the court would appoint **guardians** for the children. The court would first look for potential guardians from the ranks of immediate relatives. If suitable guardians could not be located, the court might refer the children to foster homes pending adoption. In cases of families of three or more children, courts find it extremely difficult to locate guardians willing to care for all of the children together, necessitating a breakup of the family. By executing a will, a Christian husband and wife can locate born-again relatives or friends who would be willing to assume the responsibility of caring for their children in the event that both parents should die at the same time. By locating potential Christian guardians for one's children, parents would be fulfilling their spiritual responsibility of rearing their children ''in the nurture and admonition of the Lord'' (Eph. 6:4).

Types of Wills–A will may be completed in one of three ways. First is the do-it-yourself will. This type of will is strongly discouraged, for it may be successfully challenged in the courts by disgruntled beneficiaries and ruled invalid as a result of nonconformity to technicalities in the law. The second type of will is known as a **statutory will.** Statutory wills are simple forms, often written in a multiple-choice format. By virtue of the fact that they were authored by the state, those executing wills can be confident that by completing a statutory will, they have a valid will. Statutory wills were designed for people with small uncomplicated estates. Because the forms are usually in a multiple-choice format, they tend to be inflexible. Generally speaking, statutory wills were designed for married couples who want to leave everything to the surviving spouse and make routine provisions for their young children. The third type of will is one which is completed by a lawyer. Those who are wise enough to avoid a do-it-yourself will and do not live in a state where a statutory will is available should have a lawyer draw up a legal will.

Major Provisions of Wills–Because lawyers usually charge $50 to $100 per hour, those who wish to complete a will are advised to acquaint themselves with the major provisions of a will and to approach a lawyer after they have generally decided how they want these provisions to read.

1. *Provide a personal testimony.* Christians should realize that the reading of their last will and testament will probably be their last opportunity to share the gospel of Jesus Christ with unsaved relatives and loved ones. Therefore, it is important for those who are born again to present their testimony in a clear but concise way. Many a husband, wife, child, or friend has been saved as a result of hearing the gospel presented in a decedent's will.

2. *Appoint an executor.* The **executor** of the estate is the one who has been entrusted the responsibility of seeing that the provisions of the will are carried out. Should a person die without a will, the court will appoint an **administrator** to perform the same functions. When naming an executor, be sure that he is both willing and able to carry out the job. Ask only individuals who you know are able to handle the complicated tasks of dealing with quarreling heirs, a slow court system, and demanding creditors. Also, ask someone to serve as an alternate executor in case your first choice is unable or unwilling to do the job.

3. *Appoint a guardian for all minor children.* As in the case of the executor, those whom you ask to serve as guardians for your children should be both willing and able to serve as substitute parents. Pray specifically and choose carefully. The responsibility may fall

A major purpose of writing a will is to appoint a guardian for minor children.

Trusts

A common method of reserving a portion (usually a large amount of cash, securities, or property) of one's estate for relatives or charities is to establish trusts. A trust is simply an arrangement in which one party is given control of the property involved and charged with the responsibility of managing it for the benefit of the intended beneficiary. The one charged with the responsibility of managing a trust is called the trustee. The benefactor (or ''grantor'') may choose a responsible and capable relative, friend, or associate to serve as trustee for the beneficiary, or banks often serve in this position. A trustee accepts a legal obligation to manage the trust and may be held liable for financial losses due to mismanagement.

Trusts may be established by the dictates of one's will after death (in which case they are called testamentary trusts) or the grantor may establish trusts and see that they become operational before his death (inter vivos or living trusts). The most common purpose of trusts is to make provision for one's dependent children, who as minors cannot receive a bequest directly from the estate. The grantor may then specify the time and other conditions for the paying of trust funds to the beneficiary. Trusts are also established for beneficiaries whom the grantor believes to be incapable of handling the money or property wisely for themselves. In addition, trusts may be established to support charitable organizations. Usually in this situation, earnings from trust funds are distributed periodically to the organization, thereby insuring that the gifts of the grantor will be continued long after his death.

on the guardians, and if so, they will be the ones instilling their values and character traits in your children. In addition to naming guardians for your children, you should list one or two alternates. At the time of your death, the couple you previously selected may be unwilling to serve; they may have moved and cannot be contacted; or they may have died before you. Be sure to stay informed about the lives of your children's potential guardians. Situations and values change over time, and some of these changes may require rewriting your will.

4. *List specific gifts.* If you should wish to leave certain items of property to specific heirs, it is important to describe the gift, also known as

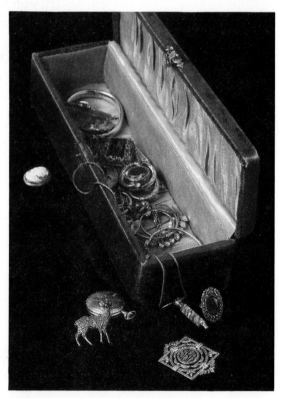

One purpose of a will is to insure that bequests—gifts of specific possessions such as jewelry, books, cars, or other special items of property—are given to the heirs which the deceased intended.

a **bequest** or **legacy,** in such a way that there is no confusion. You may also wish to provide for a substitute gift in the event the item has been lost, stolen, or destroyed. For example, "I leave my gold ring with the one carat ruby encircled with six diamonds to my grandson Bradley Allen Parker, son of Jeffrey and Sandra Parker. If for some reason the ring cannot be given, Bradley Allen shall receive the value of the ring in cash." Always include a provision to cover the eventuality that the beneficiary does not outlive you. For example "Should Bradley Allen Parker die before I do, or at the same time, the ring shall be considered part of my residuary estate."

5. *List other gifts.* Out of the money provided by the estate, you may wish to make some general gifts of cash. Since these gifts are paid out of the funds of the estate from which the decedent's bills must be paid, the writer of the will should be careful not to make the gifts too large, otherwise the court may be forced to reduce the gifts to ensure the payment of creditors. Again, be sure to make a provision to cover the eventuality that the beneficiary may not outlive you. For example, "and to my niece Kimberly Ann Parker, I leave the sum of ten thousand dollars ($10,000). Should Kimberly Ann Parker die before I do, or at the same time, the money shall be given to the Trinity Bible Church of Kennesaw, Georgia."

6. *Provide instructions on the payment of taxes and administrative expenses.* It is in this portion of one's will that the writer of the will instructs the executor in the payment of taxes and other expenses. If, for example, you do not wish for your 1964 vintage red Ford Mustang convertible to be sold to pay the estate's taxes, then it is in this section that such demands should be made known.

7. *Provide full authority to the executor.* The executor should be given full power and authority to carry out the provisions of the will including the authority to sell or lease assets, distribute specific and general gifts, and pay the estate's taxes.

Form and Detail–Note the following few final tips for writing wills:

1. Not all lawyers' fees are the same. Call several lawyers' offices for fee information before deciding on one to complete your will.

2. For married couples, it is wise to draw up *three* separate wills–one for the husband, one for the wife, and one for the couple should both die at the same time.

3. As far as form is concerned, when writing out the rough draft of your will for your lawyer, avoid the temptation to use big legal-sounding words; leave that to your attorney. Be sure that if your will is more than one page long, each page bears a page number and the sequence, for example "page 3 of 4." This makes it difficult for the unscrupulous to add pages after the fact. Each page should also be initialed or signed by the writer of the will. Be sure that all numbers are expressed both in numerals and in words, for example "I leave to my son Kenneth one dollar ($1.00)." You should sign just after the bottom line, making it impossible for extra lines or paragraphs to be added. Sign the will in the presence of at least three witnesses who are not beneficiaries of the will and who are themselves willing to sign as witnesses.

4. Under laws of **dower,** some wills may be legally overridden if your spouse is left a share of your estate which is less than the minimum required by the state. For example, if you leave your spouse only $1 and your estate is worth $1 million, your spouse is legally entitled to $400,000 anyway if the state requires that 40% of a decedent's estate go to his spouse. Children, however, in almost every state can be disinherited.

5. If you change your mind about any provision in the will, do not simply scratch through the appropriate portion and write a new entry; doing so may make the entire will invalid. Instead, one must file a **codicil,** or an amendment to the original will. Because codicils have virtually the same requirements as an original will, it would be best to draw up an

LAST WILL AND TESTAMENT OF ALAN JOSEPH DOE

Believing that faithful stewardship to my Lord and Saviour Jesus Christ is as necessary in death as well as in life, I, Alan Joseph Doe, of 211 Griffin Drive, Bedford Falls, Tennessee, state that this is my last will and testament, revoking all previous wills. On April 24, 1964, after reading Romans 3:23, "For all have sinned and come short of the glory of God," I realized that I was a sinner. Further realizing that "the wages of sin is death, but the gift of God is eternal life through Jesus Christ our Lord" (Romans 6:23), I accepted Jesus Christ as my personal Saviour in accordance to Romans 10:13: "For whosoever shall call upon the name of the Lord shall be saved." I urge all readers and hearers of this will to claim Jesus Christ as their Saviour that they may know the forgiveness of their sins and the gift of eternal life in heaven.

1. <u>EXECUTORS</u>: I appoint my wife, Jonna Doe, executor of this will. I also appoint my friend and business associate Blake Spencer to serve as a substitute in case Jonna is unable or unwilling to do so, or ceases to do so.

2. <u>GUARDIANS</u>: If Jonna dies before I do, or at the same time, I appoint my friends Ken and Janice Jones to serve as guardians of the persons and property of my children until they are eighteen (18) years of age. I also appoint my brother and his wife, Bradley and Rachel Doe, substitute guardians in the event Ken and Janice are unable or unwilling to act as guardians, or cease to do so.

3. <u>SPECIFIC GIFTS</u>: I leave all my tools to my son, Alan Joshua Doe. If the tools no longer exist at the time of my death, Alan shall receive three thousand dollars ($3,000) in cash. To my daughter Ashleigh Janine Doe I leave all my stock in the IBM corporation. If the stock no longer exists at the time of my death, Ashleigh shall receive three thousand dollars ($3,000) in cash. To my daughter Bethany Lynn Doe I leave all of my stock in the Mylan Pharmaceutical Company. If the stock no longer exists at the time of my death, Bethany shall receive three thousand dollars ($3,000) in cash. Should any recipient of any specific gifts die before I do, or at the same time, the specific gifts shall be counted part of my residuary estate.

4. <u>GENERAL GIFTS</u>: I leave to my church, Faith Baptist Church of Bedford Falls, Tennessee, the sum of fifteen thousand dollars ($15,000). Should this gift not be accepted, it shall become part of the residuary estate.

5. <u>RESIDUARY ESTATE</u>: I give all of the rest of my property to my wife, Jonna Doe. If she dies before I do or at the same time, I give all this property in equal parts to my children. If my wife and my children die before I do, or at the same time, I leave all this property to my brother, Bradley Doe.

6. <u>TAXES AND ADMINISTRATIVE EXPENSES</u>: All taxes and expenses related to my estate are to be paid out of the residuary estate.

7. <u>EXECUTOR'S OPTIONS</u>: In order to expeditiously carry out the distribution of my estate, I give my executor full power to sell, lease, mortgage, reinvest, or otherwise dispose of the assets in my estate.

Signed _____ Date Signed _____

WITNESSES: At Alan Doe's request, we met on the date inserted above to witness his signing of this will. With all of us present at the same time, he signed it and stated that it was his last will.

Signed _____ Address _____

Signed _____ Address _____

Signed _____ Address _____

entirely new will.

6. Because the decedent's safe deposit box may be sealed upon his death for several days or weeks, it is not wise to store a will in this location. Rather, a will should be kept on file with one's lawyer or with his executor.

7. Because situations such as financial holdings, number of children, names, and the like change from time to time, it is wise to periodically review one's will and rewrite it as necessary.

Life Insurance

Like a will, life insurance is a topic which most people do not like to discuss, for it, too, is connected with one's mortality, and the details are often complicated. Imagine Stanley, a 41-year-old man who works full-time at a job which pays approximately $50,000 per year. Stanley and his wife, Elaine, had elected that she be a full-time homemaker. Stanley and Elaine have two children, Andy and Sarah, aged 15 and 6 respectively. Stanley was killed as a result of injuries sustained in an automobile accident. After his death certain expenses immediately needed to be paid, including medical bills, funeral expenses, outstanding loans, etc. On her way from Stanley's funeral, Elaine shuddered to think of the financial burdens the family would encounter over the coming months and years. Before his death Stanley was bringing home nearly $3,000 per month after taxes. After his death that amount was reduced to zero. Elaine was full of questions. "How will I purchase groceries?" "How will I make mortgage payments?" "How will I clothe my family?" "What will be done when utility bills arrive and medical emergencies occur?" Without income of some sort, Elaine and her children will be impoverished in a short time.

One common misconception is that widows quickly remarry and life goes on as usual. Generally speaking, this will probably not occur. Because of the relative healthiness of their husbands, it is not the very young women who become widows. As a man grows older and his chances of dying increase, the chances of his widow's remarrying decline. Out of each 100 widows between the ages

of 30 and 39, only 40 remarry. Out of those women in Elaine's age group (over 40), 19 out of 100 remarry, leaving 81 widows to care for their families alone. Like the completion of a will, the provision of life insurance fulfills a necessary obligation of the Christian steward to care for his family in his death. As II Corinthians 12:14 says, "For the children ought not to lay up for the parents, but the parents for the children."

Estimating the Amount of Life Insurance Needed–"Who needs life insurance?" is one of the most frequently asked questions of financial planners. When a person insures his home, he is doing so in order to have the money to rebuild the home in the event it is destroyed; when a person purchases automobile collision insurance, he is doing so in order to be able to buy another car if his present one is destroyed in an accident. The main purpose of life insurance is neither to console a grieving widow nor to provide a "bonus" to be received when someone dies. The most important purpose of life insurance is to replace a family's lost income. Therefore, it is important for life insurance to be carried on all income earners in the family if the income is necessary to the family's well-being. If a person is unmarried and has no dependents, he may carry a small policy in order to defray burial costs and miscellaneous expenses.

Another frequently asked question is "how much should I buy?" Out of a fear of not having enough life insurance, too many families have become "insurance poor" by purchasing much more than they need, while others find out too late that the amount they had secured was insufficient. To determine how much life insurance is necessary, a person needs to calculate his needs for each of two areas–death-related expenses and family maintenance needs.

The first motive for purchasing life insurance is to pay for death-related expenses. Obviously, the first of these expenses is funeral and burial costs. Usually these costs average between $2,500 and $6,000. For our example let us assume that it cost $5,000 to cover Stanley's burial expenses. Estate taxes constitute the second of the death-related expenses. Currently an unlimited amount of money may be transferred to one's spouse after death, but if one's estate is over $600,000 and income is transferred to others besides one's spouse, then taxes will be due. As in Stanley's case, most people's

The death of a family's income earner can bring financial hardship if the basic provisions of financial planning have been neglected.

estates are not large enough to be subject to federal estate taxes. A third cost which occasionally arises is medical costs not covered by insurance which preceded the person's death. Stanley's medical bills came to a total of $7,000. Since his policy carried a $300 **deductible,** his estate must pay the first $300. After the deductible is paid, his insurance company will pay 80% of all bills. Because of these provisions, Stanley's estate must pay $300 plus 20% of $6,700 for a total of $1,640.

To avoid saddling one's survivors with unnecessary installment payments, the fourth death-related expense is the payment of all outstanding consumer loans. For Stanley's widow this amount totaled $4,300 including charge cards and automobile loans. Finally, probate court costs should be included. Usually these costs amount to 4% of the value of all assets distributed through the probate process. In Stanley's case his probate-distributed assets came to $350,000, making his estate liable for $14,053 in probate court costs. As a result of these expenses, the total of Stanley's death-related expenses totaled $24,993.

The second and most important purpose of life insurance is to provide financial maintenance for one's surviving dependents. The method of calculating this need is relatively easy. First one must calculate the expenses that the family will incur each month. When he was reviewing his insurance needs, Stanley determined that the family would need approximately $3,500 each month in order to pay all necessary expenses. These expenses included mortgage payments, payments for utilities such as electricity and water, purchases of food and clothing, all other household expenses, and contributions to a fund for his children to attend college.

The second step is to subtract all other incomes which are coming to the family. Stanley determined that if he were to die, his family would have two sources of income which would help meet the $3,500 need. First, he had interest income from investments which earn a steady $200 per month. Second, he discovered that monthly benefits are provided by the Social Security Administration. Since he was a contributor to the social security fund, his children would be eligible to receive cash benefits as surviving dependents. The amount of benefits paid to survivors varies with the income of the decedent and the number of his dependents. Because his income was $50,000 per year and he had two children, his wife Elaine will receive a monthly parental benefit of approximately $1,900 until her youngest child reaches age 16. When each child reaches age 16, Elaine's check will be reduced and the child will begin receiving a monthly check until he is 18. When the youngest child turns 16, checks to Elaine will stop entirely until she turns 60. She then will be eligible for a widow's pension.

In summary, when Stanley was calculating his life insurance needs, he assumed that his family would need $3,500 each month. Since $2,100 of this amount would be offset by social security benefits and investment income, Stanley would want somehow to provide the remaining $1,400 per month or $16,800 per year. Since Sarah, the youngest child, has twelve years before she reaches age eighteen, at which time she is theoretically capable of working and caring for herself, the family will need twelve year's worth of maintenance at $16,800 per year for a total of $201,600 of life insurance. Stanley, however, was not satisfied with the idea of simply multiplying $16,800 by twelve years. He believed that the amount of the annual maintenance fund would need to be adjusted for inflation. He determined that if the cost of living were to rise at a realistic annual rate of 5%, $16,800 will be required the first year, $17,640 the second year ($16,800 plus 5%), and so on. The total inflation-adjusted amount required to support the family over the next twelve years would be approximately $267,000.

Types of Life Insurance–Life insurance comes in two basic forms: term and whole life. A hybrid form has also recently entered the scene called universal life which has some of the characteristics of both.

Term insurance is life insurance which provides only death protection. Term insurance is purchased for a specified period of time. If the insured dies during the life of the policy, the proceeds are

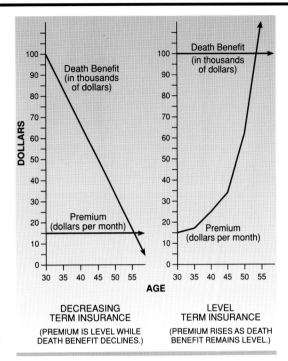

DECREASING
TERM INSURANCE
(PREMIUM IS LEVEL WHILE
DEATH BENEFIT DECLINES.)

LEVEL
TERM INSURANCE
(PREMIUM RISES AS DEATH
BENEFIT REMAINS LEVEL.)

paid to the **beneficiary,** the one named on the policy. Many insurance agents attempt to discourage potential customers from purchasing term insurance because it is less expensive than other types of insurance. As a result it provides lower commission income for the agent. Term insurance provides more death protection per dollar of payment than any other type of life insurance; however, it has no savings component. For those customers who are not disciplined enough to save money, the purchase of term life insurance may close the door on their last hope for establishing some sort of savings.

Term insurance is basically a straight contract which obligates the insurance company to provide a fixed death benefit to the insured person in exchange for a monthly payment called a **premium.** When the term of the coverage expires, the customer ceases to be insured. However, some insurance companies provide term insurance policyholders the option to renew their policies for fixed periods of time without having to have a new medical examination to redetermine their eligibility.

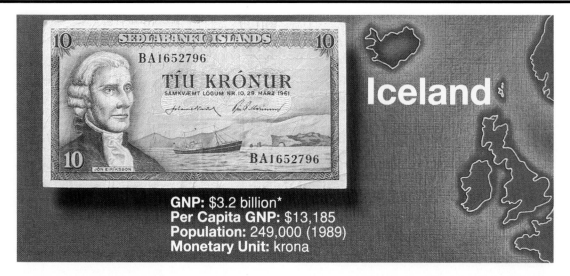

GNP: $3.2 billion*
Per Capita GNP: $13,185
Population: 249,000 (1989)
Monetary Unit: krona

Iceland is a nation whose economy is heavily dependent on fishing. About 20% of Iceland's people work either on fishing boats or in fish processing plants. Their product accounts for nearly three-fourths of Iceland's export income. Because of this dependence, the entire national economy is affected by the price of fish on the world market. In the early 1980s when the price of cod (its most profitable fish) tumbled, Iceland experienced severe inflation and the nation was thrown into heavy foreign debt. However, an improved world market for fish combined with a low interest rate on their debt in the later 1980s helped Iceland's economy to recover and prosper.

The small island-country just outside the Arctic Circle has few resources that have helped it to become a thriving, developed nation; but it has done so just the same. Although the land and climate are generally un-suited for farming, the people have found other occupations to supply their livelihood. Among them are jobs in publishing and in the manufacture of electrical equipment and of cement (the most commonly used building material). The Icelandic economy has been greatly aided by two energy-supplying natural resources. One is the water power which allows hydroelectric plants to provide 96% of Iceland's electricity. The other is a wealth of geothermal energy. The warmth brought to the earth's surface in Iceland by hot springs and geysers has been harnessed to heat about 80% of the nation's homes, among other valuable uses. These resources have helped Iceland to keep its energy dependence on the fossil fuels of other nations at a minimum, thereby strengthening its own economy.

*figure for 1986 from the 1990 *World Almanac*

Whole life insurance is the second type of life insurance. Unlike term insurance, whole life insurance provides a savings component along with the death benefit. The premiums paid on a whole life policy remain level over the lifetime of the insured. For the young person the premiums on a whole life policy are significantly greater than the premiums paid on a term insurance policy with comparable death benefits; however, as the person grows older, the premiums on term insurance grow and eventually exceed the premiums paid on the whole life policy. The managers of the insurance company take a portion of the whole life premium and apply it to the policy's death benefit and invest the difference, providing the savings component. The savings value of a whole life policy is known as its **cash value.** The cash value of a whole life policy gradually increases during the early years of the policy and later increases until the cash value of the policy equals the face value. At that point the policy is said to be paid off. Holders of whole life insurance policies may borrow from their life insurance company using the cash value as collateral for the loan.

During the late 1970s a rebellion of sorts occurred against the high cost of whole life insurance with policyholders choosing to purchase the less profitable term insurance. As a result, insurance companies in 1981 began offering **universal life insurance.** Universal life is a hybrid form of life insurance which provides policyholders with a term insurance type death benefit including a flexible savings plan. The premium on universal life is not the high unflexible premium of whole life policies. A portion of the premium (called the ''contribution'') goes toward the payment for a term insurance policy and for management charges, and a portion goes toward the buildup of cash value. The difference between the term insurance portion and the total contribution is deposited into an interest-bearing account. Unlike whole life policyholders, universal life policyholders receive periodic statements which inform them of the cost of their term insurance and the interest earned on their investment account.

Health Care and Disability Insurance

Many of us, in the midst of a crisis, have heard the saying, ''Well, at least you have your health.'' This cliché is usually considered trite until one has experienced the financial hardships of a prolonged medical problem. Writing a will and purchasing life insurance are necessary ingredients in the short-term portion of a total financial plan; however, they are useful only when the person dies. Perhaps even more serious consideration should be paid to those medical emergencies which could very quickly sap a family's lifetime of savings and investments. The most important types of health insurance coverages include disability income, major medical, and hospitalization insurance.

***Types of Health Care and Disability Insurance*–** Most responsible people study various life insurance policies, but very few even consider what is

perhaps the most important form of insurance. One of the major reasons to purchase life insurance is to supply a family with maintenance income when the provider is no longer around to do so. Likewise, **disability income insurance** provides the family with weekly or monthly payments which replace the income of someone who is unable to work as a result of an illness or injury. A family should carry disability income insurance on all members of the family who provide income upon which the family is dependent. To provide an incentive for workers to continue working on the job rather than feigning an illness or injury, providers of disability income insurance usually replace only 60% to 70% of the insured's paycheck.

Insurance companies are able to avoid paying a large amount of money on small claims made by persons suffering from illnesses or injuries that last only a short period of time. They usually require a waiting period, which may be as short as seven days or as long as one year, depending upon the choice of the insured. Those who are in the market

to buy disability income insurance can significantly lower their premium payments by selecting a policy with a long waiting period. Another factor that affects the premium is the length of time chosen for the insurance company to pay disability benefits. One may select terms as short as one year or as many years as it takes for the person to reach age sixty-five. If someone selects a policy with a long waiting period and/or a short payout period, it is important that he have a liquid cash reserve to meet the needs not covered by the disability insurance.

Major medical insurance provides benefits for virtually all types of medical expenses resulting from accidents or illnesses. It is called *major* medical insurance because the amounts of the benefits may range from several thousand dollars to millions. In order to prevent policyholders from filing relatively minor claims, major medical insurance companies require the payment of a deductible amount. For example, many policies will begin paying medical payments only after the insured person has paid $500 worth of medical bills in the same year. Some policies require the deductible for each illness or injury. In such a case the man who suffered a $400 injury in January and a $500 injury in July would receive no insurance benefits because neither of the injuries exceeded the $500 deductible amount.

Major medical insurance pays for nearly all of the insured's medical expenses. Disability income insurance provides a percentage of his income while he is recuperating; **hospitalization insurance** pays for the costs associated with staying in a hospital. Typically covered is a portion of the per-day hospital room and board charges, use of operating rooms, x-ray services, laboratory tests, and medication received while in the hospital. Usually, hospitalization insurance will cover only a limited number of days' worth of hospital charges to, perhaps, 90, 180, or 360 days.

*Sources and Costs of Health Insurance–*The basic philosophy of all insurance companies is a philosophy of spreading the risk. That is, the insurance company collects relatively small premiums from

For most families, short-term financial planning involves acquiring suitable insurance coverage to meet potential financial emergencies.

each member of a large group of people and pays for the expenses of the few who die, contract disease, or are injured. Most health insurance, therefore, is purchased on a **group health insurance** basis. Most group health insurance plans are provided by employers as a nonsalary fringe benefit. Employer-sponsored health insurance is a double blessing for employees. First, it provides the insurance benefits so desperately needed by the employees, and second, it is a nontaxed fringe benefit. If employees were to be paid the equivalent of the premiums in cash, they would receive only a fraction of the amount since the government would take its share in taxes. Then the cost of buying their own policies would be much higher since they would be buying the insurance as individuals. The business firm, however, pays lower rates for the insurance because it insures large numbers of employees. For those people with chronic health problems, employer-sponsored group health insurance can be perhaps the greatest benefit his employer provides, even greater than the paycheck.

Section Review
1. What is a last will and testament?
2. What are the purposes of life insurance?
3. What types of life insurance are available?
4. What does major medical insurance provide?

III. Long-Term Financial Planning: Retirement

The Necessity of Retirement Planning

All too many people neglect retirement planning, as they do other aspects of financial planning, until it is too late. One of the major reasons many fail to plan for their retirement is uncertainty. After all, how many in their twenties know how large their families will be, the amount of social security income they can expect to receive, the lifestyle to which they will become accustomed, and the age at which they will retire? Because of these and many other uncertainties, most Americans do not have a systematic retirement plan, and that omission can lead to tragic results. Consider the following statistics:

1. The median income of people age sixty-five and older is below that of all other age groups.
2. Even after social security income is taken into account, nearly 25% of all elderly are considered below or near the poverty level.

3. Those who retire at age sixty-five have a life expectancy of fourteen additional years.

In order to enjoy a financially secure retirement and to avoid becoming a burden upon others, it is imperative to develop a comprehensive retirement plan. A total retirement plan includes an estimation of one's needs at retirement, such as spending and housing needs, and an evaluation of one's planned retirement income.

Retirement Planning Phase One: Estimation of Needs

Living Expenses–Obviously, it is impossible to predict the exact amount of money needed for living expenses forty to fifty years from now. However, certain spending trends have been observed among the elderly (Figure 18-1). According to the Bureau of Labor Statistics, the average annual expenditures of households aged sixty-five and older in the late 1980s equaled $14,636.

Within the categories listed by the Bureau of Labor Statistics, certain trends have been observed:

Figure 18-1 Average Expenditures of Retired Families in the Late 1980s*

CATEGORY	AMOUNT	PERCENT OF TOTAL
HOUSING	$ 4,592	31 %
FOOD	2,419	17
CLOTHING AND PERSONAL CARE	760	5
TRANSPORTATION	2,528	17
HEALTH CARE	1,635	11
LIFE INSURANCE/PENSIONS	680	5
CONTRIBUTIONS	889	6
ENTERTAINMENT, READING, AND EDUCATION	596	4
MISCELLANEOUS	537	4
TOTAL	$14,636	100 %

*Source: Bureau of Labor Statistics and Select Committee on Aging, House of Representatives, Washington, D.C., 1989

Housing: If the retiree has paid off his house mortgage before retirement, the cost of housing is reduced. However, increases in property taxes may cause this figure to rise.

Clothing and Personal Care: These expenses usually decline as one no longer needs to pay the higher amounts related to work wardrobes.

Health Care: Medical expenses generally tend to increase with age. In 1988 health care costs rose to over 18% of the average retiree's budget.

Insurance: Payments for health and life insurance coverage usually rise as one ages because of the increased probability of filing claims and the elimination of employer contributions. For some, however, these increases are offset by Medicare.

Gifts and Contributions: As their incomes decline, those retirees who choose to keep their gifts and contributions at the same dollar level find that it takes up a higher percentage of their total income.

***Housing Expenses*—**As a person ages, his housing needs change. With a growing family, higher income, and increased need for space, one needs a larger home as the years progress; but as one ages and children leave the home, other needs take priority. As one's income declines and maintenance and house-cleaning chores become more troublesome, smaller homes become more desirable. After retirement, the location of housing also becomes important. Access to church, shopping centers, transportation, and medical facilities becomes more important to retirees.

The image of the elderly American living out the balance of his days in a "rest home" is quickly changing. Older Americans are asserting their independence, and their housing preference is one of the biggest reflections of this tendency. Over 90% of 5,000 Americans surveyed indicate that they want to live in their own home during retirement.

Some retirees choose to sell their homes and buy smaller homes or condominiums so that they can reduce their home maintenance concerns but still preserve their independence.

J. P. Morgan (1837-1913)
Formidable Financier

John Pierpont Morgan was born into wealth. His grandfather was a farmer who had acquired a small fortune through real estate, insurance, banking, and other business interests in Connecticut. His father, Junius Spencer Morgan, had increased the family fortune through successful banking and investment interests in New York City and London. J. P. (often called Pierpont) Morgan then used his inherited financial position and talents to rise to the top of the American business world by the turn of the nineteenth century.

While a partner in the New York financial firm of Drexel, Morgan and Company, J. P. Morgan extended his business interests into United States government financing and railroad reorganization. His solid character led him to support men and business ventures of merit without undue regard to his own monetary reward, but the results of his judicious dealings were increased riches. His financial firm was renamed J. P. Morgan and Company in 1895, and this "House of Morgan" took a leading role in the American economy. In 1895 Morgan used his resources and ideas to help President Cleveland avoid a national crisis because of a depleted gold reserve. In 1907 Morgan once again stepped in to aid the country as it faced a severe financial panic by risking his own assets to restore business confidence. In the meantime, Morgan had put together the largest corporation of its time, U.S. Steel Corporation, and taken control of other large business concerns. Because Morgan exerted influence over a large segment of the American economy, he faced opposition in his later years from a public with growing concerns over monopolies and trusts and with roused suspicions of great wealth.

Though Morgan had wielded influence over untold billions in his lifetime, his estate was valued at a relatively meager $68.5 million (plus a valuable art collection that he intended to be put in a public museum). His will set aside a $3-million trust for each of his three daughters, a half million dollar bequest for his church in New York City, and various other provisions for charities, relatives, and employees. The remainder of his estate was left to his son, J. P. (Jack) Morgan, Jr., who carried on as leader of the House of Morgan. Although Morgan had supervised his financial empire admirably, his death signaled the demise of such economic power. Fearing that future financiers would abuse their powers, the government began regulation in earnest, beginning with the organization of the Federal Reserve System. In a sense, the Fed was intended to replace the economic wisdom and stability that J. P. Morgan had provided for his country in the decades prior to World War I.

Retirement Planning Phase Two: Retirement Income

Social Security–When considering post-retirement income, the first source that often comes to mind is social security. **Social security** is a government-mandated, employer/employee-financed retirement and disability plan. Although social security provides a minimal "safety net" of income for elderly Americans, it should never be considered as one's primary source of retirement income.

The amount of one's social security benefits is determined by a complex formula. One's benefits are determined by the average earnings he received over his wage-earning career, the age at which he retired, and inflation. In addition to the benefits formula, certain adjustments may be made. For example, there is a reduction of five-ninths of 1% for each month that one receives payments before age sixty-five; therefore, if one were to retire at age sixty-two, monthly payments would be permanently reduced by 20% of what they would be if retirement were delayed to age sixty-five. If one chooses to retire later than age sixty-five, benefits are increased by one-fourth of 1% for each month past age sixty-five. To receive a history of one's earnings and an estimation of future social security benefits, one may visit his local Social Security Administration office and fill out a form SSA-7004. Within approximately one month, a statement will arrive which will show the amount of one's benefit, in current dollars, if he were to retire at age sixty-two, sixty-five, or seventy.

If one works after retirement, social security benefits may be reduced if the worker earns above a certain amount each year. For 1989 a retiree under age sixty-five could earn up to $6,480, whereas those age sixty-five through sixty-nine were permitted to earn up to $8,800. If inflation has caused the cost of living to rise for the previous year, social security benefits rise automatically in January.

Employer-Sponsored Pension Plans–Because the benefits paid by the Social Security Administration are considered to be minimal and may be subject to political forces, it would be wise for the financial planner to consider personal pension plans. One of

the first to examine is the employer-sponsored pension plan. Much like employer-provided life and health insurance, more and more employers are providing retirement funds for their employees. As one's employer contributes to the fund, the benefits accrue to the employee tax-free.

To ensure that an employee has a long-term interest in his job, employer-sponsored retirement plans have what is known as a **vesting period;** that is, after a specified number of years the employee is fully enrolled in the plan and may withdraw from his account upon termination of employment. For most firms, full vesting occurs, at the latest, after seven years.

Most employer-sponsored retirement plans are known as **defined-contribution plans** which provide an individual account for each employee. Each employee receives a document which specifies the amount of the employer's contribution to the plan.

When the employee retires, the amount in his account may be withdrawn and is considered taxable at the time of withdrawal. There exist four specific types of defined-contribution plans.

1. *Money Purchase Plan:* Your employer promises to deposit a specific amount for you each year which is usually a percentage of your wages.
2. *Stock Plan:* As a variation of the money purchase plan, your employer uses the specific contribution to purchase stock in its company under your name. The shares will be held for you until you choose to retire, at which time you may hold them or sell them at the going market price.
3. *Profit Sharing Plan:* The amount that your employer contributes is dependent upon the profits of the firm.
4. *401(k) Plan:* Under a **401(k) plan,** one's employer makes a contribution to the retirement plan and matches the amount of the contribution with a contribution from the employee's paycheck. The employee's contribution is not taxed until the money is withdrawn at retirement, beginning at age fifty-nine and a half when one's taxable income is usually lower.

Personal Pension Plans–Besides employer-sponsored pension plans, there exist two popular do-it-yourself pension plans: the individual retirement account (IRA) and the Keogh account.

An **individual retirement account (IRA)** is a retirement account which one can open at a bank or other financial institution. Deposits of up to $2,000 to one's IRA are tax deductible provided that the person is not covered by an employer-sponsored pension plan. If he is covered by such a plan, he may still make the tax-deductible deposits as long as his adjusted gross income is less than $25,000. If he is covered by an employer-sponsored plan and his adjusted gross income is greater than $25,000, his tax deduction is reduced. Interest on an IRA is not reported as taxable income until it is withdrawn. When the account holder retires, he may withdraw the entire amount at one time or withdraw it in installments over his expected lifetime.

A **Keogh Plan** is a retirement plan for self-employed people. Like the employer-sponsored 401(k) plans, payments to Keogh accounts are taken as deductions from taxable income. The maximum contribution a self-employed person may make to a Keogh account is $30,000 or 20% of his earned income, whichever is less.

Section Review

1. Why is retirement planning necessary?
2. What is social security?
3. What is a vesting period?
4. What is an IRA?

Chapter Review

Terms

financial planning
last will and testament
estate
guardians
statutory will
executor
administrator
bequest
legacy
dower
codicil
deductible
term insurance
beneficiary
premium
whole life insurance
cash value
universal life insurance
disability income insurance
major medical insurance
hospitalization insurance
group health insurance
social security
vesting period
defined contribution plans
401(k) plan
individual retirement account (IRA)
Keogh plan

Content Questions

1. What is "financial planning"?
2. Why is the writing of a will the first step in a comprehensive financial plan?
3. What are the three ways in which a will may be completed?
4. What is a bequest? What is a codicil?
5. What is the purpose of life insurance, and on whom should it be carried?
6. What is the chief difference between term life insurance and whole life insurance?
7. Why do insurance companies usually insure only 60% to 70% of a person's income in case of disability?
8. If a person chooses to retire and receive social security payments at age sixty-three, by how much will his monthly benefit be reduced?
9. What are the four types of employer-sponsored retirement plans?
10. What is the difference between a 401(k) retirement plan and a Keogh plan?

Application Questions

1. If you were to write a will today, what qualities would you consider when determining beneficiaries and their benefits?
2. Why would anyone want to purchase a whole life insurance policy?
3. What are the benefits of holding an IRA?

Epilogue: A Call for Christian Economic Thinking and Action

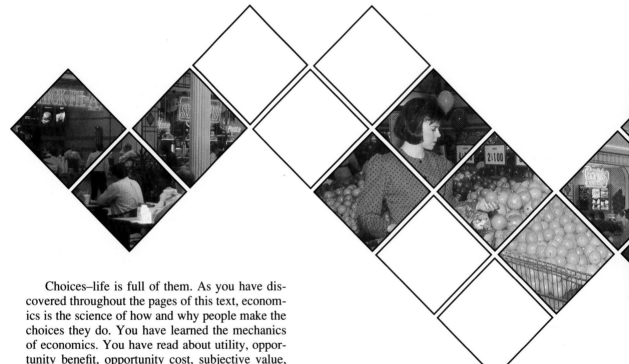

Choices–life is full of them. As you have discovered throughout the pages of this text, economics is the science of how and why people make the choices they do. You have learned the mechanics of economics. You have read about utility, opportunity benefit, opportunity cost, subjective value, demand, and supply. You have gained an essential *knowledge* of the tools of economics which, coupled with wisdom, will prove a valuable asset throughout the remainder of your life. The task now before you is to appropriate the wisdom necessary to rightly guide your choices.

Just as one must be cautious of whom he befriends, the first step in obtaining economic wisdom is the careful selection of proper role models and intellectual concepts. Proverbs 19:27 says, "Cease, my son, to hear the instruction that causeth to err from the words of knowledge." Liberal economist

John Maynard Keynes, spokesman for radical government intervention in the marketplace, recognized that everyone consciously or unconsciously apprehends the ideas and opinions of others. In his book *The General Theory of Employment, Interest, and Money* he stated that "practical men, who believe themselves to be quite exempt from any intellectual influences, are usually the slaves of some defunct economist. . . . It is ideas, not vested interests, which are dangerous for good or evil."

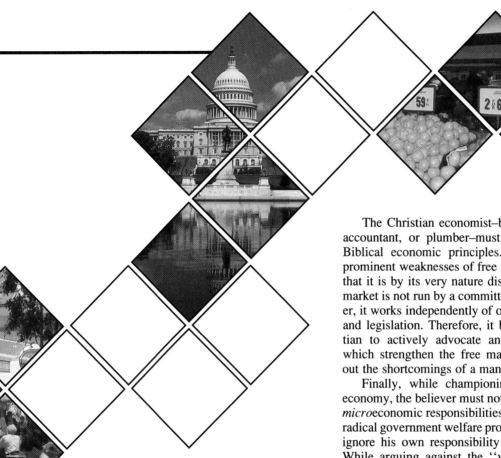

The Christian economist–be he teacher, cook, accountant, or plumber–must actively champion Biblical economic principles. One of the most prominent weaknesses of free market capitalism is that it is by its very nature disorganized. The free market is not run by a committee of devotees; rather, it works independently of organizations, edicts, and legislation. Therefore, it behooves the Christian to actively advocate and promote policies which strengthen the free market while pointing out the shortcomings of a managed economy.

Finally, while championing the free *macro* economy, the believer must not ignore his personal *micro*economic responsibilities. While denouncing radical government welfare programs, one must not ignore his own responsibility to help the needy. While arguing against the "values-clarification" curriculums of government schools, one must support and assist in his church and Sunday school. Above all, one must never come to see the propagation of the free market as an end in itself. The free market merely sets the stage for an unhindered propagation of the gospel of Jesus Christ.

What, therefore, should be the proper road map to guide the Christian's way of economic thinking? The obvious answer is God's Word, the Bible. While the Bible is not an apologetic for conservative economic principles, it does touch on certain economic principles. A second guide is common sense. Liberal economists have a tendency to allow their hearts to override their heads, such as when they advocate price controls, production quotas, and wage leveling. Just as God put natural laws in place, such as the laws of gravity and motion, He has put economic laws in place. These laws, when violated, produce undesirable outcomes. The Christian needs to use his common sense to think through both the short-term and long-term consequences of his actions.

> Therefore seeing we have this ministry, as we have received mercy, we faint not; but have renounced the hidden things of dishonesty, not walking in craftiness, nor handling the word of God deceitfully; but by manifestation of the truth commending ourselves to every man's conscience in the sight of God. But if our gospel be hid, it is hid to them that are lost: in whom the god of this world hath blinded the minds of them which believe not, lest the light of the glorious gospel of Christ, who is the image of God, should shine unto them. (II Corinthians 4:1-4)

Appendixes

COMPARATIVE STATISTICS		
	UNITED STATES	CANADA
GNP	$4,880.6 billion (1988)	$467.5 billion (1988)
PER CAPITA GNP	$19,813 (1988)	$18,015 (1988)
POPULATION	248,231,000 (1989)	26,311,000 (1989)
MONETARY UNIT	dollar	dollar (one Canadian dollar equal to .863 U.S. dollars in 1988)
CIVILIAN LABOR FORCE	121.7 million (1988)	13.3 million (1988)
UNEMPLOYMENT RATE	5.5% (1988)	7.8% (1988)
IMPORTS	$441.3 billion (1988)	$106.8 billion (1988)
EXPORTS	$320.4 billion (1988)	$111.9 billion (1988)
BALANCE OF TRADE	–$120.9 billion (1988)	+$5.1 billion (1988)
AVERAGE CHANGE IN THE CONSUMER PRICE INDEX FOR FOOD (1980-1988)	+3.9%	+5.3%

Figures from the 1990 STATISTICAL ABSTRACT OF THE UNITED STATES

Money Stock, Liquid Assets, and Debt Measures
(Averages of daily figures; billions of dollars, seasonally adjusted)

Year and month	M1 Sum of currency, demand deposits, traveler's checks, and other checkable deposits (OCDs)	M2 M1 plus overnight RPs and Eurodollars, MMMF balances (general purpose and broker/dealer), MMDAs, and savings and small time deposits	M3 M2 plus large time deposits, term RPs, term Eurodollars, and institution-only MMMF balances	L M3 plus other liquid assets	Debt Debt of domestic nonfinancial sectors (monthly average)
December: 1959	140.0	297.8	299.8	388.7	682.4
1960	140.7	312.4	315.3	403.7	717.1
1961	145.2	335.5	341.1	430.8	759.5
1962	147.9	362.7	371.5	466.1	811.6
1963	153.4	393.3	406.1	503.8	866.6
1964	160.4	424.8	442.5	540.4	929.7
1965	167.9	459.4	482.3	584.5	997.9
1966	172.1	480.0	505.1	614.8	1,065.5
1967	183.3	524.4	557.1	666.6	1,140.9
1968	197.5	566.4	606.3	729.0	1,234.3
1969	204.0	589.6	615.1	763.6	1,324.7
1970	214.5	628.1	677.4	816.2	1,414.8
1971	228.4	712.7	776.2	903.1	1,546.3
1972	249.4	805.3	886.1	1,023.1	1,701.5
1973	263.0	861.0	985.1	1,142.6	1,889.8
1974	274.4	908.5	1,070.4	1,250.3	2,061.2
1975	287.6	1,023.2	1,172.2	1,367.0	2,241.9
1976	306.5	1,163.7	1,311.9	1,516.7	2,480.7
1977	331.5	1,286.8	1,472.9	1,705.5	2,793.4
1978	358.8	1,389.2	1,647.1	1,911.2	3,166.1
1979	386.1	1,500.3	1,806.7	2,119.6	3,546.1
1980	412.2	1,633.3	1,991.1	2,327.8	3,881.9
1981	439.1	1,795.9	2,236.9	2,599.4	4,269.0
1982	476.4	1,954.5	2,443.8	2,853.5	4,660.0
1983	522.1	2,186.0	2,694.3	3,155.5	5,185.4
1984	551.9	2,367.2	2,982.2	3,523.4	5,932.7
1985	620.5	2,567.4	3,201.7	3,830.6	6,741.5
1986	725.9	2,811.2	3,494.9	4,137.1	7,597.0
1987	752.3	2,909.9	3,677.8	4,336.8	8,316.1
1988	790.3	3,069.6	3,915.6	4,672.3	9,082.2
1989	797.6	3,217.0	4,039.6		

Source: Board of Governors of the Federal Reserve System

Appendix

Unemployment Rate
(Per cent; monthly data seasonally adjusted)

Year or month	Unemployment rate (all workers)[1]	Unemployment rates (civilian workers)							
		All civilian workers	Males			Females			Both sexes 16-19 years
			Total	16-19 years	20 years and over	Total	16-19 years	20 years and over	
1948		3.8	3.6	9.8	3.2	4.1	8.3	3.6	9.2
1949		5.9	5.9	14.3	5.4	6.0	12.3	5.3	13.4
1950	5.2	5.3	5.1	12.7	4.7	5.7	11.4	5.1	12.2
1951	3.2	3.3	2.8	8.1	2.5	4.4	8.3	4.0	8.2
1952	2.9	3.0	2.8	8.9	2.4	3.6	8.0	3.2	8.5
1953	2.8	2.9	2.8	7.9	2.5	3.3	7.2	2.9	7.6
1954	5.4	5.5	5.3	13.5	4.9	6.0	11.4	5.5	12.6
1955	4.3	4.4	4.2	11.6	3.8	4.9	10.2	4.4	11.0
1956	4.0	4.1	3.8	11.1	3.4	4.8	11.2	4.2	11.1
1957	4.2	4.3	4.1	12.4	3.6	4.7	10.6	4.1	11.6
1958	6.6	6.8	6.8	17.1	6.2	6.8	14.3	6.1	15.9
1959	5.3	5.5	5.2	15.3	4.7	5.9	13.5	5.2	14.6
1960	5.4	5.5	5.4	15.3	4.7	5.9	13.9	5.1	14.7
1961	6.5	6.7	6.4	17.1	5.7	7.2	16.3	6.3	16.8
1962	5.4	5.5	5.2	14.7	4.6	6.2	14.6	5.4	14.7
1963	5.5	5.7	5.2	17.2	4.5	6.5	17.2	5.4	17.2
1964	5.0	5.2	4.6	15.8	3.9	6.2	16.6	5.2	16.2
1965	4.4	4.5	4.0	14.1	3.2	5.5	15.7	4.5	14.8
1966	3.7	3.8	3.2	11.7	2.5	4.8	14.1	3.8	12.8
1967	3.7	3.8	3.1	12.3	2.3	5.2	13.5	4.2	12.9
1968	3.5	3.6	2.9	11.6	2.2	4.8	14.0	3.8	12.7
1969	3.4	3.5	2.8	11.4	2.1	4.7	13.3	3.7	12.2
1970	4.8	4.9	4.4	15.0	3.5	5.9	15.6	4.8	15.3
1971	5.8	5.9	5.3	16.6	4.4	6.9	17.2	5.7	16.9
1972	5.5	5.6	5.0	15.9	4.0	6.6	16.7	5.4	16.2
1973	4.8	4.9	4.2	13.9	3.3	6.0	15.3	4.9	14.5
1974	5.5	5.6	4.9	15.6	3.8	6.7	16.6	5.5	16.0
1975	8.3	8.5	7.9	20.1	6.8	9.3	19.7	8.0	19.9
1976	7.6	7.7	7.1	19.2	5.9	8.6	18.7	7.4	19.0
1977	6.9	7.1	6.3	17.3	5.2	8.2	18.3	7.0	17.8
1978	6.0	6.1	5.3	15.8	4.3	7.2	17.1	6.0	16.4
1979	5.8	5.8	5.1	15.9	4.2	6.8	16.4	5.7	16.1
1980	7.0	7.1	6.9	18.3	5.9	7.4	17.2	6.4	17.8
1981	7.5	7.6	7.4	20.1	6.3	7.9	19.0	6.8	19.6
1982	9.5	9.7	9.9	24.4	8.8	9.4	21.9	8.3	23.2
1983	9.5	9.6	9.9	23.3	8.9	9.2	21.3	8.1	22.4
1984	7.4	7.5	7.4	19.6	6.6	7.6	18.0	6.8	18.9
1985	7.1	7.2	7.0	19.5	6.2	7.4	17.6	6.6	18.6
1986	6.9	7.0	6.9	19.0	6.1	7.1	17.6	6.2	18.3
1987	6.1	6.2	6.2	17.8	5.4	6.2	15.9	5.4	16.9
1988	5.4	5.5	5.5	16.0	4.8	5.6	14.4	4.9	15.3
1989	5.2	5.3	5.2	15.9	4.5	5.4	14.0	4.7	15.0

[1]Unemployment as per cent of labor force including resident armed forces
Source: 1990 Economic Report of the President

Household Incomes

Number, Median Income (in 1988 dollars), and Poverty Status of Families and Persons

Year	Families[1]						Persons below poverty level		Median income of persons 15 years old and over with income[2]			
			Below poverty level						Males		Females	
			Total		Female householder							
	Number (millions)	Median income	Number (millions)	Rate	Number (millions)	Rate	Number (millions)	Rate	All persons	Year-round full-time workers	All persons	Year-round full-time workers
1970	52.2	$30,084	5.3	10.1	2.0	32.5	25.4	12.6	$20,337	$28,002	$6,821	$16,586
1971	53.3	30,042	5.3	10.0	2.1	33.9	25.6	12.5	20,164	28,132	7,034	16,653
1972	54.4	31,460	5.1	9.3	2.2	32.7	24.5	11.9	21,085	29,824	7,356	17,131
1973	55.1	32,109	4.8	8.8	2.2	32.2	23.0	11.1	21,465	30,556	7,450	17,287
1974	55.7	30,960	4.9	8.8	2.3	32.1	23.4	11.2	20,281	29,328	7,396	17,215
1975	56.2	30,166	5.5	9.7	2.4	32.5	25.9	12.3	19,467	28,902	7,443	16,973
1976	56.7	31,099	5.3	9.4	2.5	33.0	25.0	11.8	19,597	28,814	7,435	17,281
1977	57.2	31,252	5.3	9.3	2.6	31.7	24.7	11.6	19,762	29,419	7,693	17,206
1978	57.8	32,006	5.3	9.1	2.7	31.4	24.5	11.4	19,841	29,143	7,381	17,493
1979	59.6	31,917	5.5	9.2	2.6	30.4	26.1	11.7	19,194	28,482	7,091	17,160
1980	60.3	30,182	6.2	10.3	3.0	32.7	29.3	13.0	17,989	27,526	7,064	16,641
1981	61.0	29,136	6.9	11.2	3.3	34.6	31.8	14.0	17,534	26,929	7,103	16,212
1982	61.4	28,727	7.5	12.2	3.4	36.3	34.4	15.0	17,101	26,547	7,217	16,750
1983	62.0	29,307	7.6	12.3	3.6	36.0	35.3	15.2	17,414	26,732	7,608	17,208
1984	62.7	30,096	7.3	11.6	3.5	34.5	33.7	14.4	17,762	27,331	7,820	17,559
1985	63.6	30,493	7.2	11.4	3.5	34.0	33.1	14.0	17,933	27,485	7,935	17,868
1986	64.5	31,796	7.0	10.9	3.6	34.6	32.4	13.6	18,473	27,949	8,214	18,180
1987	65.2	32,251	7.0	10.7	3.7	34.2	32.3	13.4	18,522	27,785	8,638	18,291
1988	65.8	32,191	6.9	10.4	3.6	33.5	31.9	13.1	18,908	27,342	8,884	18,545

[1]The term "family" refers to a group of two or more persons related by blood, marriage, or adoption and residing together; all such persons are considered members of the same family. Beginning 1979, based on householder concept and restricted to primary families.

[2]Prior to 1979, data are for persons 14 years and over.

Source: Department of Commerce, Bureau of the Census

Appendix

Saving by Individuals[1]

(Billions of dollars; quarterly data at seasonally adjusted annual rates)

Year or quarter	Total	Increase in financial assets									Net investment in tangible assets[7]			Less: Net increase in debt		
		Total	Checkable deposits and currency	Time and savings deposits	Money market fund shares	Securities			Insurance and pension reserves[5]	Other financial assets[6]	Owner occupied homes	Consumer durables	Noncorporate business assets[8]	Mortgage debt on nonfarm homes	Consumer credit	Other debt[8][9]
						Government securities[2]	Corporate equities[3]	Other securities[4]								
1946	24.9	19.5	5.6	6.3	0.0	-1.5	1.2	-0.8	5.1	3.7	3.8	6.7	2.0	4.0	2.9	0.2
1947	19.5	12.5	0.0	3.5	0.0	0.5	1.1	-0.7	5.4	2.6	7.0	9.4	1.3	4.9	3.5	2.4
1948	25.0	8.9	-2.9	2.3	0.0	1.0	1.0	0.1	5.3	2.1	9.5	10.2	6.9	4.8	3.1	2.6
1949	20.7	8.8	-2.0	2.6	0.0	0.5	0.7	-0.2	5.6	1.6	8.7	10.9	2.0	4.4	3.1	2.3
1950	31.8	14.9	2.7	2.4	0.0	0.9	0.7	-0.7	6.1	2.9	12.1	14.9	7.2	7.1	4.6	5.7
1951	35.0	18.9	4.6	4.8	0.0	-0.6	1.8	0.3	6.3	1.6	12.1	11.4	4.4	6.6	1.4	3.8
1952	35.9	28.7	1.6	7.8	0.0	7.4	1.5	0.0	7.7	2.8	11.7	8.7	1.9	6.4	5.2	3.5
1953	34.3	24.7	0.9	8.2	0.0	3.7	1.0	0.5	7.9	2.4	12.7	10.3	0.8	7.6	4.1	2.5
1954	27.4	21.2	2.1	9.2	0.0	0.2	0.7	-0.8	7.8	2.0	13.1	7.0	1.7	9.0	1.4	5.3
1955	36.1	28.6	1.2	8.6	0.0	6.4	1.1	1.0	8.5	1.7	17.3	12.7	2.9	12.3	7.0	6.1
1956	38.5	31.8	1.9	9.4	0.0	4.6	2.0	1.1	9.5	3.4	16.2	8.8	1.0	11.0	3.6	4.6
1957	38.0	28.8	-0.4	11.9	0.0	3.7	1.5	0.8	9.5	1.9	13.8	7.9	2.1	8.8	2.6	3.2
1958	35.1	32.5	3.7	13.9	0.0	-2.6	1.8	1.0	10.4	4.3	12.8	3.7	2.9	9.6	0.3	6.9
1959	36.8	34.5	0.9	11.0	0.0	8.4	0.6	-0.2	11.9	1.9	17.0	7.7	4.3	12.9	7.7	6.1
1960	37.4	32.7	0.9	12.2	0.0	2.1	0.0	2.3	11.5	3.7	15.7	7.3	3.2	11.4	4.0	6.1
1961	36.9	35.5	-1.0	18.3	0.0	0.8	1.1	-0.2	12.1	4.3	13.5	4.5	4.9	12.3	2.2	7.0
1962	43.2	39.7	-1.2	26.1	0.0	1.1	-1.4	-0.4	13.0	2.5	14.0	8.6	7.0	13.9	5.9	6.4
1963	46.7	45.4	4.2	26.2	0.0	-0.8	-1.6	1.3	13.9	2.1	15.5	11.9	9.2	16.6	8.5	10.1
1964	56.6	54.9	5.2	26.3	0.0	3.9	-0.3	0.3	16.4	3.1	15.7	15.1	8.8	17.4	9.5	11.1
1965	65.7	58.7	7.6	27.9	0.0	3.9	-1.6	0.8	17.0	3.1	15.3	20.2	12.4	17.1	10.1	13.7
1966	76.5	60.9	2.4	19.1	0.0	13.7	-0.1	2.4	19.3	4.1	14.5	23.2	9.9	13.4	5.9	12.5
1967	79.0	70.1	9.9	35.4	0.0	-2.5	-3.3	5.2	18.8	6.7	12.6	21.3	10.7	12.9	5.1	17.6
1968	79.5	71.6	11.2	30.9	0.0	2.3	-6.2	7.8	19.9	5.7	17.0	26.9	10.0	17.2	10.8	18.1
1969	73.9	67.0	-2.4	8.9	0.0	27.0	-2.2	10.0	21.8	3.9	17.2	26.2	13.3	18.3	10.1	21.5
1970	89.6	80.7	8.7	43.5	0.0	-5.7	-0.7	6.9	24.2	3.9	14.6	19.9	13.1	13.5	4.6	20.6
1971	99.6	105.5	12.2	67.7	0.0	-11.0	-4.3	6.7	28.0	6.2	22.3	25.7	19.5	26.2	14.1	33.2
1972	118.9	134.6	13.4	74.0	0.0	-0.5	-8.8	-1.0	48.5	9.2	29.2	34.8	26.6	38.8	19.0	48.4
1973	157.4	148.4	13.1	63.5	0.0	18.6	-4.3	9.1	39.9	8.4	33.1	41.2	31.9	44.2	23.0	30.0
1974	120.0	147.1	6.3	56.2	2.4	17.8	-2.1	13.5	43.7	9.3	27.9	29.9	14.9	34.6	9.0	56.2
1975	159.1	176.4	6.0	77.6	1.3	17.6	-6.2	-2.1	71.9	10.1	27.5	28.4	7.5	38.8	8.0	33.9
1976	164.0	206.1	15.6	107.1	0.0	8.6	-0.5	2.2	56.6	16.6	41.9	42.9	2.7	60.8	22.9	45.9
1977	190.3	253.4	19.7	106.6	-0.2	13.4	-7.3	17.2	78.6	25.4	61.0	53.3	15.2	91.5	36.7	64.4
1978	198.8	285.8	22.0	99.6	6.0	32.1	-12.5	8.7	95.0	34.9	77.8	58.8	18.9	109.4	45.1	87.9
1979	204.4	327.0	36.0	74.4	30.6	66.0	-25.5	4.8	101.8	38.8	86.7	54.0	12.4	117.1	40.5	118.2
1980	204.4	321.3	8.9	124.9	24.5	33.4	-9.9	-14.5	118.5	35.4	66.6	31.9	-6.2	96.4	2.6	110.2
1981	248.8	323.3	35.4	72.0	90.7	43.2	-35.7	-9.1	117.9	8.8	59.7	37.4	19.5	73.8	16.9	100.4
1982	263.8	379.3	24.7	119.7	82.8	69.8	-11.3	-25.8	148.0	21.3	35.6	37.2	-4.0	52.9	16.4	115.1
1983	323.1	495.4	33.4	201.8	-31.1	99.0	0.5	3.8	159.2	28.9	76.2	62.7	-11.6	120.4	49.0	130.2
1984	391.4	563.7	23.0	229.6	44.0	125.9	-53.4	0.3	157.7	36.6	95.4	98.8	14.4	136.7	81.6	162.7
1985	346.1	568.0	32.6	133.0	12.1	120.8	-34.3	51.2	185.6	67.0	97.1	117.6	1.0	157.0	82.5	198.0
1986	409.2	561.2	94.8	106.5	33.0	-2.4	16.4	37.2	202.9	72.9	114.6	125.4	3.2	216.8	58.0	120.5
1987	377.2	512.1	22.8	97.8	21.4	140.6	-24.8	28.9	195.2	30.2	134.0	115.7	-12.6	234.0	32.9	105.2
1988	432.5	569.2	8.4	159.0	18.1	177.7	-120.6	37.5	224.4	64.8	151.3	131.6	-26.4	229.0	51.1	113.1

[1]Saving by households, personal trust funds, nonprofit institutions, farms, and other noncorporate business
[2]Consists of U.S. savings bonds, other U.S. Treasury securities, U.S. Government agency securities and sponsored agency securities, mortgage pool securities, and State and local obligations
[3]Includes mutual fund shares
[4]Corporate and foreign bonds and open-market paper
[5]Private life insurance reserves, private insured and noninsured pension reserves, and government insurance and pension reserves
[6]Consists of security credit, mortgages, accident and health insurance reserves, and nonlife insurance claims of households and of consumer credit, equity in sponsored agencies, and nonlife insurance claims for noncorporate business
[7]Purchase of physical assets less depreciation
[8]Includes data for corporate farms
[9]Other debt consists of security credit, U.S. Government and policy loans, and noncorporate business debt
Source: Board of Governors of the Federal Reserve System

Federal Receipts, Outlays, and Debt
(millions of dollars; fiscal years)

Description	Actual			Estimates	
	1987	1988	1989	1990	1991
RECEIPTS AND OUTLAYS:					
Total receipts	854,143	908,954	990,691	1,073,451	1,170,232
Total outlays	1,003,830	1,064,044	1,142,643	1,197,236	1,233,331
Total surplus or deficit (-)	-149,687	-155,090	-151,951	-123,785	-63,099
On-budget receipts	640,741	667,463	727,026	788,017	855,691
On-budget outlays	809,998	861,352	931,732	971,452	997,374
On-budget surplus or deficit (-)	-169,257	-193,890	-204,706	-183,435	-141,683
Off-budget receipts	213,402	241,491	263,666	285,434	314,541
Off-budget outlays	193,832	202,691	210,911	225,784	235,957
Off-budget surplus or deficit (-)	19,570	38,800	52,754	59,650	78,584
OUTSTANDING DEBT, END OF PERIOD:					
Gross federal debt	2,345,578	2,600,753	2,866,188	3,113,263	3,319,161
Held by government accounts	457,444	550,507	676,860	814,611	961,874
Held by the public	1,888,134	2,050,245	2,189,328	2,298,652	2,357,287
Federal Reserve System	212,040	229,218	220,088	0	0
Other	1,676,094	1,821,027	1,969,240	0	0
RECEIPTS: ON-BUDGET AND OFF-BUDGET	854,143	909,954	990,691	1,073,451	1,170,232
Individual income taxes	392,557	401,181	445,690	489,444	528,489
Corporation income taxes	83,926	94,508	103,583	112,030	129,665
Social insurance taxes and contributions	303,318	334,335	359,416	385,362	421,449
On-budget	89,916	92,845	95,751	99,928	106,908
Off-budget	213,402	241,491	263,666	285,434	314,541
Excise taxes	32,457	35,227	34,084	36,154	37,634
Estate and gift taxes	7,493	7,594	8,745	9,279	9,809
Customs, duties, and fees	15,085	16,198	16,334	16,785	18,615
Miscellaneous receipts:					
Deposits of earnings by Federal Reserve System	16,817	17,163	19,604	21,086	21,107
All other	2,490	2,747	3,235	3,311	3,465
OUTLAYS: ON-BUDGET AND OFF-BUDGET	1,003,830	1,064,044	1,142,643	1,197,236	1,233,331
National defense	281,999	290,361	303,559	296,342	303,251
International affairs	11,649	10,471	9,574	14,554	18,172
General science, space, and technology	9,216	10,841	12,838	14,145	16,609
Energy	4,115	2,297	3,702	3,194	3,029
Natural resources and environment	13,363	14,606	16,182	17,499	18,168
Agriculture	26,606	17,210	16,948	14,571	14,938
Commerce and housing credit	6,182	18,808	27,719	22,688	17,184
On-budget	6,182	18,808	28,029	20,300	15,463
Off-budget	0	0	-310	2,388	1,721
Transportation	26,222	27,272	27,608	29,250	29,758
Community and regional development	5,051	5,294	5,361	8,776	7,825
Education, training, employment, and social services	29,724	31,938	36,684	37,652	41,005
Health	39,968	44,490	48,390	57,819	63,698
Medicare	75,120	78,878	84,964	96,616	98,615
Income security	123,250	129,332	136,031	146,601	153,738
Social security	207,353	219,341	232,542	248,462	264,811
On-budget	4,930	4,852	5,069	3,875	4,722
Off-budget	202,422	214,489	227,473	244,587	260,089
Veterans benefits	26,782	29,428	30,066	28,888	30,308
Administration of justice	7,548	9,223	9,422	10,489	12,608
General government	7,569	9,474	9,124	10,560	11,282
Net interest	138,570	151,748	169,137	175,591	172,979
On-budget	143,860	159,164	180,532	191,201	192,869
Off-budget	-5,290	-7,416	-11,395	-15,610	-19,890
Allowances	0	0	0	0	-1,070
Undistributed offsetting receipts	-36,455	-36,967	-37,212	-36,462	-43,578
On-budget	-33,155	-32,585	-32,354	-30,881	-37,615
Off-budget	-3,300	-4,382	-4,858	-5,581	-5,962

Source: Department of the Treasury and Office of Management and Budget

Glossary

(The page numbers refer to the first time that the term is used in the text.)

ability-to-pay principle declares a tax to be fair if it is levied on those who have the ability to pay, regardless of the benefits they receive (p. 227)

administrator a court-appointed person entrusted with the disposition of the estate of one who died without a will (p. 315)

amortization schedule a chart displaying the monthly interest costs of a loan at a given rate of interest (p. 265)

anticompetitive takeover a situation that reduces competition; occurs when business firms buy out other firms in their industry in order to eliminate the competition (p. 124)

appreciating assets goods that increase in value over time (p. 263)

artificial barrier to entry the prevention of a new firm from entering an industry because of government regulations (p. 113)

Austrian economics the school of economic thought which advocates a return to Adam Smith's concept of classic liberalism and promotes private ownership of a majority of the nation's factors of production while permitting only minimal government intervention (p. 18)

bait-and-switch deceptive advertising that draws customers into the business for an advertised product that is unavailable or unsuitable thereby providing an opportunity to sell a more expensive product (p. 251)

barrier to entry a condition that prevents a new firm from entering an industry and competing on an equal basis with established firms (p. 113)

barter the exchange of one person's goods or services for another's goods or services (p. 130)

base period the initial period of a survey, such as that for consumer prices, against which changes over time are compared (p. 206)

beneficiary the person named on a life insurance policy to receive the proceeds upon the death of the policyholder (p. 321)

bequest a gift left by a deceased person to an heir (p. 317)

Better Business Bureau an organization providing information about businesses and their products to consumers and helping consumers gain redress for unjust treatment from businesses (p. 249)

Board of Governors a group selected by the President and confirmed by Congress to guide the actions of the Federal Reserve Banking System (p. 148)

budget a tabulation of income and planned expenditures (p. 238)

budget deficit a situation in which a government, business firm, or individual receives less income than is paid out in expenses (p. 57)

budget surplus a situation in which a government, business firm, or individual receives more income than is paid out in expenses (p. 57)

business cycle an economic condition consisting of alternating periods of rising and falling real GNP and is characterized by four phases: expansion, peak, recession, and trough (p. 185)

business investment another name for gross private domestic investment (GPDI) (p. 170)

capital goods goods that are used to produce consumer goods; also called real capital (p. 69)

capital intensive description of a business firm that uses more automated equipment than human labor (p. 72)

capitalism an economic system in which private individuals own most of the factors of production and make most economic decisions (p. 83)

cartel a group of producers who agree to control the price of their goods (p. 119)

cash advance a feature of a bank card that enables the holder to obtain cash from a bank on request while increasing his bank card account debt by that amount (p. 270)

cash management the activity of accounting for cash inflows, storing short-term cash balances in the most profitable ways, and the timely payment of one's financial obligations (p. 282)

cash value the amount accumulated in the savings component of a whole life insurance policy (p. 322)

cashier's check a guaranteed check bought by a customer and drawn on the bank itself (p. 293)

caveat emptor "Let the buyer beware!" (p. 251)

cease and desist order a legal order prohibiting a party from continuing a harmful practice (p. 252)

central bank a bank that the government uses to control and accommodate the nation's finances by providing an elastic national currency, serving as the nation's fiscal agent, regulating the nation's private banks, providing a national check-clearing mechanism, serving as a bank to the nation's private banks, and creating money (p. 147)

centralized socialism a form of socialism in which the government is both the central owner and the decision maker in all economic affairs of the state (p. 89)

certificates of deposit (CDs) time deposits which carry a specific maturity date and yield a high rate of interest (p. 307)

certified check personal check for which the bank guarantees payment (p. 292)

change in demand the shifting of a demand curve experienced when demand for an item increases or decreases regardless of price (p. 21)

change in quantity demanded when the change in the price of an item causes a change in the number demanded (p. 20)

change in quantity supplied when the change in the price of an item causes a change in the number supplied (p. 31)

change in supply the shifting of a supply curve that occurs when suppliers are willing to produce more or less of an item regardless of price (p. 31)

charter an authorization for a bank to exist, issued either by the federal government or by the state government (p. 142)

checking account a non-interest-bearing transaction account offered by commercial banks (p. 285)

circular flow model a model depicting the flow of economic goods and services between households, business firms, government, and financial markets (p. 53)

classic liberal capitalism the form of capitalism allowing government only minimal ownership of resources and decision-making power (p. 85)

clearinghouse an operation organized to clear checks or send them to the banks from which they were drawn and settle accounts between banks (p. 153)

codicil an amendment to a will (p. 317)

collateral valuable goods that may be taken by a lender and resold if the borrower does not repay his loan (p. 267)

commodity money a commonly used or valued good that serves as a medium of exchange (p. 133)

communism in the economic sense, the most extreme form of socialism in which all individuals voluntarily contribute their labor for the good of society while taking from the economy only the goods and services that they truly need (p. 90)

complementary goods goods that are usually purchased or used together (p. 24)

compound interest the calculation of interest on reinvested interest as well as on the original principal (p. 300)

conditional endorsement an endorsement which stipulates the conditions under which a check may be cashed (p. 289)

consumer durable goods goods that have a life expectancy of more than one year (p. 170)

consumer finance companies finance companies that make secured and unsecured personal loans and debt consolidation loans to the general public (p. 272)

consumer goods goods that are purchased for personal use (p. 69)

consumer goods/capital goods tradeoff the allocation of limited resources to produce either consumer goods or capital goods (p. 69)

consumer nondurable goods items that are expected to be worn out or used up within one year (p. 170)

consumer price index (CPI) figures measuring changes in prices that household consumers pay for their purchases (p. 206)

consumer services intangible products purchased by consumers (p. 170)

consumerism political action in behalf of consumer rights (p. 252)

consumption borrowing the use of debt to purchase goods which will be consumed almost immediately (p. 261)

consumption expenditures the total expenditures made by all households (p. 53)

contingency an uncertain or unexpected event that may result in unplanned expense (p. 244)

corporation a business entity recognized by the government as separate from its owners or stockholders (p. 104)

correspondent banking an arrangement in which two banks have numerous regular transactions between them, and therefore they hold deposits with one another to aid the check-clearing process (p. 153)

cosigner one who obligates himself to pay the debts of another; surety (p. 103)

cosigning agreeing to pay the debt of another person if he does not pay it (p. 278)

cost of living adjustment (COLA) adjustments of wages, payments, and other sums according to inflation levels (p. 204)

cost-push inflation inflation believed to be triggered when a nation's businesses raise their prices, resulting in new demands by consumers for higher wages from their employers (p. 210)

counteradvertising advertising which a firm must produce at its own expense for the purpose of correcting prior false claims in its advertising (p. 252)

credit bureau an organization that keeps the credit records of consumers for use by credit-extending companies (p. 276)

credit limit the maximum amount a borrower may draw from an open-end credit account (p. 267)

creditor a lender to whom a debt is owed (p. 99)

crowding out a situation in which government borrowing reduces the financial capital available to business firms (p. 64)

cyclical unemployment unemployment caused by the downside of the business cycle (p. 195)

debt consolidation loan a loan used to pay all of the borrower's outstanding debts so that his monthly payments may be reduced to that of the one loan payment (p. 272)

debtor a borrower who is in debt for the credit he has received (p. 257)

decrease in demand a leftward shift in the demand curve representing a decrease in the willingness of buyers to demand an item at any price (p. 21)

decrease in supply a leftward shift of the supply curve indicating a decrease in the quantity suppliers are willing to produce at any price (p. 31)

deductible an amount which must be paid by a policyholder before his insurance will begin to cover claims (p. 320)

default failure to pay money when it is due (p. 258)

defined contribution plans employer-sponsored retirement plans which provide an individual account for each employee (p. 328)

deflation a situation in which the general price level is declining; usually caused by a reduction in the growth rate of the money supply (p. 68)

demand how many units of a product will be bought at a given price (p. 19)

demand curve a graph illustrating the various quantities of an item that are demanded at various prices (p. 20)

demand-pull inflation inflation believed to be triggered when consumers demand more products and the rising demand results in rising prices and wages (p. 211)

demand schedule a tabular model listing various quantities demanded at various prices (p. 20)

depression a severe and prolonged trough phase of a business cycle (p. 187)

Diamond-Water Paradox the riddle that asks which is more valuable, a handful of diamonds or a glass of water; solved by Karl Menger in 1871 when he proposed that value is not inherent in an object but rather is determined by the buyer (see subjective value) (p. 5)

differentiated products products that are different from one firm to another (p. 112)

disability income insurance insurance that provides one's family with weekly or monthly payments to replace the income of someone unemployed because of illness or injury (p. 323)

discount rate the interest rate charged by the Federal Reserve to banks for borrowed money (p. 157)

discounting the lending of money to banks by the

Federal Reserve Banking System (p. 157)

discouraged workers chronically unemployed people who have been out of work for six months or more (p. 192)

dissaving the action of withdrawing money from an account or borrowing money (p. 59)

double coincidence of wants both parties involved in a trade of goods or services wanting what the other has to trade (p. 130)

dower the part of a deceased person's estate which the law requires to be given to his spouse (p. 317)

duopoly an oligopoly which is composed of two business firms (p. 118)

economic Darwinism another name for the libertarian view of economic fairness allowing for a "survival of the fittest" in the accumulation of wealth (p. 76)

economic cost the value people place on a good or service (p. 4)

economic Darwinism another name for the libertarian view of economic fairness allowing for a "survival of the fittest" in the accumulation of wealth (p. 76)

contribute to its pool of wealth (p. 74)

economic model a simplification of how factors in the environment affect choices (p. 49)

economic services services that bear a positive economic cost (p. 4)

economics the science of how and why people, businesses, and governments make the choices that they do (p. 1)

effective interest rate the true rate of interest derived from compounding interest at the nominal interest rate (p. 301)

egalitarian fairness a viewpoint maintaining that each person in the nation has a right to a part of the nation's wealth simply because he is a part of the human race (p. 74)

elastic currency a money supply that can be expanded or contracted (p. 151)

endorse placing a signature on the back of a check to acknowledge its receipt by the payee (p. 287)

entrepreneurship the factor of production denoting the activity of creatively combining natural resources, human labor, and financial capital in unique ways to develop new and useful products

and services (p. 55)

equity the increased value of a home (because of inflation or improvements) beyond the amount owed on any outstanding mortgage (p. 271)

escheat laws laws which allow a state to confiscate money from a dormant account (p. 303)

escrow account a sum of money collected by a lender in addition to loan repayments for the purpose of paying for taxes and insurance to protect the mortgaged property (p. 241)

estate the assets and liabilities left by a deceased person (p. 314)

European social democracy a form of socialism in which the state takes possession of the economy's major industries but allows some private enterprise and decision making (p. 88)

executor a person named in a will to oversee the disposition of an estate according to the provisions of the will (p. 315)

expansion phase that part of the business cycle in which the nation's GNP is on the rise, the number of available jobs is growing, the unemployment rate is falling, and the national income is expanding (p. 185)

expenditure multiplier the means by which any given change in expenditures causes a greater change in national income (found by the formula $1/1 - mpc$) (p. 221)

extensive growth the ability to produce more goods and services because business firms are using more land, labor, or financial capital (p. 68)

factors of production the resources used in producing the nation's GNP; they include land, labor, financial capital, and entrepreneurship (p. 54)

fad items goods which become very popular for a short period of time, and thus their demand curves shift rapidly to the right only to shift rapidly back to the left (p. 25)

favorable balance of trade condition experienced when a nation sells more goods abroad than it purchases from foreign nations (p. 81)

Federal Insurance Contribution Act (FICA) legislation requiring the deduction of Social Security taxes from workers' paychecks (p. 226)

Federal Open Market Committee (FOMC) the agency of the Federal Reserve Banking System that is responsible for buying and selling government securities (p. 150)

Federal Reserve Banking System the government institution that serves as the central bank of the United States (p. 148)

fiat money money that is not backed by anything of value but serves as money because of governmental decree (p. 135)

final goods and services goods and services that are sold to ultimate users (p. 167)

financial capital the factor of production denoting all money loaned directly to business firms from the household sector (p. 54)

financial market the vast collection of financial institutions that receive deposits of excess funds from households and that lend to business firms; it includes commercial banks, savings and loan associations, credit unions, insurance companies, finance companies, and stockbrokerage firms (p. 59)

financial planning the process of developing and implementing plans to achieve financial objectives (p. 311)

first mortgage a home loan received with the property serving as collateral (p. 270)

fiscal agent the government's bank (p. 153)

fiscal policy the ability of the government to affect GNP and employment through the way it spends its money, taxes its citizens, and borrows (p. 217)

fixed expenses expenses which do not rise or fall as the family's income changes in the short run (p. 244)

floating-rate account a short-term savings instrument for which the interest rate may fluctuate as economic conditions change (p. 306)

401(k) plan an employer-sponsored retirement plan that is formed by both employer contributions and matching contributions withdrawn from the employee's paychecks (p. 329)

free goods goods provided freely by God in nature (p. 5)

free services services provided freely by God in nature (p. 5)

free trade a condition in which governments do not impose trade legislation and people are free to buy and sell products regardless of the nation that produced them (p. 180)

frictional unemployment unemployment resulting merely because people are temporarily between jobs (p. 194)

full-bodied coin a coin that contains an amount of gold or silver of equal worth to its face value (p. 134)

garnish to legally withhold a portion of a debtor's wages in payment for a loan in default (p. 258)

general partnership a business firm owned by two or more people (p. 101)

good any tangible thing that has a measurable life span (p. 4)

gross national product (GNP) the total dollar value of all final goods and services produced by a nation in one year (p. 167)

gross national product implicit price deflator (GNP deflator or GNP-IPD) a price index that rises as the price of all goods and services rises (p. 175)

gross private domestic investment (GPDI) the sum of all business spending on capital investment and unplanned inventories (p. 170)

group health insurance a health care policy that provides coverage for a large group of people, usually the employees of a certain employer (p. 324)

guaranteed check a check that is affirmed by a bank or other reputable backer in order to be cashed by the payee (p. 292)

guardians persons appointed by a court to care for orphaned children (p. 315)

hospitalization insurance insurance that pays for the costs associated with staying in a hospital (p. 324)

imperfect competition the condition of a market in which there are many sellers of slightly differentiated goods, sellers and buyers are reasonably aware of conditions that may affect the market, each seller has some control over his good's price, and sellers find it relatively easy to enter and exit the market (p. 116)

impulse buying making unplanned nonessential purchases (p. 238)

increase in demand a rightward shift in the demand curve representing a willingness on the part of buyers to demand more of a good or service at every price (p. 21)

increase in supply a rightward shift in the supply curve indicating a willingness of business firms to produce more of an item at any given price (p. 31)

indexing tying present wages and prices to some adjustment figure so that real wages and real prices are maintained (p. 208)

individual retirement account (IRA) a retirement account held in a financial institution and to which tax-deductible deposits of up to $2,000 annually may be made by qualified account holders (p. 329)

industry family of common concerns, groups of businesses that sell a similar product, sell to a certain group of customers, or produce their products in a similar way (p. 112)

inferior good a good which typically experiences a decrease in demand as buyers' incomes increase (p. 23)

inflation the situation in which over-expansion of the nation's money supply leads to a sustained rise in the average price level (p. 203)

insatiability the condition of having unlimited wants and thus never being satisfied (p. 2)

installment credit paying for a purchase with periodic payments according to a loan contract (p. 265)

intensive growth the ability of business firms to produce more goods or services by using existing factors of production with greater efficiency (p. 68)

interest an additional charge that a creditor demands from a borrower to cover the expense of the loan and to provide a profit; also the factor costs involving the payments made on borrowed money (pp. 56, 265)

interlocking directorate a situation that reduces competition in an industry by placing one or more directors on the boards of competing firms (p. 124)

intermediate goods goods that are purchased either to be resold immediately or to be incorporated into other goods (p. 167)

intrinsic value value ascribed to a good or service because of its nature (p. 5)

investment borrowing the use of debt to purchase goods which will increase in value, produce income in the future, or reduce expenses (p. 263)

joint account an account shared by two or more people (p. 286)

Keogh plan a retirement plan for self-employed people who wish to make tax-deductible contributions to a retirement account (p. 329)

Keynesian economics economic policies based upon the ideas of John Maynard Keynes, who believed that governments could eliminate severe conditions of the business cycle by using fiscal policy (p. 217)

L the broadest measure of the money supply including all M-1, M-2, and M-3 money along with other assets that may be used as investments, such as short-term government bonds, savings bonds, banker's acceptances, and commercial paper (p. 138)

labor the factor of production denoting all human effort that goes into the creation of goods and services (p. 54)

labor force those persons who are working (the employed) and those who are actively looking for a job (the unemployed) (p. 192)

labor intensive description of a business firm that uses a great deal of human labor relative to real capital (p. 72)

laissez faire the idea that government should generally leave the economy of a nation alone and allow the people to seek their own profit (p. 82)

land the factor of production denoting all the natural resources that go into the production of goods (p. 54)

last will and testament a legal document left by a person to indicate his desires for the disposition of his possessions after his death (p. 314)

law of demand everything else being held constant, the lower the price charged for a good or service, the greater the quantity people will demand and vice versa (p. 19)

law of supply the higher the price buyers are willing to pay, other things being held constant, the greater the quantity of the product a supplier will produce, and vice versa (p. 30)

legacy a gift left by a deceased person to an heir (p. 317)

legal tender pertaining to a government declaration that a certain form of money must be accepted by creditors if it is tendered (offered) by a debtor (p. 130)

lender of last resort an agency able to lend money to banks when a greater than expected number of depositors want to receive cash from their accounts (p. 153)

libertarian fairness a viewpoint maintaining that the only economic right to which citizens are entitled is the right to own and use property free of government interference and that the accumulation of wealth is the sole responsibility of each individual (p. 76)

limited partner a partner in a limited partnership who has no management responsibilities and no liabilities in the firm other than his total investment (p. 103)

limited partnership a partnership in which there is at least one general partner who has unlimited personal financial liability and decision-making responsibility and at least one limited partner (p. 103)

line graph a graph formed by the plotting of data involving two variables and the connecting of the resulting points to form a line of infinite information from the data (p. 52)

loose oligopoly an oligopoly in which the top four firms account for between 50% and 75% of the industry's total sales (p. 118)

M-1 a measure of the nation's money supply that is available for immediate spending and includes currency, coin, traveler's checks, and checking accounts (p. 137)

M-2 a measure of the nation's money supply that includes all immediately spendable M-1 money plus all money that is available to spend after a short delay, such as savings accounts, small time deposits, and other short-notice deposits (p. 137)

M-3 a measure of the money supply including all M-1 and M-2 money along with longer delay deposits, such as long-term time deposits (p. 137)

macroeconomics the level of economic study that is concerned with large scale economic choices and issues (p. 8)

major medical insurance health care insurance that provides benefits for virtually all types of med-

ical expenses resulting from accidents or illnesses (p. 324)

manifesto a public declaration of one's political or social beliefs and intentions (p. 89)

marginal propensity to consume (MPC) the percentage of each dollar that the average individual chooses to spend (p. 221)

marginal propensity to save (MPS) the percentage of each dollar that the average individual chooses to save (p. 221)

marginal utility curve a graphic representation of observations of utility received from some good or service (p. 14)

marginal utility schedule a tabular model displaying observations of utility received from some good or service (p. 14)

market arrangements people have developed for trading with one another (p. 111)

market equilibrium point the point at which the demand curve and the supply curve for an item intersect (p. 36)

market equilibrium price the price corresponding to the intersection of an item's supply and demand curves and at which consumers are willing to buy the same quantity that suppliers are willing to produce (p. 36)

mercantilism an economic philosophy commonly held in Europe from the sixteenth to the eighteenth centuries that advocated the accumulation of gold and silver as national wealth (p. 81)

microeconomics the level of economic study that is concerned with choices made by individual units (p. 8)

money anything that is commonly used and generally accepted in payment for goods and services; a medium of exchange (p. 130)

money market deposit accounts (MMDAs) insured accounts offered by commercial banks and thrift institutions which pay a rate of interest based on the market's demand for short-term loans (p. 306)

money market mutual fund accounts (MMMFs) accounts offered by stockbrokerage firms (p. 306)

money multiplier the factor that represents the number of times a deposit may be multiplied as it experiences the money multiplier effect (p. 156)

money multiplier effect the expansion of the money supply as a result of commercial banks lending their depositors' money to others (p. 156)

money order a small guaranteed check bought at a bank, post office, or other business (p. 293)

monopoly a form of market organization in which there is only one supplier in the industry selling an undifferentiated product (p. 121)

national industrial policy attempts by national governments to foster the growth of certain industries through the provision of low-interest-rate loans and tax advantages (p. 178)

nationalization government acquisition of the ownership of major industries (p. 88)

natural barrier to entry the situation in which new firms are prevented from entering an industry because other firms already own all of a vital natural resource necessary for the business (p. 113)

natural monopoly a monopoly that exists because one firm owns or controls 100% of some resource vital to the industry (p. 121)

negotiable order of withdrawal (NOW) account an interest-bearing transaction account offered by banks and S&Ls (p. 285)

net exports the difference between the dollar amount a nation takes in from the sale of exports and the dollar amount it pays for imports (p. 172)

net worth the value of what a debtor owns minus the amount he owes (p. 277)

nominal GNP the gross national product reported in current or *nominal dollar values* (p. 167)

nominal interest rate the stated rate of interest paid by a financial institution (p. 300)

normal good a good for which demand typically increases when the buyers' incomes increase (p. 23)

normative economics the approach to economic study involving value judgments about existing and proposed economic policies (p. 8)

nuisance goods and services goods and services that bear a negative economic cost (p. 5)

oligopoly a market in which only a handful of firms are either selling highly differentiated or undifferentiated products, sellers and buyers are not fully

aware of all market information, each seller has a great deal of control over the price, and sellers find it relatively difficult to enter and exit the industry (p. 118)

open-end credit credit from which a debtor may continually draw more money (e.g., credit card credit) (p. 267)

open market operations the purchase or sale of government securities by the Federal Reserve Banking System in order to inject or withdraw money from the money supply (p. 158)

opportunity benefit the satisfaction a person receives from a choice (p. 5)

opportunity cost the satisfaction one gives up or the regret one experiences for not choosing a desirable alternative (p. 5)

overdraft protection a financial institution's provision to extend credit (up to a predetermined credit limit) to cover an overdrawn checking account (p. 270)

partnership a business firm owned by two or more people (p. 101)

passbook account a time deposit offered by banks and thrift institutions for savers with relatively small amounts of money (p. 306)

pawnbroker a person who makes small loans at high rates of interest, taking valuable merchandise as collateral (p. 273)

payee the one receiving a check (p. 287)

peak phase that part of the business cycle in which rapid expansion comes to a halt as shortages in natural resources, high wages, low unemployment, and rising interest rates combine to create higher prices for consumers (p. 185)

per capita real GNP the nation's real gross national product divided by its total population (p. 175)

perfect competition the condition of a market when there is a very large number of sellers who are selling an identical product, when each seller and buyer is perfectly aware of all information about the market, when no seller can affect the price, and when sellers find it relatively easy to enter and to exit the market (p. 114)

personal loan a loan considered as consumption

borrowing for personal wants or needs (p. 272)

positive economics the approach to economic study involving the observation of economic choices and the prediction of economic events (p. 8)

postdated a check given a future date in an attempt to withhold payment until that time (p. 286)

premium a regular payment for insurance (p. 321)

price ceiling a barrier preventing the price of an item from rising above a certain price (p. 41)

price discrimination the selling of the same goods or services by a business firm to different buyers at different prices (p. 124)

price floor a barrier preventing the price of an item from falling lower than a certain price (p. 39)

principal the original amount of the loan received by the borrower (p. 265)

principle of diminishing marginal utility people tending to receive less and less additional satisfaction from any good or service as they obtain more and more of it during a specific amount of time (p. 14)

private corporation a corporation owned by private citizens (p. 104)

privatization the government's selling of nationalized businesses back to private owners (p. 88)

profits factor costs involving the rewards entrepreneurs receive for successful risk taking (p. 57)

progressive tax a tax that takes a greater percentage of a person's income as his income increases (p. 227)

proportional tax a tax in which all people pay the same percentage of their earnings (p. 227)

protectionists people who believe that trade deficits lead to a decrease in the number of domestic jobs and wish to protect those jobs through trade legislation (p. 180)

public corporation a corporation owned by the general public and managed by the government (p. 104)

public goods needed goods and services which private firms cannot create at a profit (p. 86)

radical capitalism the most extreme form of capitalism in which private citizens own all factors of production and make all economic decisions (p. 85)

real capital the tools business firms use to produce goods and services (p. 54)

real GNP (RGNP) the gross national product adjusted for inflation (p. 175)

recession two consecutive quarters (six months) of declining real gross national product (p. 186)

recessionary phase that part of the business cycle in which consumer purchases decline and unemployment increases (p. 186)

reconciling adjusting the account holder's check register record to balance with periodic bank statements of account activities (p. 291)

recycling turning nuisance goods into economic goods (p. 5)

redress to compensate or make amends for a wrong done (p. 252)

regressive tax a tax that taxes a smaller percentage of a person's income as his income rises (p. 227)

rent factor costs involving all payments for the use of an owner's property (p. 56)

representative money money that represents a commodity held in store (p. 135)

required reserve ratio a specified percentage of depositors' money that must be kept on hand by banks (p. 150)

restrictive endorsement an endorsement restricting the payment of the check to only one use, usually for deposit only to the payee's account (p. 288)

right of survivorship the right of one person sharing a joint account to claim the whole account balance upon the death of the other account holder (p. 286)

Rule of 72 the approximate number of years required for interest to double a deposit multiplied by the interest rate should equal 72 (p. 304)

sales finance companies subsidiary companies created by large corporations to provide credit for the purchase of the corporation's products (p. 273)

savings assignment a loan with the borrower's savings account serving as collateral (p. 269)

scarcity the condition of a good or service being finite or limited in quantity (p. 3)

schedule a table or chart explaining the relationships between pairs of variables; also called a tabular model (p. 52)

seasonal unemployment unemployment occurring when the labor force needed for certain industries or businesses expands and contracts seasonally (p. 195)

second mortgage a loan secured on a home (which already has a first mortgage) with the equity of the house serving as collateral (p. 271)

secured loan a loan with collateral (p. 267)

Series EE Bonds U.S. Savings Bonds worth $50 to $10,000 that are purchased at a fraction of their face value (p. 307)

Series HH Bonds U.S. Savings Bonds purchased at full face value by rolling over Series EE Bonds with interest paid via treasury checks (p. 308)

service an intangible function produced by useful labor (p. 4)

share draft account (SDA) a transaction account offered by a credit union (p. 285)

shortage an insufficient supply of an item as a result of its price below the market equilibrium price (p. 41)

simple interest interest compounded annually (once at the end of the year) (p. 301)

single-payment loans loans which, according to contract, must be repaid totally in one payment (p. 265)

social security a government-mandated employer/employee financed retirement and disability plan (p. 328)

socialism an economic system in which a central authority, committee, or the people in common generally own the factors of production and make economic decisions (p. 83)

sole proprietorship a business firm that is owned by one person (p. 97)

special endorsement an endorsement of a check by the payee that makes the check payable to someone else (p. 288)

staledated a check bearing a date more than six months old (p. 286)

state capitalism form of capitalism in which the vast majority of the factors of production are owned by private citizens, but the government intervenes widely in economic decisions to ensure that egalitarian goals are carried out (p. 88)

statutory will a valid will written in a standard form by the state and completed by simple indications of a person's desires for his estate (p. 315)

stock shares or portions of ownership in a corporation (p. 104)

stop payment order a request by an account holder that his bank stop payment on a check that he has written, thus prohibiting it from being cashed (p. 289)

structural unemployment unemployment occurring when worker skills do not match available jobs (p. 195)

subjective value the worth of a good or service as determined by its usefulness to the buyer (p. 5)

substitute goods goods that resemble one another and that may be used in place of each other (p. 23)

super NOW account a transaction account offering a high rate of interest in return for a high minimum balance in the account (p. 285)

supply the amount of goods and services business firms are willing and able to provide at different prices (p. 30)

supply curve a graph illustrating the quantities of an item that suppliers are willing to produce at various prices (p. 31)

supply schedule a tabular model noting the quantities of an item that suppliers are willing to produce at various prices (p. 30)

surety one who obligates himself to pay the debts of another; cosigner (p. 103)

surplus an excess of unsold products resulting from a price above the market equilibrium price (p. 37)

tabular model a table or chart explaining the relationships between pairs of variables; also called a schedule (p. 52)

tenants in common two or more holders of a joint account without the right of survivorship (p. 286)

term the period of time in which a debtor must repay his loan according to the contract (p. 265)

term insurance life insurance providing only death protection during the period covered by the policy (p. 321)

tight oligopoly an oligopoly in which the top four firms account for at least 75% of the market sales

(p. 118)

time deposits savings accounts which earn fixed rates of interest and have a specific maturity date or time period delay for account withdrawals (p. 306)

token coin a coin that contains a quantity of metal worth less than its face value (p. 134)

trade deficit a negative balance of trade experienced when a nation imports more than it exports (p. 176)

trade surplus a positive balance of trade experienced when a nation exports more than it imports (p. 176)

transaction account an account at a financial institution against which one may write a note ordering the institution to pay a specific sum of money to the one named on the note (p. 285)

transfer payments payments of money or goods from the government to individuals for which no specific economic repayment is expected (p. 57)

traveler's checks guaranteed checks bought through banks from various financial institutions as a means of safekeeping cash during travel (p. 294)

Treasury Bills (T-Bills) government savings instruments that mature from 90 days to one year (p. 308)

trough phase that part of the business cycle in which the recessionary phase has bottomed out and the unemployment rate is high while prices and incomes are low (p. 187)

trust a business combination in which a group of companies in the same industry would eliminate their competition by putting their stock into a single account and allowing a manager to look after the affairs of the group and distribute the profits (p. 123)

tying contracts a situation in which a supplier forces smaller companies to sign confining contracts with the supplier in order to give exclusive rights to the supplier and thus reduce competition (p. 124)

undifferentiated products products that are exactly alike from firm to firm (p. 112)

unemployment the state in which a person who wishes a job cannot find a job (p. 67)

unemployment rate the percentage of the labor force that is not employed but is looking for work (p. 191)

unit pricing the price per measure of the product (p. 250)

universal life insurance a more flexible kind of life insurance that combines some of the benefits of both term and whole life insurance (p. 323)

unsecured loan a loan without collateral (p. 267)

U.S. Savings Bonds bonds offered by the federal government bearing a high rate of interest and carrying the backing of the full faith and credit of the government (p. 307)

util an imaginary unit of satisfaction (p. 6)

utility usefulness (p. 5)

variable expenses expenses which may rise and fall as the family's income changes (p. 244)

vesting period the length of employment required before an employee is fully enrolled in and entitled to benefits from an employer-sponsored pension plan (p. 328)

wages factor costs involving all payments for labor used to produce goods or services (p. 56)

welfare state a nation under extreme state capitalism in which high taxes are used to provide wide social programs (p. 88)

whole life insurance life insurance providing both death protection and a means for saving (p. 322)

worker management socialism a form of socialism in which the government owns all business firms but allows the workers to make many major economic decisions collectively (p. 88)

Index

Scripture Index

Photo Credits

Cover: Suzanne R. Altizer (top, left), Gulf Oil Corporation (bottom), Republic Steel (right)

Suzanne R. Altizer: 1, 13, 29, 36, 40, 41, 57, 67, 68, 97, 98, 111, 112, 121, 140, 150, 154, 170, 187, 194, 197, 199, 229, 237, 239, 241, 257, 262, 269, 272, 273, 281, 315, 320, 324, 326

APN Photo: 90

Architect of the Capitol: 223

Bethlehem Steel Corporation: 69 (top)

Boeing Commercial Aircraft: 119

Bureau of Printing & Engraving: 129

Brad Carper: 284

Larry Carrier: 81

Cincinnati Milacron, Inc.: 30 (bottom)

George R. Collins: 4, 168

General Motors: 185

Courtesy of Tim Keesee: 224

Kitchens of Sara Lee: 69 (bottom)

Library of Congress: 42, 188, 189

Rob Loach: 89

National Archives: 135, 176

Office of Information: 148

Wade K. Ramsey: 3, 217

Republic Steel: 167

Teneco, Inc.: 54

Unusual Films: ii-iii, x-xi, xii, 10, 12, 22, 24, 25, 28, 32, 38, 46-47, 48, 49, 62, 64, 66, 73, 80, 86, 87, 94-95, 96, 100, 104, 107, 110, 116, 120, 126-27, 128, 132, 134, 136, 137, 140, 147, 161, 164-65, 166, 178, 184, 196, 202, 203, 207, 216, 225, 234-35, 236, 245, 256, 274, 280, 285, 295, 298, 301, 310, 311, 316, 322

USDA: 230

World Bank Photo: 30 (top), 74, 76, 77, 130

Marbleized paper courtesy of:

©1989 Back Street and Paula Gourley: ii-iii, 136, 147, 234-36, 256, 280, 285

Ken Brinson: 9, 61, 105, 213, 299

Dover Publications and Roger Bruckner: all other